NEWPORT PAGNELL DURING THE FIRST WORLDWAR

JOHN A. TAYLOR

NEWPORT PAGNELL DURING THE FIRST WORLD WAR

Published by Magic Flute Publications 2014

ISBN 978-1-909054-13-4

Magic Flute Publications is an imprint of
Magic Flute Artworks Limited
231 Swanwick Lane
Southampton SO31 7GT
www.magicfluteartworks.com
A catalogue description of this book is available from the British Library
Cover photograph courtesy of Ken & Joyce Graham

Contents

Acknowledgements

Especial thanks to Mr. Gerald Stratton, for vetting the original manuscript.

Zena Dan
Sue Blake
Don Hurst
Ken and Joyce Graham
Cliff Taylor
Ruth Meardon and the staff of the Local Studies Library, Milton Keynes.

NEWPORT BELLS

I returned to the town of my childhood
When my youth had passed away;
But the old familiar voices
Have altered since that day.
The children I used to play with
Are men and women grown,
And many have gone for ever
Where parting is unknown.
But soon my heart was thrilled by
An old familiar strain,
And I knew not which was stronger,
The pleasure or the pain:
For the dear old bells were ringing
In their old familiar ways.
And they seemed in my heart to echo
As they did in my childhood's days.
All other things seemed altered
And "changed with changing years,"
But they still speak of hope, and love,
And peace, that calms our fears.
For when they tell of "home, sweet home,"
I think of the home above,
Where soon, with sin and sorrow past,
We'll meet with those we love.
Those joyous bells, unchanged by time,
How clear and sweet they sound!
Though cruel war and bitter strife
Is raging all around.
Ring out, O dear old bells, ring out!
Send forth your loving call;
Ring out! Sometime, somewhere, somehow,
There's better life for all.

ESTHER BATEMAN
September 12th 1916

AIRSHIPS, AEROPLANES & AIR RAIDS

Working Model of Fire Engine by Charles Frederick Coales aged 13½

Around June 1915 William Pettit, the son of Mr. R. Pettit, the well known butcher in the town, applied to join the Royal Naval Air Service. Indeed, aviation was now becoming an established form of warfare, and in consequence in June the captain of the Fire Brigade, Mr. C. F. Coales, wrote to the Council asking if a simple form of pocket sized respirator could be provided for the firemen, in case incendiaries were dropped during an air raid. The Council unanimously agreed that the best type should be supplied, and having by early July 1915 considered two types they decided, at a cost of 1s 11d each, to purchase a dozen of the selected model. Called at the apparent request of Superintendent Pearce, at a special meeting of the U.D.C., held on Tuesday evening, August 17th 1915, a recommendation was considered from the Water, Lighting and Baths Committee 'That the Council do not undertake any lighting of the town for the ensuing year, with the exception of the lamp affixed to the Fire Station, such resolution to come into force on the 1st September next.' This was primarily for reasons of economy but the danger from air raids was also a factor, as emphasised when during his recent lecture on 'Anti Aircraft,' held at the Council Schools, Mr. W. Marsh said that he thought Zeppelins might come by way of Peterborough, Northampton, and then by Newport Pagnell and Stony Stratford on their way to London and the north. In fact it was regarding just such a visitation that a story would be circulated in the town during the last week of September 1915.

Bucks Standard September 18th 1915

Lights Out at Newport Pagnell

The very recent decision of the Newport Pagnell Urban District Council to economise in the matter of public expenditure, and to safeguard the town against air raids by the enemy has prompted a local poet to pen the following satire on the resolution adopted by the "City Fathers" to keep the town in darkness during the winter nights :—

Mr, Super, worthy councillors,
To your wisdom we submit,
But as little, struggling tradesmen,
Must admit we're being hit.

Did you plunge our town in gloom, sirs,
Just to save a fourpenny rate ?
Is it dread of German Zeppelins,
And a wish to save your pate?.

When the rates are on the rise, sirs,
The tenant finds the pelf:
Will he get a slight rebate, or
Landlord pocket it him self ?

So much gloom must causa depression,
Accidents as well, I fear;
Think of drear and dull November,
When the frost and snow are here.

What about the early workman
Groping to his daily toil?
Pitchy blackness-slipping, sliding-
Muttering curses all the while.

When a councillor-once & postman-
Slipped in Silver-street and fell,
He cried aloud : " Oh give jus light, sirs,"
And what else I dare not tell.

Light the lamps and let us see, sirs,
Give us that for which "we pay,
If it's air raids that you're fearing
I will show a better way.

Build a watch-tower on the chambers-
Please don't thinks I wish to pun-
If a Zeppelin approaches
Fetch it down with Johnny's gun,
W.S.

On a weekend leave a young soldier had arrived too late at Bletchley station to meet a train for Newport Pagnell, and so had to make the journey on foot through the night. Suddenly, on reaching Willen he heard a humming noise, and looking up saw a Zeppelin loom into view, whereupon he dived into a hedgerow and buried himself beneath a blackberry bush. Arriving in the early hours of Sunday morning he then recounted the tale to his parents at Newport Pagnell, where, with the incident seeming to reinforce this wisdom, during the month a decision was taken that where they were high the kerbstones would be whitewashed. In the interests of safety this was to make them more evident during the lighting restrictions, but at the meeting of the U.D.C. on Tuesday, October 5th 1915 the chairman, Mr. O. Bull J.P., moved that the resolution passed at the August meeting, that the street lamps should not be lit during the winter, be rescinded. He put forward the alternative "that an agreement be entered into with the Newport Pagnell Gas Company to light 24 specified lamps; eight of which shall be all-night lamps, and that the Lighting Committee be empowered to increase or alter the number when they consider the lighting necessity of the streets requires the same." This was carried, and in consequence the Lighting Committee met on two occasions to consider a modified scheme. The Gas Company were duly approached to tender for an illumination which would render the streets safe to the public, but not offer a target for air raids, and by their reply they offered to light 18 lamps from November 1st to March 31st at a cost of £60. Yet with this having been rejected by the Lighting Committee, a meeting of the U.D.C. was held on the evening of Wednesday, October 27th 1915 to approve the decision or otherwise. The result was a rejection by four votes to three. On the previous Friday, Cyril Day, the only son of Mr. and Mrs. J. Day of Newport Pagnell reported to the Admiralty, and on passing a flying test had been appointed to a commissioned rank. Thus as a sub lieutenant he was now commissioned to H.M.S. President 'somewhere in England,' but it was from Canada that he had originally travelled 'to do his bit,' since for over four years he had been the accountant of McKenzie, Mann and Co. in Toronto. However, during his leisure time he had been associated with the Curtis Aeroplane School, and having gained a good knowledge of flying volunteered at the outbreak of the war, with 10 others, to come to England. Also of an aeronautical aptitude was George Page, of Wolverton Road. In civilian life he taught at the Council School, but in November 1915 he applied to enlist in the Royal Flying Corps, which in the same month Edward Bailey, the third son of Mr. and Mrs. John Bailey, of High Street, joined as a wireless operator. From Blenheim Barracks, South Farnborough, he would be shortly sent to London for instruction, whilst as for his two brothers the eldest, John (promoted to corporal in January 1915 and then, serving on the eastern front, to sergeant in January 1916) was a farrier in the Royal Bucks Hussars. The third son was serving as a gunner in the Motor Machine Gun Section with the Royal Field Artillery at Bisley. As for their father, as a well known shoeing smith in the third week of October 1914 he had received an order from the War Office to supply as many hand made horse shoes as possible which, such that the soldiers could rough their own horses and avoid delay, were to be made for 'screws.' (Perhaps it was this work load that caused his appearance at the Newport Pagnell Divisional Petty Sessions on Wednesday, August 25th for being drunk in charge of a pony and trap at Sherington on August 21st. He had been seen by Police Constable Barnett at 7.15 p.m. but being very civil was allowed to go home in the charge of a friend. A fine of 10s was imposed.) By now the local authorities were taking the prospect of air raids very seriously, and this was emphasised in February 1916, when the chairman and vice chairman of the R.D.C. insured the Workhouse for £12,137. For a premium of £12 3s this was with the County Fire Office, and in other measures also during the month the Surveyor suggested that 'to provide for emergencies in the event of air raids' the manual fire engine should be moved from the fire station to the Council's depot, situated in Silver Street. There was even an anxiety that lamps could be used by enemy agents to signal to Zeppelins, and, with this having been foreseen by the all encompassing Defence of the Realm Act (D.O.R.A.), at the Divisional Petty Sessions on Wednesday, February 23rd 1916 Percy Brown, a miller's traveller, was summoned for carrying on his motor cycle a lamp 'capable of movement independent of the movement of the cycle.' He pleaded guilty, but said that he thought the screws were sufficient to stop the lamp from moving. Giving evidence, police sergeant Roberts said that he had seen the motor cycle in Tickford Street on February 10th, and on unscrewing the butterfly nuts of a swivel bracket found he could move the lamp upwards or downwards. Saying that he was unaware of the regulations the defendant apologised, and subsequently went to see the people at Luton who had sold him the motorcycle. They were 'almost confident' that the lamp complied with D.O.R.A., but despite a member of the Bench vouching for the integrity of the defendant, whom he knew to be a highly respected resident of Luton, a fine of 20s was imposed, with the lamp confiscated. During March 1916 another contravention of D.O.R.A. lead to a local farmer being prosecuted. This was for burning rubbish on his farm, and swiftly afterwards the Surveyor advised the Council to (not surprisingly) obtain permission from the military authorities to keep their refuse tip fire continually alight on the London Road. Having been made on February 8th 1916, under the new Lighting Order, which required householders to screen or shade their lights, so as to not throw a reflection into the street, the first local cases were heard on Wednesday, March 22nd 1916 at the Petty Sessions, with Colonel Levi in the chair.

As the first of these, Bertram Reynolds, a painter, of Bury Avenue, pleaded guilty, and giving details police sergeant Roberts said that on Sunday, March 12th, when in Bury Avenue he saw a bright light shining from the front window of the defendant's property. This was at about 8 p.m., and calling at the house he spoke to the defendant's wife who, apologising, said that because her husband was away for the weekend she had been unable to hang the green blinds to shade the light. She at once went into the house to turn off the gas, but in court Superintendent Pearce said the special constables had done their utmost to make the new order known to the residents, and as a result a fine of 10s was imposed, with the penalty in default being seven days' imprisonment.

It was emphasised that cases at the next Sessions would not receive such leniency, which therefore proved fortunate for Miss Annie Mapley who, having pleaded guilty, was also fined 10s for an unscreened light at her house on March 14th. In evidence, police constable Nicholls said at 10.15 p.m. on the Lathbury road near Woad Cottages he, in the company of police constable Barnett, had seen a bright light shining from a house in Mill Street, and on calling at the house the occupant said that she had lit the gas to go into the larder, but had forgotten to pull down the blind.

Yet despite the warning of increased penalties, on April 2nd 1916, at 8.30 p.m. special constable J. Thickpenny noticed a bright light shining from the side window of the house of William Powell, a vet. He called at the house, and on pointing out to Mr. Powell's daughter that there was only a white blind at the window she immediately apologised, and in explanation said that her father had been alone in the house when the family went to church, and, having much correspondence to deal with, had forgotten to draw the dark curtains. A 10s fine was imposed.

Then on Wednesday, May 3rd George Salmons was summoned at the Divisional Petty Sessions for having an unscreened light at his house on the night of April 27th. Not being present in court he apologised through Superintendent Pearce, whilst regarding the offence police constable Bonner said that when on duty in Tickford Street he saw, at about 10 p.m., a large gleam of light showing from the side of the house, the source of which he found to be an electric light showing down the passage.

With the door being open he called the matter to the attention of the defendant, who said the girl had gone to bed and forgotten to turn off the light. When told it would have to be reported Mr. Salmons said "Certainly," and in court a fine of 10s was imposed.

On the morning of Friday, May 12th 1916, at about 11 a.m. an Army biplane landed in Bury Field. Crowds quickly gathered to inspect the machine, which was of the latest type, and it transpired that the pilot, Captain Dowdeswell of the R.F.C., had lost his direction due to the low clouds. One of the wheels had been damaged in the landing, and a telephone message was consequently sent for mechanics to make the repairs. However, they would take awhile to arrive, and so during the afternoon hundreds of people from the town and district came to inspect the machine, the protection of which was ensured by a number of Royal Engineers who, by acting as guards, kept any persons who became too inquisitive at a safe distance. Later in the afternoon the mechanics repaired the damage, and - just before the onset of a sharp rainstorm - a few minutes after 6 p.m. Captain Dowdeswell took off, circled the town, and resumed his journey.

However, there were a couple of sequels to the incident. On his way to dinner Mr. F. W. Saunders, the traveller for the Aylesbury Brewery Company, had taken an employee of the firm, Mr. Brightman, in the sidecar of his motorcycle to see the aeroplane. Afterwards they returned via Lakes Lane, but immediately opposite Mr. Holes' dairy farm the farmer's collie dog dashed out of the gate and crashed straight into the motorcycle, taking out every spoke from the front wheel. Mr. Saunders and his companion were thrown heavily onto the road, but, although the dog died soon afterwards, Mr. Brightman escaped without injury, despite having turned a double somersault when hurled from the sidecar. As for Mr. Saunders, who was unconscious for awhile, he had sustained a fractured rib and a badly bruised right shoulder. His injuries were subsequently attended by Dr. Harry Townshend Wickham, who then took him in his car to his home in Wolverton Road.

Also related to the aeroplane incident, at the Newport Pagnell Divisional Petty Sessions on Wednesday, May 31st 1916, Dorothy Le Quelbec, a governess of Newport Pagnell, was summoned for having taken a photograph of the aeroplane without the permission of the competent military authority. Giving the details Superintendent Pearce said that the order had been made last December 1st, and having seen the defendant carrying a small Brownie camera, with which she took the photo, at his request she readily handed over the instrument and the negatives.

For his part, special constable C. Sayle said that he had been in Bury Field on May 12th when the aeroplane landed, and had asked Captain Dowdeswell if photographs of the machine could be taken. He was told no, and so when he noticed the defendant with a camera he informed her that photos were not allowed. However, later in the afternoon she told him that she had taken a picture, and explaining the reason in court she said his words had been "You won't get any today," which she took to mean because of the defective light. In reply special constable Sayle said "I cautioned you twice, and you said "Alright," and in view of this ambiguity Superintendent Pearce decided not to press the matter, but wished only to bring the ruling to the attention of the public. The governess pleaded 'guilty in ignorance,' and although no conviction was recorded costs of 10s were imposed, and the negatives forfeited.

When summoned for not screening a light of her property on May 22nd 1916, Lucy Gillespie, of The Green, Newport Pagnell, did not appear in court but sent a letter, and outlining the case police sergeant Roberts said that at 10.30 p.m. he had seen a bright light shining from an upstairs window of her house in Wolverton Road. He duly called at the premises and was told "That is Miss Lucy's room" by a Miss Frearson, who then called for her to put out the light and draw the blind. To this came the reply that she thought she had, and in her letter to the court Miss Gillespie wrote that she would be most careful in future. A fine of 15s was imposed.

As another contravention of the lighting restrictions, at the Divisional Petty Sessions on Wednesday, October 4th 1916, Raffaele Mazzone, a fish merchant of the town, was summoned for not screening the inside lights of his fried fish shop at 22, Silver Street, on September 26th. Police sergeant Roberts said that in company with Superintendent Pearce he had been on duty that night, and at 8.50 p.m. in Silver Street he saw a light shining across the road due to the defendant's door being open. When questioned the defendant said that he had screened the gas jet with a piece of cardboard, but customers were continually opening the door to enter the shop. Nevertheless, in court Superintendent Pearce said many cautions had been issued to the accused, who, pleading not guilty, was told to attend to the problem by the Bench, which imposed a lenient fine of 10s.

Yet a fine of £1 reflected the concern viewed by the Bench regarding the case of Robert Layton, a licensed victualler of the town, who, having been requested to do so by the police, had not extinguished lights in his house on September 23rd 1916.

Regarding the circumstances, police constable Nicholls said that Zeppelins had been over the country that night, and at 9.30 p.m. he received instructions from Superintendent Pearce to warn the public to put their lights out. Five minutes later he called at the defendant's premises and asked him to extinguish his lights, which he did. But at 11.35 p.m., in company with special constable Higgins police sergeant Roberts saw a bright light shining from an upstairs window of the same property, and again he told the defendant to put the lights out. He then waited for about 10 minutes, and since the lights had not been extinguished he told the defendant that the matter would be reported. In court Mr. Layton explained that shortly before the constable's second visit one of his daughters went to bed, to be shortly followed by her two sisters. Since there was no gas supply in the upstairs rooms they took candles, and when informed of the light shining from the bedroom Mr. Layton said he called twice to the girls to put out the candles. Concluding the case the Bench stressed the serious nature of the offence, but imposed a fairly lenient fine of £1, saying that he should fine his daughters for having been the real culprits.

Another serious case was heard on Wednesday, October 18th 1916 at the Newport Pagnell Divisional Petty Sessions. This involved a dressmaker of Mill Street, who was summoned for not shading the inside lights of her house on Sunday, October 1st, when Zeppelin raids were in progress. Stating the facts, special constable H. I. Middleton said that on that night he had been in charge of the patrols of special constables in the town. Special constable J. Short and another member had been posted on duty between the Neptune Inn and the first bridge, and at about 10.30 p.m. he received their report that a light was shining across the North Bridges from the back window of a house in Mill Street. He immediately went to investigate, and observing a distinct beam of light shining towards Lathbury he left the patrol on the bridge, and, with another special constable, went to the defendant's house. Harry Mapley answered the door, and when told about the light he replied "Well, we were just going to bed," after which the light was immediately extinguished.

On the following Tuesday Mr. Middleton went to the house, and the defendant told him she was only burning a candle in the room. He then explained that she should have blinds to screen the window, to which she replied that she had immediately put out the light when told to do so by her father. In court it was stated that prior to 10 p.m. the patrol had been asking people to put all their lights out due to the raid. At that period there was no light showing from the house, but since the girl had been warned on previous occasions a penalty of 15s was imposed, composed of a fine of 10s and expenses of 2s 6d for each of the special constables.

The latter amount was also the sum awarded as expenses to special constable Chapman, who brought a charge against Minnie Howard, a hotel manageress, for having 'allowed' a chimney to be on fire in the town on October 14th. A fine of 2s 6d was imposed.

Convened by the chairman, Mr. O. Bull, at a special meeting of the U.D.C., held on Wednesday evening, November 22nd 1916, the need for a modified scheme of street lighting for the winter was reconsidered. Plain speaking featured in the arguments, but with a vote having been taken it was resolved to leave the present arrangement unchanged. In fact as a 'remedy' one member said that he had gone to the 'enormous expense' of 3s in purchasing a torch, and perhaps other people in the town could do the same.

For the men from the town in the Forces, towards providing Christmas comforts an auction sale was held in the Girls' Council School on Saturday evening, November 18th 1916. Among the items were a brooch made from a piece of the Zeppelin brought down at Cuffley, and two relics from the Zeppelin destroyed at Potters Bar, and having been respectively contributed by Mrs. A. J. Simpson, of the High Street, Mrs. Carr, of Beaconsfield Place, and Mr. W. Steventon, of Stoke Goldington, these all found a ready sale.

'Suitable for lighting restrictions,' in February 1917 green paper blinds, available in all widths from 36" to 72", were available from Arthur J. Simpson, and had perhaps been used to darken those windows which were mentioned at the quarterly meeting of the Parochial Church Council, held at the Vicarage on Wednesday evening, July 18th 1917. Mr. J. Day presented the report of the finance committee, and said that apart from the window expense there had been a further cost in providing insurance against aircraft, although not the six which, in fine, sunny weather, passed over the town on Saturday, July 21st 1917, shortly after the opening ceremony of the annual fete to raise funds for Northampton Hospital.

At a special meeting of the U.D.C., on Friday evening, August 17th 1917, a proposed scheme for street lighting during the winter was considered. Previously it had been decided that 28 lamps should be lit and kept alight all night, except on full or near full moons, but this caused two difficulties, for under D.O.R.A. the Chief Constable of Bucks had no authority to sanction all night lighting, and, with a depleted staff, the Gas Company would be unable to undertake extinguishing the lamps in the late evening, and then relighting them for the benefit of the workmen at 5 a.m. It was ultimately resolved - subject to the sanction of the police authorities - to have 22 lamps alight during the evenings until 11 p.m., with a recommendation that the lamp at the dangerous Cannon Corner should be kept burning all night.

Thus in September 1917 the Gas Company said they were prepared to light the evening lamps suggested by the Council for a cost of £52 10s with - subject to labour conditions - the extinguishing of the lamps to begin at 10.15 p.m. and be complete by 11 p.m. Of this the Chief Constable had approved, although he wanted to know whom to contact to extinguish all the lamps in the event of an air raid. The Council duly accepted the tender, and in the event of an air raid they would immediately notify the police to extinguish the lamps, which would first be lit on October 3rd. During the month at the meeting of the U.D.C. the seal of the Council was duly affixed to the contract of the Gas Company, but there was soon a concern, for at the November meeting of the U.D.C., held on the evening of Tuesday 6th, a letter was read from the Superintendent of Police, complaining that during a recent air raid alert it had taken half an hour from the Gas Works being notified before all the street lamps were extinguished. However, on the letter being forwarded to the secretary of the Gas Company, a reply would be received stating that arrangements had been made to prevent any reoccurrence.

On the domestic scene lighting transgressions were still occupying the attention of the Divisional Petty Sessions, as on Wednesday, March 20th 1918, when Gladys Fish, the manageress of the International Stores, pleaded guilty to not screening the inside lights of the shop on March 9th. The previous occupants of her position had been repeatedly warned, but since she had only recently arrived in the town no conviction was recorded, although costs of 5s 6d were imposed, and any further occurrence would incur a heavy fine.

In glorious summer weather the town's Red Cross Gala Day and Gymkhana took place on Whit Monday 1918, but an unscheduled event was the appearance of an Army Observation Balloon which, having first been spotted at a distance, caused great excitement when it descended onto the sports field. Aboard were five officers on an instructional flight from London, and once the balloon had been deflated and packed away it was transported on a lorry lent by Messrs. Adkins to the railway station, from where the cargo and its crew would begin their return journey on the 5.20 p.m. train.

For the purchase of aeroplanes, or other weapons, which would be named after those towns or villages which subscribed the required amounts, special efforts were now being made to raise money through the increased sale of War Bonds and War Savings Certificates. For this purpose a representative committee, with power to add to its number, was appointed for Newport Pagnell and district, and, with the objective being to raise £30,000 during the seven day period commencing Monday, July 8th 1918, it was decided to call the endeavour 'Aeroplane Week.' The men appointed to the committee were the Reverend Gunnery, chairman, Messrs. G. Tayler, P. C. Gambell, F. W. Taylor, J. O. Butler, O. H. Bull, T. H. Sim, H. I. Middleton, A. W. Goodman, and J. J. Day, whilst the female members would be Mrs. Symons, Mrs. Mitchison, Mrs. Roberts, Miss A. M.Coales, Mrs. Wellesley Taylor, Mrs. Shoebridge, Mrs. Brandon, Mrs. Hedges, Miss Neill. Additionally, Messrs. A. E. Garratt, E. Whittaker, and L. W. Jeacock would represent the village associations, with the post of honorary organising secretary to be occupied by Miss James.

Further arrangements for Aeroplane Week were made at a committee meeting held on the evening of Monday, June 10th 1918, where at the Urban Council Offices, and with the Reverend Gunnery presiding, several leaflets

Bucks Standard, Saturday, July 6th, 1918

and other literature from headquarters were read. With their decisions binding on all the advertising and literature to be issued, it was decided that Messrs. J. O. Butler, J. Short, and T. H. Sim should act as an Advertising Sub Committee, with Messrs. F. W. Taylor and J. J. Day elected to make the arrangements for a Special Selling Centre. As a sub committee responsible for the sale of all securities Messrs. J. O. Butler, F. W. Taylor, L. Salmons, T. H. Sim, and C. R. Line were appointed, and given power to add to their number. As for the immediate monies, Mr. Butler said that he already had promises of about £2,000, and Mr. Short reported that the Foresters' Friendly Society, of which he was secretary, would invest £700. Mr. L. Salmons, who further promised to arrange for special slides and films, gave permission for speeches to be introduced into the programmes at the Electric Theatre, both in the week prior to and during the effort, and Lady Farrar promised to ask her daughter, the famous cellist Miss Gwendoline Farrar, if she could bring a concert party from London to perform a special free entertainment. This would also provide an opportunity for an address on War Savings to be given by a speaker from headquarters, for, as Miss James explained, many people had the wrong impression in the town, thinking they were expected to give the £30,000 without realising that it was an investment, which would bring a greater return than the Post Office Savings Bank.

Consequent to the meeting much progress was made, and at 7 p.m. a week later, and at the same venue, Mr. F. W. Taylor reported that Miss Geary had given permission for 41, High Street to be used as the Special Selling Centre. This would be open from 2 p.m. to 9 p.m. each day during the week, and Mr. Wilford had not only promised to assist with providing the office furniture, but had also undertaken to erect the Result Indicator outside, which would be under the charge of Mr. Sim. A further committee meeting for Aeroplane Week was then held in the Urban Council Chamber on Monday evening, July 1st 1918, where, with Miss James announcing that financial promises in the town had amounted to £10,000, it was agreed that the Special Selling Centre should be formally opened on Monday, July 8th at 1.45 p.m. In fact shortly before that time, as an omen of good fortune an aeroplane flew over the assembled company, and perhaps provided an added incentive to save, since for every £10,000 that was subscribed the Government would name an aeroplane 'Newport Pagnell.' In front of a fairly large attendance the Reverend Gunnery, as the chairman, gave a brief introductory speech, and after this the opening ceremony was performed at 2 p.m. by Mrs. Doyne-Ditmas, of Great Linford, who was accompanied by her husband, Major Doyne-Ditmas. In a short address she wished the 'Week' every success, and, saying that £11,000 had been promised to date, she raised applause by adding that she and her husband would invest another £1,000.

On the evening of the previous Thursday, at the Electric Theatre Mr. J. Short had briefly addressed the audience on the subject of War Savings, and on the Saturday evening Mrs. Trevor took the chair when Mr. O. H. Bull gave a further talk on the subject. Then on the evening of Wednesday, July 10th special War Saving films were screened, with the first being 'The adventures of Dick Dolan.' However, there was only a moderate attendance to which Lady Farrar, who (supported by local worthies) presided, introduced Miss Chamberlain from the National Council of War Savings, whom, to applause, she announced was a daughter of the late politician Joseph Chamberlain. Miss Chamberlain duly dealt with her subject in an able fashion, and in a simple and homely style sketched the events that had lead to war in the form of a word picture, which she called 'Mrs. Britannia and her children.' The villain of the piece was 'Mr. Germany from Hunland,' and with frequent bursts of enthusiasm punctuating her talk she concluded with a forcible address, saying "You all mean to win the war. Then you can win it more quickly by not spending your money uselessly and by lending every penny you can spare." This was greeted with more applause, and on the initiative of Lady Farrar three cheers were given, after which Miss Chamberlain had to leave to catch her train. Sung by Mr. C. R. Line, with the audience joining in the chorus *Rule Britannia* further aroused the patriotic ambience, and afterwards Lady Farrar read out the list of contributions from the town and villages. The amount to Wednesday evening was £32,644 8s 6d, and to applause she said she hoped they would soon reach £50,000.

The Reverend Gunnery then thanked her for having taken the chair, and also expressed his appreciation to the proprietors of the Electric Theatre.

At 9 p.m. on Saturday, July 13th 1918, the Aeroplane Week concluded, and, with over £5,000 having been raised by the working class of the town, was deemed to be a great success. Of the total of £55,326 12s 6d, the amount invested at Barclays Bank totalled £50,600 16s, and at the Post Office and Special Selling Centre £4,616 4s 6d. The overall figure included £1,100 from the Unionist Club War Savings Association, £64 13s from the Congregational Girls' Club Association and £5 8s 6d from the Parish Church Girls' Club Association. Amongst those who had given invaluable help were Mr. J. O. Butler, the manager of Barclays Bank, Mr. J. White, the postmaster, and two members of his staff, Miss M. Thompson and Mr. T. Tame. Throughout the week they had been on duty at the Selling Centre, where those giving clerical assistance included Miss James, the honorary organising secretary, Mrs. Gillam, Miss Gee, Miss M. Butler, and Messrs. J. O. Butler, F. W. Taylor, J. J. Day, and T. H. Sim. As for the writing of the notices of meetings, and the house to house delivery of special appeals, handbills, etc., great assistance had been given by the senior girls of the Council Schools. They had been under the supervision of Miss James, who at the final committee meeting of Aeroplane Week, held at the Girls' Council School on Tuesday evening, July 23rd 1918, reported that the total investments amounted to £55,326 12s 6d. She then read a letter of congratulation from Mr. E. C. Streatfield, the County War Savings Secretary, and in the same tone a letter had also been received from the Headquarters of the National War Savings Association, which, with the actual expenditure being £9 16s 9d, had allowed £10 for expenses. In a cloudless sky, on the afternoon of Monday, July 29th 1918, an airship, built 'somewhere in England,' was seen over the town performing 'certain evolutions' in the brilliant sunshine. Thinking it to be a Zeppelin some ladies became very concerned, but thinking the same German prisoners, engaged on agricultural work in the locality, began to dance with joy, until their guard exclaimed "You — fools, don't you see it's one of ours."

On Tuesday evening, September 3rd 1918, at the meeting of the U.D.C., held at the Council Chamber, High Street, a letter from the secretary to the Gas Company was read, stating that the price to light 22 lamps during the winter would be £57. This was accepted, and in further lighting matters with the end of the war, and therefore of lighting restrictions, there was now no objection to fixing a light in the porch of the Council Offices, so that the steps could be seen. Also with the end of the war, with a more certain future wartime romances could now blossom into marriages, and thus on Thursday, December 12th 1918, Miss Ida Mary Powell, the eldest daughter of Mr. W. J. Powell, M.R.C.V.S., and Mrs. Powell, married Captain Ernest Grimes, R.A.F. He was the elder son of Mr. and Mrs. Grimes, of East Dulwich, but before the war had been living in Canada. At the outset of hostilities he then came to England in 1914 with the first Canadian Contingent, with which he continued to serve until 1917. However, for the last 11 months he had been on active service with the R.A.F., and having acted in France for awhile as his observer Lieutenant Bruce Martin, R.A.F., was his best man, with Kathleen Powell as the bridesmaid. She was the younger sister of the bride, who for her big day wore a dress of wine coloured taffeta, and a fawn velour hat. In the afternoon the couple then left by motor car for Bletchley, en route for a honeymoon in Bournemouth.

Another R.A.F. bride would be Miss Elsie Stanton, the youngest daughter of the late Mr. C. Stanton of the town, who on Saturday, February 15th 1919 married another resident of the town, Corporal David Hackett, R.A.F. He was on a brief leave from the Front, and would shortly return to the headquarters of the R.A.F. in Cologne. Having served a printing apprenticeship at the Bucks Standard, on August 8th 1914 he had voluntarily enlisted in the 6th Bedford Regiment, and for 10 months saw much fighting in France. Invalided home after an accident, he returned to the Western Front in September 1917, and posted to the 4th Bedfords again saw much fighting, until contracted out with trench fever. Part of his convalescence would be spent at the Tickford Abbey V.A.D. Hospital, but despite being discharged as B3 he was ordered back to France, and on his transfer to the R.A.F. was given the rank of corporal, and an important post in the quartermaster's department.

As for the monies raised so enthusiastically during Newport Pagnell's Aeroplane Week, in reply to this question in October 1919 Captain G. Bowyer received a letter from the Air Ministry, stating that a 140 h.p. two-seat aeroplane of the R.E.8 type had been named after the town. A photo was enclosed, and the town could feel justifiably proud of their patriotic effort. Therefore it was perhaps best that they could not have known that within 20 years their dedication would again become necessary, when once again the clouds of conflict loomed. The first serious exercise of the town's air raid wardens took place on Monday evening, May 22nd 1939, and following the outbreak of war in view of the greatly increased threat of air attack Ouse Bank (now Ousebank) would become the Report Centre, with the first air raid warning in North Bucks sounded on Wednesday morning, September 6th 1939. But that's another war and, of course, another story.

ALIENS

On Wednesday, October 21st 1914, since the outbreak of the war the Newport Pagnell Bench of Magistrates dealt with the first case in North Bucks under the Aliens' Restriction Order. In the dock was John Steyskal, an Austrian subject who, having been in the country for 29 years, was described as a motor accessories maker of Northampton. His offence was having on October 19th travelled beyond the five mile limit without the required permit and speaking very good English in court he pleaded guilty and said he had a permit to come to Newport Pagnell on October 17th but didn't use it. Giving evidence, Superintendent Pearce said that on October 19th the prisoner called at Newport Pagnell Police Station and, issued by the Chief Constable of Northampton, produced a permit to travel to Newport Pagnell between 6 p.m. and 11 p.m. on October 16th. However, he was told that since he had no permit to travel on the 19th he would be arrested. In the subsequent enquiries the Chief Constable of Northamptonshire informed Superintendent Pearce that several permits to travel to Newport Pagnell had been issued to the prisoner, but only on one occasion had he complied with the Aliens' Restriction Order by reporting to the police on his arrival. In his defence the accused said that Mr. Goldsmith, a police inspector at Northampton, had assured him it would be alright but Superintendent Pearce had ascertained that this was not true. An altercation in court then ensued, with the prisoner saying, "I express myself sometimes not quite plain; I don't think I said that." After further disputes Alderman Bree of Northampton then spoke in favour of the prisoner, but nevertheless a sentence of six months imprisonment was passed without hard labour.

In February 1917, Francisco Attena, a motor fitter of Hampstead Road, London, was summoned as an alien for having failed to notify his change of address. In fact he registered his address on arrival in London but didn't declare his move at Newport Pagnell. Until discharged on medical grounds, for some years he had served in the Italian Army and it was stated in court that he originally registered at Newport Pagnell Police Station under the Aliens' Order in February 1915. However, when police sergeant Roberts visited 9, Church Passage, Newport Pagnell, on the morning of February 2nd 1917, he found that the man had left three weeks before. A fine of 10s was imposed.

At the Newport Pagnell Divisional Petty Sessions, on Wednesday, December 12th 1917, Annie Rebinstoff, of 1, Greenfield Road, Newport Pagnell, was summoned for failing to notify a change of her address at Newport Pagnell on November 16th. German by marriage, this was under the Aliens' Restriction Order and she pleaded not guilty. Police constable Marsh said that on November 16th at 6.30 p.m. she had called at Newport Pagnell Police Station and there handed in her travelling permit from Luton to no. 1, Greenfield Road. Superintendent Dibben said that he was the Alien Registration Officer for the Division and having on November 17th received a communication from Luton Borough Police, notifying the change of address of the defendant, it was due to a query regarding her actual whereabouts that he had made enquiries. Eventually she was located by Wolverton police and at the request of Superintendent Dibben she attended Newport Pagnell Police Station on November 23rd. There it was revealed that she had been residing at Wolverton from November 16th to the 20th and he pointed out that under Article 19 1c of the Aliens' Restriction Order she, within a certain number of hours, should have furnished the Registration Officer of any change. However, saying that she knew nothing about this she countered that Wolverton was within the five mile limit for daytime travelling. Concluding the case the chairman said that it was a technical offence, since Article 21 of the Order said nothing about the need for a permit, but nevertheless a fine of 5s was imposed.

(At the Stony Stratford Petty Sessions on Friday, December 14th 1917, Ralph Hopkins, a grocer, was summoned for failing to notify the presence of an alien at his residence. He was a special constable and wrote to say that he had not known of the requirement. In fact the 'alien' was Mrs. Rebinstoff, the cousin of his wife, and he was fined 2s 6d. As for Mrs. Rebinstoff, born at Hanslope, where her father still lived, she had met her husband at Ostend and being at Bruges when the war broke out she got to England by the last boat.)

At the Petty Sessions on Wednesday, January 9th 1919, Herman Frederiksen, a labourer of Caistor, Lincolnshire, pleaded guilty to having failed to notify his change of residence as an alien at Newport Pagnell on December 7th. Registered as a Dane he had been engaged on agricultural work at Emberton but left to go to Lincolnshire. His employer had expressly told him to notify the police but he didn't. His knowledge of English was not very good and perhaps in view of this he was fined 5s with 2s 6d costs.

Residing at 27a, Mill Street, Newport Pagnell, Nellie Riese, the wife of an interned alien, was summoned at the Divisional Petty Sessions on Wednesday, March 5th 1919, for committing an act 'calculated to prejudice the discipline' of a certain prisoner of war on February 23rd. Superintendent Dibben said that under Section 46Ag of the Defence of the Realm Act this was the first case of the kind to come before the court and involved a man named Bitonski. Having been interned as a German P.O.W. on the Isle of Man he was released for employment of national importance and duly arrived at Great Linford to be engaged on timber work. As for Mrs. Riese, with five children to keep on 25s a week she had written to the Board of Guardians seeking extra relief but at their meeting on Wednesday, February 27th 1918, it was stated that she was already receiving the maximum and no extra could be allowed. In consequence she asked if soldiers could be billeted at her house and although this request was refused by Superintendent Dibben he said that if there was an opportunity to send lodgers under the Aliens' Act then he would do so. Consequently he sent Bitonski but only under certain conditions which included not being allowed out of the lodgings after 9 p.m. However, as a result of some transgression he had to order Bitonski to return to his quarters at Great Linford, to live with other aliens in an unoccupied cottage, but it was subsequently discovered that the man was not stopping at Great Linford but returning to 27a, Mill Street, Newport Pagnell, for his meals. As a result Mill Street was put out of bounds. Yet on Sunday, February 23rd when Superintendent Dibben sent police sergeant Roberts and police constable Nichols to Bitonski's quarters at Great Linford, where it should have been possible to find him at 9 p.m., they found the quarters empty. Thus at 10 p.m. the officers were sent to Mrs. Riese's house and with the constable going to the rear of the premises the sergeant knocked at the front door. Thereupon Bitonski bolted out of the back door, only to be stopped by the constable. In response to the commotion Mrs. Riese said "I know what you've come for; don't make a scene" whilst as for Bitonski he made no comment. It transpired that after the Armistice, Bitonski had told Mrs. Riese that he could now board with her on condition that each evening he went home before 9 p.m. Having been under police regulations, which she strictly kept, she was unaware that army regulations were being broken but a plea of guilty was entered. However, it was considered that the German was more to blame and although the case was dismissed any further cases would not be treated so leniently.

BELGIAN REFUGEES

Towards raising funds for the plight of Belgian refugees, under the auspices of the P.S.A. Brotherhood an enthusiastic public meeting was held in the Electric Theatre on Sunday evening, September 6th 1914. On the platform, which was decorated with the national colours, Mr. J. Boswell, of Crawley Grange, presided, and was supported by Lady Farrar, Mrs. Boswell, the Reverend F. Gunnery, Colonel A. Good, Dr. H. Wickham, and many other local notables. The meeting opened with the first verse of the National Anthem, and with this followed by *'Onward, Christian Soldiers'* the Reverend Gunnery then offered prayers, saying in his address that they were facing probably the greatest crisis since the Armada, and it must be remembered that Belgium need not have come into the conflict at all. She might have stood aside and said, "Let those other people fight their battles." She didn't do so, but rose most nobly to the call and had suffered terribly for this country.

After stirring addresses and songs a collection was then taken, which raised a total of £28 10s for the Belgian Relief Fund. With clothing, furniture etc. provided, and their maintenance guaranteed by well known residents in the town, by mid October 1914 three Belgian families were living rent free in a house in Tickford Street. They were Msgr. Joseph Gielen, his wife Madame Elisa Gielen, their daughter, Mdlle. Maria Gielen, Msgr. Eugeen Vergaelen, his wife, Madame Maria Vergaelen, their 2½ year old son, Lucien, and Msgr. Paul Jansens and Madame Caroline Jansens. They had all come from Antwerp and spoke of a nearby village which had been in German hands for nine days. On arriving the enemy had demanded all the food and commandeered all the wine, and amongst the 150 villagers taken prisoner was the father of Msgr. Vergaelen.

Ordered by the Germans to dig a well, the captives, wearing only slippers, trousers and a shirt, had their hands tied behind their backs by the German soldiers, and were then made to stand at the mouth of the well. There they were shot, with their bodies thrown into the well and covered up. Also taken prisoner had been the brother of Msgr. Vergaelen and his mother, but although she had managed to escape, her whereabouts was now unknown. Another village had been bombarded by the Germans for three days. Those buildings that were not destroyed were set alight, whilst in the vicinity of Antwerp at another place 11 bombs dropped by Zeppelins killed 10 people, wounded two policemen and blew a man's arm off; "We saw aeroplanes every day, which threw things down, and the worst was when they bombarded the town. Eight days before the bombardment all the inhabitants slept in the cellars because they were so afraid of the bombs. Then the English soldiers came with their cannon and they cheered us up. Then we saw a fight in the air with some aeroplanes. There was one German aeroplane at first, then four English machines went up and they all seemed to meet in the air. The German seeing he could do no good rushed off. He was pursued but was not captured. All the week prior to the fall of Antwerp we had these things going on and on Wednesday at midnight the Germans began their bombardment of the city with the big siege guns. We shall never forget it; it was terrible. The shells were simply hailing upon us and around the Town Hall and Law Courts. About three o'clock in the morning all the inhabitants fled in the direction of Holland - men with their parcels and the women with their children in their arms. We left our houses at four o'clock and didn't know where to go. Then we saw a friendly boat which took us to Quelque. At 8.30 we arrived at Hansvert in Holland and waited three hours on the station for a train to Veissinque.

"The train was absolutely crammed with refugees, and 350 were waiting on the station when we arrived. The heat in the train was absolutely awful. At Veissinque we were taken in and provided with beds. The women had the beds and the men slept on the floor. At Veissinque we had something to eat for the first time since we left home - nearly 24 hours."

On Saturday morning they were taken to Folkestone by boat, and having been examined by a doctor passed through Customs. They were then given bread, meat and coffee, and, telling of the kind reception they had received in London, said how happy and grateful they were to be in Newport Pagnell. Further funds for the Belgian Relief Fund were raised during the month when, as the first of their winter session, the Newport Pagnell P.S.A. Brotherhood held a musical afternoon at the Electric Theatre. The attendance was such that people even stood in the entrance and exit doors, and with Mr. Arthur Bullard occupying the chair, supported on the platform by the Belgian refugees in the town, the meeting was opened by the playing of the National Anthems of Belgium, Russia and France by Miss Amy Harris. Amongst others on the platform were Lady Farrar, Mrs. Boswell, Mrs. and Miss Trevor, and Miss Tidmarsh. At the outset Mr. Bullard said that a sacred concert and collection would be held in the evening, so as to avoid disappointing those who had been unable to get into the meeting. Continuing, he said that he had visited Belgium as a delegate several times, and it seemed impossible that such a lovely country was now in ruins. The assembly was then addressed by Msgr. Quintin, a Belgian exile, and throughout the event as an accomplished pianist and charming vocalist his daughter, Mdlle. Quintin, would provide contributions including, in her native tongue, the Belgian song 'Avont Groet.'

By the kindness of Colonel Butler, seen in the foreground, Belgian refugees were accommodated at Tickford Abbey

Then in a speech Msgr. Quintin expressed his gratitude for the hospitality afforded by the English and the Brotherhood, saying "We have no words, and surely you need to be in our place to feel our gratitude. You are so happy in this nice, generous England, where we too are happy to be received as you have received us in Newport Pagnell. We have lost everything. Just as we appear now we may look all right, but we have no money; we have nothing. It is a good thing to have such societies as yours. We bring our best thanks and cheers to England and the English people." At the evening meeting, where many had to stand, Mr. F. Sharp was in the chair, with on his right two of the Belgian families who were housed in the town. The proceedings began with the singing of the National Anthem, and during the event Mdlle. Quintin again displayed her talent as a brilliant pianist. The singing by Miss Eva Garratt and Miss Grace Middleton was also greatly appreciated, and in Flemish Msgr. Paul Jansens addressed the meeting through Madame Rippinstoff, a native of Hanslope who, before the war, had lived in Belgium for 14 years. He thanked the English people for their assistance, and said that at home he had helped in the electrification of Antwerp, laying electric wires around the city. Msgr. Quintin also expressed thanks, and said "When we come here we find it so safe. We feel glad to come to a country where you live so happy. If we go back to Belgium we will tell our families what good people you have here. We are so happy that we have not words to tell you how we feel." A collection was then taken, and £20 was raised by the two meetings.

For the accommodation of two Belgian families, the business premises of 18, High Street had now been placed by Mr. and Mrs. W. Lee at the disposal of the Belgian Refugee Committee, which, by the decision of a special meeting of the members of the Newport Pagnell Co-operative Society, held on Monday evening, October 26th 1914, also acquired the use of five rooms of the Society's drapery and boot establishment. In fact providing them with accommodation and sustenance for 15 weeks the Society had applied for six refugees, and if the situation had not improved by then the term might be extended. Through the generosity of Colonel Butler, in November 1914 a family of Belgians was accommodated at Tickford Abbey, comprised of George Morian, his wife, his aged parents, his two boys, his niece, and two servants. When the war broke out they had been at the seaside, and since it was impossible to return to their home, north of Lille, they had been compelled to escape to England in October. After staying a while at Folkestone they then had to seek help, when their funds were almost expended. Locally, for the fund for the Belgian refugees on Wednesday, November 25th 1914 the Newport Pagnell Branch of the National Farmers' Union held an agricultural jumble sale. Miss Payne had lent her field near the centre of the town, at the back of the Cattle Market, and Mr. P. C. Gambell gave his services as auctioneer, he being the resident representative of George Wigley and Sons. The expense of the appeals sent around the district was defrayed by Mr. J. Higham, and amongst others who helped was George Taylor, the blacksmith of Tickford Street, who not only lent his horse and trolley to collect the various gifts, but also permitted the services of his workmen. Farm animals, produce, and implements were all amongst the items, and also offered was a model of a church made by Ernest Miller, a crippled inmate of the Workhouse. This was sold for 2s, and the total of £150 raised by the event would be forwarded to the Daily Telegraph Shilling Fund for Belgian Relief.

From Ostend, a few days before Christmas 1914, another family of Belgian refugees arrived in the town, to be accommodated in the five well-appointed rooms above the drapery department of the Co-operative Society, in St. John Street. They were Monsgr. Jean Bapt Goss, Honorina, his wife, their two children, Mabel and Willy, aged three and one, and Mdlle. Vauleke, the sister of Madame Goss. As a pilot on the sea, Monsgr. Goss had been away on his boat when his family was driven from their home, and it had been due to a falling shell that his wife and children had to flee in terror, clad in only their night clothes.

During the last week of 1914 a party of local vocalists, consisting of Mrs. J. Price, Miss Bailey, the Misses Whiting, Miss Freda Coales, Mr. Lucas Salmons, Mr. O. Critchard (tenor), Mr. A. Bullard and Mr. C. K. Garratt (bass), visited the town and neighbouring villages, and by singing carols raised £11. Of this, £1 was expended on Christmas dinners for four resident

NEWPORT PAGNELL

Pound Day

FOR THE

Belgian Soldiers.

A Pound Day for the Belgian Soldiers at the Front is being organised by the Newport Pagnell Belgian Relief Committee on

Saturday, Aug. 7th.

GIFTS will be received at

St. Peter's School, Priory Street,

Between the Hours of 10 a.m. and 8 p.m.

Please bring one pound of groceries, such as coffee, cocoa, chocolate, lump sugar, biscuits, dried fruit, cereals for puddings, lentils, split peas, haricots, or tinned supplies, such as meat, jam, salmon, meat, extract, fruit, &c.

All particulars will be found in the leaflets distributed in the town and neighbourhood.

Bucks Standard, August 7th, 1915

A local Belgian appeal in 1915.

families bereaved by the war, with the remainder being given to the Newport Pagnell Belgian Refugees Relief Fund. As for raising funds to bring relief to the destitute women and children in France and Belgium, on Sunday evening, February 28th 1915 a concert was held at the Electric Theatre by the Newport Pagnell P.S.A. Brotherhood. Once again so many attended that some had to stand, and, with Mr. C. K. Garratt as the pianist, the artistes included Miss Maude Willby, of the Sheffield Choir World Tour, Frank Webster, of St. Paul's Cathedral Choir, and Miss Winnie Cotton, a promising local musician who gave a pleasing piano solo.

The event was staged under the patronage of Lady Farrar, who presided, and she was supported by amongst others Mr. W. Hichens, the chairman of Messrs. Cammell, Laird and Co. shipbuilders, Alfred Bullard, who had been primarily responsible for organising the concert, and several of the Belgian refugees who were staying in the town. Opening the proceedings Mr. Garratt played the National Anthem of the Allies, and after the singing of the first verse of God Save the King a short address was given by Lady Farrar. All the musical items were of an extremely high standard, and during an interval Mr. Bullard explained the purpose of the concert, with Mr. Hichens pointing out in a speech the perils of labour disputes in the factories, which disrupted the output of essential war supplies. In aid of the destitute and starving poor in Belgium, at the Town Hall on Tuesday evening May 6th 1915 a concert was held, for the success of which the Misses Allfrey had worked very hard. Plants and flowers loaned by Mr. F. Allfrey decorated the stage, and among the artistes were Msgr. Alfred de Reyghere, the Belgian violinist, and his violinist son, Master Alfred de Reyghere. The contralto songs of Madame Dora Newell were greatly appreciated, also the performance of the elocutionist, Miss Ruby Bower. During the interval Belgian favours offered to the audience raised £2 17s. Having for the past five months been organising and collecting food and clothing, during the first week of May 1915 the committee of the Newport Pagnell P.S.A. Brotherhood despatched five tons from the town, for the relief of the destitute and poor in Belgium and France. This was being sent to the order of Monsieur Maurice Calmeyn Adinkerque, via Dunkirk, for the Commission de Ravitallment, La Panne, Belgium, and would be the 11th such expedition undertaken by the Brotherhoods of England.

In fact the need for organised relief had been witnessed at first hand by Mr. A. Bullard, who had accompanied the 10th expedition to Bruay, Bethune, Givenchy and Vermilles. Sadly, on the afternoon of Wednesday, July 14th 1915 the funeral took place in Newport Pagnell Cemetery of Madame Van Yoos, a Belgian refugee who, with her husband and children, had been guests of the local Co-operative Society. The compounded effects of escaping the Zeppelin raids on Antwerp, plus the illness that she was suffering at the time of the German invasion, had led to an intervention of consumption, and it was from this that she died on July 10th, aged 30. Amongst the many mourners were the Belgian refugees from the town, Miss Quinlan, Mr. J. Tattam, secretary of the local Co-op, many of the Co-op members, and 'A few English neighbours.' The Reverend Father Walker, of the Wolverton Roman Catholic Church, conducted the burial rites, and among the floral tributes were those placed on the grave by the bereaved husband and the two children. Apart from the Belgians, under the auspices of the Newport Pagnell War Charities Committee relief for the Serbians would also be raised in the town, with two grand concerts in aid of the Serbian Relief Fund being held in the Electric Theatre on Tuesday, February 1st 1916. Mr. C. K. Garratt was the organiser, with support for the concerts being given by Lady Farrar, Lord and Lady Euston, and other well known people of the district. Through the kind offices of Lady Farrar, Madame Ada Crossley, the world famed contralto, came down from London, and other artistes included Miss Gune Atkinson, from Cosgrove Priory, 'a charming soprano,' Miss Gwendoline Farrar, an accomplished cellist, Alfred Heather, the principal tenor of the Beecham Opera Company and the Royal Choral Society, Charles Tree, the popular baritone, and George Blackmore, a clever entertainer.

Played by Mr. Garratt the programme opened with the Serbian and British National Anthems, and during an interval tea was served, under the direction of a ladies' committee headed by Mrs. Allfrey. At the crowded afternoon performance the sale of programmes by the Misses Helen and Muriel Farrar, Miss Wickham, and Miss Lawley realised £4 14s 6d, and with members of the Royal Engineers acting as stewards the evening concert was packed, such that by the combined collections Mr. C. K. Garratt would be able to forward a cheque for £110 0s 6d to Mr. W. Chantler, J.P., the honorary treasurer of the Newport Pagnell War Charities Committee. As for the Belgians, there seems little further information available, but no doubt after the war they were able to return to their native land, for in 1919 it was requested that anyone who had lent furniture to the Belgians at 63, Tickford Street, should fetch it away by Monday afternoon, March 3rd. Yet interestingly some years after the war the town would again become acquainted with another refugee who had escaped to England. He was Raphael Henri Remon, who as a 13 year old boy had fled from the advancing German cavalry at La Basse in 1914. At Calais he boarded a ship for England, but that night the vessel unfortunately struck a mine and sank, and, since at the time it was believed that everyone aboard had drowned, his parents gave him up for dead. However, he had been rescued and was subsequently brought to England. After the war, whilst working in London he made friends with a son of Mr. and Mrs. Joseph Goodman, of Broad Street, Newport Pagnell, and having recently married he and his bride then came to stay with the family for their Christmas holiday. During this time they made many friends in the town, and with his story having aroused local interest renewed attempts would be made to try and trace his parents.

BUCKS VOLUNTEER DEFENCE CORPS

Following the outbreak of war in August 1914 some 70 men of the town, being representative of the business community, volunteered to perform two or three hours of duty each night, guarding such places as the water works, gas works, post office and local bridges. Then in support of the movement for establishing a North Bucks Battalion of the Volunteer Defence Force, this being for the defence of the homeland in case of emergency or invasion, a well-attended public meeting was held in the Masonic Hall on Monday evening, February 15th 1915. Local farmers, tradesmen, men above military age and a large contingent of special constables attended and lucid speeches of explanation were given by Lieutenant Colonel W. G. Bowyer, Commandant of the North Bucks Battalion, and also by the adjutant Mr. W. Trevor, who said: "The defence of the locality could not be better done than by men who knew every inch of the country. And in those counties where a landing might be attempted the organised volunteers would be of immense value."

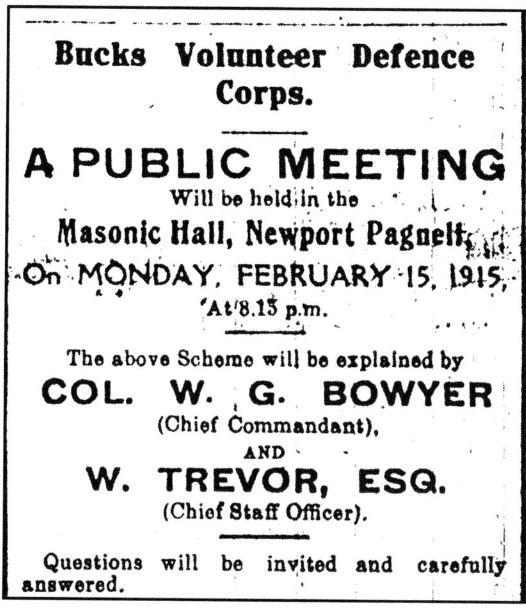

Bucks Volunteer Defence Corps.

A PUBLIC MEETING

Will be held in the

Masonic Hall, Newport Pagnell,

On MONDAY, FEBRUARY 15, 1915,

At 8.15 p.m.

The above Scheme will be explained by

COL. W. G. BOWYER

(Chief Commandant),

AND

W. TREVOR, ESQ.

(Chief Staff Officer).

Questions will be invited and carefully answered.

Bucks Standard, February 13, 1915

In his address Lieutenant Colonel Bowyer said: "The object of the movement was that any invader of this country should feel that he had to meet not only the regular forces that were left for the protection of the country, but that all the able bodied inhabitants would be to a great extent drilled and skilled enough in arms which with their knowledge of the country would make them a very formidable foe." Explaining the background to the assembly, he said that in the wake of a meeting called by the Lord Lieutenant of the county a wish was expressed, after some discussion, that three battalions should be raised in Buckinghamshire, to be called the Buckinghamshire Defence Corps. These three battalions would be raised in the three parliamentary divisions of the county and he had been asked by the Lord Lieutenant to raise that for the north. Written authority to fight would be given by the War Office but with the need to make arrangements for expenditure a central committee, supported by wealthy men, had been formed in Bucks, in consequence of which some 2,000 rifles had been purchased.

In time it was hoped to have the men attired in uniform and whilst this was permitted by the War Office no badges of rank were to be worn, with the only identification to be a distinctive armlet with the letters G.R. on the left arm, this being the warrant of the War Office that a man was under their organisation and control and entitled to bear and use arms. With no age limit or medical, Lieutenant Colonel Bowyer said that any man who wished to join should visit the police station, where the roll was kept, and sign a form of declaration. There would be three drills a week and to meet the criteria a man would have to attend 40 drills of an hour each, plus qualifying as a second class shot on the miniature rifle range . By March 1915, with Mr. W. Uthwatt as the captain and Mr. Murray Gordon as the honorary local secretary, some 20 youths from the town aged 15 to 19 had enrolled in the 'Newport Pagnell Company of the County Volunteer Defence Corps,' with the drill instruction being given by Mr. John O. Butler, who lived with his wife, Adeline, at The Bank House, Newport Pagnell. Being also the auditor of the Newport Pagnell Gas and Coke Co., in his daytime employment he was the local manager of Barclay and Co's. Bank and so the drills had been arranged for the evenings of Tuesdays at 8 p.m. and Wednesdays and Saturdays at 6.30 p.m. Including John Odell, George Tayler, F. W. Taylor, Percy Taylor, A. Bullard, F. O.Butler, E. Glanley, C. H. Glanville, F. Wilford, C. Wilford, T. Blagg, J. Higham and H. Middleton, by the beginning of April 1915 the company had 78 members and whilst all had been issued with the official 'G.R.' armlets, many of the older members had additionally been supplied with rifles and bayonets. Soon Mr. Butler was promoted from the ranks to be platoon commander and as such on Sunday afternoon, August 22nd 1915, took part in a route march and drill which comprised the members of the Newport Pagnell and Olney Companies of the Bucks Volunteer Defence Corps. Carrying arms, and many wearing the regulation head dress, the companies met at Cross Albans Hill and after over an hour of drill, carried out in a field tenanted by Mr. R. Mayes, then marched back to their respective headquarters.

Under Commandant W. Trevor, accompanied by Platoon Commander F. O.Butler and Section Commanders H. I. Middleton and E. Naylor, the Newport Pagnell platoon of the Bucks Volunteer Defence Corps went on another march on the afternoon of Sunday, September 12th 1915. With other sections this was to a field lent by Ben Whiting at Willen, where, after useful field operations, the 70 members of all ranks took part in a charge.

It was perhaps as a debrief to this exercise that on the following Tuesday evening Commandant W. Trevor gave a lecture to the officers and men of the Newport Pagnell platoon on field operations. As for those local men in the regular forces, these included Mr. Butler's son of whom it was stated in the London Gazette on Thursday night; July 27th 1916, 'W. Riding Regt. Cadet John Goodwin Butler, from Inns of Court O.T.C., to be second lieutenant (on probation), 23rd July 1916.' From employment on the local staff of Barclay and Co's Bank he had joined the Officers' Training Corps on July 19th 1915, and would leave for the Western Front in October 1916. One of the largest patriotic meetings in the town since the war began took place on Market Hill on Friday, August 4th 1916. This, with Mr. O. H. Bull presiding, had been convened by the U.D.C. and amongst those supporting him on the platform were Mr. W. Trevor, J.P., wearing the uniform of the Bucks Volunteer Regiment, of which he was now 'Commanding Officer of the North Bucks (3rd) Battalion.' In a patriotic speech he said that during a meeting of the Territorial Force Association, held that day, he had received

Newport Pagnell, Wolverton and District Model Building Society.

AN APPROPRIATION by Sale will take place at The Poplars, after the usual Subscription Meeting on Monday, 26th November, 1917.

MYRTILLO WARREN,
Secretary.

Advertisement in the Bucks Standard November 17, 1917

Below:

The Poplars, until lately a video shop

orders 'to do his level best' to get recruits for the Bucks Volunteer Regiment. However, for three new members they had little choice for, having at the Urban Tribunal on Wednesday evening, August 9th 1916, been granted three months' military exemption, this was conditional on joining that body.

The stark realities of active service were tragically emphasised when it was announced that on Thursday, March 29th 1917, Mr. Butler's son, Second Lieutenant John Goodwin Butler, of the Duke of Wellington's (West Riding) Regiment, had died of wounds received in action. He was aged 20. On Wednesday evening, December 19th 1917, at the meeting of the Newport Pagnell, Wolverton and District Model Building Society, held at The Poplars, his father was appointed an arbitrator in place of the late Mr. F. J. Taylor and during the same month Mr. Nicholls, a surveyor of the R.D.C., was appointed Quartermaster and Honorary Lieutenant in the 3rd Bucks Volunteer Regiment. On the occasion of the King's Proclamation being read, on Sunday, January 6th 1918, the Newport Pagnell Platoon of the Bucks Volunteer Regiment, under Lieutenant H. I. Middleton, were amongst those present at the Soldiers' Church Parade, as also when they formed a guard of honour at the Red Cross Sale held on Market Hill on Wednesday, April 24th 1918. On this occasion they were dressed in their newly arrived uniforms but the incentive of new uniforms seemed insufficient to encourage the attendance of some members, for at the meeting of the U.D.C. on Wednesday evening, October 30th 1918, Lieutenant Middleton, speaking on the question of Volunteer training conditions, said that a number of the men who had been granted military exemption had 'never been near' to carry out their duties. In fact several had been arrested and threatened with detention at Oxford Barracks, a measure which seemed to cure their reluctance. Recruits had to put in 14 drills a month of one hour each (with this being 10 for 'efficient men') and Sunday sessions from 10 a.m. to 12.30 p.m. counted as 3½ drills. Yet the following month with the signing of the Armistice there would be no further need for such commitment and it would be with a proud record that the Newport Pagnell Company of Volunteers, under Lieutenant H. I. Middleton, with Captain Tanguy, adjutant, and Dr. H.T. Wickham, Medical Officer, attended the special thanksgiving services for the cessation of hostilities on Sunday, November 17th 1918. Then at the disbanding of the Newport Pagnell Company of Special Constables on Saturday evening, October 25th 1919, thanks were expressed to Lieutenant Butler, and also Captain Wilford, for having done so much to bring the town's company to perfection.

C. KENNETH GARRATT

An only son, Charles Kenneth Garratt was born in 1885, and at the age of seven began his long association with the Newport Pagnell Parish Church Choir, of which he would be boy solo for five years. As a boy soprano, with blackened face he also sang with the Newport Pagnell Diamond Jubilee Minstrels and on May 3rd 1898, in an entertainment given by them for the benefit of the Football Club he contributed, 'When mother puts the little ones to bed.' He studied the organ firstly under Mrs. Alfred Bullard and then successively Mr. C. J. King, of St. Matthew's Church, Northampton (he being a well known organist, who was conductor of the Northampton Musical Society), Dr. Stanley Roper, M.V.O., F.R.C.O., organist to His Majesty's Chapels Royal, London, and then Dr. Alcock, a one time organist at Salisbury Cathedral. When his voice broke at the age of 15 he became the organist at Chicheley Church, where on Thursday, August 10th 1905, at a service to dedicate the bells and organ he played the newly overhauled and retuned instrument, to which two new stops had been added. After the service, on the Vicarage lawn his string band then played music for dancing.

In 1906 Mr. Garratt conducted his first work, 'The Mikado,' and in March 1908 he succeeded Donald Reid (who became a member of St. Paul's Cathedral Choir) as organist at Newport Pagnell Parish Church. In fact it was here that on the afternoon of Thursday October 5th 1911, he married Miss Gladys Evelyn Cotton, the daughter of Mr. W. Cotton of Newport Pagnell. With the catering by Mr. H. Roddis, of the Anchor Hotel, on the previous evening the groom had invited the senior members of the choir to dinner at the Masonic Hall, and afterwards the ladies joined the company for entertainments to include piano duets by the bride's sister, Miss Winnie Cotton, and Mr. Garratt. During an interval the Vicar then presented Mr. Garratt with a handsome arm chair, subscribed for by the choir as a wedding gift.

As for the wedding service, this was conducted by the Reverend Gunnery assisted by the Reverend U. J. Easson, of Chicheley. The service was fully choral and one of the hymns had been specially composed for the occasion by Donald Reid. Attending the bride were Miss Cotton's two sisters, and at the reception, held at the Town Hall, a model of the parish church surmounted the wedding cake. Afterwards a short whist drive was followed by dancing, with the couple then leaving for a honeymoon in Penzance, the Scilly Isles and Torquay. Including 'The Pirates of Penzance,' from 1909 Mr. Garratt organised and conducted many operas in the town and following the outbreak of the First World War he would organise numerous entertainments for the raising of funds and morale, many of which are detailed elsewhere in this book. At the Congregational Church, on Monday, August 30th 1915, his cousin, Miss Elsie Garratt, the second daughter of the late Mr. Barker Garratt and Mrs. Garratt, married Arthur Roberts, the second son of Mr. and Mrs. John Roberts. Miss Garratt had a long association with the Congregational Church, being a teacher in the Sunday School and a former member of the choir, whilst the groom, having for 17 years been an official of the town's governing body, was deputy clerk of the U.D.C. Additionally he was the local agent for the Board of Trade and Unemployment Insurance, an active member of the P.S.A. and financial secretary to the Hospital Week Committee. Her uncle, Thomas Garratt, gave the bride away and after the service a reception for about 40 guests took place at her home in Silver Street. Then in the early evening the couple motored to Bletchley station, to board a train for a honeymoon in Folkestone. The bride's only bridesmaid had been her sister, Miss Eva Garratt, who on Thursday, February 17th 1916, in the Wesleyan Schoolroom would be among the artistes at an entertainment staged by the Wesleyan Royal Engineers, in which her songs included 'My love is like a red, red rose,' and 'Till the boys come home.'

Tragically, just as the war was coming to a close the town was struck by the influenza epidemic and with Mr. Garratt falling victim he was duly nursed by his wife. However she then became ill and died aged 31 on October 24th 1918, at her home 'Concordia,' 26, Lovat Street. The funeral took place on the afternoon of Monday October 28th, and the details are given in the Influenza Epidemic chapter.

Eventually Mr. Garratt recovered from his illness, convalescing at Bournemouth, and, resuming his interest in the local entertainments, would be responsible for the afternoon and evening concerts which, on Monday, March 3rd 1919, were performed at the Electric Theatre. These were in aid of the town's Nursing and Good Samaritan Society and Mr. Garratt opened the afternoon programme by playing Grieg's Wedding Day on the piano. During the performance the soprano Miss Desiree Ellinger, of the Sir Thomas Beecham Grand Opera Company, made her first appearance in the district, and the event would raise £40 12s 6d.

As the organist and choirmaster of the parish church, the first of an anticipated series of organ recitals by Mr. Garratt was given at Evensong on Sunday, October 26th 1919, and on Wednesday, November 5th 1919, he was also present at a meeting to consider the formation of an Orchestral Society for Wolverton and district. This was held at 7 p.m. in the large hall of the Infants' School, Aylesbury Street, Wolverton. Mr. Garratt was also continuing to instruct private pupils, amongst whom in November 1920 Miss Winifred Rout, of Silver Street, obtained honours in pianoforte playing in the Senior Division of the Trinity College of Music Examinations. These had been held recently at Northampton and she scored 37 marks out of 40 for playing and 19 out of 20 for studies.

As for other successes, as a pupil of Miss N. Watkins, of Lovat Street, in July 1918 she had obtained the Pitman's Theory Certificate for Shorthand. In 1921 Mr. Garratt became honorary conductor of the Newport Pagnell and District Choral Society (holding this position until 1940), and in 1922 was appointed director of the Wolverton Science and Arts Institute and District Choral Society, a position he would hold until 1940, when overtime duties meant that members were unable to attend for practice.

In his daily employment Mr. Garratt was a clerk in the accounts department at Wolverton Works, and on September 14th 1922, he married Gracie Jenkins, the eldest of the four daughters of Mr. Henry C. Jenkins (of The Firs, Wolverton), who had come to Wolverton Works as chief accountant in 1910. Held at 9 a.m., with Mr. Julian Mann, of Olney, as best man the ceremony was of a quiet nature and attended by two of her sisters, the Misses Vera and Dilys Jenkins, the bride was given away by her father. Afterwards a reception for relatives and those immediately concerned took place at Tickford Abbey, which had been kindly lent by Mr. and Mrs. Ward. The honeymoon would be in Cornwall and a daughter would be born to the couple on May 22nd 1923.

When the Temple of Music was built in the grounds of Tyringham House in 1929 Mr. Garratt became the honorary organist, and his subsequent performances would raise hundreds of pounds for the Tyringham Pension Fund, instituted by the Konig family. The following year, in January he then gave an organ recital in the Congregational Church, being assisted by his recently formed choir of glee singers. In fact one of the members was his cousin Miss Eva Garratt, a daughter of the late Barker Garratt, the brother of his father Thomas Garratt.

Appointed as the conductor of the Bletchley Choral Society in 1935 (retaining this position until 1941) the following year for somewhat different skills he received the gift of an electric clock, as an appreciation for having since 1925 organised the clerical staff annual outings of Wolverton Works. His home was now The Elms, in the High Street, where on the morning of September 5th 1942, his mother, Lucy, died at the age of 80, 13 years after her husband. She had lived at The Elms for the past eight years, and having been ill for a while had been bed ridden for the last three weeks. Born in Sherington in 1862 she was the youngest daughter of Mr. and Mrs. John Coleman, and apart from being a devout church person she had also been greatly involved in the local branch of the Mothers' Union. The funeral took place at Newport Pagnell Parish Church on the Tuesday afternoon, with her body laid to rest in the grave of her husband.

On the last Thursday of February 1945, Mr. Garratt retired after 46 years as a member of the accountants staff of the L.M.S. at Wolverton Works. His one time boss and father in law, Henry Jenkins, had retired in 1931, but sadly he died only a few months after the retirement of his son in law, who attended the funeral at St. Albans in October 1945. After retiring Mr. Garratt continued to officiate as organist and choirmaster at the parish church which fortunately had not been damaged during the war. However in 1941 during an enemy air raid bombs straddled the railway line and seriously damaged the front portion of St. Luke's Church, which served, and still serves, the Red House district of the town.

Thus on Whit Monday 1948, an event to raise money for repairs was held, and in the Fancy Dress competition Mr. Garratt's daughter, Jean, came third in the 'walking children up to 5' group, dressed as 'Make Do and Mend.' Before a packed attendance, on Sunday, July 11th 1948, in the lower hall of the Newport Pagnell Church House a public presentation was made to him by Mr. H. Mason, the people's warden. This was in honour of his 40 years' service as organist and choirmaster at the parish church, and, having been subscribed for by the people of the parish, comprised a cheque for £50 and a framed photograph of the church choir.

Looking towards the chancel, Newport Pagnell Parish Church.

Maintaining his musical association with the town, during the same year Mr. Garratt was instrumental in reforming the Newport Pagnell and

The commemorative plaque, mounted beside the organ in Newport Pagnell Parish Church.

District Choral Society, of which he would remain the conductor until 1956. In further musical acclaim he would also be president for five years of the Bedfordshire Organists' Association, and in 1950 twice conducted 'Elijah' for the Northampton Musical Society, when their conductor fell ill. In 1952 he then retired as organist and choirmaster of Newport Pagnell Parish Church and at a private party given to the choirboys, held on Saturday, March 22nd, the senior choirboy, Master Brian Berrill, made a speech on their behalf to mark the occasion. Thanking Mr. Garratt for his good work and his kindness, he presented him with a Parker Duofold pen and a magnificent blotter, inscribed in gold leaf, 'To C. K. Garratt from his choirmen.' Wishing him and his wife a happy retirement Brian then asked Mrs. Garratt to accept a silver trinket dish. This was a gift from the choirboys for the many parties afforded to them over the years by herself and her husband, who additionally received a monetary gift from the bellringers.

The Elms, High Street

Yet Mr. Garratt still remained active on the local music scene and when after the sale of Tyringham House the new owners, the directors of the Australia and New Zealand Bank, gave permission for the fourth of a series of music concerts, to be held on the afternoon of Sunday, August 10th 1952, Mr. Garratt as the honorary organist of the Temple of Music was the accompanist, as well as playing many pieces. On Easter Saturday 1953, Mr. Garratt's only daughter, Jean, who was Head Almoner of the Hitchin hospitals, married James Kingston, the son of Mr. and Mrs. W. Kingston of Laragh House, Bandon, County Cork, with one of the wedding gifts being appropriately from the Newport Pagnell and District Choral Society. The ceremony took place at St. Ippolyts church, Hitchin, and as one of Mr. Garratt's former pupils Bert Thickpenny, who was now organist at Stoke Goldington and Gayhurst, presided at the organ. Jean was given away by her father and the honeymoon would be spent touring in France and Spain, after which the couple would make their home at Great Snoring, near Fakenham, Norfolk.

Jean had been educated at Bedford High School and Edinburgh University and, after completing her training as an almoner through the Institute of Almoners, she secured her first post at Luton and Dunstable Hospital. Whilst at Luton she became a member of the Luton Choral Society and when later appointed Head Almoner of the Hitchin Hospitals she then joined The Thespians, an operatic society of the town. As for the groom, having graduated at Trinity College, Dublin, he was a civil engineer and during the war served abroad as a Flight Lieutenant with the R.A.F. Presently he held a post with the Air Ministry Works Directorate, following three years with the Anglo Iranian Oil Company at Abadan.

Having never fully recovered from a serious illness at Christmas, on Good Friday 1959, Mr. Garratt suddenly died at his home, The Elms, aged 74, having taken to his bed on Tuesday week. Apart from his musical activities, as a prominent Freemason he had been the oldest member of the S.S. Peter and Paul Lodge of Newport Pagnell, instituted in 1909, and apart from being Lodge organist for many years was twice Worshipful Master. In fact the previous year he had been appointed as an officer of the Grand Lodge of England. The funeral took place on the Tuesday morning and among the many mourners was his brother-in-law, Mr. H. Jenkins.

After the death of Mr. Garratt the directors of the Australia and New Zealand Bank at Tyringham allowed several of his ex-pupils and friends to carry on the Temple of Music concerts, and no doubt these included Peter Harris, the only son of Mr. and Mrs. R. Harris of Lincoln Lodge, Silver Street, who would continue Mr. Garratt's musical legacy by becoming the organist at the churches of Willen, Walton and Woolstone.

CHURCH INSTITUTE & THE TOWN INSTITUTE

With nearly 40 of the members now serving in the Forces, for the forty-eighth time the members of the Newport Pagnell Church Institute were entertained to a supper on New Year's Eve 1914 by Mr. F. J. Taylor, of Lovat Bank. However, in his absence his nephew, Frank Taylor, presided, and amongst those present were John Odell, the vice president of the Institute, and several members in military uniform. With the customary distribution of Tom Smith's crackers, the supper was served by Messrs. C. Lawman and Son, and once the tables had been cleared the chairman proposed the loyal toasts. Afterwards further toasts were proposed, and among the stirring speeches was that made by the Vicar, the Reverend F. Gunnery. Being afforded a cordial welcome Private Percy Odell said it was a privilege to appear in uniform that night, for during the past few weeks he and his comrades had been preparing themselves and getting fit, such that when the hour arose they would be a credit to the town. Another fitting response to the toast was made by Lance Corporal C. Darlow, and at the conclusion of these formalities the rest of the evening was given up to songs, with Mr. C. K. Garratt presiding at the piano. In aid of funds for the Church Institute, in the Masonic Hall a concert was given by Mr. A. Levin's concert party on Wednesday evening, October 20th 1915.

Then at the same venue on Tuesday evening, December 28th 1915, there was a happy gathering of the Royal Engineers stationed in the town. This was for the formal opening of the building as a recreation, games and refreshment centre for the military, and the soldiers gave three rousing cheers when the vicar announced that the library and billiards table of the Church Institute, which was situated on the floor below, would be open to the men. For the funds of the 'Newport Pagnell Church Institute and the Melanesian Mission,' by permission of the Reverend R. S. and Mrs. Mitchison the annual sale of work was held on Thursday, June 15th 1916, in the grounds of Green Lodge. The members of the Church of England's Men's Society (C.E.M.S.) gave invaluable help, and in bright summer weather the ladies at the stalls enjoyed good business in the shade of the trees, with the secretarial duties being undertaken by Mr. H. Middleton. Directed by Miss Wilford, and with Miss West at the piano, the children performed delightful songs and dances, and the entertainment also included two charming performances by Madge Proctor, whose rendering of the song 'My precious Teddy Bear' earned high praise. A play was acted by the Misses Allfrey and the Misses Savory (from Emberton) and of the various attractions a sweet stall was the province of the Misses Gunnery, assisted by Miss Shepherd and Mademoiselle Le Quilbacq, with hoop la under the charge of Miss D. Odell and Miss Connie Saunders. During the afternoon a fancy rummage came under the wing of Mrs. H. Middleton and her daughter, Miss G. Middleton, whilst in the evening Mr. H. Middleton conducted a rummage sale. Then in further activities that year, on Saturday, December 16th 1916 a charity football match was played at the town between the local Church Institute and the Royal Engineers, raising £3 14s for Northampton Hospital.

On Thursday afternoon, June 14th 1917, the grounds of Green Lodge, kindly lent by the Reverend R. S. and Mrs. Mitchison, were again the venue for a sale of work and garden party in aid of the Newport Pagnell Church Institute and the Melanesian Mission. This had been arranged by Mrs. P. C. Gambell, and with the stalls located about the lawn there were also guessing and other competitions, as well as a rummage sale arranged by Mrs. Gambell, picturesque dances given by the Council School girls under the direction of Miss James, and music in the evening by the Excelsior Silver Band. As for the dances, seven 'little dots,' dressed as babies in long white nightgowns and night caps, scored a big success in their piece 'It's no joke to be a baby.' In fine weather the occasion was greatly enjoyed, and raised a commendable sum of £64.

Representing the various religious bodies in the town, a meeting was held on the evening of Wednesday, July 25th 1917. This was at the invitation of the Vicar, who said that only by the generosity of the late Mr. Fred Taylor had the Church Institute been kept going for so many years. Now on the present lines it could not be self supporting, and, being willing to waive his position as president, he asked for opinions as to whether the Institute was necessary, and if so how it should be run. Presently they were solvent, but it being stated that the cost would be about £100 a year, plus ideally another £50, Mr. H. I. Middleton, the secretary from 1902, gave details of the finance, management, and membership. Praising the work of the Institute, Mr. O. H. Bull stressed the need for its continuance, especially in the interests of the young and old, and after discussions between the vicar, Mr. O. H. Bull, Mr. H. I. Middleton, Mr. F. W.

Proposed Newport Pagnell Town Institute.

A MEETING will be held in the Church Institute on WEDNESDAY next, DEC. 12, at 8 p.m., to receive the report of the provisional committee appointed by a previous meeting.

All interested in this important matter are particularly requested to attend.

JOSEPH SHORT,
Chairman of the Urban District Council.

Bucks Standard, December 8, 1917

Taylor, Dr. Wickham, Mr. F. Allfrey, the Reverend A. Seys Howell, Mr. Francis Littleboy (manager of the town's branch of Barclays Bank), Mr. W. Cowley, Mr. F. J. Sharp, Mr. M. Warren, Mr. F. O. Butler, and Mr. T. Garratt, the meeting pledged to put a resolution, regarding the formation of a Town Institute, to the members at the half yearly meeting in September 1917.

The Church Institute, at the top of Silver street. Partly timber framed, the premises were destroyed by fire in 1934. Photo courtesy of Don Hurst.

Steps would then be taken to wind up the present Institution, with a further meeting to be held to establish the Town Institute. Thus on Wednesday evening, December 12th 1917, a public meeting duly took place, at which was considered the report of a provisional committee that a Town Institute should be established, and then carried on as an experiment for one year from January 1st 1918. Mr. J. Short, the chairman of the provisional committee, occupied the chair, and including a number of the youthful members of the Church Institute those present were the Reverend Gunnery, the Reverend Mitchison, Dr. Wickham, Dr. Bailey, and Messrs. F. Allfrey, F. W. Taylor, F. Littleboy, F. J. Sharp, W. Cowley, T. Garratt, S. Ratcliffe, R. Gordon, E. Feasey, O. H. Bull, and H. C. Cummins. Meeting with the assembly's approval the report was unanimously adopted, and in consequence the Masonic Hall Company would be approached both with a view to renting the whole of the Hall, and to ascertain the price for its purchase. For making these enquiries Messrs. F. W. Bull, W. J. Coales, and Mr. J. Short were appointed as the sub committee, with Messrs. F. W. Bull, F. Littleboy, and F. W. Taylor appointed as the sub committee to draw up an appeal for subscriptions. As for the draft rules, these, drawn up by the

Reverend Gunnery, Mr. W. Cowley, and Mr. T. G. Puryer, were submitted at the second meeting of the provisional committee where, being practically the same as at present, except for lowering the age of admission to 15, they were recommended for adoption. In other business Mr. F. Littleboy reported that £18 4s in donations for immediate use had been promised, plus promises of £25 as annual subscriptions, and in a letter the Masonic Hall Company had offered to let the present Church Institute and gym for £28 p.a. As for the use of the whole of the Masonic Hall this would be £50 p.a., or £750 for the purchase.

After due consideration it was resolved to recommend taking over the present Church Institute at £28 p.a., with the landlord paying rates. So that a fresh start could be made Mr. Allfrey, who had been a member for 40 years, generously offered to clear the debts of the Church Institute up to December 31st of the present year, and with all the matters now resolved it was moved that a Town Institute should be formed on the lines recommended by the provisional committee. In consequence Mr. F. W. Taylor suggested that without re-election the members of the Church Institute should be considered members of the new Town Institute, and any others who wished to join could send in their names for election at a meeting of the Institute in the first week of January. Ultimately the vicar proposed, and Mr. F. J. Sharp seconded, that a committee of six be appointed from that meeting to meet a committee of six to be elected by the Church Institute, with these 12 members to form the first committee of the new Town Institute. The former six would be the Reverend A. Seys Howell and Messrs. F. Littleboy, J. Short, W. Cowley, F. J. Sharp and A. Bullard, whilst for the latter these would be the Reverend Gunnery and Messrs. F. Allfrey, G. Tayler, F. W. Taylor, J. Odell, and O. H. Bull, as was decided at a special general meeting of the members of the Church Institute held on Saturday evening, December 15th 1917. Occupying the chair, here the Reverend Gunnery referred to the generous offer made by Mr. F. Allfrey to clear the whole of the liabilities of the Institute, and in an appropriate response a hearty vote of thanks was adopted. It was then proposed by Mr. Allfrey 'That an inventory be taken of the property of the Church Institute, and that it be leased from January 1st, 1918, to the Town Institute from year to year at a nominal rent of 1s per annum payable to the Vicar, and to be surrendered to the Vicar and the Parochial Church Council in as good condition as now, fair wear and tear excepted, in case of the new Institute falling through within three years from January 1, 1918.'

This was then carried unanimously having been seconded by Mr. T. Garratt, on whose proposition, seconded by Mr. M. Warren, it was agreed that the provisional committee should be empowered to wind up the Church

Institute. Mr. P. C. Gambell would be asked to undertake the inventory, and thus the inauguration of the new Town Institute took place in the Lower Room of the Masonic Hall on Monday evening, January 7th 1918. Amongst the large attendance were the Reverend Gunnery, the Reverend R. Mitchison and Messrs. J. Short, F. Littleboy, F. Allfrey, G. Tayler, J. Day, T. Garratt. A. J. Simpson, O. H. Bull, J. West, A. Fairweather, J. Odell, F. O.Butler, A. Inwood, E. Feasey, P. C. Gambell, F. W. Taylor, A. Bullard, S. Ratcliffe, W. J. Line and J. Gregory. Also present were a good number of the lads who would benefit. Letters of apology had been received from Messrs. F. W. Bull, W. Cowley, and F. J. Sharp, and, having been proposed to the chair by the Reverend Gunnery, Mr. J. Short, chairman of the U.D.C., said in his opening remarks that, having himself been first acquainted with the old Institute some 40 years ago, they met to give a good send off to the new Town Institute, where he hoped some of the older men would from time to time attend, so as to instruct the younger members. After his address he then declared the Town Institute open, following which Mr. O. H. Bull wanted to know if the committee entrusted with the arrangements had prepared a draft of the proposed rules, and what the terms of membership would be. As the acting honorary secretary the Reverend Gunnery then read the proposed rules and regulations, which he said were largely based on those of the old, and it was suggested that lads aged from 15 to 18 should pay 1s a quarter, those over the age of 18 the sum of 1s 6d per quarter, and honorary members not less than 10s per annum.

ASPLEY HEATH, Beds,
One mile from Woburn Sands Station, L. & N.-W. Rly.

MESSRS. FOLL & BAWDEN
Are instructed by Mr. Inwood, who is relinquishing the Fullers Earth Works,
To Sell by Auction, on the premises,
On WEDNESDAY, MARCH 1, 1916, at One o'clock precisely,

MACHINERY, TOOLS, and PLANT, including a capital 22h.p. Crossley oil engine, shafting, belting, pulley wheels, water tanks, wheelbarrows, sacks, iron plates and bars, hoists, corn mill, timber-built sheds, corrugated iron, and miscellanea.

Catalogues of the Auctioneers, Woburn Sands and Bletchley.

Bucks Standard, February 1916

With business continuing almost as usual, in September 1914, a 'very cheap' 6 h.p. De Dion car was offered for sale by Foll and Bawden, auctioneers at 58, High Street, Newport Pagnell. However, once it became clear that the war was going to be a protracted conflict there was a continuing need for men for the Army and in the last week of October 1915, Vivian Gardner, a clerk in the offices, was accepted for the Army Ordnance Corps. He had previously tried to enlist five times, including at Dunstable and Finsbury Barracks, but had been rejected on each occasion. In early 1916 it was announced that the business carried on in the town for the last six years by Foll and Bawden would shortly pass to Geo. Wigley and Sons. This was principally because Lieutenant T. Bawden, who was in partnership with Mr. W.A. Foll, was expected to soon leave for foreign service, since he had accepted a commission in the Army Service Corps in the autumn of 1915. In fact it was perhaps in consequence of this that on April 24th 1916, at the Swan Hotel a daughter was born to his wife, who in January 1917 required a young girl as a general servant at 'Ingleside,' Wolverton Road. A year later it was announced that Lieutenant Bawden, who for some months had been commanding a Horse Transport Company in France, had been promoted and it was thus as Captain T. Bawden that he sent a cheque for £1 1s for the funds of the new Town Institute. This had been inaugurated on Monday evening January 7th 1918, and in the letter he said; "I have been a member of the Church Institute for some years and I think, even in these times, it would be a great pity if the old Institute had to shut up altogether." Before enlisting Captain Bawden had been a special constable in the town and at a supper to mark the winding up of the movement, held at the Swan Hotel on Thursday evening, February 6th 1919, he was amongst those who spoke of how valuable this training had been for his subsequent Army service.

At the meeting on Thursday evening, January 24th 1918, held at 8 p.m., the chairman said that Mr. Gregory would be the caretaker, but since they had been unable to find a secretary the Reverend Gunnery had offered to temporarily assume the role, until the general meeting. The following morning Mr. Short then unexpectedly received a letter from Captain T. Bawden, who was serving in France. Enclosed was a cheque for £1 1s towards the Town Institute funds, and in the letter he said "I have been a member of the Church Institute for some years and I think, even in these times, it would be a great pity if the old Institute had to shut up altogether." Nevertheless, the first half yearly meeting of the members of the Town Institute took place on Wednesday evening, August 7th 1918, in the reading room where, in the unavoidable absence of the president, Mr. J. Short, the chair was taken by the vice president, Mr. F. Littleboy. Now being the honorary secretary Mr. T. G. Puryer gave the report for the half year commencing January 7th 1918, the date on which the Institute had opened, and with a complement of 90 members both the library and gym had been well used. The total income was revealed as £105 1s 5d, with the expenditure being £99 16s 10d., and for the prizes for a billiards tournament, which had been offered by Mr. Reginald Odell, Mr. Chapman and Mr. F. Bavington were appointed to assist in making the arrangements. After the war, in September 1920, the directors of the Masonic Hall then offered the facility, including fixtures, to manufacturers or persons requiring good premises, and as per the advert the main building comprised three rooms on the ground floor, a gymnasium, store shed and urinal. On the first floor was the Assembly Room with a stage, and there were two dressing rooms. One had a w.c., and there was also a w.c. on the ground floor. Sealed bids were to be delivered on or before September 25th to Mr. C. Clare, the secretary, High Street, although it was stipulated that the lower rooms and gym were still let to the Town Institute at £28 p.a., with the ground rent being £2 p.a.

60, High Street

COUNCIL & COUNCILLORS

The Council Offices

Newport Pagnell Urban District Council was established in 1897 and after the outbreak of war at the Council Offices, 60, High Street, men aged 19 to 30 who wished to enlist could give their names to Sergeant Lucas, the recruiting sergeant. Also at the Council Offices, on Wednesday evening, September 30th 1914, a meeting of the Newport Pagnell Parochial Distress Relief Committee, which dealt only with local cases of distress occasioned by the war, was held.

Then on Tuesday evening, April 6th 1915, at the monthly meeting of the U.D.C., held in the Council Chamber, the Surveyor reported that a horse had been secured on trial. Thought to be very reasonable for such an animal the price was £60 but although the horse had been tested satisfactorily one member thought it was rather short in the neck. Nevertheless the animal was purchased. However, by June 1915 it was reported that the Council's grey mare had 'gone bad all round' and the veterinary surgeon said the only remedy was to 'fire' her in all four legs. A horse would be hired in her place.

For the undertaking of the National Registration Act, a national survey, qualified persons wishing to be enumerators were to apply on Saturday, July 24th 1915, at the Council Offices, 60, High Street, between 10 a.m. and 1 p.m., or Monday, July 26th between 10 a.m. and 4 p.m. In essence the Act provided a basis for the 'Derby Scheme,' whereby before the introduction of conscription men could 'attest,' or confirm, their willingness to enlist. However, in the concluding days of the scheme on Thursday night December 16th 1915, so many men applied at the Council Offices that there was insufficient money to pay the accepted recruits, with the military authorities having to provide a loan.

With the introduction of conscription those seeking military exemption could initially state their case at Local Tribunals held at the Council Offices, where, being the first time since its formation, on Tuesday evening, August 1st 1916, the U.D.C. met on the lawn at the rear of the premises.

On Tuesday evening, April 17th 1917, at the annual meeting of the U.D.C. Joseph Short was elected chairman whilst in other matters £3 15s was accepted as the price for cleaning the Council Office windows for the coming year. This had been forwarded in writing by Messrs. Feasey and Goodman and was the same as their previous amount.

As for other routine housekeeping, there was tragedy at the Council Offices on Wednesday morning, May 29th 1918, when the caretaker, having had occasion to go outside whilst engaged in washing, was found lying ill.

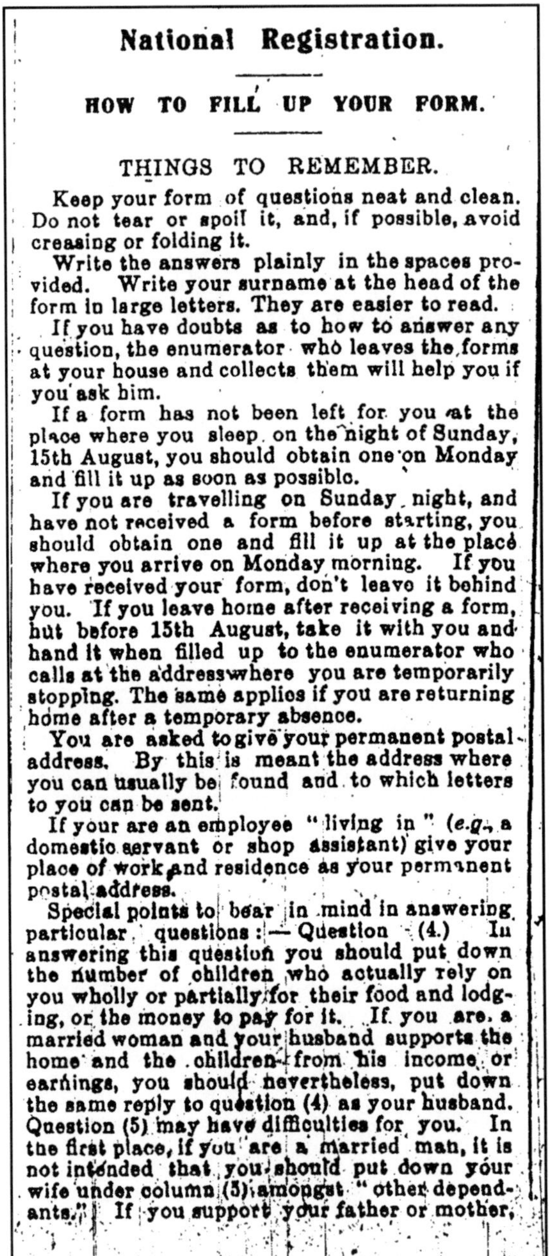

National Registration.

HOW TO FILL UP YOUR FORM.

THINGS TO REMEMBER.

Keep your form of questions neat and clean. Do not tear or spoil it, and, if possible, avoid creasing or folding it.

Write the answers plainly in the spaces provided. Write your surname at the head of the form in large letters. They are easier to read.

If you have doubts as to how to answer any question, the enumerator who leaves the forms at your house and collects them will help you if you ask him.

If a form has not been left for you at the place where you sleep on the night of Sunday, 15th August, you should obtain one on Monday and fill it up as soon as possible.

If you are travelling on Sunday night, and have not received a form before starting, you should obtain one and fill it up at the place where you arrive on Monday morning. If you have received your form, don't leave it behind you. If you leave home after receiving a form, but before 15th August, take it with you and hand it when filled up to the enumerator who calls at the address where you are temporarily stopping. The same applies if you are returning home after a temporary absence.

You are asked to give your permanent postal address. By this is meant the address where you can usually be found and to which letters to you can be sent.

If your are an employee "living in" (*e.g.*, a domestic servant or shop assistant) give your place of work and residence as your permanent postal address.

Special points to bear in mind in answering particular questions:—Question (4.) In answering this question you should put down the number of children who actually rely on you wholly or partially for their food and lodging, or the money to pay for it. If you are a married woman and your husband supports the home and the children from his income or earnings, you should nevertheless, put down the same reply to question (4) as your husband. Question (5) may have difficulties for you. In the first place, if you are a married man, it is not intended that you should put down your wife under column (5) amongst "other dependants." If you support your father or mother,

Bucks Standard, August 14th 1915

She was 48 year old Mrs. Kate Clarke, widow of the late Mr. W. Clarke, and, having been concerned at her prolonged absence, the discovery was made by her sister, who lived with her. Almost at that moment Dr. White happened to be visiting the Council Offices but nevertheless she had passed away before he could arrive. No inquest was held, for having been in indifferent health for several months she had been under the care of the doctor. By her death three sons were bereaved. Two were in the Forces - one in Salonica and one in Egypt - with the youngest employed at Salmons.

With the subsequent need for a caretaker, applicants were to apply in writing with two recent testimonials to Mr. Ernest Ward, Clerk to the Council, by Saturday, August 31st 1918, and by the meeting of the U.D.C. on Tuesday evening, September 3rd 1918, thirteen hopefuls had applied. Of these, four were disqualified for not complying with the terms of the advertisement with the nine remaining being Mrs. Bass, Mrs. Mayne, Mrs. Daniells, Messrs. J. Adams, J. Cooper, W. Barnwell, C. Page, J. Stevens and J. Short junior. With regard to the latter the chairman, Mr. J. Short, withdrew from the meeting and the Council then went into committee, reaching a final decision that the post should be offered to Mrs. Mayne, a devout churchwoman, member of the Mothers' Union and a keen worker for the hospital fetes.

With the end of the war, in November 1918 it was agreed that a light should be fixed in the porch of the Council Offices, so that the steps could be seen, and on Saturday, July 19th 1919, at the Peace Day rejoicings in the town an illumination on the front of the Council Offices featured the letters G.R. as the centrepiece. Mrs. Mary Elizabeth Mayne would remain as the caretaker for many years and died, aged 80, in 1944, two years after suffering a seizure which greatly affected her health. Her wish to be buried in the churchyard of her native village, Lower Heyford, was complied with.

Ernest Paul Ward

Ernest Paul Ward, Clerk to the U.D.C. since its formation in 1897, died on Monday morning, March 29th 1920, at his residence in Broad Street. On Sunday he had been in usual health but during the afternoon suffered a seizure from which he didn't recover. Previous to becoming Clerk he had for some years been in the office of the late Charles Powell, when he was Clerk to the Newport Pagnell Board of Guardians and R.D.C., and amongst many other duties was relieving officer for many years for the Newport Pagnell District and during the war the clerk to the town's Military Appeal Tribunal. As a cripple he couldn't take part in sport although he enjoyed bowls, being a member of the town club from the start. As for other activities as a Freemason he had been a member of the Hygeia Lodge, London. Many prominent persons from the Council and town would be present at the funeral and he left a widow, a son and also three daughters; the Misses Mary, Dorothy and Phyllis Ward. Sadly the latter died the following year on March 19th at The Sanatorium, Peppard Common, aged 23.

William Rogers Chantler

After a long illness, on Friday, January 4th 1918, William Rogers Chantler J.P. died at his residence 'The Elms,' Newport Pagnell. He was 71 and on the day of the funeral as a mark of respect the blinds of all the private houses were drawn as the cortege proceeded from 'The Elms' to the cemetery, lead by the Fire Brigade in full uniform. He was born in 1846 in the house long associated with his father's business at the corner of High Street and St. John Street and after local schooling was sent to the then principal school of the Society of Friends at Ackworth, near Pontefract. Having later spent a year in Northampton to gain experience he then assisted his father in his business as chemist and druggist, which was conducted for many years in a shop just a few yards from his home, to where he eventually retired in 1906. In his younger years he played cricket for the town and was a competent skater.

Apart from his daily profession he was involved with the fire service, having joined the Volunteer Fire Brigade in 1870, and became a member of the Brigade Committee in 1888. Then in 1904 he acted as chairman of the Fire Brigade Committee when the Brigade's management was taken over by the U.D.C. In fact he was made the first chairman of the U.D.C., relinquishing the post in 1914 due to ill health. Two years later he then resigned from the North Bucks Liberal Association, of which he had been President for awhile, on finding the attitude of the official Liberal Party with regard to the Military Service Acts contrary to his political and religious views. In other interests for many years he was a manager of the old British School and was amongst those elected to serve on the School Board at the advent of that body. In other appointments he was made a county magistrate, performed a great deal of work on the Hospital Week Committee and in January 1916 became the treasurer of a committee formed to 'authorise, organise, and superintend' appeals of all kinds for money for charitable assistance during the war,' the intention being to stop rogue appeals. William's wife also took an interest in local organisations to include the Newport Pagnell Diamond Jubilee Nursing and Good Samaritan Society and the British Women's Temperance Association. She also helped in the Y.M.C.A. canteen whilst as for her own culinary needs in August 1917 she advertised for a good general servant 'who understands plain cooking. Good references needed.'

Joseph Short

Born at Filgrave, as an infant Joseph Short came with his parents to Newport Pagnell where, walking daily to Cranfield at the beginning of his career, he would serve for nearly 40 years on the postal staff. Defective eyesight would cause his eventual retirement, at which not only would the indoor and outdoor staff present him with a handsome gift but he would also be awarded the King Edward medal for long and efficient service. As for his other lifetime pursuits in 1898 he was elected a member of the Parish Council and in 1904 became secretary of Court 'Unity,' Ancient Order of Foresters, a position he would hold until June 1926. Until it was replaced by the Public Assistance Committee he served on the Board of Guardians and would often be appointed to represent the Board at the Poor Law conferences. Additionally, practically from inception he became a member of the Newport Pagnell Old Age Pensions Committee, was an original member of Newport Pagnell Bowling Club, of which he served as honorary secretary for a long while, and in other sporting activities was for a long period secretary to the Amateur Swimming Club, this being at a time when it held a very high place in the Midlands and Home Counties. Following the outbreak of World War One, on Thursday night, September 3rd 1914, at a recruiting meeting held on the Market Hill he was a prominent speaker and in January 1915, he was a speaker on the occasion of the transference of Court 'Unity,' Ancient Order of Foresters, from the Masonic Hall to The Poplars, where, at a convivial meeting at the Railway Tavern, he addressed officers and members on the progress and the sound financial position. On Saturday, December 11th 1915, a batch of 90 men from Newport Pagnell were sent to Wolverton by train and although all the eligible men from the Newport Pagnell Post Office staff offered themselves for enlistment, Joseph was rejected due to an insufficient chest measurement. However he became a special constable and further assisted the war effort in early 1916 when elected as the U.D.C.'s representative on the district Agricultural War Committee. Then at Aylesbury, on Thursday, February 8th 1917, he was appointed as the town's representative on Bucks County Council, a position he would hold for nine years. In other appointments he was associated with the Council Schools, a member of the Newport Pagnell Rural District Tribunal and on the evening of Tuesday, April 17th 1917, at the annual meeting of the U.D.C. he was elected chairman, a position he would hold three times. On Wednesday evening, June 27th 1917, he then became a man of property when at a sale of business and residential accommodation in Newport Pagnell and Stantonbury, held at the Swan Hotel, he purchased 72, London Road. A brick and slated residence this was in the occupation of Messrs. Salmons and Sons, or their under tenant, with the purchase price being £230. Mr. Short also took an active interest in the social life of the town and in 1917 at the annual fete to raise funds for Northampton Hospital, held at Bury Field on Saturday, July 21st, his auction sale raised £52. On Tuesday, August 21st 1917, he was appointed as a member of the committee for food control by the U.D.C. whilst on Wednesday evening, December 12th 1917, he occupied the chair at a meeting to consider establishing a Town Institute. This would replace the old Church Institute and in due course as chairman of the provisional committee he occupied the chair on Monday evening, January 7th 1918, when the inauguration of the new Town Institute took place. Also during the month he was present at The Poplars, where at the year's first monthly meeting of Court Unity, Ancient Order of Foresters, he presented the Court with a complete set of Officer's Ribbons. When news of the Armistice arrived in the town it would be Mr. Short who convened a public meeting that evening in the Electric Theatre. Then on Thursday evening, February 6th 1919, when the Newport Pagnell special constables were provided with a first class supper it was he who presided, as also at a meeting on Friday evening, February 21st 1919, which, convened by the U.D.C., was to consider the question of a permanent memorial for the fallen from the town. A few months later from the platform of a lorry he would then announce the signing of the Peace Treaty, having been handed a telegram containing this momentous news at the town's annual effort to help the funds of the Northampton Hospital. As an honorary member, on Monday evening, September 29th 1919, he was present at the Masonic Hall for an important meeting of the N.F.D.D.S.S. (forerunner of the British Legion) and in December he convened a meeting representative of the corporate bodies of the town to discuss a 'welcome home' for the town's servicemen. This was duly given on Saturday, January 24th 1920, with Mr. Short having played a major role in creating the event. In May 1920 came his appointment by the Ministry of Food as district food officer for the newly constituted area. His headquarters would be at Newport Pagnell and his duties would begin on July 1st when the local Food Committees ceased to exist. By the recommendation of the Lord Lieutenant of Bucks, on June 28th 1920, he was made a Justice of the Peace but would still continue as the secretary of the Court 'Unity,' Ancient Order of Foresters, of which the head office was transferred to 60a, High Street, adjoining the U.D.C. offices, in December. Sadly his wife, Jane, died at 13, Tickford Street, in the early hours of Friday, February 3rd 1922. She was aged 65 and succumbed to pneumonia, having contracted influenza the previous Sunday morning. The funeral took place on the Tuesday afternoon and although confined to his house for almost two weeks by illness Mr. Short was allowed to attend by his doctor. The other mourners included Miss Janet Short and Mrs. Ferrett, daughters, Mr. J.W. Short, son, and Miss Maisie Noakes, his adopted daughter. As for Joseph Short, he died at his home in Tickford Street in December 1930 aged 71, having not recovered from a breakdown of health in the summer. Nevertheless except for the last couple of months he had been able to attend to some of his public duties, until a recurrence confined him to his house.

CRIMES & PUNISHMENT

At Newport Pagnell Police Court, on Wednesday, January 20th 1915, an ex-soldier of the Hussars, who shortly after the outbreak of war had enlisted in the 3rd Hussars, and who at the time of his arrest was in training with his regiment, was charged on remand. This was for having on July 25th 1914, stolen 18 handkerchiefs, one box and a quantity of brushes, a total value of £1 10s. The property belonged to Isabella Wright, a widow, of 11, Paggs' Court, Silver Street, and giving evidence she said that on Monday, July 20th 1914 the man had come to her house to lodge, and occupied a bedroom with a man named Webb. Five days later he left, after which she discovered a box of handkerchiefs and some paint brushes were missing, which she kept in a drawer of the dressing table in her room. Charles Ratcliffe, the stationmaster at Newport Pagnell, said that at 7.15 p.m. on July 25th the man had called at the booking office and asked the time of the next train to London. Carrying his collar and tie, his pockets being bulky, the man seemed to be under the influence of drink and said he was going for a weekend. However, he only bought a single 3rd class ticket. Police constable Bonner said that on January 13th when the Greenwich Police had detained the man he read him the warrant, but the prisoner replied that he didn't know anything about it. However on the way back to Newport Pagnell he said, "I might as well tell the truth about it. I took the handkerchiefs and brushes from the house and took them home. I am very sorry but I was in drink." In court he pleaded guilty, and asking for the case to be dealt with that day said that he had never been in trouble before. He would pay the cost of the goods and wished only to serve his country. If he went to prison the separation allowance for his wife and seven children would be stopped, and in view of his willingness to rejoin his regiment, and because in a wire his commanding officer had assessed his character as 'fair,' he was let off with a fine of £2.

On Sunday, September 26th 1915, at 2.30 a.m. police constable Bonner, in company with police sergeant Roberts and police constable Barnett, met three labourers in Mill Street and said to them: "I suspect you of coming from land where you have been in search of game, and I shall search you under the Poaching Prevention Act." Nothing was found on two of the men, but in a pocket of the third he found four pegs which, being wet and muddy, seemed to have been in recent use. The use with nets was the inference, and giving evidence in court police constable Bonner said that at 11.15 p.m. the previous night he saw the three men go down Mill Street and across Bury Field. Addressing the Bench, the man found with the pegs said, "You never saw the case of a man brought before a Bench for carrying pegs like that. It is only because we are poor. There has never been such a case." Nevertheless he was fined 20s, with the case against the others dismissed.

James Martin, of no fixed abode, faced a charge on May 3rd 1916 of having acted as a pedlar without a certificate. Special constable W. C. Chapman said that when on duty in Tickford Street, at 5 p.m. on Tuesday afternoon, May 2nd, he saw the accused hawking postcards door to door. When asked if he had a licence the man said he thought he didn't need one. Consequently brought to the police station, in court when asked by the chairman as to why he didn't get a regular occupation, since there was plenty of work, he replied that he would try. Imprisonment for seven days was imposed.

Charged with maliciously breaking two panes of glass, a man of no fixed abode appeared at a special police court at Newport Pagnell on Saturday, June 24th 1916. Giving evidence, Mrs. Ada Harris said that when the man called at her house in Priory Street she gave him a pair of buttonhole scissors to grind, saying that if the work was not done properly she would not pay him. Later he returned the scissors and asked for two pence, but she refused to pay claiming he had spoiled them. The man then said if she didn't pay he would break every pane of glass in the house, and he consequently put his soldering iron through one pane, and his fist through another, causing damage to the value of 10s 4d. Pleading guilty, he was sentenced to 14 days' hard labour.

At a special police court at Newport Pagnell, in August 1916 the wife of a lance corporal of the Royal Engineers, now encamped at the town, faced a charge of fraud. On July 4th, whilst on a visit to her husband she was paid the credit of 11s at the post office, but an entry in the bank book was subsequently found to have been altered from £2 to £2 10s. Her arrest took place at her home village of Calstock, Cornwall, at the post office of which she alleged that having made a deposit of £2 10s, on leaving the office she found she had only been credited £2. On drawing this to the attention of the counter staff, in her presence Miss Dorothy Cox made a correction. However, this was denied, it being pointed out that the writing and the ink in the alteration were different to the original entry. Pleading not guilty the woman asked for the case to go to a jury, but after consulting with her solicitor decided to settle the case that day. The Bench imposed a fine of £8, or a month in prison, in consequence of which her husband, who was in court, having been invalided from the Front, applied for time to pay, with a month being allowed.

Having retired to bed, on the night of November 12th 1916, Mr. Ellingham was roused at about 11 p.m. by footsteps on the path of his house in Park Avenue. Opening the window he asked a young lad what he wanted, and received the reply, "Do you know there is a key in your shop door in the High Street?" However, on visiting his premises on Sunday evening, on leaving just before 6 p.m. Mr. Ellingham had locked the door and taken the key with him, and told the lad he must be mistaken. Nevertheless, he got dressed and went with the boy to the shop, where he found a key in the lock which he could not remove. The lad said he had been to a party, and saw the key whilst lighting a cigarette when walking by. In court Gertrude Roberts, a shop assistant, said at 9.45 p.m. she was standing near Mrs. Phillips' shop in the High Street when she heard someone trying a key in the lock of Mr. Ellingham's shop. She saw the boy, but did not know him. Police sergeant Roberts said on Tuesday 14th when questioned the defendant initially denied trying to enter Mr. Ellingham's shop, but afterwards said "I put the key in the lock and could not get it out again. I saw a man and asked him where Mr. Ellingham lived. I went to him and told him there was a key in the lock of his shop door. I took the key from Mr. Gibson's stables about 8.15, and I went up the street." Police sergeant Roberts then charged and cautioned him, to which he replied "I have been reading Nelson Lee's book and that is the cause of this. I have told the truth." When asked by the chairman, the lad said the book was a detective story about a robbery, and when the chairman queried "Breaking into somebody's house?" replied "Yes." The chairman then told the boy they would treat him kindly because they wanted to give him a chance. He should go back to school and "be a good boy and get some better books to read." Aged 16 years and nine months the defendant had been in a reformatory, to a representative of which he was then handed over.

For having on December 1st 1916 thrown dough about on the Wolverton Road, five boys aged between 12 and 16 were summoned at the Divisional Petty Sessions on Wednesday, December 13th. They pleaded guilty, and in evidence police constable Nicholls said that on December 4th the lads, consequent to his enquiries regarding a number of complaints, admitted having thrown dough at each other. One of the boys was employed at a baker's shop, and to the bake house of this some of the boys went to assist him in the evenings. They had taken some dough when they left, and females living alone on the Wolverton Road had been greatly annoyed when pellets of the same were thrown at their windows. After a good ticking off in court, in which the need to conserve food was emphasised, they were each fined 2s 6d costs.

Herbert Hawkins, of 13, London Road, was summoned for having allowed a stray dog to be on the highway in the town on December 17th 1916. Since the accused was engaged on munitions work at Bedford his father appeared in court, and admitted that he had personally taken the dog for a run. However, it got loose and was found in Silver Street by special constable A. Lott. The case had been brought because of much sheep worrying in the district.

The case involving a cowman with an artificial limb, and a milk seller, at the Newport Pagnell Divisional Petty Sessions on Wednesday, January 24th 1917, serious charges of milk theft were heard. Regarding the former, aged 38, on January 28th he was alleged to have stolen milk valued at 3s 6d from his employer, Mr. Alfred Bullard. The other defendant, aged 58, of 114, Tickford Street, was charged with having received the milk knowing it to be stolen. Police sergeant Roberts said on Tuesday, January 23rd he and police constable Crockford were keeping observation near the Workhouse when they saw the cowman driving a horse and cart. Two churns of milk were on board, and he was travelling from the direction of his employer. At the corner of North Crawley road the man then stopped and poured some milk into a pail held by the other man, whose cottage was some 30 feet away. The recipient then handed something to the cowman, who put it in his pocket. About 7.45 a.m. police sergeant Roberts then questioned the cowman at Mr. Bullard's house in Tickford Street, to where he had brought the older man. In the presence of both defendants he asked Mr. Bullard if he had given permission to sell any milk and was told "No, I have not." Before being taken to the police station and charged the cart driver apologised, and said "I am a fool. I would not have had this happen for any money." In court Mr. Bullard said the man, who had the responsibility for the milking and delivery of the milk at the railway station, was employed as cowman and foreman on his farm, and had 32s a week, a house, garden, and milk for his family. The accused pleaded guilty, and when the case of the other defendant was the man said that at the time he bought the milk for 2s 6d he thought it was all right. Every morning since Christmas he had received two gallons, with one gallon every morning for a week before Christmas. Mr. Bullard said the defendant had asked if he could supply some milk, but was told there was none to spare. An appeal for leniency was made by Mr. Bullard on behalf of the younger man, since he had worked for him for several years and had a wife and three children, two of whom were of school age and the third a cripple. As for the older man, having known him all his life he was hard working and of good character. In conclusion each prisoner was fined £10 or in default two months' imprisonment, being allowed until the end of March to pay, as long as the instalments were kept up.

At the Newport Pagnell Divisional Petty Sessions, on Wednesday, February 21st 1917 a schoolboy of 28, Priory Street was charged with theft. It was alleged that from a shop in Tickford Street he stole about £1 in money from Mr. R. Pettit, a butcher, on February 10th, and also charged was a boy of 4, River Side, for receiving 3s from him, knowing it to be stolen. Police sergeant Roberts said that he saw both prisoners on the 14th and on telling them he was making enquiries about Mr. Pettit's stolen money the boy said,

"I took it and I suppose I shall have to tell the truth now." It transpired that in the evening his mother had sent him to the shop to get 2d of suet, but on arriving he was told by the manager, John Read, that he hadn't got any. However, he was told to wait, during which Mr. Read left his ten year old daughter in charge. When her back was turned the boy then put his hand in the drawer and took out a note and some silver. On Monday evening, telling him they had some money he saw the other boy and they bought two flashlights, had tea, bought a pocket book, two oranges, two jellies, two packets of chocolate, half pound of cheese, some bread and biscuits. The latter he bought from the shop of Mrs. Betsy Tooth at 79, Tickford Street, and when he spread a pound note on the counter he said in reply to the woman's query that his mother wanted it changing, so as to send some to his uncle in France. In court the parents of the boys asked for the case to be dealt with by the Bench, who in consequence of a guilty plea sentenced the boy who had stolen the money to eight strokes of the birch, and the other to four.

On the afternoon of Friday, March 30th 1917, sensational allegations regarding the theft of Army food were partly heard at the Newport Pagnell Police Court, which had the appearance 'of a small provision merchant's shop.' In fact before the magistrates, and alleged to have been stolen from the Royal Engineers messing quarters at Newport Pagnell, was displayed a huge quantity of foodstuffs, including flour, tea, currants, raisins, sugar, potted meats, a case of corned beef, a quantity of plates and basins, a small bag of potatoes, 40 tins of herrings, bottles of pickles, custard powder, Lyle's golden syrup, cheese cake, Yorkshire relish, H.P. sauce, about 92 lbs. of jam, butter beans, onions etc. In the dock a lance corporal employed in the Royal Engineers' mess was charged with stealing a quantity of provisions, the property of H.M. Secretary for War. By his side stood a depressed looking woman of 10, Northampton Terrace, Priory Street, who was charged with having received the provisions from the man, who was billeted at her house. Superintendent E. Dibben said that on Wednesday 28th he made enquiries regarding a boy and the female prisoner. They had made two deliveries to the town's railway station, and there he subsequently found a leather case consigned to an address at Manor Park, Essex, and a tin trunk consigned to an address at Bournemouth. Taking possession of both he found the leather case to contain various Army provisions valued at 16s 8d, and in the tin trunk provisions valued at £2 15s 8d plus a letter apparently addressed to the prisoner's daughter at Bournemouth, stating those items that were for her. Also found was a torn slip of paper asking for the wrapper to be sent back for re-use. On the following day, with a search warrant Superintendent Dibben then visited the house of the female prisoner, where the property produced, with the exception of a few articles about which enquiries were ongoing, was identified as Army stores. The male prisoner subsequently admitted that the label on the case was written by him, and during the search he was told by the woman "You know you brought the things here." Both prisoners were remanded to Northampton gaol until the Petty Sessions on Wednesday next.

The Newport Pagnell Police Court was packed on Wednesday, April 4th 1917, when for over four hours the Bench heard the serious charges against a widow woman and a lance corporal of the Royal Engineers. In court was displayed a large collection of provisions which, allegedly stolen by the soldier from the Royal Engineers messing quarters in the town, comprised provisions valued at 16s 4d, and also from between October 30th and March 29th those valued at over £17. Against the woman were three charges:

1/ Receiving from a soldier a quantity of Army provisions to the value of £1 17s 1d about March 28th 1917.

2/ Between October 30th 1916 and March 29th 1917 receiving from a soldier a quantity of provisions and utensils valued at £15 16s 7d, issued for the use of soldiers stationed at Newport Pagnell.

3/ On or about March 28th 1917 assisting a soldier in making away with provisions valued at 16s 4d issued for soldiers stationed at Newport Pagnell.

Heard first were the charges against the woman, on whose behalf Mr. A. Darnell, a Northampton solicitor, entered a plea of not guilty. Superintendent Dibben said that on Wednesday, March 28th he made enquiries regarding a small leather trunk, and a tin trunk, which the woman's son, Sidney, had taken to the town railway station. That night he then went to the station and in the passenger booking office found the leather case (produced). When opened this was found to contain provisions, and by an attached label was destined for Mrs. Davey of 83, Harcourt Avenue, Manor Park, Essex, she being a sister-in-law of the soldier. A label attached to the tin trunk bore the name and address 'Mrs. Ballard, 24, Bennett Road, Bournemouth. With care. Glass,' the intended recipient being the woman's daughter. This also contained provisions and a letter addressed to 'My dear Alice,' from which extracts included 'Well, dear, I am sending you a few things but you will have to pay for the carriage. I have 7lb. of jam, which I know you will be glad of. ... Let me know if you receive this stuff. P.S. You will be able to make Henry an onion pudding and bacon. He will like that.' (Laughter.) In consequence of these discoveries Superintendent Dibben took out a search warrant and, accompanied by police sergeant Roberts, searched the woman's four bedroomed premises. Under the stairs came the discovery of large quantities of tinned food, which were duly taken out and piled on the floor. The woman then walked to the parlour door and said to the soldier, who had been billeted in her house since October 30th 1916, "Here. You had better come and look what he is doing." The soldier looked but said nothing, and on going into the front room she went up to him and said, "You know you brought the things here." He made no answer. A quantity of jam and sundries was then found in the cupboards in the front room, but it was in the back bedroom, which she occupied, that the majority of the produce was discovered. By the chimney, covered up, was a tub containing 51 lbs. of flour, and on the floor nearby a bag of potatoes, which the woman said she had grown for seed. However, on examining these Superintendent Dibben found them to be cooking potatoes, to which she said she had grown them in her garden. Under the bed a black basket contained more provisions, and the Superintendent then took possession of the whole stock. As for police sergeant Roberts, he found plates under the chest of drawers in the bedrooms, and 12 basins variously about the house. Then in the front bedroom where the soldier slept the policemen found more provisions, and following this the prisoners were arrested. Asked if she wished enquiries to be made about the apparent non Army items the woman, with her initial explanations proving incorrect, said that the crockery came from the camp in Bury Field, at the time this was broken up the previous autumn. In fact during the court proceedings it was revealed that she had been employed there cooking for the officers. Regarding the soldier, who was employed as a mess corporal under James Gault, a quartermaster sergeant in the Royal Engineers, he was allowed to draw his rations weekly and take them to his billet, and although the woman at first denied having sent other consignments by rail, she eventually admitted that she had. As for the cooking utensils, these were to replace her own which had been broken. The proceedings revealed that her husband had been killed in a motor lorry accident at Wolverton, whilst of her sons two were in the Army in France, with another son, Sidney, at Newport Pagnell, engaged to fetch the rations for the soldiers in a hand truck from the messing quarters. Taking the stand, on reading from a prepared statement the soldier corrected a claim made by the Superintendent that the woman had said "You brought these things into the house." He said the correct version was "You didn't bring all these things home, did you?" after which he motioned for the woman to 'hold her tongue.' Having enlisted in the Army at the age of 16½, he served through the South African War and 12 years with the Gloucester Regiment, and after leaving the Army with an exemplary character had been employed in the Post Office, and under the Metropolitan Asylums Board as a telegraphist. He joined the Royal Engineers at Newport Pagnell in June 1916, and was appointed lance corporal in November 1916. A week after the Royal Engineers had gone into billets in the town he was sent to the messing quarters, and presently had charge of the central messing room. With his conduct satisfactory his commanding officer allowed him to take his food to his billet, these rations being drawn every Saturday afternoon by the woman's son. During his questioning the soldier said that rations were issued carelessly, such as large tins of jam being given out instead of tea and sugar, and it was inevitable that over time there would be an accumulation of produce. A case of corned beef had lain around the messing quarters for days, because although it was intended for the men they said "Put it in the swill bin." If found guilty he said this would be his first crime, and overcome with emotion he was unable to finish reading the statement. Nevertheless, it was strictly forbidden for a soldier to sell any left over food, which had to be returned to the storekeeper. After retiring the Bench then gave their verdict. Unanimously they found the woman guilty but in a lenient view imposed a fine of £5 on each of the three charges, or a month in prison for each case. For the soldier they took into account his good record but unanimously passed a verdict of guilty. For the first offence a fine of £10 was imposed, or two months prison with hard labour, and for the second a fine of £25, or three months with hard labour. On asking for time to pay the Bench allowed the woman to pay £5 down, with two months for the remainder.

On Saturday, May 5th 1917, at a special police court three men of no fixed abode, one describing himself as a pedlar, faced a charge of drunkenness in the town on the previous day. In the morning one had been found intoxicated by special constable W.C. Chapman, and was fined 10s with 2s 6d costs, whilst for the offender arrested for being drunk and disorderly by police constable Bonner, he suffered a fine of 10s. The last of the drunks had been found at 11.30 p.m. by special constable T. Sim, to whom he explained he had not gone into lodgings because the £9 15s in his possession might be stolen. He was fined 10s and 2s 6d costs but elected for the alternative of seven days in prison. However, under a new order the Bench could deduct a fine from the money found on a prisoner, and this was the course pursued.

At a special police court on Saturday, May 19th 1917, a 48 year old married woman, of The Butts, Coventry, was charged on remand with stealing on August 7th 1916 two blankets, two sheets, one mackintosh, and £10 in money from her husband, of Union Street, Newport Pagnell. Charged with aiding and abetting her, in the dock stood a man also of 27, The Butts who, formerly in the Royal Engineers, and billeted for a time with the woman and her husband, was stated to be a deserter from the regiment. Regarding the woman's husband, he gave his occupation as a labourer, and said he had been married for 27 years to his wife. However, on the night of Saturday, July 29th 1916 he had occasion to have words with the soldier, and in consequence the following night in reply to her husband the woman denied having been walking out with him. On August Bank Holiday 1916, leaving his wife indoors the husband got up at 5.30 a.m. to leave for work half an hour later, but when he returned just after 6 he found her missing. No one knew her whereabouts, and he then noticed certain items were missing. As for the soldier, he left on the Bank Holiday and was supposed to be in camp on Bury Field. Giving evidence the couple's eldest daughter, who lived next door, at 41, Union Street, said between 9 a.m. and 10 a.m. at her parent's address on August Bank Holiday she saw her mother, who said she was going to her brother's at Shoreham by Sea, thinking that if she went away then the 'bother' on the Saturday night would blow over. However, the daughter later received a letter bearing a Northampton postmark but no address, and although her mother could not write her name appeared in the contents, which stated she was going to Coventry to work, but mentioned nothing about returning. Giving evidence, Harry Boughton, of Newport Pagnell, said on August Bank Holiday he saw the woman on the station where he, being the porter, labelled her tin box for Northampton. Also he saw two single tickets for Northampton purchased by the woman, but he did not see the man with her. In her evidence Mrs. Maria England of 8, Monk's Pond Street, Northampton, said the woman visited her on August 7th 1916. They had met some time before at Northampton Hospital, and the woman explained that her husband was dead and she had married again, the man being with her at the time. Until September 4th the woman remained at Mrs. England's home, where, with the couple having the front parlour, the man visited her each weekend. During this time the woman worked at the Barracks, where when she eventually left the house she said she was going to sleep. Mrs. Amy Evans of 14, Semilong Road, South Northampton, said on September 4th the woman called at her house and asked if she could have a room, as her husband had gone to France. Subsequently she stayed five weeks, and, dressed in khaki, the man stayed at the house on the first day and again clad in khaki at week ends. During this time the landlady bought a mackintosh for 12s and a blanket for 2s from the woman, who said her son had given her the former, with the latter being her own property. On being detained by the Coventry police, on Wednesday, May 16th the two prisoners were read the warrant by police constable Barnett, after which the woman confirmed she took one blanket and two sheets: "My boy in the Army gave me the mack. I never had the money. The old man never had £10." When told he would be charged with aiding and abetting, the man made no reply. During the return railway journey the woman said she pawned the sheets at Northampton, and sold the blankets to a woman at Northampton for 4s. In court the pair pleaded not guilty, with the woman saying she took the things because they were her property. She had worked for them, and didn't take anything from her husband. The man said, "I am not guilty. It was six weeks before I went with this lady. I know nothing whatever about what she took from the house. She said she had the blankets and sheets from the Mothers' Meeting. She used to go out washing and the money she was paid she paid into the Mothers' Meeting, which was how she got the blankets." After retiring the Bench found the woman guilty of taking property which belonged to the house, such items being part property of her husband, but the chairman said they appreciated she was a hard-working person with no previous record, and felt the blame attached more to the male prisoner, "partly owing to his sex." A fine of 40s was imposed, with a month to pay. As for the man, who had a previous conviction for felony, the court said he was far more to blame in aiding and abetting, and "It ought to have been your business to have tried to prevent the woman from committing a folly. You knew all about it, and the seriousness of the offence you yourself were committing." A sentence of three months prison with hard labour was imposed, with no option of a fine. Superintendent Dibben then said that since October 16th 1916 there was the further charge of being a deserter from the Royal Engineers. On this count the man would be handed over to a military escort at the completion of his sentence.

At a special police court on Friday, June 1st 1917, the case was partly

38, Greenfield Road.

heard of a woman wearing the uniform of a nurse. With the name on the charge sheet differing from the name she had given the magistrates' clerk, she was charged in custody with between March 18th and May 30th stealing from a house in Greenfield Road the sum of £18, the property of a soldier from Catterick, Yorks., who was a private in the Oxon and Bucks Light Infantry. Police sergeant Roberts said on Wednesday at 10.30 a.m. he received information that £18 in gold, with a cash box, had been stolen from a tin box at 38, Greenfield Road, and on visiting the house he found the lock on the tin box had been forced, and the money missing. Going into the bedroom occupied by the prisoner on searching a dress basket he found the small cash box, and in consequence of further enquiries at 9 p.m. the defendant was detained at the police station. The soldier had struck up a friendship with the woman whilst at Cheltenham, and brought her to his home at Newport Pagnell because she was 'seeming to want a rest.'

At a special police court, on Monday, June 4th 1917, in the uniform of a V.A.D. nurse a woman was charged with the theft of money and a cash box, the property and life savings of Private Reginald Clarke, 4th Reserve Battalion Oxon and Bucks Light Infantry, of 38, Greenfield Road, Newport Pagnell. She was offered a chair, but preferred to stand throughout the 2½ hours. In evidence the soldier said on January 1st he was stationed at Cheltenham, where he made the acquaintance of the prisoner whom he knew as Miss Jean Campbell. Whilst there they 'walked out' for ten nights, and he maintained a correspondence after leaving Cheltenham on January 10th for camp at Catterick. By arrangement on March 12th he then met her at Bletchley station, and as his 'young lady' brought her to his mother's home at Newport Pagnell. There she stayed for two days, before leaving about two hours after his return to military duties on March 14th. Before leaving, putting the keys in a drawer in his bedroom he locked his tin trunk in which, containing about £20 in gold, was a locked cash box. Wedged into this box, to stop the contents rattling about, was a label from a packet of Murray's straight cut cigarettes, the brand he smoked before joining the Army some 15 months ago. Also before his departure he gave his mother a sovereign. This was in the presence of the woman, and she was also present when on March 12th he changed a pound note for his sister. After returning to camp in Yorkshire the soldier continued writing to the woman at Cheltenham, and then later at Langley Marsh, Bucks, from where in a letter she said she was going to visit his mother's house. However, he subsequently received a communication from Yorkshire police, and having returned home on a Sunday found the tin trunk forced open. The gold and the cash box were missing, although the woman had never been told what money he had. Giving evidence his brother, Arthur, said that being temporarily discharged from the Army, for agricultural work, he lived at the house with his mother. On coming home from the Army on March 19th he asked her about his brother's watch, and when she gave him the key he unlocked the trunk. Not finding the watch he then opened the cash box from which, containing two watches and 18 sovereigns, he took out the required timepiece, locked the box and the trunk, and returned the keys to his mother. The trunk was in the bedroom that he occupied each night and he was at home when the woman came to visit. She stayed until May 26th but when he went in search of her on Tuesday night, May 29th he found her in the company of a soldier at Stony Stratford. When he said he wanted a word she did not stop, but left the soldier and went off down the road. On the following morning he then went to inspect the tin trunk. In her evidence his sister, Alice Clarke, a domestic servant, said that one midday during the woman's stay she had occasion to go upstairs, and in doing so saw her walking from Albert's bedroom along the landing without wearing shoes. Frequently the daughter went shopping in the town with the woman, and she always seemed to have plenty of money, principally in notes but no gold, which she freely spent. Mary Clarke, a widow, of 38, Greenfield Road, said she had received a letter and postcard from the woman asking to stay for a week. The woman duly arrived on May 7th, and a payment of 10s per week in Treasury notes was agreed. On May 10th she helped with the housework and made the beds, including that which the brother slept in, and on May 18th having helped with the housework she agreed to go for a morning walk in the town with the daughter. Taking some time she then went upstairs to get ready, and with no one else being upstairs it was during this while that, when in the scullery, the daughter heard a noise as if the woman had dropped something. They then went for a walk with the children, but returned around noon since she complained of feeling hot and tired. About half an hour later the woman received a telegram. She said it was from her father, who had been serving in Egypt with a Red Cross unit, and was forwarded to Newport Pagnell from the Red Cross hospital at Cheltenham. It had been sent there from Euston, to where the woman then said she had to go. Consequently she left the house about 12.45 p.m. but returned at 2.30 p.m., having supposedly sent a wire to the stationmaster at Euston. If her father came back with her, she asked Mrs. Clarke if he could be accommodated, and this was agreed. Taking only her handbag the woman then left the house about 3.30 p.m., saying if she could arrange for her father to come she would return that night. However, she did not return but on Wednesday, May 30th, sent a telegram from Paddington stating; "Coming by last train to Wolverton. Shall have to walk. Jean." Informing she would be in Red Cross uniform, another telegram arrived later that day, with this being the date that Mrs. Clarke missed the cash box from her son's trunk. She was consequently present when police sergeant Roberts unlocked the woman's dress basket and found the empty cash box. Mrs. Mary Gardner, the manageress of a clothing and boot establishment in the town, said the woman came to her shop on May 26th and bought a pair of shoes, leaving her old ones to be repaired. She gave the name of Cameron and tendered a sovereign as payment, to which when the manageress exclaimed "Oh, gold" she replied "Yes, I have had to break into my bank." Mary Oswell, of 98, High Street, Stony Stratford, a boarding house keeper, said on May 26th the woman came to her house with a Sergeant Knowles. They said they were man and wife, and she agreed to accommodate them until the following Tuesday. The pair duly filled up the Alien Registration form in the name of Knowles and were each charged 10s for the stay. As payment the woman tendered a sovereign, and they both stayed until Wednesday morning. Stationed at Catterick, but due to return to France on Thursday, Sergeant Henry Knowles, of the Gloucester Regiment, said he had been acquainted with the woman, whom he knew as Edith Paule, for about nine months, and on May 26th when he came to visit her at Newport Pagnell they met near the entrance to the town. After a short conversation, at her suggestion and purporting to be to her father he sent and paid for an express message to Euston, where, with a platform number given, she asked to meet him. After sending the message he then met up with her at the railway station, and they left by train for Wolverton. From there they walked to Stony Stratford and stayed at the boarding house as man and wife. He then left on Wednesday, May 30th when she said she was going back to Newport Pagnell to pack up her 'stuff,' before going to London for an appointment with a lady regarding a situation. Throughout the time they were together she had plenty of money, all gold coins, which she said was her savings. Frequently she went shopping, always buying something, and her attitude was "I pay my way and you pay yours." Giving his evidence, police sergeant Roberts said that at 10.30 a.m. on May 30th he received information that a cash box containing £18 had been stolen. He went to 38, Greenfield Road and in a bedroom found a tin trunk forced open, by seemingly using a pair of tongs from the fireplace. In the presence of Mrs. Clarke, in another bedroom he found a locked dress basket, which by obtaining a key he opened and found amongst the contents the cash box, empty except for a piece of a cigarette packet. At 9 p.m. that night he then saw the prisoner detained at Newport Pagnell police station, to where she had been brought from Bletchley railway station by Inspector Callaway. In consequence he read her the warrant, but when charged and cautioned she said she was not guilty, and when shown the cash box she said she had paid 6½d for it, and produced the key. However, she couldn't remember where she bought it. Searching her property police sergeant Roberts found new clothing, an account for a Red Cross coat, purchased for £2 7s at Oxford on May 30th, and another of the same date at the same shop for 8s 2½d. For this, which she was wearing when he found her in custody, she had tendered a pound. Also found in her possession was a gold sovereign, 3s 6d in silver, 9¾d in copper, a postal order for 10s, issued at Wolverton on May 30th, eleven 1d stamps, and twelve ½d stamps. She was wearing a new wrist watch and also had a new despatch case and writing case, and when remanded on Saturday said she cashed a cheque for £4 6s 3d from her late employer at Slough. In court, in reply to the chairman Mrs. Clarke said that before May 30th plain clothes was the attire of the woman, who at the conclusion of the proceedings, and having nothing to say, was committed for trial at the Bucks Summer Assizes. Two days later she was duly indicted at Aylesbury before the Hon. Sir Charles Montague Lush, one of the justices of the High Court of Justice. In the dock she pleaded guilty to stealing £20, and the prosecution mentioned that there was another warrant against her regarding a larceny in the Slough Division. Expanding on this, Superintendent Dibben said he held the warrant, which regarded the theft of clothing etc. from a former place of employment at Langley, and with the value estimated at £5 10s she asked for this to be taken into consideration. She also admitted a previous conviction of two months' hard labour at Gloucester Assizes in October 1916, this being for three charges of larceny, and also at Gloucester City Quarter Sessions for the theft of a brooch, for which she was sentenced to 21 days' hard labour. Moreover, at the police court at Cheltenham on September 19th 1907 she had been bound over on a charge of stealing clothing. Superintendent Dibben said she was a married woman whose husband was an inmate of the Gloucester Lunatic Asylum. She had three children, of whom two were in Dr. Barnado's Homes, with the other in the care of a woman at Cheltenham. Sentenced to nine months' in prison with hard labour, she was told that if she continued this class of offence, and if she appeared before him again, she would receive penal servitude.

For having on June 18th used abusive and profane language at the town, on Wednesday, June 20th 1917 a man of no fixed abode was charged on remand. Additionally, and relating to the same date, there were also summons for begging alms and for peddling without a certificate.

At 8.45 p.m. on Monday he was seen trying to enter the playground of the infants' school, and for becoming very abusive when challenged he was taken to the police station. Giving evidence, a lady of the town said the prisoner called at her home during the morning and asked if she wanted any mats mending. When she said she didn't he then begged for food. From fingerprints, Superintendent Dibben had obtained the prisoner's previous record from Scotland Yard, and now would be added 14 days hard labour for using bad language, 14 days hard labour for begging, and a fine of 10s, or seven days' in prison, for peddling without a certificate.

On Wednesday, June 27th 1917, at the Divisional Petty Sessions a builder of the town was charged with having been drunk and disorderly on June 26th. Police constable Bonner said at 7.15 p.m. whilst on duty in Tickford Street he saw the man drunkenly approaching Priory Street, 'rolling and staggering about,' and when the constable told him to go home he said "All right." However, after going a little distance he returned and became abusive to the officer. He was again told to go home, and after more bad language he walked away. Later, at 7.35 p.m. the officer saw him near the 'Picture Palace' and the same occurred. Then at 8 p.m. in Silver Street he came up to the officer and being very abusive struck him by the side of the eye. Thereupon the officer threw him to the ground and with the assistance of two other officers took his assailant into custody. Superintendent Dibben said the man was very drunk and excitable when brought to the police station and wanted to be put into the exercise yard to fight it out with police constable Bonner. In court it was stated that this was not the first occurrence, and the man was sentenced to a month in prison with hard labour.

At the Leicester Quarter Sessions, on Monday, July 30th 1917, a car conductress pleaded guilty to stealing a diamond ring and a gold wedding ring. She also admitted a previous indictment for felony at Oldham. In prosecution a Leicester jeweller gave evidence that she came to his shop asking to see some wedding rings. She then wanted to see some diamond rings, and placed an order for a diamond sapphire ring, priced at about £8. She gave the name and address of Miss Wilks, of Melton Mowbray, and when asked for a deposit said this would not be necessary, since she was coming to Leicester on Saturday to have her wedding dress fitted. After she left he then discovered that two rings valued at £5 13s were missing. One of these, a diamond ring, she was wearing when eventually arrested, and the other, a wedding ring, she had pawned for 25s. As for her motive, she said she committed the offence because a man was continually following her about. Two further charges were also taken into account, one for stealing a lady's coat at Blackpool, and the other for the theft of a lady's rolled gold watch at Newport Pagnell on June 18th. Passing a sentence of 18 months' hard labour the Recorder said he hoped that that someone would get hold of the scoundrel who had poisoned her life, and why she returned to him when she came out of prison, instead of seeking police protection, he couldn't make out.

In a case, which had been before the competent Military Authority, who authorised the proceedings, Edwin Sellick, a motor engineer of Stantonbury, was summoned at the Divisional Petty Sessions on Wednesday, September 5th 1917, this being for having used motor spirit for a purpose not authorised by the Petrol Control Committee. Superintendent Dibben said that at

12.24 p.m. on Saturday, August 11th, he saw the man driving a hackney motor car, which drew up at the entrance of Newport Pagnell Parish Church and picked up a party of wedding guests. He took the number of the car and later at the police station asked the man to produce his permit from the Petrol Control Committee. Mr. Sellick duly produced a permit listing a series of authorised purposes, and said he had taken the wedding party to Mrs. Coleman's, in Broad Street. When informed this was not an authorised purpose he contended that he was nevertheless entitled, because his wife had taken the order and, until he arrived in the town, he knew nothing of its nature. He said the booking came under Public Duties and added, to laughter, that at the present time he considered getting married was a public duty. On first hearing of the regulations he applied to the Petrol Committee of the Board of Trade for a permit to run his cars, which, having specifically asked if this would include wedding parties, and with no reply to the contrary, was duly issued. Regarding the alleged offence, he had first driven the bridesmaids from Stantonbury to Newport Pagnell Parish Church and then after the ceremony took the bride and bridegroom home. He next returned for the guests at the church, where he was surprised to see Superintendent Dibben inspecting the vehicle. In consequence, after his hire duties he then drove to the police station to enquire the reason. Giving a verdict of a technical offence the Bench imposed a fine of £1.

As a contravention of the Defence of the Realm Act, at a Special Petty Sessions on Saturday, November 3rd 1917, a man was charged for unlawfully wearing naval uniform, an accusation which he contested. Police sergeant Roberts said that on the previous date at 7 p.m. he saw the man coming from the Y.M.C.A. Hut, and when he asked him what he was doing the man replied, "I have signed an agreement with the Admiralty to go with trawlers." As for the uniform: "They issue them out to us on our discharge. I am making my way to Baker Street for my pension." He then produced a seaman's discharge book but since it was dark he was advised to come to the police station by the officer, who on noticing the words 'H.M.S. Pekin' on the man's hat was told, "Well, I am entitled to wear it, and yet I am not." On being asked where H.M.S. Pekin was he said, causing subsequent laughter in court: "That ain't a ship at all; that is the cookhouse where they send you all when you join up." Explaining his situation, the man said he was a Grimsby fisherman, and although he belonged to a trawler he could leave on giving 24 hours'notice and join another boat. He was entitled to wear the uniform because the clothes issued to him showed a distinction between a fisherman and the Admiralty's naval men. However, he admitted he had been absent from the trawlers for about two weeks. In court, to laughter, Superintendent Dibben said that the man was in Northampton police station on Thursday night, but they turned him out as a conundrum. Remanded for enquiries to be made, the man then appeared at the adjourned hearing on Wednesday, when it was stated that a message from Grimsby police confirmed he was entitled to wear the Naval uniform with the distinctive badge, having signed on as a fisherman under Admiralty agreement. With reference to the charge of being a possible absentee, in the absence of any information he was discharged.

At a special police court on Wednesday, November 21st 1917, a member of the Royal Engineers, formerly encamped with the Signal Section at the town, was charged with the theft on July 9th of a gent's bicycle and bell, valued at £3 10s. This was the property of Fred Chapman, a bootmaker of 28, Caldecote Street, who also hired out bicycles. In the book he kept of such transactions there was an entry on July 9th regarding the man, who giving his home address as 42, Pelham Road, Wood Green, London, came to the shop at about 1.30 p.m. and asked to hire a bicycle to go to Fenny Stratford. He said he wanted it for about an hour and a half and would pay on his return, but he didn't come back. On the following day a warrant was issued for his arrest, and eventually on Friday, November 16th police constable George Marsh received instructions to proceed to Bedford Borough Police Station, where finding the man in custody he read him the warrant. In reply the man said he did not steal the cycle but it had been taken at about 6 p.m. whilst he was in a tea shop on the London Road at St. Albans. He told the people at the shop, but since "I could not report it to the police as I should have been had as an absentee," he completed his journey by motor bus. Subsequent to the reading of the warrant he was taken to Newport Pagnell police station and detained. In court he pleaded not guilty and said that he went to Fenny Stratford to enquire from the postman, and also the orderly room, about a parcel, since it apparently depended on what he received by post at Fenny Stratford as to whether he went to London, where he was living with a woman. In court the lieutenant and adjutant of the Royal Engineers said the man had been dealt with by the Army authorities on July 9th for being an absentee, and this was an offence for which he was still wanted, since he had escaped from the guard room whilst waiting a regimental court martial. It transpired in court that during his 'freedom' he had made a living as an accompanist at al fresco concerts, 'in khaki and singing,' whilst for his part during the proceedings the man said he told the police at Stafford that the cycle had been stolen: "I surrendered, after ten weeks' absence, at Wood Green, and when I was brought before the O.C. I told him about the bike. I lay in the guardroom for three weeks and I didn't say anything more about it until I was questioned by the Stafford police. I had the bicycle but I won't be accused of stealing it." "When I went to London it was not my intention to desert. It was what happened afterwards." A sentence of one month in prison with hard labour was imposed.

For having on November 11th ridden a cycle without lights, Thomas Shakeshaft, of Port Fields Farm, Newport Pagnell, was summoned at the Divisional Petty Sessions on Wednesday, November 28th 1917. Police constable Crockford said he saw the defendant at 10.20 p.m. riding on the London road, and when stopped the man said he thought the rear light was alight but knew the front lamp was out. He had only ridden a couple of miles, in which distance he had to light the front lamp twice. Following his plea of guilty a fine of 10s was imposed. As for another lighting offence, Richard Pettit, a butcher of Newport Pagnell, was summoned for driving a horsed vehicle without white lights at the front, and a red light at the rear, on November 19th. Police constable Nicholls said at 5.05 p.m. he witnessed the pony and trap being driven through the town by the man, who explained that he had been delayed at his farm feeding cattle, and, lighting up time being at 4.37 p.m., didn't know it was so late. Pleading guilty he received a 10s fine, but said he had been only 200 yards from home, and thought the law made allowances for farmers.

At the Divisional Petty Sessions on May 1st 1918 a woman of Priory Street, Newport Pagnell, was brought up in custody, charged with an offence in respect of a member of the Forces. With the offence having allegedly taken place between April 2nd and April 30th he was now in hospital suffering from venereal disease. Superintendent Dibben said the warrant was issued that morning on information supplied by Captain Mowatt, the Officer Commanding the Royal Engineers in the town. A medical certificate from Dr. White, the Medical Officer, was produced, and police sergeant Roberts gave evidence of arresting the prisoner at 11.15 that morning. Superintendent Dibben then asked for a remand of one week, and with this granted by the Bench the prisoner was to be transferred to Northampton gaol until Wednesday next. Subsequently on Wednesday, May 8th the woman, who had a previous conviction of a month in prison at Sheffield for immorality, was sentenced at a Special Sessions at Newport Pagnell to four months' in prison.

A man of no fixed abode was charged with being intoxicated on the highway in the town on May 5th 1918. Special constable T.H. Sim said that on Sunday May 4th at 10.15 p.m. he found the man lying hopelessly drunk on the path near the Post Office, and in consequence he took him to the police station. A fine of 5s was imposed plus 2s 6d special constable's expenses.

At a special police court on Thursday, May 16th 1918 a laundress, from Clewer, was brought up in custody, charged with being a common prostitute and behaving in an indecent manner in a public place at Newport Pagnell on May 15th. A private in the 7th Battalion Oxon and Bucks Light Infantry was also brought up in custody, charged with aiding and abetting. The woman pleaded guilty and the man not guilty. Police constable Barnett said at 9 p.m. on Wednesday, May 15th he saw the two under the influence of drink in the High Street. Later he saw them behaving in an indecent manner in Bury Field, and on that evidence Superintendent Dibben asked that she be remanded to gaol for a week. She had only been in the town for 36 hours, and he wished to make enquiries about her. She was consequently remanded to Northampton gaol until the next Wednesday. Home on overseas leave the soldier was released on recognisance of £5, since the Superintendent had no wish for him to spend his well-earned leave in prison. From remand in Northampton gaol, on Wednesday, May 22nd the woman was charged at a Special Petty Sessions with behaving in an indecent manner in a public place on May 15th. Superintendent Dibben said having communicated with the police at Clewer he discovered that while there she was of no fixed abode, and had a previous conviction for indecent behaviour and being drunk and disorderly. Regarding the present charge she pleaded guilty and a sentence of a month in prison with hard labour was imposed. As for the soldier, who was on leave from Salonica, and was to report the next day at Cowley Barracks, Oxford, having answered his bail he was fined £1.

At the Divisional Petty Sessions on Wednesday, May 29th 1918 William Walton, a motor cab driver of Bedford, was charged with the unauthorised use of motor spirit at Newport Pagnell on May 14th. Additionally, George Langley, the owner of the cab, was charged with allowing the cab to be used outside the limits of the area where it was licensed. Both pleaded not guilty. Police constable Nicholls said at 2.15 p.m. on May 14th he saw the cab outside the Swan Hotel, and when questioned the driver said the vehicle was being used, as for the last year or two, by the Army Service Corps on Army contract. His orders he took from the order book in the yard, and his journey had been to Aylesbury and Fenny Stratford with an Army officer to inspect hospitals. Mr. Langley said he was contractor for Eastern Command and on the day in question the cab was being used by the Assistant Director of Medical Service. The vehicle was requisitioned and he was obliged to supply it. He owned five cars and sometimes used hired cars and sometimes motor cabs. Acknowledging that motor cabs were not to travel further than the three mile limit he admitted that he had not obtained a permit, although it would have been possible to do so. The Bench dismissed the case against the driver and imposed a nominal penalty of 2s 6d against Langley, whom they considered had only committed a technical offence. In other cases a man of Manor Farm, Woolstone, was summoned for the unauthorised use of motor spirit to ride a motor cycle at Newport Pagnell on Wednesday, May 15th. He also failed to produce his driving licence, and as a further offence the acetylene lamp was not obscured. Police sergeant Roberts said he saw the man on the motor cycle in the High Street, and on investigation found the lamp had been whitewashed over with five holes made in it. The driving licence had expired on March 18th, but the man said this was an oversight. He had been to market after doing the milking and had other business to attend to. He was fined 5s for the licence and 5s for the lamp, but the other charge was dismissed. A farmer of Lavendon Grange Farm was summoned for unauthorised use of motor spirit to drive a motor cycle at Newport Pagnell on May 11th. In court, police sergeant Roberts said at 11.15 a.m. in the High Street he questioned the man, who said he was going to Aylesbury to see the Clerk of the Tribunal. His father was appealing for him, and he was going to fetch the necessary form since there was insufficient time to apply by post. He wanted to get his form as he didn't want to join the Army. However, at this the defendant interrupted, saying "That's a lie!" Continuing, police sergeant Roberts said he directed the man to the Council Offices where he could get the form from the Clerk to the Tribunal. During this evidence the man was lolling in the dock with his hands in his pockets, and speaking sharply to him the Magistrates' Clerk said "You might take your hands out of your pockets!" The chairman then asked "Do you want to join the Army?", and receiving no as the reply said "Well, the sergeant's evidence is correct as far as that's concerned." Making a statement the man said his father had permission from the War Agricultural Committee to appeal for him. There had been no time to apply by post so his father said he had better go and fetch it. Then after police sergeant Robert's advice he instead obtained one from Mr. Glanville at Newport Pagnell. The case was dismissed.

Having been remanded in prison for seven days, on Wednesday, June 5th 1918 at the Special Petty Sessions a 32 year old man, who described himself as a jobbing gardener, of Cosgrove, was charged with stealing by means of a trick 5s in money, a packet of onion seed, and ½ pint of peas, all the property of Mrs. Knott of Newport Pagnell. The offence had been committed on May 22nd and in evidence Cecil Petts, of Sherington, an employee of Messrs. Oldham and Co., mineral water manufacturers, said on that day he was coming along the Newport road in the van when a pedestrian asked him for a lift to Newport Pagnell. Claiming to be a discharged soldier the man said he lived at an address in the High Street, and on being given a lift to the town at the Ram Inn he helped to carry six dozen minerals into the pub. While Cecil was making out the ticket the man asked "Is it 2s a dozen?" and was told it was. The man then accompanied Cecil to the Y.M.C.A. Hut, and whilst there Mrs. Knott came across the road and asked if she could have two or three dozen minerals. However, she was told they were all for customers. Aboard the van the man heard the conversation and then travelled with Cecil to Mrs. Higgins' in Station Road, where he helped to carry some more minerals. He then said he wanted to go home but would return in a few minutes. He didn't come back and Cecil next saw him at about 5 p.m. that evening on the Wolverton Road in Great Linford parish, where he said "I have been waiting for you." The man explained that he had to see someone at 5.30 p.m. about a job and it was the following Sunday evening on leaving 'The Case is Altered' pub at Stony Stratford that he was again seen by Cecil, who said "Hold hard, I want to see you. Come out in the back yard. Have you got the money which you drew off Mrs. Knott?" The man said he hadn't but giving his name as H. Stewart told Cecil to call at 10, Queen Anne Street, Stantonbury, the next morning. He said he was drawing £7 10s Army pension at 8 a.m. that day but on calling round in the evening Cecil found the address to be an empty house. In court Mrs. Knott confirmed the events at the Y.M.C.A. Hut and said that in the afternoon the man came into the shop and asked her for the money for three dozen lemonades, which he said they would bring when they came back the second time. She told him that if she was not at the shop they could be left at the next door neighbour's. She gave him 5s in silver and copper and, saying he would be back on Saturday, he also had ½ pint of peas, of 7½d value, and an ounce of onion seed, valued at 1s 3d. She thought he was learning the round, and had not seen him since. Police sergeant Govier said on May 27th he received information respecting the charge, and from the description given visited a Cosgrove address early the next morning. The man was not at home but the house was kept under observation, and when he returned at 12.30 a.m. on May 29th he was charged with the offence, to which he replied, "A paltry 5s. I saw the lad last Sunday and promised to pay it him yesterday." He was then taken to Newport Pagnell police station. In court the man pleaded guilty and said although he rented the house at Cosgrove his proper home was at Clapham Junction. Of the prisoner's past criminal record, Superintendent Dibben said he was bound over on a charge of larceny in 1910, sentenced to 21 days prison on a similar charge in 1912, served six months' hard labour for embezzlement in 1915, and for similar offences further periods of six months and three months respectively in 1916 and 1917. Presently he was living at Cosgrove with a woman that he had picked up at Luton, having due to 'domestic troubles' deserted from the Army at Abbey Wood. At the conclusion of the proceedings Superintendent Dibben received a telephone message confirming the man had deserted from Abbey Wood since November 1st, and sentencing him to six months' hard labour the chairman said his record was shockingly bad.

At the children's court of the Petty Sessions, on Wednesday, June 12th 1918, five schoolboys of the town were summoned for causing malicious damage to the windows and woodwork of a cottage in Clay Lane, the property of General Butler. The damage amounted to £2 10s 9d and one of the boys pleaded guilty to throwing stones, but not doing any damage, and the others pleaded guilty. They and possibly others had lately caused a great deal of trouble, and a fine of 5s was imposed on the parents of each of the boys, who were bound over for six months to be of good behaviour. Two other boys pleaded guilty to damaging trees in the town the property of General Butler between February 1st and June 6th. This damage was estimated at £1 and each culprit was fined 5s and bound over for six months. Of the adult cases, for the unauthorised use of motor spirit on May 30th Mervin Ballam answered a summons. He was a water works manager, of Berkhamstead, of which town Arthur Codgbrook, a gas works manager, also appeared, charged with having allowed the motor spirit to be used. Both pleaded not guilty. Police sergeant Roberts said that whilst on duty in the High Street, at 1 p.m. on May 30th he saw Codgbrook seated in the sidecar of a motorcycle driven by Ballam, who said they were using the petrol for business purposes, and, because the train service was not convenient, he was bringing his friend to see some machinery at the Gas Works. He said he possessed a licence for two gallons of petrol a month for business purposes, and Codgbrook also had a licence, as he wished to visit Newport Pagnell to see 'a one man stoking scoop' at work. It was his petrol that was used for the journey. From the Bench it was stated that the pair had been instructed by the Directors to see this machinery, but nevertheless each was fined 10s.

Having been remanded on July 15th, David Umney, a labourer of the town, was brought up in custody at the Petty Sessions on Wednesday, July 24th 1918, charged with stealing on July 13th a bicycle belonging to Horace Tebbutt, valued at £3. In evidence Charles Tebbutt said he lived at 77, Caldecote Street, and the cycle was the property of his son, Horace, who was on active service in Ireland. When he left home on Saturday the bike was in the house but when he got home at night it was gone. His wife, who was an invalid, 'made a communication' to him respecting the bike and in consequence he saw police sergeant Roberts the next day. Of the St. Albans City Police, police constable Thorpe said he was on station duty that Saturday night when, accompanied by a special constable, the man came to the police station and complained of being attacked by two American soldiers. Allegedly at 11.55 p.m. in St. Albans they asked him to sell the bike and having given him £1 then rode off. However, shortly afterwards they returned and made enquiries about the machine, in reply to which Umney said he had bought it from a Mr. Green of Stoke Goldington, and had ridden over to see his sister. In a grip that nearly throttled him the soldiers then retrieved the £1, thrust 3s into his hands, and rode off. Explaining that he was training with the American troops in Hertfordshire, in court Private Albert Cavasino said that having suspected the bike to be stolen they took back the £1 they had paid the man, and having given him 3s rode the bike to camp, where the sergeant was told about it. Superintendent Dibben said that with the consent of Mrs. Tebbutt the defendant had borrowed the bike to go to Woburn, but he didn't come back and sold it for £1. As for the defendant, he said he wasn't guilty of stealing the bike as he had only borrowed it, and in reply to the Bench said he got rid of the machine because it had no lights. With the time being three minutes to midnight he was afraid the police would stop him. He was sentenced to 21 days' hard labour.

(Charles Tebbutt was locally renowned for his interest in birds, and at the annual summer show of the Northants Good Intent Ornithological Society, held on Saturday, July 13th 1918 at the Fanciers' Club, Northampton, he took 1st, 2nd and 3rd prize in Class 1, 'heavy breeds, old birds.' In Class 2, 'light breeds, old birds,' he gained 1st, 3rd and highly commended, while in Class 3, 'heavy breeds,' he gained 1st and highly commended. He would then win further prizes with his poultry at the Northampton Show on November 16th 1918.)

From a week's remand in gaol, a 48 year old 'iron dresser' of 47, Moseley Street, Blackburn, was brought up at the Petty Sessions on Wednesday, August 14th 1918, charged with obtaining a sum of money by false pretences from Elizabeth Webb on August 2nd, and from Ellen Daniells on August 3rd. Elizabeth Webb said she lived at 59, Greenfield Road, and the prisoner called at her house about 4.30 p.m. on the Friday afternoon. He said he had just left her son, serving in the Royal Welsh Fusiliers, in Egypt, and had promised he would come to see her. Saying he had come from Market Harborough he gave his name as Hargreaves, and on hearing that he expected he would have to walk home Mrs. Webb gave him 3s, all the silver she had. Believing his story she gave him a good tea, and was further taken in when he said, "Your son always wrote my letters for me and called me 'Dad.' He has got his ticket and you will have a pension of 17s 6d per week, and when he gets home he is going into munitions work" Elizabeth Reynolds said the prisoner called at her shop at the corner of Greenfield Road on Friday afternoon, August 2nd, and asked if she knew anyone in the street who had a son in Salonica. She said she didn't know, but a little girl who was in the shop thought Mrs. Daniells might have. The man then left and went up Greenfield Road. Ellen Daniells, of Spring Gardens, said the prisoner called at her house between 9 a.m and 10 a.m. on Saturday morning. He said he had left her son and George Baxter, of Caldecote Street, in a rest camp at Salonica, for having suffered an attack of malaria their discharge was pending. They should have travelled on the same boat as him but were allegedly not well enough. She asked if he wanted any food but he said "I daren't have solid food. I have to have a special diet for my complaint, but if you care to give me anything towards my expenses you can do so." She gave him a shilling, but when she told her husband at dinner he said "It's a fraud." Superintendent Dibben said the Luton Borough Police had apprehended the prisoner, who in court made a rambling statement regarding troubles with his wife, of being in hospital etc. Superintendent Dibben then said that the prisoner joined the Army on December 23rd 1914 and was discharged from the Royal Welsh Fusiliers on August 28th 1917, with his papers marked 'a hard working man.' The Superintendent had received a letter from the Chief Constable at Chesterfield regarding two similar charges, and requesting that these be taken into consideration it transpired that last December the man was telling the same story in Lancashire. He was entitled to a pension of 8s 3d a week, and drink had undoubtedly been his downfall. A sentence of four months in prison with hard labour was imposed, with the chairman adding "I wish I could give you more."

Stationed in the town, a member of the Royal Engineers reported sick on July 25th 1918, and was found to be suffering from venereal disease. In consequence on August 6th Captain J.B. Mowatt, the commanding officer, gave instructions for a warrant to be issued for the arrest of a 21 year old married woman from Moulsoe. The following day at 9.30 a.m. she was apprehended by police sergeant Honour, and having been remanded on bail appeared in court to answer a charge under D.O.R.A. Regulation 40D. She pleaded not guilty, and with Dr. H.T. Wickham having found no indication of the disease, when he examined her at her home on August 13th, the Bench remanded her for a further seven days, to allow time for a report from the Medical Research Association to be obtained. Subsequently she appeared at the Petty Sessions on Wednesday, August 21st, and with the report confirming Dr. Wickham's findings the case was dismissed.

On Thursday, August 22nd, at the Petty Sessions a private in the Labour Company was charged with having on August 19th stolen a quantity of bacon and tea, the property of H.M. Army Council, from the Staple Hall Depot, and also charged, for having received these goods, and for being in possession of an Army blanket, was a woman of Newport Pagnell. Giving evidence, James Ransom, of the Labour Corps, said that he was employed as sergeant cook at Staple Hall Depot, and on the day in question a quantity of bacon was drawn from the stores by the accused, who worked in the cookhouse. After the bacon had been boned, the man left at about 5.45p.m., but also gone was some tea in a tin caddy, which the sergeant cook had placed ready for use the next morning. Acting on information from Newport Pagnell, on August 19th Inspector Callaway and police constable Hedges then kept watch on a house in Aylesbury Street, and at 6.50 p.m. saw the two prisoners leave the premises and, with the man carrying a dress basket, walk into Vicarage Lane (sic). When stopped, the woman, whose lawful husband was serving in France with the Army Veterinary Corps, said that she was the wife of her companion, and while both were being taken back to the house the bacon and tea were found in the basket. The house belonged to a widow, Hannah Diddams, and when they arrived she was told by the woman that "The police want to see the lodger form." As for the man, he duly admitted taking the goods from Staple Hall Depot, and at the police station a further search of the basket revealed several letters relating to the prisoners. However, in evidence an officer of the Labour Corps spoke of the excellent military character of the man, and perhaps in view of this although a sentence of six weeks in prison was imposed, this would be without hard labour. Lieutenant Thomas Sylvester, quartermaster at Staple Hall Depot, then identified the blanket as Army Council property. This had been found in the woman's house at Newport Pagnell, and in explanation she said that it came from South Africa, having been brought to her by a man billeted in her house about a year ago. In fact she had made a statement to that effect, and pleaded not guilty. Nevertheless, other items had also been found in her house, and it was duly discovered that these had been taken over a period of time from a house in Newport Pagnell, where she had assisted the domestic servants. It was further revealed that one of her children was being looked after by her parents at Newport Pagnell, and the other by friends, and as the supposed wife of the male prisoner she had come to Fenny Stratford to live with him in a house in Aylesbury Street. In concluding the case, the charge regarding the blanket was dismissed, but for receiving the bacon and tea the woman was sentenced to six weeks hard labour in prison. As for the other charges, these would warrant a further three weeks.

At the Petty Sessions, on Wednesday, September 18th 1918, a member of the Labour Company attached to the Royal Engineers in the town was brought up from prison on remand, charged with stealing on the night of September 6th two £1 and one 10s Treasury Notes. These were the property of Sapper Jones, who stated that whilst under canvas in the camp at Newport Pagnell he drew £2 arrears of pay and 15s ordinary pay. This had been on Thursday, September 5th, and he put two £1 and one 10s Treasury Notes in his wallet before retiring to rest about 9.50 p.m. However, the prisoner, who slept in the same tent, heard him tell his other two occupants that he had drawn a good amount, and when the man arose at 6.15 a.m. he discovered, at about 7 p.m., that the notes were missing. He reported the theft to the commanding officer and the police on the Saturday morning, and in consequence Inspector Bailey of the Northants Constabulary saw the prisoner detained on Monday, September 9th at Wellingborough police station. Having received information from Superintendent Dibben he questioned the man, who explained that he was paid 10s before he left Newport Pagnell. He further claimed to have paid 4s 6d for the hire of the bicycle. Yet when searched he was found to have 13s in silver, and accounting for the difference he said his mother had sent him 5s 6d in a registered letter. Saying "I would not rob a child" he denied any knowledge of a robbery at Newport Pagnell but was told that his mother would be seen, with enquiries to also be made at Earls Barton and from the girl with whom he had been to Northampton on the 7th. In the wake of these investigations he then admitted the theft. In court Superintendent Dibben said the man was absent from the Royal Engineers at Newport Pagnell without a pass, whilst in his evidence Captain Mowatt, commanding officer of the Royal Engineers at Newport Pagnell, said the man enlisted at Northampton on August 31st 1915, being posted the following month to the 3rd Northants Regiment. In November 1915 he went to France and in June 1916 was treated in England for wounds in the left foot and face. In December 1916 he returned to the Front and in June 1917 was again wounded. Later put in a Labour Company, he had been in Newport Pagnell for about three weeks before committing the offence. His conduct was not satisfactory and his character bad, but there was no criminal record. Pleading guilty he was sentenced to a month of hard labour, and the chairman, who told him it was contemptible to steal from a chum, especially in war time, said had he not been wounded twice the sentence would have been harsher.

At the Petty Sessions on Wednesday, October 2nd 1918, the British and Colonial Motor Company, of Long Acre, London, was charged with allowing petrol to be used by Joseph Kopuit of Forest Gate, a motor driver who was summoned for the unauthorised use of the fuel at Newport Pagnell on September 11th. A plea of not guilty was entered. Superintendent Dibben said on that date at 3.45 p.m. he saw a small second-hand car being driven in the High Street by the defendant, who said he was employed by the British and Colonial Motor Company, which had sent him to Sheffield to drive the car, which they had purchased, to London. His route had been via Leicester and Northampton, but he didn't have a special permit for the journey. The man was joining the Army in a fortnight, and the solicitor acting on his behalf read a letter from the Controller stating that although permits had previously been issued, they were now unnecessary for firms engaged in the trade. Knowing nothing of this Superintendent Dibben said he would like to make enquiries, and the Bench adjourned the case for a month.

At the Petty Sessions on Wednesday, May 18th 1919, a man, late of the Royal Engineers at Bedford, was summoned by a single woman of 36, Mill Street, Newport Pagnell, to explain why he should not contribute to the support of her illegitimate male child, of which he was the alleged father. At first he denied being the father but reversed this when two of his letters were read out, in one of which he told her that he had been doing orderly corporal's duty, and she shouldn't be surprised if he came home a field marshal. Whilst billeted in Newport Pagnell he had walked out with the woman for five months, despite being married with two children. Recently demobilised he was now out of work, but nevertheless the Bench made an order for 5s a week until the child was 14, and directed him to pay the costs of £4 17s 6d.

At a special police court, on Wednesday, December 17th 1919 a sergeant in the Royal Fusiliers, wearing four service chevrons, the Delhi Ribbon, the D.C.M. and other decorations on his breast, was charged with having unlawfully obtained charitable contributions at Newport Pagnell on December 8th, contrary to the Vagrancy Act. He pleaded not guilty. Miss Alice M. Coales, of Beechwood, Newport Pagnell, said that when he called on her on the evening of December 8th he said he had been unable to find work in London and, having walked from Luton, wanted a little assistance for a night's lodging, before making for Birmingham. She gave him some tea and 1s 6d in money, and later introduced him to the local secretary of the National Federation of Discharged Soldiers and Sailors, Fred Lane, who said in court that when she brought him to his house he advanced him 5s. This was on condition it was repaid, and he also provided him with a bed at a respectable house in the town. However, not availing himself of this the man travelled that evening to Northampton by the 6.25 p.m. train, as testified by the booking clerk at Newport Pagnell station. Superintendent Dibben gave evidence of having received the prisoner in custody on the night of Monday, December 15th, and on being charged the man, admitting he was unable to repay the money, said he had been in Northampton since leaving Newport Pagnell on the 8th. He had no Army papers about him, but on oath claimed to have enlisted in the 2nd Battalion Grenadier Guards in 1902. He allegedly went to France on August 4th 1914 and although discharged after being wounded on November 18th 1914 enlisted in the Leicester Regiment, and was severely wounded at Neuve Chappelle. After serving in France he was re-engaged for Russia, from where having arrived in April 1919 he returned with General Robinson during October, the month he was demobilised. It was during a visit to his brother at Kettering that he claimed he lost all his papers and £21 in money. In order for Superintendent Dibben to make enquiries he was remanded until Friday, December 19th, on the morning of which he was brought up in custody, but refused to plead. However, the Bench found him guilty of having unlawfully obtained food and charitable contributions, and consequent to his recent enquiries Superintendent Dibben stated the man's correct age to be 31. Having enlisted in the Grenadier Guards in 1911 he was discharged for misconduct, but in 1914 enlisted in the Leicester Regiment and was transferred to the 9th Battalion Royal Defence Corps in 1917, where he seemed to have redeemed his character. He re-enlisted on April 10th 1919 in the Royal Fusiliers, but held the rank of corporal, not sergeant. Found by the Kettering police in a hovel in that town, the Superintendent then produced the prisoner's protection certificate and discharge book, by which was shown, excepting a mention of the North Russian ribbon, that he was entitled to wear all the decorations. He had only drawn one instalment on his protection certificate, £30 4s 4½d being due to him, and on October 24th had corresponded with the War Office as 'Corporal Curtis,' regarding proceeding to America. Consequent to a complaint of trying to obtain charitable contributions, on December 8th he was detained by the Bedford Borough Police, whilst as for his previous record, on April 4th 1919 he had been fined £1 at Kettering for obtaining 10s by falsely claiming that his wife and children were starving, and that his landlord had thrown him out. In fact he was not married but cohabiting with a woman. Previously he had been charged with larceny and put on probation, and was twice fined by the Kettering Bench for larceny. In court the chairman, Mr. Carlile, told the man that he should be grateful to Superintendent Dibben for taking him into custody, for it had been the means to get his papers back, and there was now no reason why he shouldn't go straight. He was fined 5s and allowed a week to pay, which would allow him to return to Kettering and draw the money due to him. By the opinion of the Bench he had been walking about disgracing the King's uniform.

ELECTRIC THEATRE

In 1912, in conjunction with Alfred Bullard, a local entrepreneur, at the top of St. John Street the owners of the Salmons' coachworks purchased a private house, Clifton House, which had been built in the 1860s on the site of an old pub, The Bell. The house had once been owned by Benjamin Tarry, a retired farmer, and after his death his widow lived there until she died at the age of 82 in 1911.

Opened in 1912 on December 20th the cinema was built over the large gardens at the back of the house and having fashioned the flashing sign for the façade Harry Bardett, as the foreman engineer, worked the apparatus. During the First World War the cinema became a venue for many patriotic meetings and concerts with the Misses Edith, Mabel and Emily Holland amongst the staff. The chief of these was Mr. W. Webb for whom in view of his long and serious illness the proprietors arranged a benefit performance

in 1916 on Wednesday evening, November 22nd. The first part comprised pictures, with, arranged by Mr. C. K. Garratt, the second part being a concert in which all the performances were contributed by the Royal Engineers. Several battle scenes were amongst the films screened during the war and some years after the war there was sounds reminiscent of artillery when one Friday afternoon a terrific thunderstorm broke over the town. At the time Mr. J. Wilcox, an inspector of the British Acoustic Company, was examining one of the projecting machines when a bolt of lightning came down the ventilator bursting into a flame which leapt three feet high. Mr. Wilcox was partially stunned and attributed his escape from the fact that the motor he was examining was earthed and the floor of the operating box covered with rubber material. The battery room was filled with smoke and a door in the upper part of the building torn from its hinges and blown five yards. The chimney was shattered and brickwork crashed through the roof of the adjoining stationer's shop. After a refurbishment in 1939 the premises were renamed the Electra Cinema and closed in 1988, being subsequently developed into an arcade of shops.

During the silent era of films, Mrs. F. Shedd, formerly Miss Dorothy Higgins, was the pianist at the cinema. She had married Frank Shedd on Christmas morning 1915 and their home would be 9, Station Road. However, in 1917 at the age of 25 he was killed in action serving with the Bucks Battalion of the Oxon and Bucks Light Infantry. When the 'talkies' arrived Mrs. Shedd continued at the cinema until the early 1930s, operating the gramophone. For over 25 years her father had been the self taught organist at the Wesleyan Chapel, Newport Pagnell, and she received her early music lessons from Walter George of the town, a piano dealer, tuner and teacher. An accomplished musician she was accompanist at many dances and concerts and also conducted her own orchestra. In her daily employment for some years she was a school teacher at Sherington and Simpson, and for a long while kept a small thatched general store in Station Road. As for her musical activities, she was organist at the Wesleyan Chapel, then Moulsoe parish church and for 12 years at the Congregational Church, from which position she retired in 1959. She died in February 1963 at Renny Lodge Hospital aged 72, having been in failing health for some time.

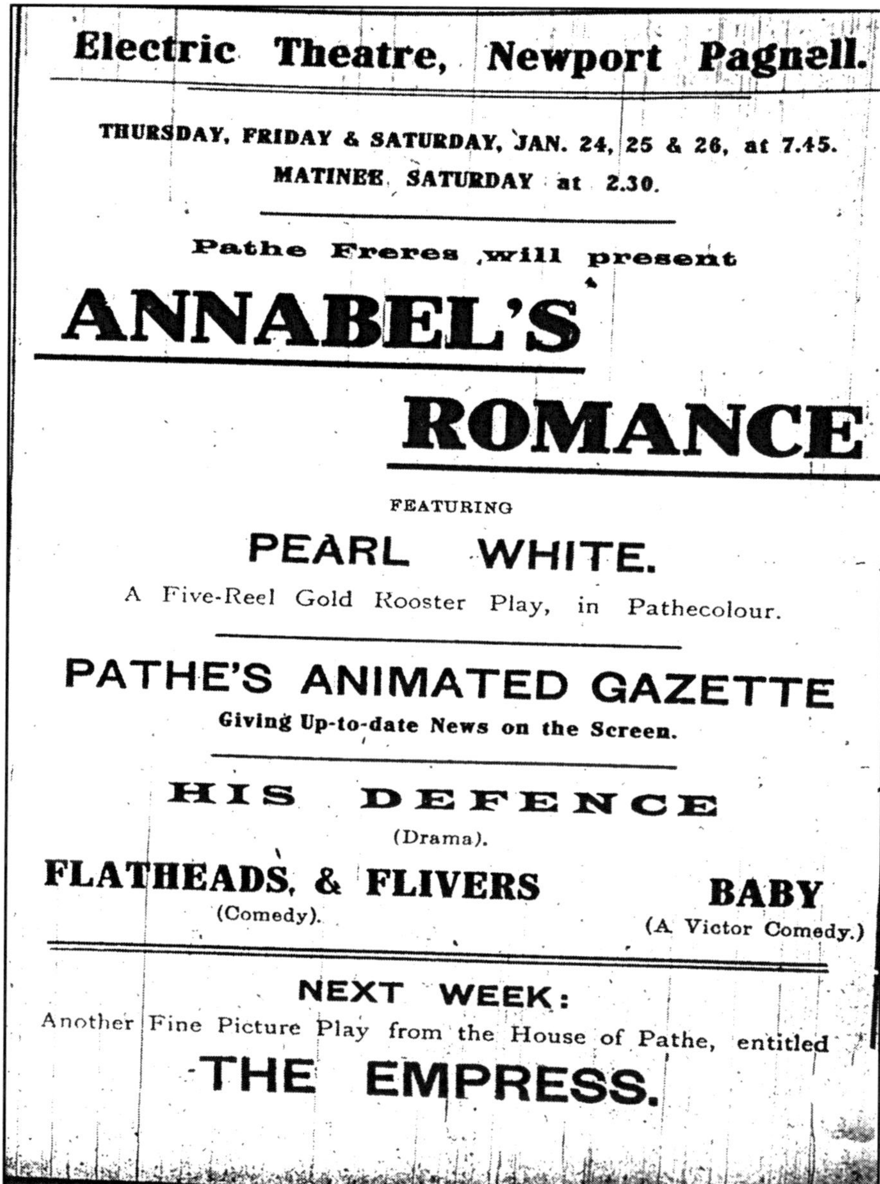

Electric Theatre, Newport Pagnell.

THURSDAY, FRIDAY & SATURDAY, JAN. 24, 25 & 26, at 7.45.
MATINEE SATURDAY at 2.30.

Pathe Freres will present

ANNABEL'S ROMANCE

FEATURING

PEARL WHITE.

A Five-Reel Gold Rooster Play, in Pathecolour.

PATHE'S ANIMATED GAZETTE

Giving Up-to-date News on the Screen.

HIS DEFENCE

(Drama).

FLATHEADS, & FLIVERS
(Comedy).

BABY
(A Victor Comedy.)

NEXT WEEK:

Another Fine Picture Play from the House of Pathe, entitled

THE EMPRESS.

Above: An early advertisement from the Bucks Standard describing a typical showbill from the period.

Seen on p. 79 The Electric Theatre circa 1912.

Seen on p. 80 The present day premises.

FIRE BRIGADE

As a member of the Bucks National Reserve, during the first week of December 1914 Reginald Odell, the son of John Odell, the local ironmonger, offered his service for the defence of the country. He was also a member of the Fire Brigade, which on Monday evening, January 4th 1915, suffered the sad loss of Samuel Lilley Coales who, after a few days illness, died at 31, High Street, aged 68. The son of the late William Peck Coales, he had been in business for many years as a jeweller etc. in the town, but his public prominence was due to his deep interest in the work of the Newport Pagnell Fire Brigade, which, when it was still a volunteer organisation, he had joined in 1866. As second officer he served for several years under Mr. F. J. Taylor, and on the latter's resignation he took over as chief officer in 1891. Then on the completion of 40 years with the brigade, in recognition of his service he was presented on August 24th 1905 with a solid silver gadroon-shaped tea service and cake basket. It was his ambition to equip the brigade with a modern steam fire engine, and, with the fund having been started by his only son, Second Officer C.F. Coales, this intention was realised in 1912, with the purchase made possible by subscriptions acquired mainly from persons in the town and district. Of the fires attended by the new appliance, the small blaze which broke out at the International Stores on Tuesday afternoon, January 12th 1915, had been apparently caused by a lighted gas jet igniting a match board ceiling, but the prompt arrival of the brigade and three men, under Second Officer C.F. Coales, quickly contained the incident. The following month Fred Platt and Fred Moore were appointed as members to replace Reginald Odell and E. Whitmee. They had joined the Forces (Mr. Whitmee having served in the Boer War with the Wolverton Company of the Bucks Volunteers) and the month also witnessed another loss when, being one of the pioneers who had established the brigade, and in his early years had been a member of the Sanitary Committee, William Bromwich died on Tuesday, February 23rd aged 82. Having more than 50 years ago succeeded his late father, Martin Bromwich, as head of Messrs. Bromwich and Sons, tailors and outfitters, he had been the oldest businessman in the town, but for the last few years had entrusted the management of the shop to his eldest son Mr. J. Bromwich.

In April 1915, in succession to his late father Mr. C.F. Coales was appointed as chief officer of the brigade, and it was by his suggestion that Messrs. W. Pettit and L. Mitchell were appointed as additional members. Yet apart from their fire-fighting skills members of the brigade could also render medical assistance, as when Nurse Johnson, of St. John Street, met with an accident in 1915 on Friday, May 21st. While attending a case in Bury Avenue she had slipped and broken the small bone of her leg just above the ankle, and, with Dr. C. Bailey summoned, initial assistance was given by members of the ambulance section of the brigade, who superintended her conveyance on the ambulance litter to her home. With the increasing menace of the German Zeppelins, in June 1915 the captain of the brigade wrote to the Council asking if a simple form of respirator could be provided for the firemen. These would be carried in their pockets in the event of incendiaries being dropped, and in unanimous agreement the Council resolved to purchase the best type available. Thus having considered two types of respirator, in July 1915 the Council decided to purchase a dozen of the chosen type at a cost of 1s 11d each. Of those members of the brigade who wished to enlist in the Army, on Monday, June 14th 1915 there had been disappointment for Fred Shelton, the son of Mr. C. Shelton, when he applied to join the Beds Yeomanry for, as on two previous occasions, he failed the medical test. But across the nation there was no lack of volunteers, for patriotic fervour was still running high. Indeed, on Wednesday evening, August 4th 1915, a large and patriotic crowd gathered on Market Hill where, with the brigade present in full uniform, a pledge was made to carry the war through to a victorious conclusion. Yet despite such fervour, with the continuing attrition of trench warfare the need for conscription arose, and at the Military Tribunal in June 1916 the U.D.C. asked for three members of the brigade to be exempted. However, for the military Captain Green said instructions had been received from the War Office that the place of volunteer firemen could be undertaken by special constables, and in addition one of the men applied for had been passed for garrison duty. But in response the chief officer of the brigade said that since he was now four men short both men were indispensable, and in view of this six months was given for the man passed for garrison duty. As for the other two they were exempted until August 1st, on which date for the first time in its formation the U.D.C. met in the open air on the lawn at the rear of the Council Offices. In the ensuing business it was agreed that two new lengths of hose should be purchased for the brigade, whose complement would now include Messrs. C. Pidgen and B. Reynolds, as replacements for the two members who were joining the Forces.

One of the largest patriotic meetings since the beginning of the war took place on Market Hill on Friday, August 4th, 1916. Fronting the platform were the members of the brigade in full uniform, but this would be the last such occasion that Frederick James Taylor, of Lovat Bank, would witness, for after a long illness he died in 1917 on Wednesday evening, March 23rd, aged 83. Being for a long period its chief officer, until a few years ago he had taken a great interest in the brigade, and it was largely due to his efforts that the town had been equipped with not only a magnificent steamer but also the most modern of fire fighting appliances. In fact the engine had been christened 'Lovat' in the grounds of his home at Lovat Bank. On Monday afternoon, March 26th 1917 he was laid to rest in the family vault in Newport Pagnell Cemetery, and at the funeral the brigade was fully represented by the firemen in full uniform, and also two retired members. On Tuesday evening, July 31st 1917, at the monthly meeting of the U.D.C. a tender from Merryweather was accepted for replacing the brigade's defective hose, and for the two 60 foot lengths the cost would be £15 10s 4d. Then at the November meeting of the U.D.C., on the evening of Tuesday, November 6th 1917, Mr. A. Levin, a member of the brigade for the past 21 years, tendered his resignation, since he was contemplating leaving the town at the end of the year. Another departure would be that of William Chantler, for he died on Friday, January 4th 1918. Having joined the Volunteer Fire Brigade in 1870, in 1888 he became a member of the Brigade Committee, and when in 1904 the U.D.C. took over the management of the brigade he acted as chairman of the Fire Brigade Committee. As for his daily employment, for many years he assisted his father in his business as chemist and druggist, and eventually retired to his home, which was situated only a few yards from the shop. The funeral was held on the Tuesday afternoon, with the coffin preceded by the members of the brigade in full uniform.

On Tuesday evening May 7th 1918, at the monthly meeting of the U.D.C., held in the Council Chamber in the High Street, a special report of the Fire Brigade Committee was considered. This had been prepared subsequent to a report by the chief officer, in which he stated that a recent fire at Lathbury could not be attended because horses hadn't been available. Therefore in the wake of this Salmons had been asked to provide a suitable motor vehicle for trial, and so also at the meeting a report from Chief Officer Coales on the subsequent test was read. With the route being up Chicheley Hill, Chicheley, North Crawley, and then home, this had taken place on the evening of Saturday, May 4th, and since the 30 h.p. Daimler had proved a great success Messrs. L. Higgins and H. Wise, two persons of competent expertise, were asked to examine the condition of the vehicle. Their findings revealed all to be in order except, due to bad driving at a previous date, two worn gear wheels. However, Salmons had provided a written agreement that they would be pleased to replace the gear wheels if the Council decided to purchase the car, and after discussion it was decided to appoint a committee of Messrs. Coales, Tayler, Bull, and Short, to carry through the negotiations. On the evening of Tuesday, June 4th 1918, at the monthly meeting of the U.D.C. the chairman, Mr. J. Short, presented long service medals and bars to certain members of the brigade. He said that in the days of the old Volunteer Brigade it had been customary to present members with a bronze medal on the completion of 20 years service, with a bar for each additional ten, and thus the Council, who now had control of the brigade, were continuing the custom. He then presented a bar to Mr. W. Coverley, who had joined in 1882, a bar to Mr. T. Shelton, who had joined in 1883, and a medal each to Mr. Albert Clarke, 1898, and Mr. F. Mayne, 1897. In fact except for a short break a member of the Mayne family had been a member of the brigade since its inception in 1855, with Mr. W. Mayne, the grandfather of the present member, having served from 1855 to 1870, and Mr. T. Mayne, the father of the present member, having served from 1870 to 1891. There was also a medal for Mr. G. Procter, who had been unable to attend. With it having been agreed to purchase the Daimler from Salmons, the asking price of £200 had been negotiated to £195, and the vehicle, fitted with its new fire brigade body, was delivered by the firm to the fire station on the early afternoon of Friday, August 2nd 1918. In fact it would be in action only a short while later, for at about 3.30 p.m. the brigade received a call to attend a hayrick fire at the farm of Mr. George Tayler. Due to the vehicle they were swiftly on the scene, and duly managed to save one rick and the greater part of another. The garaging of the Daimler at the fire station now meant that the ambulance had to be accommodated in a room at the back, and, since this unsurprisingly caused problems of accessibility, at the meeting of the U.D.C. on Tuesday evening, September 3rd 1918 Mr. C.F. Coales, the chief officer of the brigade, requested in a communication that an alternative location should be found. The porch of the parish church or the police station were suggested, and in due course Superintendent Dibben would agree to the latter.

Special thanksgiving services for the cessation of hostilities were held at the parish church on Sunday, November 17th 1918, with the brigade being amongst those present, under Chief Officer Coales. Yet shortly after this joyous occasion there was sadness when, after a short illness, Bertram Reynolds died on Friday, December 15th 1918 at 15, Wolverton Road. Aged 33, he left a widow and two children. By trade a painter and decorator, he had been employed by Salmons, and having been rejected by the Army on medical grounds not only associated himself with the local company of the Volunteers, but also until a short while ago had served as a member of the brigade. On Saturday, July 19th 1919, the Peace Day rejoicings took place in the town, and the procession which paraded the principal streets included the brigade in their uniforms under Chief Officer Coales. As for those members who had returned from military service, at the parish church on Monday, August 9th 1920 Frederick Shelton, who having been originally rejected by the Army served in the Royal Engineers, married Miss Mary Mason, the eldest daughter of Mr. and Mrs. Harry Mason. Both families had long been connected with the business life of the town, and, having for several years been on the teaching staff of the Girls' Department of the Council Schools, the bride was presented by the children with a case of ivory-handled tea knives. Strewing flowers in their path, schoolchildren formed a guard of honour as the couple left the church, and a reception for some 40 guests was later held at the bride's home in Silver Street. In the afternoon the couple then motored to Bletchley station for a honeymoon in Brighton. Concluding this period, after an association of 25 years with the brigade, having been its Chief Officer for the past eight years, Mr. C.F. Coales retired, and on behalf of the members of the brigade on Saturday evening, April 14th 1923, was presented with an upholstered armchair by the new Chief Officer, E.P. Whitmee. From membership of the brigade he had joined the army early in the war and during his service in France with the 2nd Oxon and Bucks Light Infantry was wounded on three occasions and promoted on the field to sergeant, a rank that he held on demobilisation.

FOOD, FARMING AND FLOWERS

For the fund for Belgian refugees, on November 25th 1914, the Newport Pagnell Branch of the National Farmers' Union held an agricultural jumble sale, with the cost of the appeals sent around the district defrayed by Mr. J. Higham. Situated near the centre of the town, at the back of the Cattle Market, the venue was a field lent by Miss Payne, and, as the resident representative of George Wigley and Sons, Mr. P. C. Gambell gave his services as auctioneer. George Taylor, the blacksmith of Tickford Street, lent the services of his workmen, and also lent his horse and trolley to collect the various gifts, which included farm animals, produce, implements and also a model of a church made by Ernest Miller, a crippled inmate of the Workhouse. This was sold for 2s, whilst in total the event would raise £150 for the 'Daily Telegraph Shilling Fund' for Belgian Relief. The end of the year saw hundreds of local agricultural acres under water due to heavy rain. At one point Caldecote Street, Station Road and the High Street from the Railway Tavern to Lakes Lane were practically impassable on foot, and there was tragedy one Sunday afternoon when, whilst playing with a school friend, on the bridges spanning the River Lovat, and its tributary at Caldecote, the seven year old son of Harry Welch, of Wepener, Newport Pagnell, accidentally fell into the water and drowned. His father and others had rushed to the scene but no trace could be found, and, with both the river and the adjoining stream having overflowed, it was assumed that he had been washed away by the force of the water. Under the direction of the police dragging operations were carried out, but it was not until two weeks later that the body was found.

At the Swan Hotel, on Wednesday afternoon, January 27th 1915, the annual meeting of the Newport Pagnell branch of the National Farmers' Union was held, with George Tayler occupying the chair. Mr. P. C. Gambell presented the balance sheet, which showed a healthy situation, and of the resolutions unanimously approved was one to press the Bucks Education Committee to, albeit with the consent of their parents, allow boys to leave school at the age of 12 to work on the land. During the evening the annual dinner was held at the same venue, with the toast 'Our Imperial Forces' proposed. This was submitted by Mr. J. Payne, who coupled it with the names of Mr. J. Whiting, who had fought in the Boer War, Mr. F. W. Taylor and Mr. W. J. Hobbs, both of whom were special constables and had sons who were expected to soon go to the Front. Also mentioned was Mr. P. C. Gambell, the lieutenant of the local corps of special constables, and as one of those replying to the toast Mr. A. Bullard, to laughter, said he was proud to be a member of the N.F.U., for it brought him into contact with the most prosperous and contented body of men in the district. Later he was amongst those contributing songs to piano accompaniments by Mr. C. K. Garratt. Also at the Swan Hotel, with the committee re-elected en bloc, plus the addition of Mr. Fleming, of The Hyde, Olney, the 20th annual meeting of the Newport Pagnell Shire Horse Society took place on Wednesday, February 10th 1915. However, because many of the members were in the Forces the usual dinner was not held, and due to the war the Foal Show had not taken place. Nevertheless the general account showed a balance of £146 9s 8d, and in other matters for the next season the well bred horse 'Redlynch Martinet,' by 'Lockinge Forest King,' had been hired from Messrs. Forshaw. In February 1915 it was announced that Mr. Alfred Bullard was shortly to travel to inland France as the representative of the National P.S.A. Council. With the Newport Pagnell Society having promised a ton of potatoes, the mission was to assist the distribution of foodstuffs to the civilian population in stricken areas, and on Wednesday, March 31st 1915, Mr. Bullard duly left for a location only a few miles from the firing line.

As for other charitable measures, from his agricultural friends and neighbours in March 1915 Mr. George Tayler, of The Kickles, undertook a collection in the Newport Pagnell district for the Red Cross, this being to help the stricken people of Serbia. Shortly after midday there was a severe thunderstorm on Tuesday, August 3rd 1915, and once again the agricultural acres were threatened with flooding, since the deluge lasted for half-an-hour and the drains were unable to cope. Then in mid August 1915 came another scourge, in the form of a plague of wasps nests of which Mr. A. Franklin, the gardener at Westbury, would destroy 27, and Mr. J. Bocock, of the Red House, 16. One, as big as a football, he found to contain 3,000 broods, which were then distributed among his customers for fishing purposes. In fact Mr. Bocock was renowned as a local beekeeper and one Tuesday in the month at the Northampton Beekeepers' Show he secured one first, one second and one third prize. His wife also enjoyed success, for she won fourth prize in the class for cakes made with honey! Mr. Bocock also had an interest in horticulture, and lent the field for the first show of flowers, fruit and vegetables held at the Red House on Saturday, August 28th 1915. At 5 p.m. the opening ceremony was performed by John Roberts and during the event the Newport Pagnell Excelsior Silver Band played musical selections for dancing. Mr. A. Lott, the gardener to Mr. F. J. Taylor, of Lovat Bank, and Mr. A. Franklin, gardener to Mr. H. Sim, of Westbury, acted as the judges and amongst the 175 entries were many fine specimens of produce from the allotment holders of the Red House, Fox Gate Piece and Great Linford. Indeed of these James Moseley won 16 prizes with his 19 exhibits, whilst for a remarkable dish of onions Mr. Alfred Chapman, a Fox Gate Piece tenant, secured the special prize of a live duck for the best exhibit in the show. Then on Saturday, September 4th 1915, the 5th annual flower show of the Unionist Working Men's Club took place, with the judges of the curtailed schedule being Mr. E. Golding, the head gardener at Tyringham House, and Mr. C. Leach, the gardener at Cranfield Court. Mr. F. J. Taylor, of Lovat Bank, gave the prizes for both the table decoration and the wild flower collection by the children of the members, and other donors of special prizes were Mr. A. Corbett, Mr. Cecil R. Line and Messrs. Toogood and Sons. During the school summer holiday about 30 male pupils helped local farmers with the harvest. Their services were much appreciated and on Sunday, September 26th 1915, harvest thanksgivings were offered at St. Luke's Mission Church, which had been especially decorated by members of the congregation with fruit, vegetables and flowers. The Reverend W. St. John Lindars, the priest in charge, was the celebrant, and the day opened with the celebration of the Holy Communion at 7 a.m. Then for the same purpose the annual thanksgiving services were held at the Parish Church in 1915 on Sunday, October 3rd, with the fruit and vegetables of the decorations distributed among the sick and poor of the town on the following morning. In October 1915 the root crops grown at the sewerage farm were sold for £44 1s 6d, although the previous year the sum had been £59.

However, this had been due to an extra yield of mangolds from two acres and the oat crop would counteract this deficiency. Heavy and continuous rain caused extensive flooding in the town and district during the third week of December 1915. From Stony Stratford to Olney the area resembled a miniature sea, and rain fell steadily throughout Wednesday, December 15th, when the committee and members of the Newport Pagnell Branch of the Farmers' Union held a gigantic agricultural jumble sale. This through the sale of farm produce, implements etc. was to raise funds for the British Farmers' Red Cross, and Miss Payne had granted the free use of her field adjoining the Market Place, where amongst the livestock were all manner of farm animals and even mongrels and two guinea pigs. Opening the sale, Lady Farrar stressed the need in the present situation for women to take up work on the farms, and said, "Out in Africa I look after many things on the farm. I feed the chickens and the pigs and there is no nicer work in which a woman could be engaged." In the form of a red cross, at the end of the opening ceremony she was handed a bouquet of red and white carnations and ferns by Miss D. Wickham, which she then graciously donated to the sale. At £4 this was subsequently bought by Donald Fraser, and he again put it back until, with each bloom offered separately, only the framework was left. Nearly all the carnations made 5s a piece, and total sum realised by the bouquet of £11 19s 6d contributed to the £551 made by the most successful event, despite the mire of the market place. At The Poplars, a special meeting of the Newport Pagnell Horticultural Society took place on Thursday evening, December 23rd 1915, with Mr. F. Saunders, the chairman, presiding. However, due to the war it was decided not to hold any further summer exhibitions. On Wednesday afternoon, February 16th 1916, the A.G.M. of the Newport Pagnell Shire Horse Society took place at the Swan Hotel, where, with a balance of £84 2s 3d in the bank, the statement of accounts showed the expenditures to include £240 for hiring the services of 'Redlynch Martinet.' All of the 20 agriculturalists who had acted as the previous year's management committee were re-elected en bloc, with the addition made of Mr. J. Gilbert. There was heavy snow in the district on Wednesday morning, February 23rd 1916. It lay five inches deep in the streets and people had to take care not to slip and fall. Yet it wasn't snow and ice that caused an accident to Ernest Wood, a dairyman and shopkeeper of Priory Street, on the evening of Friday, February 25th 1916, for whilst cutting hay to feed his cows, on his small holding on Chicheley Hill, his ladder broke and in the tumble the hay knife cut a piece of his kneecap, and grazed the bone of his leg. Fortunately a military officer nearby came to his assistance and took him in his car to Newport Pagnell from where, after the wound had been treated, he was taken to, and detained at, Northampton Hospital.

Following a rapid thaw during the previous day, there was a heavy fall of snow on Friday, March 3rd 1916. Then on Saturday morning the storm was the worst that could be remembered for many years, and a keen east wind drifted the snow to a considerable depth at the roadsides. Overflowing their banks the Ouse and Lovat flooded hundreds of acres of low lying land and no doubt caused consternation to Mr. J. Short, for he was elected as the representative of the U.D.C. on the district Agricultural War Committee. At the Swan Hotel on Wednesday afternoon March 22nd 1916, the A.G.M. was held of the Newport Pagnell branch of the N.F.U., which would pay the subscriptions of the eight members who were in the Forces. Mr. George Tayler, J.P., presided, but since he was also on the local Tribunal he had now decided to step down, despite pressure for him to continue. He would be succeeded by Mr. W. Eyles with Mr. W. Brice Shakeshaft elected as vice chairman, and also the Branch delegate at the executive meetings of the N.F.U. In other business a resolution was passed requesting that two practical farmers should be appointed to the Tribunal, primarily to hear appeals for military exemption in Bucks. In the Electric Theatre, some 400 women assembled on Friday afternoon, March 17th 1916, to hear the Government scheme explained for employing women on the land. As district representatives on the County Women's War Agricultural Committee this had been arranged by Mrs. Wellesley Taylor and Lady Farrar, who, presiding, in her opening address emphasised the role that women in the towns were playing: "We in the country know one thing we can do, and which the farmers in a way think we can't do. We can help them in the work of the farm." As the principal speaker Miss Gardner, the chief organising secretary of the Board of Trade and Board of Agriculture scheme, said the Women's Work organisation had been formed to cope with the shortage of labour on the land. The proposal intended to register every woman willing to work on the land in every village of every county in the country and, with one woman in each village to be responsible for canvassing that village, she stressed the need for women farm workers. Mrs. Wellesley Taylor said the organisation had only just commenced in the Newport Pagnell district, and they had registrars in 27 of the 28 parishes. So far five women had registered to work anywhere as full time workers, 50 women had registered as part time workers, and within a month they hoped to have the scheme fully operational. The first full time worker in the town had undertaken to look after six horses whilst another was to take part in general work on a farm in Devonshire. As for two full time workers from Great Linford, aged 16 and 22, they were ready to go anywhere. Lady Farrar mentioned the menace of submarines and the shipping losses and said food production was becoming imperative. Representing agriculture at the meeting were Mr. D. Fraser, of Tickford Park, Mr. G. Tayler, J.P., Newport Pagnell, Mr. J. Howson, of Warrington and also Mr. A. Bullard who, as a local farmer, said that although he was not enthusiastic about female labour, a woman who had assisted milking his cows for many years had proved fully competent.

Supporting this view Mr. J. Howson said no farmer employed more women than he did, and before he came to Bucks the 20 women employed on his farm in Cumberland proved their worth in all aspects of farm work. Mr. Tayler, one of the most prominent of farmers in the district, and also Chairman of the Board of Guardians and Rural District Council, said that despite being very much 'chaffed' by his farming friends he entirely agreed with the motive of the meeting, and as a member of a local Tribunal he knew that 40% of men were being taken from the land for military service. Appropriately, many of the ladies acting as canvassers and registrars in the villages were present, and also in attendance were three clergymen. In Fox Gate Piece, whilst digging on his son-in-law's allotment Thomas Sharman, aged 73, collapsed and died on Tuesday afternoon, April 4th 1916. His wife had died about two weeks earlier and since then he had been residing with his daughter, Mrs. Whitlock, at 2, Greenfield Road. Having been an agricultural labourer he previously lived at Willington, near Bedford. Giving evidence at the inquest Sapper James Gordon, of the Royal Engineers, said that whilst taking a walk round the allotments he had seen him fall. By the middle of the month nine women in the Newport Pagnell district had been placed on farms. 166 were registered as willing to help local farmers on the land, whilst as for the sewerage farm the Surveyor reported that four beds had been dug, despite a delay caused by the bad weather. The oats were in and the mangel wurzel would be planted in the dug beds at once. However in early June the Council's Visiting Committee reported that the seeds in the sewerage beds were not coming on at all well. This was also the case with the wurzel, where the replanting of the kohl rabbi (sic) was suggested. More pleasingly though the petrol-driven plough was in satisfactory use on the farm. On the domestic scene a 'good gardener,' ineligible for the Army, was needed at once by Allfrey, Bury Lawn, but the need was hardly as urgent as that for agricultural labour, especially the employment of women on farms. By June 1916 quite a number were engaged in hoeing and light work, and on their books Mrs. Traill, Mrs. Littleboy, and Miss Bailey, of Newport Pagnell, had the names of several women and girls willing to work on the land. In fact at the meeting of the U.D.C. on Tuesday evening, June 6th Mr. George Tayler, J.P., spoke highly of the work of the women on his farm, and the Surveyor agreed with his suggestion that the Council should set an example by employing women on their farm.

As for the male contribution, with the immediate need for about 10 poles of allotment particulars were required in late June 1916 by Mr. F. W. Saunders, of the Cannon Brewery, and in early September 1916 a tenant occupying three acres of land on the sewerage farm field was given permission to erect a barn on his holding. For members of the Unionist Working Men's Club, the 6th annual show of flowers and vegetables was held on Saturday, September 2nd 1916. Despite many of the members being in the Forces there was a good entry and many donations had been sent by interested persons. The sale of the produce would be for the soldiers' tobacco fund, and among the events was an archery tournament for a bunch of grapes, which raised £1 6s 8d. In connection with the Newport Pagnell Adult Schools, a harvest festival was held on Sunday, September 3rd 1916, at The Poplars. Here a fine collection of flowers, fruit and vegetables had been arranged by members of the men's and women's schools, and at the meeting for men in the morning the first half hour was conducted by Mr. G. Rippener, he being a schoolmaster at Byfield and an ardent Adult School worker at Woodford. Mr. F. Littleboy, president of the Men's School, occupied the chair, and he was supported by Mrs. Littleboy, President of the Women's School. For the Wesleyan Church, their harvest thanksgiving services were held on Sunday, September 10th 1916. Mrs. Shedd presided at the organ throughout the day and for church expenses the collections amounted to over £4. On Monday the gifts of flowers, fruit and vegetables were then sold, realising high prices. In November 1916 it was announced that the crops from the sewerage farm had sold well, but seven pickling cabbages had been stolen from the Union Allotments. Between the town and Wolverton, heavy rain on the night of Saturday, November 5th 1916, then on Sunday, and again on Tuesday, caused such a rapid rise in the level of the Ouse and the Lovat that animals had to be hurriedly moved to higher ground by the farmers. Hundreds of acres were under water, but nevertheless on Monday morning, November 27th 1916, six women were needed to thresh corn on the Port Fields farm of T. B. Shakeshaft, where a couple of weeks later two women would be required 'to get up swedes' at 14s per acre. Due to the war, this year the Newport Pagnell Christmas Fat Stock Show Committee had decided not to offer prizes among the breeders of cattle in the district. As for the Show, attended by buyers from a wide district, this was held on Wednesday, December 6th 1916. In January 1917, at 3½d each, six for 1s 7d, or 12 for 3s, new laid eggs were for sale from the Council's Surveyor, Mr. C. A.Branford, at 23, Silver Street. Also during the month the U.D.C. was asked to obtain information regarding the demand for seed potatoes from small scale growers in the district, and persons interested were to send details of the type and the quantity they required to the clerk, Ernest Ward. Mr. George Tayler, J.P., of The Kickles, had now declined the town's nomination for the vacancy on Bucks County Council, caused by the death of Mr. E. Mitchell. Apart from farming several hundred acres he was chairman of the Board of Guardians, the R.D.C., a member of the U.D.C. and a member of the Bucks County War Agricultural Committee, and understandably these commitments fully occupied his time.

An extraordinary general meeting of the Newport Pagnell Branch of the National Farmers' Union took place on Wednesday, January 24th 1917. Presiding, Mr. W. Eyles, chairman of the Branch, said this was to both consider organising pigeon shoots throughout the district, and receive the committee's report on the arrangements for a big Red Cross sale in the town on March 21st. Additionally Mr. J. Butler, the manager of Barclay and Co.'s Bank, would explain how they could make money, and, to laughter, how to buy War Loans when they had no funds to do so. However, for the time being this was perhaps of little concern to Mr. W. J. Hobbs, the well known Newport Pagnell cattle dealer, for he was confined to bed, having been kicked on the thigh by a bullock whilst attending King's Lynn market. The A.G.M. of the Newport Pagnell Shire Horse Society took place on Wednesday afternoon, February 14th 1917, at the Swan Hotel, where the Selection Committee reported the hire from Messrs. Forshaw, of Carlton on Trent, of 'Blackthorn King.' In fact this would prove a wise decision, for their choice would be the winner on Tuesday, February 20th 1917, of the first prize in the class for stallions over four and under ten years of age at the Shire Horse Society's Show, held at the Agricultural Hall, London. In other matters it was resolved to invest £50 in the War Loan, and the outgoing committee were re-elected with Mr. W. Brice Shakeshaft appointed secretary, a position he had held for 22 years. On the same afternoon, at a meeting of the Newport Pagnell District War Agricultural Committee concern was expressed at the number of men being taken from agriculture for the Army. Regarding those cases discussed by the Local Tribunals, in consequence Sir Herbert Leon moved a resolution requesting that the War Office grant permission for these to be re-opened where the applicants were not to be called up till April 1st. As for those men who were called up on January 1st, they should be released. This was approved, and it was just as well that in late February 1917 George Tayler, J.P., of The Kickles, was appointed by the Board of Agriculture as agricultural representative for the northern part of the county, to watch the interests of farmers on the Bucks Appeal Tribunal. By the beginning of March 1917, the Clerk of the Council had applied to Aylesbury for £40 2s 9d worth of seed potatoes. However, since the War Agricultural Committee was unable to supply three of the types only £26 15s 6d worth could be forwarded, with the money received for small quantities being returned to some 30 applicants.

As for the potatoes grown last summer on the Council farm, these had been sorted, and, with the rest to be sold by public auction in the Council yard on Saturday afternoon March 31st, those of seed size would be planted on the farm. An extraordinary general meeting of the Newport Pagnell Branch of the N.F.U. took place on Wednesday afternoon, February 28th 1917. As set out in a recent speech by Lloyd George, the Prime Minister, this was to consider the policy of the Government with regard to agriculture, and to a large attendance of local farmers the chairman, Godfrey Eyles, said the speech seemed favourable to agriculture. Nevertheless details of the start date would need to be known, and also what constituted 'an able bodied man' under the weekly wage proposal of 25s. Also details regarding boy labour, and whether they would have to pay for beer for certain work done on the land, in view of the higher 25s wage. A great deal of discussion ensued and a resolution was passed worded: 'That this meeting of the Newport Pagnell Branch of the National Farmers' Union heartily approves of the scheme put forward by Mr. Lloyd George in connection with agriculture.' A meeting of the Newport Pagnell District War Agricultural Committee was held at the U.D.C. Offices on Wednesday afternoon, March 7th 1917. With George Tayler, J.P., in the chair letters were considered from the Board of Agriculture regarding the loan of horses for agricultural work, and also discussed was the employment on the land of conscientious objectors, who would be housed and fed by their employers. Of lesser, yet no less important matters, five ducks had gone missing since Monday, March 19th. Three being white, and two brown, they belonged to Miss Cowley of 100, Caldecote Street, and a reward awaited the finder. Under the auspices of the Newport Pagnell Branch of the National Farmers' Union and the Town Committee of the Red Cross Society, a large agricultural and general auction jumble sale took place in the town on Wednesday, March 21st 1917. For equal division between the British Farmers' Red Cross Fund and the Bucks Branch of the Red Cross Society about £1,150 was raised, and the details are given in the Nursing chapter. At the monthly meeting of the U.D.C., on Tuesday evening, April 3rd 1917, the Surveyor reported that the potatoes, recently sold in 14lbs lots to town residents, had realised £8 8s. Also, a letter had been received by the Clerk of the Council, Mr. E. Ward. This stated that under the conditions laid down by the Board of Agriculture the seed potatoes, ordered under the County Scheme, would be sent in quantities of not less than four tons to one consignee at a railway station convenient for distribution. This had been sent by Mr. C. Watkins, secretary to the County Education Committee, and, enclosing a card for him to accept responsibility, he nominated Mr. Ward as consignee for those intended for Newport Pagnell and district.

The Committee would refund the expense of distributing the potatoes in 1cwt sacks to neighbouring stations, and Mr. Ward said a consignment had already reached Newport Pagnell station, although he was awaiting instructions as to where they should go. In the Newport Pagnell district, some of the farmers had now begun to pay the enhanced wage of 25s a week for agricultural labourers, and there was also pleasing news for farm workers in the B categories for, in the present circumstances, no more would be called up, as stated at the Newport Pagnell Rural District Tribunal on Tuesday afternoon, April 3rd 1917. At the monthly meeting of the U.D.C., on Tuesday evening, May 1st 1917, the Surveyor produced his lists regarding the costs of potato sprayers. Instructions were subsequently given to obtain one from a local tradesman, and for authorisation to use the machine on the town allotments applications were to be made to the Surveyor by the second week of June. However, operators would have to cover the cost of the lotion needed to prevent blight. The two pigs fed by the Council were to be auctioned the following day in the market although would perhaps not be subject to the new regulations for food control under the Defence of the Realm Act. These duties were to be carried out by the Council's Surveyor, Mr. C. A.Branford, who at the U.D.C. meeting on Tuesday evening June 5th 1917, said the work of repairing the allotment fences had yet to commence, since the necessary materials were not available and there was a shortage of labour. In early June 1917 an attempt was made to organise an association for allotment holders in the town. The committee of the Fox Gate Piece allotments, with Mr. W. King as secretary, was moving the matter, and a meeting of those interested took place in the allotment field on Saturday afternoon, June 9th. On a wider scale, at the request of the Local Government Board the Council had agreed not to place any hindrance on agricultural motor tractors using the public roads, and at the end of the month it was proposed to employ women in parties of six or eight on farms in the district. Those interested were to send their names to the Registrar, Miss Bailey, at The Elms, Newport Pagnell. Seventeen lots of potatoes had been sprayed by the end of the first week of July 1917, and such was the continuing demand that the Surveyor reported the need for another machine. Therefore on the recommendation of the Clerk, and the sanction of the Finance Committee, another had been ordered, although through difficulty in procuring the chemicals Mr. Branford had to apply to the Food Control Committee for a supply.

Bucks Standard Nov. 3rd 1917

By early July there was a marked improvement in the appearance of the sewerage farm. Cleaning out of the beds was progressing as rapidly as possible and the oat crop had greatly improved. As for the allotment this had been cleaned and properly cultivated, and, with the two pigs fed by the Council having been sold at market for £18 2s 6d, after all expenses there was a profit of £5 1s 4d. From a peck of Sir John Llewellyn seed, purchased from John Odell, a crop of potatoes dug in mid July by George Moseley yielded nine bushels on his Fox Gate Piece allotment. For other produce, persons requiring a supply of 2lb

'Kilner Pattern' glass jars, for preserving fruit and vegetables, could apply to the U.D.C. Offices, 60, High Street. This would need to be on or before Wednesday, August 1st 1917, in fact just in time for a demonstration on fruit bottling and preserving vegetables which, organised by the Bucks Agricultural Executive Committee, and with free entry, was to be given by Mrs. Smith, the Board of Agriculture Demonstrator, in the Girls' Council School on Tuesday, August 7th at 8 p.m. Films on the importance of women in farming were shown at the Electric Theatre on the evenings of Friday, August 4th and Saturday, August 5th and perhaps suitably motivated farmers would contact the Registrar, Miss Bailey, at The Elms, for women workers to help in the harvest. In fact possibly amongst their number was the lady at 5, Station Road, who, having been employed in large gardens for two years, in mid July 1917, sought three to five hours gardening work daily at 4d per hour. On Wednesday, August 15th 1917, at the meeting of the R.D.C. there was a detailed consideration of the Ministry of Food's scheme for sugar distribution. In consequence, later in the month the R.D.C. local food control committee required an Executive Officer for the scheme, with the appointment to be primarily until December 31st at £2 10s a week. With a clerk paid for by the committee, an office would be provided in Newport Pagnell, and those hoping for the appointment were to apply to Mr. C. H. Glanville, Clerk to the Council, at 60, High Street. This would have to be not later than August 28th, with applications to be in their own handwriting, and accompanied by copy testimonials. A special meeting of the R.D.C. was convened on Wednesday morning, August 22nd 1917, to receive a report from the provisional committee which had been appointed under the Sugar Control scheme. Then at the meeting of the U.D.C. a selection committee was appointed to select 12 members to serve on the Sugar Control body for the district, and the committee as recommended was appointed.

On the evening of Wednesday, August 29th 1917, at the sitting of the Local Tribunal an appeal was lodged by the head gardener at a private house in the town. Married, with one child, he had been passed for general service, but asked for a short exemption to lift crops. Comparing his work with that of the younger men on the land, who were given six months exemption, he said he produced three crops each year from the two acres, which was more than the farmers did, and supporting the application the chairman, Mr. O. H. Bull, said the vegetables were given to the V.A.D. Hospital at Tickford Abbey. Due to this six months was granted. Also helping in the war effort were the pupils of the Council Schools, who had a day's leave from their studies on Thursday, September 13th 1917, to gather blackberries. These were to be used for making jam for the troops, with a small sum paid for every 1b. Elsewhere, two carrots grown by Arthur Proctor, of Bury Avenue, weighed 3lbs 14ozs, whilst the nine fine specimens from the Fox Gate Piece allotment of Tom Bavington, the cemetery caretaker, made 10s when given to a charity scheme. Weighing 2¾ lbs a huge potato of the May Queen variety was dug up by Mr. J. Smith, of Abbey Terrace, and having planted four potato shoots also doing his bit was the Surveyor of the Council, Mr. C. A.Branford, who in mid September 1917 lifted a crop weighing 2½lbs. As for Private Rupert Warren, whose home was in the town, during the same month he was awarded an artistic and appropriately designed diploma by the French military authorities. This was for having the best garden in the Calais area which, with the plot principally used to grow vegetables for the troops, he cultivated whilst serving with the 1st Garrison Battalion Hampshire Regiment. By posting bills on the Council allotments, also in September the Committee of the Fox Gate Piece Seed Club agreed to invite tenants of the garden plots to become members. Based on co-operative principles, the organisation aimed to secure garden seeds at advantageous prices, with the secretaries being Mr. Percy Sharpe, of Wolverton Road, and William King, of Bury Avenue. The Newport Pagnell and District War Agricultural Committee now announced that, having completed their training, a number of skilled women workers - milkers etc. - were presently available, and their services could be obtained by applying to Mrs. Wellesley Taylor, of Sherington Manor.

Under the auspices of the Newport Pagnell P.S.A. Brotherhood, and through the generosity of Mr. Alfred Bullard, this year a potato growing competition had been organised among the members. The idea was to encourage working men to grow as much food as possible, and presented by Mr. Bullard the 20 bushels or so of King Edward seed potatoes were sold at a nominal cost of 1s a peck. The money was then allocated to a prize fund for the heaviest crop lifted from 12 roots grown in succession, and also for the largest yield from any one root grown under any conditions. On Saturday, September 15th and Sunday, September 16th 1917, members of the P.S.A. Committee then dug and weighed the potatoes, and in the class for 12 roots Mr. F. J. Sharpe easily won the first prize. The weight of 80lbs. 12ozs was over 15lbs greater than the weight for the second prize, which for the single root was won by Mr. Sharpe, whose entry at 9lbs 2ozs was just 6ozs less than that of Mr. Bullard, who took first prize. In late September 1917, a man was required to thatch corn ricks at the farm of T. B. Shakeshaft, Portfield, and also regarding straw the annual services of harvest thanksgiving were held in the parish church on Sunday, October 7th. At the beginning of November a group of ladies began a small soup kitchen in the town. This was to help those old people on small incomes, with the soup, which contained meat and vegetables, being provided at 1d per pint twice a week to a selected list of 45 people. Further deserving cases would be considered by the sub committee of Mrs. Gunnery, Mrs. Digby White, and Mrs. Littleboy. At the monthly meeting of the U.D.C., on the evening of Tuesday, November 6th the Surveyor reported that the crops grown on the sewerage farm, and auctioned by Wigley, Sons and Gambell, had made £86 3s 6d. In other matters 22 applications had been received for the allotments formed by splitting the three or so acres of farm land on the Willen road, and this left about an acre still to be let. On Wednesday, November 28th 1917, Lady Farrar took the chair at a well attended meeting of the Registrars of the Newport Pagnell Women's War Agricultural Committee, held at the U.D.C. Chambers. Here Miss Pott, the travelling inspector for the Board of Trade, gave an address on the work of the Committee, and asked for consideration to be shown to the many National Service farm workers who were now amongst them. Mrs. Wellesley Taylor said that in the report of the previous month the number of farm workers in the Newport Pagnell area was 259, and speaking as well for Lady Farrar she thanked the Registrars for the splendid way in which they had carried out their work, and urged that more workers, both local and National Service, should be employed by the farmers. After heavy snowfall, in the third week of January 1918, much of the town was flooded. This had been due to a rapid thaw and rainstorms, and a variety of vehicles had to be requisitioned to convey pedestrians through the submerged streets.

During February it was announced that persons requiring an allotment should contact the U.D.C. offices at 60, High Street, whilst as for men on active service, Mr. A. Bullard had undertaken to dig the allotments of two of their number. On Wednesday, February 6th 1918, at the Divisional Petty Sessions a motor driver of Bedford was summoned for the unauthorised use of petrol, or petrol substitute, at Newport Pagnell on January 30th. In the same case four butchers of Bedford were charged with causing the petrol, or petrol substitute, to be used. They pleaded not guilty. Giving the details Superintendent Dibben said on January 30th he saw a motor cab in the High Street and on being questioned the driver said he had been hired off the rank near St. Peter's Church, Bedford, by four men who wished to try and buy some meat at Newport Pagnell. Superintendent Dibben told him he was more than three miles out of the district for motor cabs, and, stating the date to be January 10th, corrected the man's reply that the Order didn't come into effect until February 10th. The man was then taken to the police station, and in court the defence said that a car hired from a garage could go any distance for professional business, or certain other purposes, and therefore the only offence committed was having hired a taxi. As for the reason, there was a shortage of beef at Bedford and the four butchers understood they could obtain some at Newport Pagnell. Being too late to catch a train they agreed to share the expense and hire the taxi, the driver of which said that no instructions at Bedford had been received about the Order. The Bench dismissed the charge, although they agreed that Superintendent Dibben had been right to bring the case. At the Electric Theatre, on the evening of Sunday, February 17th 1918, the principal speaker at a conference of the P.S.A. was the chairman of the Baptist Association of America, Mr. G. Coleman, of Boston, U.S.A. There was a large attendance, and presiding Lady Farrar was supported on the platform by Messrs. W. Ward, Hon. International Secretary of the P.S.A. Brotherhood, and Messrs. J. Short, J.P., chairman of the U.D.C., A. Bullard, F. J. Sharp, F. W. Coales, W. J. Coverley, F. Maslin, A.W. Goodman, F.L. Mayne, and A. Ablett. Having announced that the Newport Pagnell Brotherhood would contribute £10 to Mr. Ward's Continental Fund, she then pressed for the cultivation of more land for food production, and, after warning of the increased submarine menace, spoke of the scheme that she had proposed two years ago for the marketing of surplus vegetables, and which she and Mrs. Taylor were now introducing in the district.

Newport Pagnell District War Agricultural Committee.

TO FARMERS.

Ploughing, Hedging and Ditching.

FARMERS desirous of obtaining German Prisoner Labour, with Horses and Ploughs, or Labour for Hedging and Ditching, should at once apply to

MR. PHILIP C. GAMBELL,
87, High Street, Newport Pagnell.

The Ploughing will be charged at per acre and Hedging and Ditching at per chain.

By order of the Committee,
C. H. GLANVILLE,
Newport Pagnell, Secretary.
15th Feb., 1918.

Bucks Standard, February 16, 1918

She and Mr. Ward and the artistes were then afforded a vote of thanks by Mr. F. J. Sharp. As per a notice from the Newport Pagnell District War Agricultural Committee, of which Mr. C. H. Glanville, 60, High Street, was the secretary, in March 1918, three motor tractors would become available for ploughing in the district. They could be hired on application to Mr. Philip C. Gambell, 87, High Street, who, with forty having arrived in the town during the first week of March, to be accommodated in the stables at Westbury, was the person farmers should contact for the hire of German prisoner-of-war labour. Mr. Gambell was responsible for arranging their work details, either with horses and ploughs, or for hedging and ditching, and ploughing would be charged per acre, and hedging and ditching per hour. Meanwhile at Bank House there was now the need to hire or purchase a pony lawn mower. 'Apply secretary.' On Tuesday evening, March 5th 1918, at the U.D.C. meeting, held in the Council Chamber, permission was granted for the Newport Pagnell Seed Club to put up notices on the various allotment fields. This was to enable the committee to contact the members more quickly, whilst as for the produce from the sea, during March in St. John Street large consignments of fresh and dried fish of all descriptions were being received by Bull and Son, fishmongers. These would be sold at controlled prices although for bloaters, kippers and fresh herrings the price would be less whenever market conditions allowed. For Food Cards, many residents of the town had yet to send in their application forms. Saturday, March 9th, was the deadline, and applications were to be forwarded to Mr. E.P. Ward at the Local Food Office, 60, High Street. The annual meeting of the Newport Pagnell Shire Horse Society was held in the Swan Hotel on Wednesday afternoon, March 6th 1918. In the chair was Mr. J. Robinson, who had helped to start the Society, and he was supported by Mr. W. Brice Shakeshaft, the honorary secretary, who, on behalf of the Selection Committee, reported that having visited Messrs. Forshaw's they recommended the hiring of Prince Forester for the next season. In fact this was subsequent to an interview at which four members of the Towcester Society had confirmed, having previously hired him, that being an exceedingly well-bred horse, by Redlynch Forest King, he was of excellent character and his stock had been successful both in the show ring and at the sales. Mr. Shakeshaft then read the 23rd annual statement of accounts, which, with all arrears paid off, showed a total balance of £106 9s 4d, including £17 10s invested in War Loan.

The Foal Show Account had a balance of £30 18s 3d, and as a tribute to his abilities Mr. Shakeshaft was re-elected as honorary secretary, with the committee re-elected en bloc. At the same venue an extraordinary general meeting of the members of the Newport Pagnell Branch of the N.F.U. took place on the afternoon of Wednesday, March 6th 1918. There was an excellent attendance and in the chair Mr. W. Eyles was supported by Messrs. P. C. Gambell and W.B. Shakeshaft, the joint honorary secretaries. Towards forming a County Executive Branch 17 delegates had been appointed to attend a meeting at Aylesbury, and as one of these Mr. Shakeshaft now reported on the result, which confirmed the intention. On the night of Wednesday, March 14th, or the early hours of the following morning, five fowls belonging to Mr. F. W. Saunders, the manager of the Newport Pagnell Branch of the Aylesbury Brewery Company, were killed by a dog, and when discovered four were lying in the hen house with one on an adjacent rubbish heap. Portions of each had been eaten, and although at first a fox had been thought to be the culprit, experts later pronounced it to be the work of a dog. For assisting the starving children of Palestine, the Congregational Church Girls' Club, under the superintendence of Miss. A. M. Coales, organised an entertainment at the Council Schools which, before a large attendance, took place on the evening of Friday, March 22nd 1918. Due to several members being on leave the Royal Engineers Orchestra was unable to appear and so the event was opened with a piano solo by Miss A. Harris. In the dressing of the much admired pageant play, which included the uniformed nurses Kathleen Tattam, Frances Hine, Rose Lane, Joyce Sayle, Winnie Mynard, Nora Symons, Winifred Pearce, and Gertie Westley, both Mrs. Ablett and Miss L. Goodman had assisted. As for the other performances, on renewing his acquaintance with a Newport Pagnell audience Corporal Uttridge received an enthusiastic response, with all of his elocutionary items being encored, and as a result of the event a substantial sum would be sent to the Syria and Palestine Relief Fund.

Attended by a large number of parents and friends, an open day was held at the Girls' Council Schools on the afternoon of Tuesday, March 26th 1918. After a few words from the headmistress, Miss James, a talk on food was given by Miss McIver, and the exhibits included wartime cookery, with substitute dishes such as carrot marmalade, apricot jam from swedes, potted meat from lentils, lentil sausages etc. Laundry work and housewifery were also highlighted, and the event incorporated a short musical programme by the pupils. For persons wishing to grow their own produce, early seed potatoes, as well as those for eating, were now available from Arthur Sewell, of 44, Greenfield Road. His day job was as an engineer, but for another resident of the town, who was now serving with the colours, around the beginning of April 1918 ten men began enthusiastically digging over his 20 pole plot on the Willen road allotments. This was in response to an offer made by the local P.S.A. Brotherhood, and, with the applications having totalled 230 poles, one of the subsequent letters of thanks would read: "Newport Pagnell. To the Committee. Will you please accept my sincere thanks for the great kindness you have rendered me and mine by so kindly undertaking the working up of our allotment. I can only say that you have solved for me a tough problem, seeing that labour is both scarce and dear, when obtainable. My husband feels most grateful to you, and wishes me to tender his sincere thanks, and trusts the day is not far off when he can do so himself personally. Wishing the P.S.A. Brotherhood, and all its undertakings, every success." Such was the commitment of the members that the work would be complete by the end of the month. Also during the month a special effort was to be made by the Newport Pagnell Branch of the Farmers' Union and the Town Branch of the Red Cross Society. This was for the Red Cross Funds, for which to a crowded attendance the Parish Church Girls' Club held an entertainment at the Electric Theatre on the evenings of Tuesday and Wednesday, April 9th and 10th 1918. For many weeks Mrs. Mitchison, assisted by Miss M. Coales, Miss Bale (who through illness could not attend the performances), Miss P. Taylor and Miss E. West had been busy training the girls in their roles, and this was quite apart from making most of the old fashioned costumes for nearly a hundred different characters. Mr. C. K. Garratt was the musical director, and of the performances by Miss Bertha Richens her splendid singing was encored each evening.

Also rapturously received was the song scene from Martin's 'Songs of the Fair,' and also excellently presented was the amusing 'A House warming in War Time,' with 'The Fairy Dreams' as another pleasing rendition. As a most capable violinist Miss Daisy Frost brilliantly rendered 'Gipsy Melodies and Dances,' and at the piano Archie Naish made a successful first appearance at the town, with his humorous sketches and musical monologues vociferously encored. Splendidly presented was the historical pageant 'Women in Britain,' and, having written the words, each evening the Reverend G.F. Sams, of Emberton, recited his composition in an impressive manner. Also impressive was the final procession and grouping of the whole of the characters, presenting a magnificence which, together with the inspiring and patriotic sentiments of the epilogue, enthused the audience to a pitch of fevered patriotism. For considering the best way to dispose of surplus vegetable produce a meeting, with Mr. J. Short in the chair, was held in the Central Hall of the Girls' School on Thursday evening, April 18th. The intention was to form a local scheme in conjunction with the Buckinghamshire Branch of the Women's War Agricultural Committee, and as the North Bucks representatives Lady Farrar and Mrs. Wellesley Taylor were both present. In opening the meeting Mr. Short said that a while

MISS BERTHA RICHENS

(Pupil of Mr. Victor Beigel, of London),

Is open to receive Pupils for

SINGING and VOICE PRODUCTION

And will visit

WOLVERTON and NEWPORT PAGNELL Weekly.

For terms and particulars apply—

MISS BERTHA RICHENS,

Emberton House,

Newport Pagnell.

Bucks Standard, April 28th, 1917

ago a meeting had been held and a committee appointed, but it was felt that the committee also needed working men who took an interest in allotments, essential at the present time. The object of the scheme was to collect fruit and vegetables from the local villages and bring them into the town, where a shop or stall would be opened for one or two days a week. Thereby those people unable to grow their own produce could obtain what they needed. Miss Day, of the Board of Agriculture, Food Control Department, then delivered an address in which she stressed the need to grow as much food as possible, and outlined several of the schemes now being carried out in the country. She emphasised that the produce should be properly graded, the highest quality being sold for the best price, and suggested that the vegetables could be taken to a central depot in each village, where two or three persons could 'turn down the poor stuff.'

Also she dealt with the question of preserving, canning and bottling fruit and vegetables and concluded by saying that due to being on a fixed income many of the population were now worse off than before the war. Therefore it was essential that they had a good supply of vegetables. She then answered various questions, and additional names were added to the committee. On Market Hill, under the auspices of the Newport Pagnell Branch of the N.F.U. and the Newport Pagnell Red Cross Committee, a sale was held on Wednesday, April 24th 1918. In fine sunny weather the event included 'Agriculture Cars,' and details, with brief mentions of the Women's Land Army, are given in the chapter on Nursing. It being stated that this should be undertaken more than once a week, to collect house refuse for pig food a council employee by the name of Archer was now going around the town with his hand cart. Then on Friday, June 21st 1918, the Newport Pagnell and district committee for the disposal of surplus fruit and vegetables commenced a stall on Market Hill. This would be open each Friday until 8 p.m. at the Brewery Malting, kindly lent by the Newport Pagnell Brewery

Newport Pagnell District War Agricultural Committee.

WOMEN LABOUR (Skilled).

IN view of the present call of the Army for Grade 1 Agricultural Workers, the attention of Farmers is particularly drawn to the fact that there are a number of Skilled Women Workers (Milkers and otherwise), who have completed their training and are now available for farm work.

The above Committee strongly urge farmers in this neighbourhood to take advantage of their services.

Applications should be made, at an early date, to:— MRS. WELLESLEY TAYLOR, Sherington Manor, Newport Pagnell.

C. H. GLANVILLE,
Secretary to the Committee.

60, High-street, Newport Pagnell,
12th June, 1918.

Bucks Standard, June 22nd, 1918

Company Ltd., and due to a paper shortage purchasers were requested to bring their own receptacles. Those donating produce would be paid the full price obtained, less a commission of 2d in the 1s for working expenses. Arranged by Mrs. Symons, at her residence, 'Brooklands,' a garden fete was held on Thursday, June 30th 1918, for sick and wounded war horses. The proceeds would be for the R.S.P.C.A. Fund, but since the weather was inclement in the hope that the rain would hold off the fete was continued on Friday. Unfortunately the day proved to be showery but nevertheless the sum of £18 16s 3d was made. Apart from the stalls and games, boating on the Ouse was enjoyed. The boats had been lent by the Misses Taylor, of Lovat Bank, and amongst the boatmen were the Reverend Mitchison and Inspector Fordham, of the R.S.P.C.A. In fact also for the welfare of horses, in August 1918 the New Horse Order would be made. This decreed that no more than six persons could ride in a horse drawn carriage, for the reason that due to the restrictions of corn etc. horses were presently not as well fed as before. On Tuesday evening, July 16th 1918, at the meeting of the U.D.C., held in the Council Chamber, High Street, it was reported that the new allotments at the sewerage farm were in excellent condition. Two women engaged via Mrs. Wellesley Taylor were weeding carrots and eight German P.O.W.s were doing very good work, although there was still much to be done. On the evening of Tuesday, September 3rd 1918, at the meeting of the U.D.C. instructions to repair the gates and fences of their allotments were issued to the Surveyor, Mr. Branford, who said that a lot of pilfering was going on. He had mentioned this to the police and not only was it rife at the allotments but also amongst the mangolds, etc. at the farm, where notices would now be posted stating that offenders would be prosecuted.

At 36, Caldecote Street, R. W. Johnson presently wished to buy any quantity of blackberries at 3½d per lb. Elsewhere the 7th annual flower and vegetable show for the members of the Unionist Club took place in the Concert Hall of the Club on Saturday, September 7th. Afterwards practically all the exhibits, plus the 'not for competition' fruit and vegetables given by other members, were sold by auction, making £5 for the Christmas Presents Fund for those members serving in the Forces. A show of vegetables was held at the Workmen's Social Club on Saturday evening, September 21st, with Messrs. E. Golding, of Tyringham, and W. Bavington, of Newport Pagnell, as the judges. In addition to the vegetables a number of members contributed various produce, which was then sold for the benefit of the Soldiers' Fund of the Club. At Bury Field, with all fees to be paid on that day restocking would take place on Friday, October 11th. This was stated by William Fleet in a notice to the public, who were also advised by the Newport Pagnell Rural District Food Control Committee that, with these to come into use on November 18th, the new ration books could not be issued unless they had sent in their ration book reference leaves. The person to contact was Mr. J. Short at the Local Food Office, 58, High Street. By the end of the second week of October 1918, Bucks schoolchildren had collected 90 tons of blackberries. According to the Ministry of Food, the Army and Navy consumed one and a half million pounds a day, and the failure of the fruit crop had made it imperative for the education authorities to continue their efforts. Mr. O. H. Bull being the Central Agent for Newport Pagnell, Great Linford was the first in the Newport Pagnell area to reach a ton, to be closely followed by the boys of Newport Pagnell, who reached a ton on Tuesday, October 15th 1918. Later in the month it was announced that on Thursdays at 7.30 p.m. in the Boys' Council School Mr. P. Mann, the County Council Lecturer, would give a series of lectures on Food Production. Then in late December 1918 food production was also one of the needs for the European refugees returning to their looted and ransacked homes, and for their assistance the local branch of the N.F.U., responding to an appeal from the French Red Cross, held a meeting one Saturday evening at the Swan Hotel. Here, with Mr. W. Eyles in the chair, Mr. A. Bullard said that although the P.S.A. Brotherhood was doing something similar he would be willing for them to join with the N.F.U. in this cause, and he promised to lend his store in St. John Street where the collected goods could be taken and packed. It was then duly decided that the P.S.A. should be asked to undertake the collection of goods in the town, with the men of the N.F.U. committee to organise both the collection in their respective villages and the delivery to the depot at 16, St. John Street. The appeal and collection would be made in 1919 between January 1st and 4th inclusive, and in this work Mrs. Geo. Tayler, Mrs. F. Littleboy, Mrs. Digby White, Mrs. F. J. Sharp, Mrs. Gambell, Miss Webster, Miss A. M. Coales and Miss Bailey would be asked to co-operate with the committee of the Farmers' Union and the P.S.A.

Then concluding the formalities, on Sunday, December 15th 1918, a well attended meeting of the Newport Pagnell P.S.A. Brotherhood, with Mr. A. Goodman presiding, confirmed that the P.S.A. would join with the town branch of the N.F.U. for the collection of goods on behalf of the French refugees. Of more local matters, Mr. William Fleet now gave notice that all stock must be removed from Bury Field on Monday, December 23rd 1918. Any remaining after that date would be put out to keep and the same duly charged. Following the end of the war some major changes in the local agricultural scene took place in March 1919, with it being reported that Mr. George Tayler, one of the most prominent of farmers in the district, was giving up The Kickles and Lakes Lane Farms. The farm animals and equipment would be consequently auctioned on Tuesday, April 8th, and then on August 29th 1919, Wigley Sons and Gambell were instructed to auction at Tickford Lower Farm 70 head of cattle, including 40 young cattle and 30 dairy stock, on the instructions of Alfred Bullard, who was giving up milking. As for the local Food Committees, they ceased to exist on July 1st 1920, but for Joseph Short, the man who had been the local Food Officer, in May 1920 he had been appointed by the Ministry of Food as district food officer for a newly constituted area which embraced the Newport Pagnell Urban and Rural districts, Bletchley Urban, Linslade Urban and the Leighton Buzzard districts. His headquarters would be at Newport Pagnell and his role would begin when the local Food Committees ceased to exist.

The Kickles & George Tayler

Resident at The Kickles, Mr. George Tayler, one of the best known agriculturalists in the district, presided on Wednesday evening, August 26th 1914, at the Town Hall, where an adjourned meeting to consider restarting the Rifle Club took place. Then at a recruiting meeting held on the Market Hill he was one of the speakers on the evening of Thursday, September 3rd 1914. In other pursuits he occupied the chair at the 1915 annual meeting of the Newport Pagnell branch of the National Farmers' Union, held at the Swan Hotel on Wednesday afternoon, January 27th, and was amongst those who joined at the formation of the Newport Pagnell Company of the County Volunteer Defence Corps. From his agricultural friends and neighbours, in March 1915 for funds for the Red Cross he undertook a collection in the Newport Pagnell district to help the stricken people of Serbia and the following month having been vice chairman was appointed as chairman of the Board of Guardians, the meetings of which he had attended for 25 years. On Wednesday, February 9th 1916, a special meeting of the Newport Pagnell R.D.C. was held to appoint a local tribunal to deal with cases under the Military Services Act 1916. The existing tribunal, which had been appointed to deal with the cases under Lord Derby's Scheme, was appointed and since Mr. Tayler was included he decided, despite pressure to continue, to stand down as president of the Newport Pagnell branch of the N.F.U. at the A.G.M. This was held at the Swan Hotel on Wednesday, afternoon March 22nd 1916, and his successor would be Mr. W. Eyles. Yet he would still continue farming and at the meeting of the U.D.C. on Tuesday evening June 6th 1916, spoke highly of the work of the women on his farm and, with the Surveyor in agreement, advised them to set an example by employing women on their own farm.

In other matters he took part in a rifle shooting match between the officers of the Royal Engineers (Signal Section) stationed in the town and a town team on the range of the Rifle Club on Thursday evening, July 6th

1916. However with heavy rain and bad light it was only possible to fire at 500 yards and in improved weather the match was completed on Thursday evening, July 20th. The soldiers won by a score of 66. In other military matters, having been prepared through Mr. Tayler's initiative in August 1916 a roll of honour, commemorating the men from the town who were serving in the war, was hung in the porch of the parish church. 470 names were included and on a separate roll were given the names of the 38 fallen. The monthly meeting of the R.D.C. and Board of Guardians was held in the Boardroom of the Workhouse on Wednesday, January 3rd 1917, but on this occasion Mr. Tayler, the chairman, was absent, being on a visit to Margate to spend a while with his nephew. He had just returned from the Front and also to be involved in the war effort was Mr. Tayler's niece, Miss Gladys Tayler, working in France under the direction of the British Committee of the French Red Cross Society. Other relations were also serving for in June 1915 a wounded soldier from Hanslope had found himself being tended in hospital by Mrs. John Tayler, formerly of Milton Keynes but then of Nash Court Farm, Margate. A widow, she had been a Red Cross nurse at the military hospital since the beginning of the war and was a sister in law of Mr. Tayler. As for her eldest son, Lieutenant John Tayler, he had joined the O.T.C. (Inns of Court) in the winter of 1914, being gazetted after training at Berkhampstead to the Middlesex Regiment. Around mid 1916 he then went to France and after much hard action suffered dangerous machine gun wounds in the legs, thigh, forearm and side. Nevertheless it was in cheerful terms that from a French hospital in May 1917 he wrote to his relatives in the Newport Pagnell district. Meanwhile in the town during the previous month Mr. Tayler had declined the town's nomination for the vacancy on Bucks County Council, caused by the death of Mr. E. Mitchell. The reason was that apart from farming several hundred acres he was chairman of the Board of Guardians, the R.D.C., a member of the U.D.C. a member of the Bucks County War Agricultural Committee and in February 1917 had been appointed by the Board of Agriculture as the agricultural representative for the northern part of the county, to watch the interests of farmers on the Bucks Appeal Tribunal. Being unable to attend, Mr. Tayler had asked the chairman to request at the monthly meeting of the U.D.C. if the members would accept a printed roll of honour of the men from the town who had fallen and those who were still serving with the colours.

This was held on Tuesday evening, November 6th 1917, and the gift, which had taken a great deal of trouble and expense to prepare, was unanimously accepted. Great trouble and expense were also the factors on Friday afternoon, August 2nd 1918, when at about 3.30 p.m. the Newport Pagnell Fire Brigade received a call to a blaze at one of two large hayricks on

Mr. Tayler's farm. Fortunately the greater part of the burning rick was saved and the second remained undamaged. However perhaps the fire contributed to his decision to now leave The Kickles, which would be auctioned by Messrs. W. Brown and Co. on Wednesday, September 25th 1918, at 4 p.m. at the Swan Hotel. On Monday, November 11th 1918, some time before noon news of the Armistice arrived in the town and in consequence in the evening a public meeting was held at the Electric Theatre. Here as chairman of the R.D.C. Mr. Tayler said he was proud to stand before them that night and congratulate them that the war was at an end and at a successful conclusion. This was greeted with loud cheers and continuing he said no one could have thought of the cost or that it would last four years. He praised the courage and spirit of the fighting men and expressed thanks to them and also the soldiers, including some wounded, that he could see among them that night. When the war broke out England only had a peace time Army but armies had been raised and trained and equipped and 'it had been done.' Trying times lay ahead but these he did not fear for he had an abiding faith in the good sense of the people of this dear old land of theirs. He hoped they had crushed Kaiserism, militarism and brutality forever and he asked them to lift up their hearts with thankfulness to God, who had given them such a splendid victory. Mrs. Tayler had also played her role in the war and at the Public Library, Northampton, was amongst the workers in the Y.M.C.A. movement at Newport Pagnell who were presented with service badges by the Honourable Mrs. Stuart Wortley. Mr. Tayler was a prime mover in organising a first class supper at the Swan Hotel on Thursday evening, February 6th 1919. This was to mark the winding up of the Special Constables in the town and also being wound up was Mr. Tayler's involvement with The Kickles and Lake's Lane Farms, the farm animals and equipment of which would be auctioned on Tuesday, April 8th. Nevertheless he remained involved with the town's activities and on Saturday July 19th 1919, for the Peace Day rejoicings on Bury Field the huge bonfire had been built with the wood he procured by cutting a 'Peace avenue' through the bushes at the far end. With the benefit of a supply of town water, and an electricity generating plant, after the war The Kickles was purchased in 1919 by William Godfrey Eyles for £8,000. In 1931, after his death the farm, then in the occupation of Mrs. J. Dover, was auctioned at the Swan Hotel, Newport Pagnell, but did not reach the reserve figure of £6,000. However, supposedly it was then sold by private treaty half an hour later to Mr. W. Millard, of Milton Bryan. Having retired from farming it would be at The Kickles that John Dover, late of Milton Keynes, would take up residence and where, after a long illness, he died in 1934 aged 74.

Mr. W. J. Hobbs

Shortly after the outbreak of war Joseph Hobbs enlisted and passed into the Civil Service Corps. He was the younger son of Mr. W. J. Hobbs, of 'Buryville,' Newport Pagnell, who was amongst the first to join the Special Constables of the town. In his normal business he was one of the largest cattle buyers in the midlands district and whilst attending the King's Lynn market in late January 1917 was kicked on the thigh by a bullock, being consequently confined to bed for some days. Joseph had enlisted in the Civil Service Rifles with a friend, who in late September 1918 as Corporal Mason, M.M., was staying with him at Newport Pagnell as one of the survivors from the Galway Castle, which had been recently torpedoed. They had seen service together in France but being made permanently deaf through shellfire Joseph had been discharged whilst having been later blinded at the Front his friend had been trained at St. Dunstan's Hostel as a poultry farmer. With his mother he was proceeding to South Africa on the Galway Castle when it was torpedoed. The women, children and the helpless were put on the first boat away and having in peacetime been a keen oarsman he volunteered to row. In fact clad only in his pyjamas he assisted in the rowing for over three consecutive hours and in the Daily Mirror would be published a photo of him being welcomed back to St. Dunstan's by the cheering nurses. After the war, on Thursday evening, February 6th 1919, the Newport Pagnell Special Constables were provided with a first class supper at the Swan Hotel. This marked the winding up of the movement in the town and Mr. W. J. Hobbs was amongst those who had organised the event.

INFLUENZA EPIDEMIC

In November 1916 a long letter from Mr. O. H. Bull, the headmaster of the Council Schools, had been sent back from the authorities at Aylesbury for consideration by the Managers. This regarded his desire to close the school due to the absence of two teachers from illness, but although one had since returned the other was still away with influenza. Therefore as a temporary measure a teacher from the infant department had been transferred to the boys' school, and it was suggested that the classes might be re-organised. However, there was a far more serious outbreak of influenza in 1918, which in the last week of October had spread rapidly in the town. In fact there were over 500 cases, and, with several of the staff being ill, and the pupil attendance less than 50%, on Wednesday, October 23rd, it was decided to close the schools until Monday, November 4th, with the Sunday Schools to be closed as well. Indeed such was the seriousness of the epidemic that two deaths had occurred from pneumonia following flu. Leaving four children, of which the youngest was four months, Mrs. Beatrice Mary Walden, the wife of Fred Walden, of 16, Greenfield Road, had succumbed aged 32 on Wednesday morning, October 23rd, whilst the following morning Mrs. Gladys Evelyn Garratt (nee Cotton, whose parents, Mr. and Mrs. W. Cotton, lived in the High Street) died aged 31 early on Thursday morning, October 24th at 'Concordia,' Lovat Street. She was the wife of Mr. Charles Kenneth Garratt, a talented musician, and, having nursed him for the same illness all the previous week, she had been taken ill on the Saturday.

On Tuesday evening dangerous symptoms then developed, and early the following morning the condition worsened. The funeral was held on Monday afternoon, October 28th 1918, and proceeding to the church the cortege passed business premises that as a mark of respect were closed, and private houses where for the same deference the blinds had been drawn. Prior to the service, conducted by the Reverend Gunnery, Mr. O. H. Bull (acting as church organist during Mr. Garratt's illness) played Dr. Sparke's Elegy, and then following the service the Dead March, as the body was being removed for interment in Newport Pagnell Cemetery. From the office staff at Wolverton Works four of Mr. Garratt's fellow clerks acted as bearers, and, with Mr. H. C. Jenkins, the chief accountant, also present, the mourners included Mr. and Mrs. W. Cotton, the parents of the deceased, Miss R. Cotton, sister, and Mr. and Mrs. T. Garratt, father and mother-in-law. Amongst the many wreaths was a floral cross worded 'To my darling wife, with fondest love, from Ken. O rest in the Lord.' With the epidemic raging, held in the Central Hall of the Girls' School on Thursday evening, October 31st 1918, there was consequently only a small attendance at a public meeting. This was to support John Scurr, the prospective Labour candidate for the Division, but for many in the town politics was now the least of their concerns. With there seeming to be no end to the scourge, on November 25th 1918 due to pneumonia after influenza Dennis Higgins, the youngest son of the late Mr. A. Higgins and Mrs. Higgins of 131, London Road, died aged 29 at Huntingdon where, having learned his trade as a trimmer at Salmons, he had moved eight years ago for employment at the Portholme Aircraft works. However, for 13 months he had served under Commander Locker Lampson with the Armoured Motor Car Squadron in France, where he was discharged. His death left a widow and a daughter aged 2 years 3 months, and on November 29th at the funeral at Huntingdon one of the wreaths was worded 'To dear Daddy, from Doris; Gone to Bye-byes.'

Another was 'From Commander Locker Lampson and three Petty Officers of the Squad to which Dennis Higgins belonged, in memory of his good comradeship and gallantry during the Great War.' Within two hours of each other, on Saturday, December 7th 1918 Mrs. Annie Dorrill, aged 40, and her five year old son, Ronald, died of influenza, and compounding the tragedy when the deaths occurred her husband, Bombardier Joseph Dorrill of the Royal Horse Artillery, who throughout the war had served on the Western Front, was marching with the victorious British troops into German territory. He was the son of Mr. and Mrs. J. Dorrill of Lathbury, six of whose sons served in the war, and the bereavement left two daughters aged seven and 2½ at the family home at 29a, Mill Street. Then at Northampton Hospital on Sunday, December 8th Mrs. Louisa Woolhead of London Road, the daughter of the late Mr. C. Daniells, died aged 34 of pneumonia following influenza. Her husband was serving in India as overseer of a regimental tailoring department, and the funeral took place at the parish church on December 14th. On service with the B.E.F. in Flanders, and on the eve of his anticipated return to civilian life, 21 year old Private George Daniells, R.A.S.C., (Ammunition Column), died on January 16th 1919 at No. 32 Casualty Clearing Station. This was from pneumonia following influenza, and his burial took place in Valenciennes cemetery on January 17th. In May 1915 he had enlisted in the Oxon and Bucks Light Infantry, but on account of his health was transferred to the Ammunition Column two months later. He had been on the Western Front for nearly two years, and before enlisting was employed in the town by Dr. C. Bailey. Thus in the space of eight months Mrs. Daniells had lost her husband and her younger son, who had been killed in action on April 26th. Another soldier who would survive the war but fall victim to the epidemic was Sergeant Alfred West, M.M., of the 2nd Battalion, Oxon and Bucks Light Infantry.

He was the eldest son of Mr. and Mrs. A. West, of Broughton, and being on the Special Reserve at the outbreak of the war he mobilised with his

The grave of Sergeant A.E. West, Newport Pagnell cemetery.

regiment, and, wounded in the retreat from Mons, subsequently experienced much hard fighting in France and Flanders. He received his promotion on the battlefield, and was awarded the Military Medal for carrying his officer to safety under heavy fire. After the Armistice he served with the British Army of Occupation, and was on his way home, to begin work on the farm of Mr. Adams at Broughton, when he contracted his illness. Aged 27 he died on February 27th at the Military Hospital, Gravesend, from where his body was brought for interment in Newport Pagnell Cemetery on Wednesday, March 5th. Several soldiers who had seen active service were amongst those present, and the mourning was especially poignant since only nine months ago he had married Mrs. Lake, of Priory Street, Newport Pagnell, whose first husband had been killed early in the war. On April 27th 1919 Miss Mabel Dant, the eldest daughter of Mr. and Mrs. E.F. Dant, of the High Street, was laid to rest in Newport Pagnell Cemetery, where amongst those grieving were her parents, brothers and sister. Of a bright and cheerful disposition she had died from influenza aged only 17, having been ill for just a few days. Even in 1922 influenza was still claiming victims, and in the early hours of Friday, February 3rd Jane Short, the wife of Joseph Short, died at 13, Tickford Street. She was aged 65, and had fallen ill on the previous Sunday morning. The funeral took place on the Tuesday afternoon, and although confined to his house by illness for almost two weeks Mr. Short attended by permission of his doctor. Others mourners were Miss Janet Short and Mrs. Ferrett, daughters, Miss Maisie Noakes, adopted daughter, and Mr. J.W. Short, son.

MEDICAL MATTERS

(INCLUDING THE BUCKS 48 V.A.D & TICKFORD ABBEY V.A.D. HOSPITAL, & THE ROYAL ENGINEERS HOSPITAL)

Following the outbreak of war, Miss Dorothy Wickham, the daughter of Dr. H.T. Wickham, began organising a special course of nursing lectures for the women of Newport Pagnell. Her father and Dr. C. Bailey were to give their services as the class instructors and persons interested were to contact Miss Wickham at The Close, Newport Pagnell. In consequence, with some 60 ladies having given their names Dr. Wickham gave the first lecture on the evening of Tuesday, August 25th 1914, and subsequent lectures would be held on Tuesday and Friday evenings. The ladies of the town were also contributing to the war effort in other ways, and by the end of August had made various articles for the wounded. Thus of these Mrs. S. Williams, the secretary, had been able to despatch to the St. John Ambulance Association a large parcel of pillows and pillow cases, with another parcel of sheets and shirts to hopefully follow shortly. In fact for the moment no further needlework was required, although financial donations to purchase sheets would still be welcome. Then on Monday, September 7th 1914, at the meeting of the Newport Pagnell Ladies' Work Committee the definitive totals of the items sent by Mrs. Williams were given, being 33 wool pillows, six feather pillows, 102 white pillow slips, 40 sheets, 20 night shirts, 20 flannel day shirts, 20 pyjama suits and bed coats, 24 small invalid cushions, and socks and bed socks. The annual church parade of the members of the local Friendly Societies and the corporate bodies in the town took place on Sunday afternoon, October 4th 1914, and lead by the Excelsior Silver Band the procession wended the principal streets to attend Divine service at the Parish Church. The collection was in aid of Northampton Hospital and in other fund raising events £4 was made at the Workmen's Social Club on Saturday evening, January 23rd 1915, when before a large attendance a concert arranged by Mr. C. K. Garratt was given for the St. John Ambulance Association.

Having been in business for many years in the town as a grocer, John Daniels, a zealous worker for the Wesleyan Church, and a long standing member of the P.S.A. Brotherhood, died on Friday, January 29th 1915, aged 65. This was following an operation at Northampton Hospital, to where for the wounded soldiers a box of cigarettes, tobacco etc. was sent on Saturday, April 17th 1915, having been collected from his customers at the Railway Tavern by Mr. R.J. Layton. On Friday, May 21st 1915, the medical skills of

Dr. Bailey were called upon when, whilst attending a case in Bury Avenue, Nurse Johnson, of St. John Street, slipped and broke a small leg bone just above the ankle. After first aid treatment members of the ambulance section of the local Fire Brigade then supervised her removal on the ambulance litter to her home. In June 1915 it was announced that the 'Ladies of Buckinghamshire Ambulance Car' had been accepted by the War Office. Mr. Barnard had specially enlisted to drive the vehicle which before being handed over had the word 'Buckinghamshire' written in large letters on the side. In fine summer weather, on Saturday, June 26th 1915, the annual fete to raise funds for Northampton Hospital was held. The occasion had previously taken place in Bury Field, but since certain rights were held by Mr. J. Knapp, of Linford Hall, who was of the opinion that during the period of war such jollification and festivities should be abandoned, the venue this year was in a large field at Woad Farm, granted by Mr. John Adkins. With an attendance of thousands the event proved much on the lines of previous years, but included the addition by the Reverend W. St. John Lindars (curate) of a pageant in which about 250 children, wearing 'dainty costumes and ingenious and characteristic get-ups,' paraded the crowded principal streets of the town, lead by the Excelsior Silver Band. Also along the streets slowly travelled a car representing the Allies, which was followed at intervals by cars respectively illustrative of nursery rhymes, Japan, a hospital and Britannia. The horses and trolleys were lent for the parade by the Newport Pagnell Brewery Company, Messrs. F. Coales and Son, T. & C. Shelton, W. Wagstaff, Wilford Bros., Salmons and Sons, and H. West, and also included were 'Peace and the Seasons,' May Queens, flower girls, ancient Romans, Indians, cowboys, butterflies, nurses and comic characters etc.

The opening ceremony was performed by the Mayor of Northampton, accompanied by his wife, and immediately afterwards the pageantry children were grouped on the sports enclosure to be judged for prizes by Mrs. Carlile, Mrs. W. Trevor, Mrs. Wellesley Taylor, Mrs. Good, the Mayoress of Northampton and the Mayor of Northampton. In fact he was so taken by the effort of the participants that he gave special cash prizes for those who had narrowly missed an award. One of these was Rosalind Bicknell of Clifton Reynes, who attracted much attention as a cowgirl mounted on a fast moving pony. After the ceremony the children then skilfully performed a series of dances. These they had been by amongst others Mrs. Gillam and Miss E. Bailey, who had given much assistance to the temporary headmistress of the Girl's School, Miss Amos, who herself had provided much assistance in the dressing of the girls. With Mr. C. K. Garratt at the piano, music was provided by his orchestra, composed of Messrs. O. Burnell, double bass, Webb, flute, P. Sharp, violin, and Miss Gladys Lindars, violin, and during the event the entertainments included clever trapeze acts performed by Mons. Bellini, who also performed juggling acts. Athletics were another feature of the event (although no one eligible and fit for service in the Forces was allowed to compete!), and, organised by Mr. A. Levin, a troop of minstrels gave four entertainments in a marquee on the fete ground. During the afternoon in the garden of Woad Farm a baby show was held, judged by Nurse Cresswell and Mrs. Harley, whilst for infants and older children a pony and a donkey, lent by Mrs. Hedges and Mr. Arthur Mills, of Great Linford, gave short rides. A pet lamb reared by Miss Pettit, of Woad Farm, trotted amongst the crowd and by means of Red Cross boxes raised £1 16s 6d. Miss Eva Garratt had organised an archery tournament for a pig and a sheepdog puppy, both of which were given by Mr. Duncombe, and throughout the afternoon and evening various amusements were on offer, such as skittles and also shooting, at the galleries of which Mr. Corrie Boswell, of Crawley Grange, gave his services. By storing cycles at the Neptune Inn, Mr. and Mrs. Pettit raised 9s 9d, with their little daughter contributing 8s 8d by the sale of roses. Organised by Mrs. Arthur Simpson, on Saturday, July 17th 1915, a penny house to house collection in the town made £15 8s 2d for the British Red Cross Society and St. John Ambulance Association. As for other fund raising endeavours at the recent town charity fete Charles Tucker, an employee at Salmons, had collected £1 5s 7d for Northampton Hospital.

During July 1915, the Higher Education Committee announced their proposal to hold a class in Home Nursing, with the intention being, under the regulations of the St. John Ambulance Association, for participants to obtain a certificate for admission to Voluntary Aid Detachments. Mr. H. Middleton, of The Lamblies, was to be the organiser and for the class to proceed not less than 20 candidates, aged over 16 years, would need to enrol. The fee for the course, of not less than 10 hours, would be 2s 6d. The annual thanksgiving services for the harvest took place at the Parish Church on Sunday, October 3rd 1915, with Mr. C. K. Garratt presiding at the organ. The church interior had been decorated by the ladies of the congregation, and the collections of £29 12s 8d would be forwarded to Northampton Hospital, with the fruit and vegetables of the decorations to be distributed among the sick and the poor of the town on Monday morning. At the Electric Theatre, there was a large assembly on Sunday evening, October 31st 1915, when the Newport Pagnell Hospital Week Committee (a body of voluntary workers which had already raised thousands of pounds for the Hospital during its some 10 years of existence) organised a united service to raise funds for Northampton Hospital. The Reverend F. Gunnery presided, and with Mr. C. K. Garratt at the organ, and a combined choir leading the singing of the hymns, the service opened with 'Soldiers of Christ arise,' followed by prayers from the Reverend A. Seys Howell. In late January 1916 Dr. C. Bailey wrote to the Council saying that he had joined the R.A.M.C. and therefore asked for leave of absence to be granted for the duration of the war. This was readily granted with Dr. Wickham to act in his place.

Formerly a girls' school, this premises in the High Street became the Vicarage in 1875. In the summer of 1904 this became the home of the Reverend Frederick Bernard Gunnery when, having previously been curate in charge of St. John's, High Wycombe, he came to the town as Vicar. It was through his efforts that the Mission Church of St. Luke's was erected at the Red House end of the town, opened in 1910. Of his many appointments he would be chaplain to the Workhouse, President of the Good Samaritan and Nursing Society, and during the First World War chairman of the committee which did much work to raise money for the British Red Cross Society and the Soldiers' and Sailors' Christmas Presents Fund. After the war, in October 1921 he accepted the living of Wath on Dearne, in the Diocese of Sheffield. This was in the gift of the Dean and Chapter of Christ Church, Oxford, and with a population of 10,000 the community formed part of an important mining district in Yorkshire. Prior to leaving Newport Pagnell, on the evening of Tuesday, November 22nd 1921 at St. Paul's School he was presented with a cheque for £115 18s. This was a gift from the townspeople, and large congregations attended his farewell sermons, preached on Advent Sunday, November 27th. At the beginning of 1927 he was appointed rural dean of Wath on Dearne.

In February 1916, at The Poplars the statement of accounts and balance sheet for the past year of Court 'Unity,' Ancient Order of Foresters, one of the oldest in the London United District, was issued and revealed a capital of £6,711 and a small loss of £39. However, the claims for sickness and funeral benefits had been high. Of the 800 membership, 146 were in the Forces and paid no subscription and tragically six had been killed. The Juvenile Branch had a membership of 137 boys and 55 girls, and from the Benevolent Fund seven guineas had been sent to Northampton Hospital, with amongst other donations a guinea each to the Newport Pagnell Good Samaritan Society and Bedford Hospital. For a service conducted by the Reverend F. Gunnery, attending the Parish Church on Sunday afternoon, March 12th 1916, were the members of the Newport Pagnell P.S.A. Brotherhood. Mr. C. K. Garratt presided at the organ and the offertory was for the benefit of Northampton Hospital via the Newport Pagnell Hospital Week Committee.

The annual meeting of the Newport Pagnell Diamond Jubilee Nursing and Good Samaritan Society was held in the Vicarage on Saturday evening, April 1st 1916. The Reverend F. Gunnery presided, and amongst those present was Mr. A. J. Simpson, the secretary. Here it was stated that the Nurse had made 3,237 visits to 73 families (76 patients), 70 articles of nursing appliances had been lent to 50 patients, assistance had been given in seven surgical cases, and four in patient letters and 25 out patient letters had been used for Northampton Hospital. With Mr. Cole now leaving the district Mr. A. Ablett would be the collector, and in other business the Reverend Gunnery was re-elected president and Mr. F. Littleboy as treasurer. Thanks were expressed to those who had given gifts of old linen, whilst as for Nurse Cook there was nothing but praise for her dedication, for which she would be sent a letter of appreciation. Since the outbreak of the war the Newport Pagnell Habitation of the Primrose League had refrained from all political work. Instead it focussed on charitable causes, to include the St. John Ambulance and the Red Cross, and a prominent lead had been given by Colonel A. Good, Ruling Councillor, Mrs. Wellesley Taylor, Dame President, Miss Bailey, secretary, and Miss D. Wickham, juvenile secretary.

On the evenings of Wednesday 3rd and Thursday 4th May 1916, these officers, with the co-operation of their wardens, then held two whist drives at the Unionist Club for the benefit of the Bucks Territorials' Comforts Fund. Colonel Good acted as M.C. on Wednesday and of the 90 or so players a prize was awarded to Mrs. Ivester Lloyd, after a cut with Mrs. Harvey Norris. Mrs. Gallows, a soldier's wife, qualified for the booby prize! This was presented to her by Mrs. Wellesley Taylor, who on Thursday evening in referring to the work done by the Newport Pagnell Habitation said they began by teaching the children to be patriotic, and to know what was going on in their country. Question papers had been issued to some 250 children, and for the best a prize giving, at which all the children enjoyed tea, was held in January 1915, during which month a whist drive for the St. John Ambulance and Red Cross raised £7. In September 1915 she had written a personal letter to the members in the Habitation asking them to make a gift for the wounded soldiers and sailors in the hospitals, and in consequence 1,230 were received. Thus an evening presentation of the gifts was made at the Electric Theatre, where during the occasion Mr. Crowe, the secretary of the Primrose League, gave a lantern lecture regarding the war and a collection raised £6 for the St. John Ambulance and Red Cross. Then in December 1915 the Juvenile Branch by selling primroses throughout the Habitation raised £19, especially pleasing since the sellers of the flowers and emblems had been little children. Having concluded her resume Mrs. Wellesley Taylor then presented Mr. and Mrs. Arthur J. Simpson, the Habitation's late secretary and treasurer, with a pair of handsome silver candlesticks and a list of the subscribers, with the address worded:

> 'Primrose League, Newport Pagnell Habitation 624.
> Presentation made on May 4, 1916, to Mr. and Mrs. Arthur Simpson in token of their valuable services as hon. secretary 1913-1916, and hon. treasurer, 1914-1916.'

As Mrs. Simpson stepped forward to receive the gift there was hearty applause, and expressing their thanks Mr. Simpson said they were sorry to sever their official connection but hoped to do their best for the work in the future. Sadly Mr. Trimmer, a member of the Habitation, had been killed at Gallipoli but with his widow still being a member the Grand Council, in appreciation of their work, had allowed the Grand Star of the Primrose League to be awarded. The annual fete for Northampton Hospital was held on Saturday, June 21st 1916, with Wilford Bros. having erected the arch and streamers of bunting at the entrance to Bury Field which, by permission of Mr. J. Knapp, J.P., who had relented from his views of the previous year, provided the venue. Mr. W. Chantler, J.P., was treasurer of the management committee, John Roberts, secretary, and Mr. F. Mayne, amusements secretary, and in his address the chairman, the Reverend Gunnery, said that since November 1914, 1,560 sick and wounded soldiers had been treated at the Hospital. However, since the Government allowances did not cover the cost of the treatment it was estimated that at the end of the financial year there would be a deficit of £4,000. Continuing he said that Mr. Konig had sent a cheque for £5 and he hoped that everybody would make this fete a great success. He then extended a cordial welcome to Lady Farrar, who having been preceded into the field by the Excelsior Silver Band performed the opening ceremony from the platform of a wagon which, also to be used as the auctioneer's rostrum, had been lent by F. Coales and Sons. Before a large attendance Lady Farrar said that with the possibility of a big push in France there might be considerable casualties, and the hospitals would need more money.

After this address Miss U. Gunnery, the Vicar's little daughter, stepped forward and presented her with a handsome bouquet (a gift to the committee from Messrs. Ramsbotham and Co.) and a purse of £20, which Lady Farrar handed to the funds. Thanks were then afforded to her and to the donors of the gifts by Mr. J. Knapp, and with this being seconded by the Reverend A. Seys Howell three cheers were given. Between the showers sports were held and in the tug of war, which featured two Royal Engineer teams - England and Ireland - and a town team, Ireland won against England, only to be defeated in the final by the town. The prizes had been provided by tradesmen in the town and in other activities dances, under the supervision of Miss K. James, the headmistress, were performed by girls from the Council School, with a bonny baby competition taking place, by permission of Mrs. Traill, in the garden of the Manor House, where the judges were a sister of the Crippled Children's Institute, Northampton, and Nurse Abbott. A new feature of the fete was the introduction of a sale of natural roses instead of artificial, as in previous fetes, and with the blooms sent in by the townspeople the instigators, Mr. and Mrs. Tracy Higgins, were accordingly kept very busy. Young ladies and children were the voluntary vendors and £18 2s 0½d was raised. The gifts for the sale had been collected by Mrs. G. Tayler, Miss F. Payne, and others, and despite the rain the auction proceedings, for which Messrs. J. Odell and A. Bullard lent weighing machines, were commenced by the Mayor of Northampton together with Councillor J. Pearse, J.P., and two Northampton Hospital workers, who had journeyed from the fete at Raunds to be present. After his introduction the Mayor began the auction by offering a hen and brood of chickens which, having been sold to Mr. Hobbs and then resold to Mr. A. Bullard were finally auctioned for 10s.

In other events an amusing play, 'Mangling done here,' was presented by the Misses Allfrey and the Misses Savory, and entertainments were also performed by the Magpie Concert Party. Other amusements included roundabouts, goal kicking, coconut shies, and skittle tables, and teas and light refreshments were served on the field under canvas. Contributions to the funds were also raised by Miss K. Tate, portrayed as Britannia, Miss Tooth, by the sale of an original poem, and Madge Proctor, who with her little pet dog collected several shillings. Other monies were collected by Mrs. C. Pettit and her young daughter, whilst other revenue came from the sale by schoolchildren and others of scented cards, arranged by Mr. J. Roberts, the secretary. Despite the heavy rainstorms during the day £1 6s was raised from a fruit and ice cream stall by Mr. R. Mazzone who, for raising further funds, had lent two barrel organs, one of which, mounted on a horse and trolley loaned by Mr. George Taylor, was paraded around Bradwell, Wolverton and the neighbouring villages. Cycles were stored in the field by Mr. W. Harris, and at the Railway Tavern by Mr. R.J. Layton, and in the evening despite torrents of rain hundreds of supporters arrived by train from Bradwell and Wolverton, their contributions helping towards the total of £230 raised by the event. The dedication festival of the Parish Church was continued on Sunday, July 2nd 1916, and in the afternoon the usual children's flower and egg service was held. The large number of beautiful flowers and the contribution of 333 eggs were then taken after the service to Northampton Hospital whilst the offertory of the service, amounting to £1 3s 7d, would, less expenses, go to the Hospital Week Committee. The offertories throughout the festival were on behalf of the Oxford Diocesan Fund and amounted to £34 11s 6d.

On the afternoon of Thursday, October 19th 1916, the attentions of the school nurse were required when a small boy named Daniells, of Greenfield Road, fractured a leg when, whilst playing with other children, he fell on the hard asphalt of the Council School playground. Doctor White was called and the lad was then taken to Northampton Hospital. For the benefit of the British Farmers' Red Cross Fund and the Bucks Branch of the Red Cross Society, a large agricultural and general auction jumble sale took place in the town on Wednesday, March 21st 1917. This was held under the auspices of the Newport Pagnell Branch of the National Farmers' Union and the Town Committee of the Red Cross Society, and many farmers had sent gifts of livestock, agricultural implements and produce and also money. Local worthies and residents of the town also gave generously as did Mr. F. J. Taylor, who sent a cheque for £100, Salmons and Sons, who contributed 50 guineas, and the pupils of the Council Schools, via a collection organised by the head teachers. Employing the services of his lady clerks - Miss Geary and Miss Cox - Mr. P. C. Gambell was the honorary auctioneer, with assistance given by Mr. A.W. Merry and Mr. Clifton. Members of the Royal Engineers acted as sale porters and Miss Payne, as on previous occasions, had lent her field adjoining the Cattle Market to accommodate farm produce, implements, carts, poultry, dogs and rabbits. Mrs. Fraser, the wife of Donald Fraser, of Tickford Park, had been invited to perform the opening ceremony, and, as a gift from Mrs. W. Hedges of Great Linford, she was presented with a basket of eggs by the Reverend F. Gunnery, who on behalf of the Farmers' Union and Town Committee thanked her for her kindness. He then announced that a telegram wishing the sale every success had been received from Lady Farrar, from whom, with applause greeting this announcement, a cheque for £5 would be forwarded. Mrs. Fraser then graciously handed the basket of eggs to be sold by Mr. Gambell and when four eggs had been bought at a sovereign each, and two others at 10s each, the next egg was purchased by Mr. J. Mann, J.P., of Olney, who having been to the Magisterial Bench stopped his car and wrote out a cheque for 10 guineas. A little later Mrs. Fraser paid £15 for an egg and in total the clutch raised £32 10s 6d.

Including three sets of harness donated by Mr. F. W. Taylor, other articles in the sale included a cigar of the late King Edward VII, presented by Mr. R. Pettit. Sold several times over this was finally bought by Mr. H.T. York of Olney for £3 17s 6d whilst an autographed letter from General Sir Douglas Haig made £2 2s. A candelabra given by Mr. F. Allfrey realised £6, an antique tea caddy given by Miss Coales, 22s, 12 beautifully made English toy ambulances and wagons, a gift from Mrs. G. Salmons and Mrs. L. Salmons, fetched £2 18s 6d, a case of cider from John Odell made £1, four tons of regulation flour, from Messrs. Coales and Son, millers and merchants, went to the Newport Pagnell Co-operative Society for £97 12s, and a dog cart given by Major W. Trevor, J.P., of Lathbury Park, made £5. Despite frequent snowstorms, throughout the day the Ladies' Committee worked hard selling Red Cross flags and catalogues, and, with Mrs. P. C. Gambell, Mrs. Digby Clark and Miss D. Odell amongst those carrying the trays, the flags alone realised £36 18s. In the evening, by being sold and resold at the Royal Engineers smoking concert a box of 50 cigars, given by Mr. A. Marshall, tobacconist, made £34 4s 6d, which contributed towards the total raised by the event of about £1,150. On Saturday evening, March 24th 1917, the annual meeting of the Newport Pagnell Diamond Jubilee Nursing and Good Samaritan Society was held at the Vicarage. The Reverend F. Gunnery occupied the chair and also present were Mrs. Gunnery, Mrs. F. Littleboy, Mr. and Mrs. W.R. Chantler, Miss A. M.Coales, Mr. T. Meadows and also Mr. T. Sim, the secretary, who was assuming the double office of Mr. A. J. Simpson, secretary, and Mr. A. Ablett, collector, both of whom were resigning. Respects were paid to the late Frederick Taylor, and a proposition to send sympathies to his family was carried in silence. In the 18th annual report it was stated that the nurse had made 2,287 visits to 70 patients (68 families), 60 nursing appliances had been lent to 40 patients, surgical assistance had been given in seven cases, and five in patient and 16 out patient letters for Northampton Hospital had been granted. Once again Nurse Cook had carried out her duties with complete satisfaction, and following the details of the finance the Reverend Gunnery was unanimously re-elected as President, with the committee also re-elected.

Including a number of soldiers there was a large attendance at the Parish Church on Tuesday afternoon, March 27th 1917, when in a full choral service Miss Dorothy Elaine Wickham, the only child of Dr. H. Wickham and Mrs. Wickham, of The Close, Newport Pagnell, married Lieutenant Temple George Hillyard of the Devon Regiment. He was the only son of the Reverend A. Hillyard and Mrs. Hillyard, of The Parsonage, Upton Pyne, Exeter and during 1915 had seen much hard fighting in France. Subsequent to being seriously wounded at the end of April 1916 he spent some time in Netley Hospital and on recovering joined the Reserve Battalion of his regiment, with which he was presently serving at Devonport. Mr. C. K. Garratt presided at the organ and the nuptials were performed by the Reverend A. Hillyard, father of the groom, assisted by the Reverend C. T. Wickham, the uncle of the bride, and the Reverend Gunnery. Lent by her uncle, the bride's veil was from the family's heritage and in her other attire she wore a gown of ivory tinted Liberty satin, into the belt of which was tucked a beautiful Bucks lace handkerchief, the gift of Miss Fleet. Given by Mrs. Hugh Gillespie and Miss Gillespie, two antique pearl buckles fastened the train on the shoulders and as the gift of the groom she carried a sheaf of Harrissii (sic) lilies. The groom's two sisters were the bridesmaids and as the bridal party left the church a squad of 16 Royal Engineers, taking their orders from Corporal Keay, formed up in two lines. They were marshalled by Lieutenants Roberts and Robey and as the newly weds left the church the soldiers brought the long poles they carried (used in their work with telephone wires) smartly to the slope. In the absence of a formal reception Mrs. Wickham entertained the relations of the couple, plus a few intimate friends, at The Close, and during the afternoon the couple left by motor car en route for Oxford, the bride taking with her a brown suede bag as the gift of Captain and Mrs. Huddart, and a spray of pink carnations. These had been given by Nurse Eastwood and also Nurse Cook, who in her professional capacity employed her skills following an accident which befell Mr. Harry Watson, a tobacconist of the High Street, on the night of Sunday, June 3rd. Having slipped whilst coming downstairs he had fallen heavily to the bottom, and as well as dislocating his shoulder suffered a cut on the face and severe bruising. Tragically his wife had recently died following an accident, and he was placed under the care of Dr. White and Nurse Cook. However as assistant nurse she would resign the following month due to her impending marriage.

At the meeting of the U.D.C. in June 1917 the following letter was read;

"The Lamblies, Newport Pagnell.

Dear Sir,

When the Emergency Hospital at the schools was started to deal with possible air raid casualties, two stretchers were purchased from Messrs.

Salmons and Sons for £4 4s. These have recently been paid for, and as officer in charge, after consultation with Dr. Wickham, the medical officer, I wish to hand them over to the Urban District Council for the use of the town. If the Council accept the offer I would suggest that for the duration of the war one of the stretchers be kept at the V.A.D. Hospital. At the present time one is kept at the Fire Station and the other at the Police Station.

Yours truly,
H. I. MIDDLETON."

The Council accepted the offer and a vote of thanks was passed. However relations between the Vicar and certain inhabitants of Wolverton proved less harmonious that month, as evidenced by letters to the local press:

"Re. Alexandra Rose Day.

Dear Sir,

I understand that some of our ladies who visited Newport Pagnell on Saturday last to sell roses were ordered back by the Vicar. Did he act on behalf and with the approval of the Newport Hospital Saturday Committee? If so we Wolvertonians would be quite justified in preventing the annual barrel organ parade of our streets for that cause and other collections for Newport from time to time.

I quite agree there should be no overlapping, but the Vicar's action in this case appears to be very one-sided, especially as the ladies in question had permission.

Yours faithfully,
"WOLVERTONIAN"."
Wolverton,
June 12."

The Vicar duly replied:

"Dear Sir

Allow me to answer the letter of "Wolvertonian" in the "Bucks Standard" of June 16th.

My action had nothing whatever to do with the Hospital Week Committee. I acted as chairman of the Newport Pagnell War Charities Committee.

In 1915 this committee consisting of representatives from the various corporate bodies of the town - the Urban Council, the religious bodies, friendly societies, &c. was formed to authorise, organise, and control flag days, street collections, and public appeals for charities connected with the war. We were anxious to avoid overlapping, which I am glad to see that "Wolvertonian" deprecates, and to protect the town against the well-meant but possibly too frequent appeals for the many worthy objects which this war has created. It has no police powers. We can only ask our neighbours kindly to co-operate with us and to respect the wishes of the town as expressed by this representative body.

Your correspondent seems to suggest some lack of courtesy on my part by the expression "ordered back." What I did was to request the ladies to cease collecting, at the same time explaining my reason. Even then I only acted when complaint was made to me.

With regard to the "permission," doubtless the sellers had the necessary Police sanction. That might be and would be granted to 20 different organisations for the same day. Moreover, the Police cannot impose any conditions. They are concerned only with the bona fides of the collection. But probably we are all agreed that to be solicited on behalf of several different objects, however good, on the same day and in the same streets might be a real nuisance. It is to avoid this very thing that our committee exists. As it was, we had already granted permission to the Salvation Army for their Flag Day on June 9th.

If Wolverton has or should have a representative committee to authorise and control street collections I should certainly feel morally bound to get its permission before collecting funds there.

I will only add that a year ago a letter was written by our Secretary asking that in the future our approval should be sought before another Rose Day. I have since learnt that it never reached the Wolverton Committee. But I did write some months ago to the Bucks Standard announcing the existence and objects of our organisation in the hope that the fact might thus become generally known.

Yours faithfully,

FREDERICK B. GUNNERY."

At the request of the Newport Pagnell Hospital Week Committee, Mrs. Mitchison organised a Rose Day which, held on Saturday, July 1st 1917, raised £18 10s for Northampton Hospital. All the roses were grown in local gardens and acting as the sellers were members of the Parish Church Girls' Club. Then in beautiful summer weather in Bury Field on Saturday, July 21st 1917, the annual fete to raise funds for Northampton Hospital took place. At the entrance to the field Messrs. Wilford Brothers had erected the arch - bearing a message that wished success to the fund - and barrel organs lent by Mr. Mazzone for the occasion were taken around the villages, with one mounted upon a horse trolley provided by George Taylor, shoeing smith. Mr. John Roberts was the secretary of the Hospital Week Committee, Mr. C. Page treasurer, Mr. Frank Payne sports secretary, and Reverend Gunnery chairman, who as president was supported by amongst others Mr. J. Boswell, J.P., Mrs. Boswell, the Mayor and Mayoress of Northampton, and Mrs. Trevor and Miss Trevor of Lathbury Park. In his address he emphasised the valuable work performed by the Hospital in treating soldiers and said that unfortunately this year they had not been able to obtain the popular roundabouts because all the engines were on war work. Making a donation of 10 guineas to the fund, in the presence of the large gathering Mrs. Boswell, of Crawley Grange, declared the fete open from a contractor's trolley, after which little Gladys Mayne, the daughter of Mr. F.L. Mayne, handed her a purse containing £15. The sum had been collected in the town for the funds of the fete and was accompanied by a beautiful bouquet of carnations marked, 'A small contribution, wishing you every success.' This had been donated by Alfred Cockerill, a well known nurseryman and florist of Northampton, and having handed the money to the Vicar, Mrs. Boswell, acting on a suggestion, offered the bouquet for sale. This was duly bought by the Vicar for £2 5s and then handed back for auction in the evening. The Mayor of Northampton next proposed thanks to Mrs. Boswell, as well as to all the donors and helpers, and giving an address remarked upon the rivalry with Olney. This town had come first last year and in his address Mr. J. Boswell said they must try to beat Olney, "a very nice place."

Having on occasion gone around the wards and chatted to the patients, Mr. Short paid tribute to the work of the Hospital, and - not least to beat Raunds and Olney - asked everyone to bid heartily at his auction and re-offer the articles for re-auction. Shortly after the opening ceremony there was an unintended, but not unwelcome distraction, when six aeroplanes passed over the town in the direction of London but the first scheduled item of the fete, repeated later in the afternoon, consisted of character dances by girls of the Council Schools trained by Miss James and her staff. Then under the direction of Mrs. Mitchison, assisted by Mr. C. K. Garratt, members of the Parish Church Girls' Club gave two performances of a sketch entitled 'A New Decree,' 'of Japanese influence.' With prizes donated by local tradesmen, in the sports the open one lap handicap for men of the Forces proved popular, whilst two convalescent soldiers from the V.A.D. hospital at Tickford were successful in the final. However, in the tug of war the Royal Engineers were hopelessly outclassed by a team lead by Tom Bavington, who in such events had been a successful coach in years gone past. Of the other events there were races for the ladies and for girls and boys, and in a heel and toe contest the bandsmen joined in the fun, playing their instruments as they made a tour of the track. Scouts including J. Dunbabin assisted at the many stalls and that selling flowers and vegetables did excellent business during the afternoon and again in the evening, since people from the town had contributed some choice cut blooms, with a variety of produce supplied by the allotment holders.

Dating from 1699 the old King's Arms in Tickford Street. It was demolished for road improvements. The premises of the new King's Arms were once the home of Mr. Visscher. Photo by courtesy of Mr. G. Stratton.

With Mrs. G. Page as president, and Miss A. M. Coales as superintendent, this was under the auspices of the Congregational Church Girls Club, members of which, including Miss Bertha Garratt and Miss Maisey Ellingham, sold buttonholes on the field during the afternoon, as they had in the streets during the morning. Before and on the day of the sale the Misses Layton sold buttonholes and scented cards, with Miss K. Layton selling a record 29 dozen of the latter. Teas and refreshments were available on the field and with valuable gifts of milk supplied by Mr. Trevor, of Lathbury Park, and Mr. Geo. Tayler, of The Kickles, amongst other donations residents had given butter and eggs, and Messrs. F. J. Taylor mineral waters. For the amusements the Adult School, the Workmen's Social Club and Mrs. Collier, of the King's Arms, lent skittles, and there was also a billiard table, two weighing machines, hoop la, children's boats, football goal kicking, coconut shies and a shooting range, this being in the charge of Leonard Rose and Harry Thickpenny. Mrs. W. Hedges of Great Linford had lent her donkey to give rides to the children, who could also at a nominal sum ride the pony of Master Reggie Smith, which he paraded around the ground. He was the son of the landlord of the Beehive Inn, who was in the Forces. In other fund raising ventures Miss K. Tate, of Priory Street, sold copies of an original poem. Under the direction of Lieutenant A. Speight, tenor, three concerts were given by the Royal Engineers, and with Mr. C. K. Garratt as accompanist among the items were songs rendered by Miss Bertha Richens, and, of the humorous variety, by Lance Corporal Aspinwall. In the evening the auction sale organised by Councillor Joseph Short took place and the first lot was the auctioneer's hammer used for many years by the late Mr. J. Goodwin, of Newport Pagnell. Purchased by Mr. J. Clare for 25s he then presented it to Mr. Gambell as a memento of the fete. Other goods in the auction ranged from a suckling pig and geese to easy chairs, vegetables and fruit, whilst an egg laid on the field by a hen was repeatedly sold and raised 15s. Given by Mr. J.A. Price half a ton of coal made 19s and a load of sawn wood, donated by Mr. W. Goodman, of Chicheley, was purchased for £1 by Mr. P. C. Gambell. Coales and Sons gave twenty 14 lb bags of flour, and with all the auction lots disposed of £52 was raised.

In an old English skittle competition for a live pig, only a few seconds before 8.30 p.m. just as a tie of the highest score of 16 was about to be played Mr. J. Dorrill junior, from Lathbury, paid his 3d for three balls, 'trundled up the improvised alley' and to the chagrin of the tie holders scored 17! The day then concluded with dancing to the Excelsior Silver Band in the sports enclosure. The fete had proved a great success and the total of £276 18s 4d included the monies received by Mr. R.J. Layton, of the Railway Tavern, and Mr. G. Darby for storing cycles, plus a donation of 10s from Clarence Hayllar. Postponed from August Bank Holiday, due to the Bathing Place being in flood, a grand water carnival organised by the Newport Pagnell Hospital Week Committee took place on Thursday afternoon, August 23rd 1917. In a programme in which the Royal Engineers gave assistance the schoolboys' swimming tests, for monetary prizes given by the Misses Taylor of Lovat Bank, proved popular and the championship of the school was won by William Ellingham. In fact he had only recently learned to swim, and for his achievement received a watch given by the H.M. Inspector of Schools. Despite having only one arm Leslie Brooks was loudly cheered for his successful completion of the 20 yards back swimming test, and the watery events, despite a sharp thunderstorm midway through, included exhibitions of diving in which a town team were successful against a Royal Engineers team, raised by Lance Corporal Keay. The annual meeting of the Working Men's Club took place on Wednesday evening, February 27th 1918, over which Mr. W. Carlile presided. The balance sheet was considered satisfactory, audited by both Mr. H. I. Middleton, the schoolmaster, and the assistant to Mr. F. W. Taylor, the chemist, Mr. J. J. Marshall. However, the latter was in a less healthy condition, for he was presently in hospital, having fractured his knee cap on Thursday evening, February 21st. The accident happened in the Unionist Club when, whilst stepping from the entrance hall to the side passage, he fell over a bicycle being taken down the passage. Assistance was quickly given and at his lodgings, which were quite close by, he was later attended by Dr. H. Wickham and Dr. Digby White, being removed on the Saturday to Northampton Hospital for an operation.

The annual meeting of the Newport Pagnell Nursing and Good Samaritan Society was held at the Vicarage on the evening of Saturday, March 23rd 1918, with the President, the Reverend Gunnery, in the chair. Also present were Mrs. Gunnery, Mrs. F. Littleboy, Miss J. Taylor, Miss A.

M.Coales, Messrs. A.G. Ablett, T. Meadows, C.R. Line, and T.H. Sim, the honorary secretary, and having been printed and circulated the 19th annual report was taken as read. The Nurse had made 2,557 visits to 106 patients (100 families), 60 nursing appliances had been lent to 40 patients, and three in patient and 17 out patient letters to Northampton Hospital had been granted. With the report and balance unanimously adopted the election of the officials then took place and the Reverend Gunnery and Mr. S. Smith Harvey were respectively re-elected as president and vice president. Mr. F. W. Taylor, Mr. W. J. Coales and Mr. F. W. Bull were appointed as additional vice presidents and Mr. F. Littleboy was re-elected treasurer. Re-elected on the committee were Mrs. Chantler, Mrs. Gunnery, Mrs. F. Littleboy, Miss A. M.Coales, Miss J. Taylor, Messrs. A.G. Ablett, T. Meadows, and A. J. Simpson, whilst as for Miss French and Mr. C.R. Line, they were added to the committee. On Monday, April 15th 1918, at the Parish Church Miss Winifred Emily (Freda) Coales, the younger daughter of Mr. and Mrs. W. J. Coales, of The Lodge, married Lieutenant Hilary A. Agnew. Serving with the Highland Light Infantry he was the only son of the late Mr. and Mrs. H. Agnew, of 'Rocquaine', Newport Pagnell and having been involved in much heavy fighting, and wounded twice, he had been in the Forces since the beginning of the war. In fact he unexpectedly received orders to proceed to the Front on Wednesday and in consequence the ceremony would be of a quiet nature, performed, assisted by the Reverend Gunnery, by the Reverend R. Bale. He was the cousin of the bride who was given away by her father with her brother, Lieutenant J.L. Coales, of the Munster Fusiliers, acting as best man. As a member of the Tyringham V.A.D. since March 1915 Freda had been a V.A.D. nurse at the Stanmore Military Hospital, and from the headquarters of the St. John Ambulance Association she had been sent with five other nurses around December 1915 to France, where by a coincidence at Boulogne she was conveyed from one station to another in a motor car subscribed for by the Bucks farmers.

Since February 1916 she had been nursing at No. 2 Red Cross Hospital at Rouen and also the Duchess of Westminster's Hospital at Le Touquet. After the marriage ceremony the newly weds left the church by the north door, to find the Commandant of Tickford Abbey V.A.D. Hospital, Miss McFerran, the Quartermaster, Miss Wood, and the nursing staff and wounded soldiers all lined up as a Guard of Honour. On Market Hill, in fine sunny weather a sale for the Red Cross was held on Wednesday, April 24th 1918, under the auspices of the Newport Pagnell Branch of the N.F.U. and the Newport Pagnell Red Cross Committee. The proceeds were to be equally divided between the British Farmers' Red Cross Fund and the Bucks Branch of the Red Cross Society, and, as stated in an appeal issued earlier in the month, £1,000 was the target. Yet even before the sale began donations of £105 had been received from Mr. F. Konig, £100 from Donald Fraser and £50 from Messrs. R. Wylie and Co. Together with other donations this made over £650 and about £72 had been raised by Mrs. Mitchison's Girls' Club Concert. Mr. P. C. Gambell acted as the honorary auctioneer and his office staff - Miss Geary, Miss Cox, Miss Inns and Mr. Hedge - all worked hard throughout the day. Gathered around the temporary platform, which had been decorated with flags and bunting, hundreds of spectators watched the opening ceremony at 2 p.m., with a guard of honour formed by the Newport Pagnell Company of the Bucks Volunteer Regiment, under Lieutenant H. I. Middleton (wearing their new uniforms,) and the Newport Pagnell Company of Special Constables, under Captain C. M. Wilford and Lieutenant F. O.Butler. Arranged on one side of the platform were the soldier patients from Tickford Abbey, together with Miss McFerran, Miss Wood, Dr. H.T. Wickham (the Medical Officer) and several of the nursing staff, whilst on the other side were a number of local workers of the W.L.A. under Mrs. Wellesley Taylor, she being the representative for North Bucks. Members of the Royal Engineers formed three sides of a square, outside of which the large crowd was kept, and Superintendent Dibben, police sergeant Roberts and several of the Bucks Constabulary were on duty to keep order.

Having lunched at the Vicarage, the Marquis of Lincolnshire firstly inspected the Guard of Honour of the Volunteers and Special Constables and after a similar inspection of the W.L.A. and wounded soldiers was then welcomed on the platform by the chairman of the Executive Committee, Mr. G. Tayler. From the platform in the presence of other worthies he expressed thanks for his kind invitation, and having recalled his boyhood memories of the district praised the Army, Volunteers, Special Constables, W.L.A. and nurses, saying that although for three years he had acted as Lord Chamberlain to Queen Victoria, thus attending many Drawing Rooms, he had never seen a better group of young women than the representatives of the W.L.A. Being indisposed he said his wife was unable to attend, but she sent an affectionate message. Ending his address he then called for three cheers for the King, plus an extra cheer for the Prince of Wales. After this the National Anthem was played by the town band, which subsequently paraded the streets with the 'Red Cross car.' Arranged by Mr. Walter John Coales, of The Lodge, this aroused considerable interest and not least because of Mr. R. Fergusson as 'the wounded soldier patient' and Miss Clara Adams and Miss Florrie Shelton as 'the nurses.' At the sale the 'V.C. Cockerel,' Mr. Fyson's famous bird, (sic) was then put up for sale by the Marquis, having during its previous 103 sales raised £8,212 for the Red Cross. After a bid of £5 from the Marquis, Mr. Gambell then took over and a sum of £60 6s was obtained.

The Red Cross Sale on Market Hill on Wednesday, April 24th 1918

Photo courtesy of Ken & Joyce Graham

Here we are again.
Keep the Fires Burning till the
Boys come home again
I am only a small
COCKEREL
I am a Native of "Ramsey"
I have already gained the VC

Left: Mr. Fyson and his famous bird

Later in the afternoon at a meeting of the Farmers' Union he again offered the bird and this time a further £69 10s 6d was secured, plus a further £23 7s 6d in the evening. In other lots a framed photo of a pedigree Shorthorn cow in Yorkshire, which had given birth to four calves last August, this being a unique record, was bought by Mr. Gunnery for 10s. This had been presented by Mr. Gibson, a veterinary surgeon of the town, and amongst the other lots were a sheep dog given by Mr. Ward, which made £4, a pig given by Major Trevor, £5 15s, and a clock given by Messrs. Coales and Sons, jewellers, £2 2s. In total £370 was made and apart from the auction there were numerous side shows, competitions etc., organised under the direction of Mr. C. M. Wilford. The attractions included hoop la, a cake competition, skittles, bran tub, bumble puppy, swings, doll competition, weighing machine and electric shocks and in the charge of Mrs. Mitchison and Miss Bale the 'hidden treasure' brought in £2 18s 2d. Stalls for the sale of fancy and useful articles were the jurisdiction of Mrs. G. Tayler and her assistants, with the tea and refreshment stall superintended by Miss A. M.Coales assisted by amongst others Mrs. F. Littleboy and Miss Margaret Coales. This made £3 1s 10d, whilst £14 6s 6d was collected by Mrs. Durrant and the Misses U. and K. Easson, who, attired in their W.L.A. uniforms, toured the town with a barrel organ lent by Mr. Mazzone.

As the proceeds from the afternoon sale of teas at the Corner House, Mrs. Dyer gave £2 12s 3d, and additional monies were raised during the day by the sale of flags by ladies under the direction of Mrs. Gunnery. The large marquee erected on Market Hill had been lent by Messrs. C. Lawman and Son, and brakes had been

The premises opened in August 1915

provided by Mr. R.J. Layton to fetch those members of the band who were employed at Wolverton Works. Concluding the occasion a dance was held in the Council Schools in the evening, at which over 200 persons were present. Held under the auspices of the N.F.U. and the Town Red Cross Committee, and in conjunction with the Royal Engineers Wireless Depot in the town, in glorious summer weather the Red Cross Gala Day and Gymkhana took place at Newport Pagnell on Whit Monday 1918, attended by over 4,000 people from the town and local district. Woad Field had been kindly lent by Messrs. Adkins Bros., and the hardworking committee, of which the Reverend Gunnery was chairman, deserved especial praise, as also Messrs. C. K. Garratt and T.H. Sim, the joint honorary secretaries. Having been assembled in Station Road, and lead along the crowded High Street by the Excelsior Silver Band, the afternoon's proceedings began with a procession of decorated cars etc. organised by Mrs. Mitchison and marshalled by Sergeant Major Harrod, Sergeant Hockaday, and Sergeant Mildmay. Decorated by Mrs. Mitchison, Mrs. Huddart, Mrs. Hillyard, Miss West, Miss M. Coales, Miss Odell and Miss P. Taylor, the cars had been contributed by Newport Pagnell and comprised the 'Red Cross Car,' the 'nurses' being Clara Adams, Florrie Shelton, Norah Mayne, and the 'patient' Percy Goodman; the 'Agriculture (Past)' car, aboard which were Millie Bass, Alice Tandy, Ethel Mason, Florrie Petts, Lily Holes, Rose Petts, Winnie Fisher; the 'Masque of the Centuries' car, staffed by Phyllis Attkins, Kathleen Petts, Gladys Harper, Lily Pratt, Ivy Wagstaff, Violet Thickpenny, Eva Bass, Jessie Childs; the 'Britannia and her Allies' car, carrying Norah Daniells, Dolly Earl, Minnie Smith, Doris Chapman, Ada Mitchell, Maggie Stagg, Nellie Bavington.; the 'Agriculture (Present)' car, arranged by Mrs. Wellesley Taylor of Sherington, with a crew dressed in their W.L.A. uniforms of the Misses K. Easson, Mooney, Newsholme, Hickson, Basley, Hollis, Payne, Pope, and Catt. In the form of a camp, under Senior Patrol Leader Norman Saunders the Lathbury troop of Boy Scouts had also entered a car. Troop members marched along with the vehicle and also present was their Scoutmistress, Miss D. Trevor, who by touring the streets and the field with a small pony raised £2 2s 6d in her collecting box.

Boys of the Council School under Lieutenant H. I. Middleton also took part in the procession, as did members of the Parish Church Girls' Club who, by selling flags and badges in the field, made over £12. Prizes had been offered for the best decorated cycles but since no one competed these were therefore added to those awarded to the cars, the judges being Mrs. Vaughan Harley of Walton Hall, Mrs. Trevor of Lathbury Park and Mrs. Field of Milton Keynes Rectory. The prize of £2 2s, presented by Messrs. C. Coales, W. Cotton, and A. J. Simpson, went to the 'Agriculture (Present)' car and this sum the Women's Land Army workers handed back for the funds. Prizes of the value of £1 1s, given by Mr. A.H. Rickard, and 10s 6d, by Mr. F. J. Sharp, went to the 'Agriculture (Past)' car, and each girl on the 'Masque of Centuries' car and 'Britannia and her Allies' car was presented with a Red Cross Tombola ticket by Mrs. Harley and Mrs. Trevor. After arriving at the field the decorated cars formed up and the opening ceremony took place from two wagons specially prepared for the occasion. As chairman of the Town Committee the Reverend Gunnery presided, and amongst those supporting him were Mr. G. Tayler, Mr. J. Short, Major and Mrs. Doyne Ditmas, Colonel A. Good, Captain J.B. Mowatt, and Mr. and Mrs. Carlile. Following God Save the King, played by the band, the Reverend Gunnery then introduced Sir Arthur Lawley, representative of the British Red Cross in France, who had formerly been Governor of Madras, Governor of Western Australia, and Lieutenant Governor of the Transvaal. He was accompanied by Lady Lawley, Lady Farrar and Mrs. Baird (the sister of Lady Farrar and the wife of Brigadier General Baird, Gordon Highlanders) and before his address the Reverend Gunnery's small daughter, Ursula, presented Lady Lawley with a bouquet of carnations, provided, through the offices of Mr. J. Short, by Mr. A. Cockerill of Northampton. Sir Arthur then thanked the assembly for their welcome and said that he had been pleased to accept the invitation of his friend of long standing, Lady Farrar. Saying he had only returned from France a few days ago he spoke of the righteousness of the war, the assurance of victory, and the comradeship that he had witnessed in the trenches, remarking that these had seen the burial of the old prejudices and barriers. There was now the birth of new ideals, for the "toff" had done his bit and the "scallywags of the slums" had proved themselves heroes. Men of all sorts and conditions of life had faced death and hardship for the honour and glory of their magnificent Empire, and the "comradeship of the trenches" would prove a precious element in the future social fabric of the country." He then praised the work of the Red Cross and the V.A.D.s. and declared the fete open.

Having been carried in the procession on the Agricultural (Present) car, and given by Mr. G. Duncombe, Mr. P. C. Gambell next offered for sale a small pig and two shepherd dog puppies, one of which Lady Farrar bought twice over. Lady Lawley purchased the other for £4 4s. As for the pig, this was finally purchased for £5 5s by the Reverend R. Mitchison. Amongst the other lots, two cockerels given by Lady Farrar for one of the Agricultural cars were repeatedly sold and the total raised by Mr. Gambell was nearly £40. Another feature of the programme was an exhibition of war trophies and relics, around which parties were shown by Company Sergeant Major Harrod. The items included a German field gun captured on the Somme, a lifebuoy from H.M.S. Hogue, German helmets and rifles, and a machine gun from a Zeppelin. Some of the items had been contributed by Major Doyne-Ditmas whilst the inkstand used at the signing of the deliverance of Jerusalem was loaned by Major Clutton, of Sherington. Mr. Walter Carlile exhibited fragments of windows from the Cloth Hall and Cathedral at Ypres, and amongst other items were fragments of the Zeppelin brought down at Cuffley. Additionally, a Turkish rifle, bayonet, clip of cartridges and a Turkish cricket ball bomb from Gallipoli were exhibited by Captain Mowatt M.C., who was referee for a programme of sports held on a track of a ¼ mile circumference. These events included a skipping competition for girls under 11 and a gymnastic display performed by the Royal Engineers. However not on the programme was the appearance of a balloon which, first spotted in the distance, then descended onto the sports field. On an instructional flight from London, the craft, with five officers aboard, was an Army Observation Balloon, and after landing it was deflated, packed up and taken to the railway station on a lorry provided by Messrs. Adkins, to be returned with the officers on the 5.20 p.m. train.

Under Miss James, accompanied by the band and each equipped with a flag the girls of the Council Schools gave a display of marching on the lines of a military tattoo. This was then followed by Old English dances and folk songs, with Mrs. Gillam as one of the helpers. Despite the distraction of the balloon an afternoon concert arranged by Mr. C. K. Garratt took place at 4 p.m. and among the artistes were Miss Bertha Richens, Miss M. Wilford, Mr. C.R. Line, and Miss Marjorie Line. The accompaniments were played by Miss M. Knott, A.L.C.M., Mr. Garratt, and Pioneer Picton, and in the evening before a large attendance another concert took place, arranged by Mrs. P. C. Gambell. For this a stage had been erected by Mr. Compton, assisted by Mr. T. Nottingham, and with a piano lent free of charge by Mr. J. Thickpenny the performers included Mr. D. Ashton Davies. At 7.30 p.m. the prizes were then presented by Lady Farrar, to whom a vote of thanks was proposed by Captain Mowat, seconded by Mr. Garratt and carried with enthusiastic cheers. Lady Farrar suitably responded and then called for three cheers, which were heartily given. Throughout the event the many sideshows had been superintended by Mr. C. M. Wilford, with Mr. Reginald Odell amongst those kept busy with the popular swings. Mrs. Gunnery had superintended the refreshment tent and throughout the afternoon musical selections were played by the Excelsior Silver Band, under Bandmaster Green. Of the many persons responsible for the day's success thanks were due to Mr. R. Pettit, who, with a temporary bridge erected over the brook, had allowed the use of his field at the North Bridges as a pedestrian entrance to the ground. Messrs. Lawman and Son had loaned all tenting, in the erection of which, as with the preparation of the sports ring, invaluable assistance had been given by members of the Royal Engineers. They also assisted Messrs. Lawman and Son to take down and pack the tents on the following day, and in other activities on Saturday, June 29th 1918, they played St. Andrew's Hospital, Northampton, in their home town at cricket and easily won, with Corporal Dennis taking seven wickets for 34 runs.

The annual fete in aid of Northampton Hospital took place on Bury Field on Saturday, July 20th 1918. The weather had been dull in the morning but proved fine just before 2 p.m., when the Excelsior Silver Band marched to the venue from North Bridges. Supported by the Hon. Mrs. Denis Farrer, the Hon. Daphne Mitford, Mr. and Mrs. W.A. Swannell, the Mayor of Northampton (Councillor A. J. Chown), and Messrs. F. Allfrey, J. Short, and O. H. Bull, at the opening ceremony the chairman of the Hospital Week Committee presided, with the speeches delivered from a wagon lent by Messrs. F. Coales and Son. Firstly the Vicar welcomed Mrs. Farrer and thanking her for coming to open the fete said that the Northampton Hospital had been a blessing to Newport Pagnell, from where 37 in patients and 91 out patients had been treated during the past year. With suitable words Mrs. Farrer then performed the opening ceremony and was presented with a bouquet by little Phyllis West, the daughter of Albert West, a member of the committee. Next the Vicar formally presented a purse containing £25 to the fete funds and said that his wife could not be present as she was attending a meeting at Northampton on nursing work. Giving an address the Mayor of Northampton then gave figures for the past contributions from Newport Pagnell, and said that despite treating large numbers of soldiers Northampton Hospital had not reduced the accommodation for civilians. His hearty vote of thanks to Mrs. Farrer, and to all the donors of gifts and services, was seconded by Mr. O. H. Bull, and in her response Mrs. Farrer referred to the importance of district nursing and infant welfare. Mr. Short then proposed, "That this gathering records its great appreciation of the splendid work done by the Northampton Hospital, both for those living in this town and neighbourhood and for our sick and wounded soldiers and sailors," and in his address advised those present to spend their money liberally that afternoon for the intended cause. This was seconded by Mr. F. Allfrey, who mentioned that he had been a subscriber to Northampton Hospital for over 40 years.

As for the events of the fete, under the direction of Miss James 88 girls of the Council Schools, each carrying a flag, gave a display of marching on military lines, and with Miss Winnie Rout at the piano this was followed by several Old English dances and folk songs. Later in the afternoon Maypole dances were performed by children of the Infants' Department under the supervision of Miss Mills, the headmistress, who also played the piano accompaniments. An afternoon programme of sports had been arranged, which included a skipping race, a potato race for ladies, a land boat race, an egg and spoon race for ladies, a tug of war between three teams of Royal Engineers, and a three legged race for men in the Forces. Also during the afternoon in a large marquee a concert arranged by Mrs. P. C. Gambell took place, in which Miss M. Knott and Miss V. Cameron played a piano duet, songs were performed by Miss K. Powell, Mr. D. Ashton Davies, Miss V. Cameron and Miss Marjorie Line, and Miss M. Wilford rendered a recitation. These artistes then also featured in the two evening concerts, in which Sapper Morgan gave a piano solo as well as an encored recitation. Before a large crowd a new item for the fete took place at 5 p.m. This was a singing contest for school children and in making the introductory remarks Mr. O. H. Bull hoped that in a year's time they would also have prizes for violin and piano playing. After the judging, carried out by Miss Bertha Richens, Mr. J.W. Britton, of Emberton, and Mr. D. Ashton Davies, Mr. F. W. Bull then presented the prizes. The chairs for the contest and concerts had been lent by the Town Hall Company, The Poplars and the Y.M.C.A., and as a result of the three concerts and the singing contest £12 4s 8½d was raised. During the event a stall for the sale of flowers and vegetables attracted splendid business and under the superintendence of Miss A. M.Coales this had been arranged by members of the Congregational Girls' Club, some members of which, including Miss E. Garratt, had sold buttonholes in the town during the morning and in the field in the afternoon. Throughout the occasion, tea and refreshments were available in a large marquee and in view of the rationing the provision of sugar was greatly appreciated by the visitors, as was the consignment of mineral waters and lime juice sent by Mr. F. W. Taylor.

Of the various sideshows, coconut shies and hoop la were a feature and in the Old English Skittle Competition the prize of a pig was won by Mr. J.W. Bocock. The Unionist Club had lent two skittle boards, the Co-op and John Odell lent weighing machines and the swing boats were by courtesy of Mr. C. Sayle. As for two piano organs lent by Mr. Mazzone, one, in the charge of Messrs. S. Brown, A. Hammond, F. Rainbow, and J. Richardson, toured Willen, Woolstone, Woughton, Simpson, Walton, Milton Keynes and Broughton whilst the other, in the charge of the Misses Harris and Mills, went to Wolverton and Stantonbury, around the town, and then to the venue. The total raised by these was £21 16s 5d and in addition Mr. Mazzone made £1 5s for the funds by selling ice cream in the field. In other fund raising ventures Mrs. Pettit, of the Neptune Inn, who was amongst those who helped to store cycles, sold scented cards to the value of £1 9s and she also obtained £2 1s in her collecting box. Having played during the afternoon the Excelsior Silver Band, under Mr. A. Green, performed for dancing in the sports enclosure in the evening, the small charge for which raised £2 4s 11d of the combined grand total of £170 8s 11d. For the safe gathering in of the harvest, special services of thanksgiving were held at St. Luke's Mission Church on Sunday, September 29th 1918, with the offertories being for Northampton Hospital. The premises had been decorated by the lady members of the congregation and on Monday the fruit, vegetables and bread were distributed to the old people in the Almshouses. In October 1918 Superintendent Dibben confirmed to the Council that he would be pleased to find room at the police station for the ambulance and in other matters regarding accommodation at the Swan Hotel, on the instructions of Alfred Bullard, on the evening of Wednesday, October 30th 1918, Wigley, Sons and Gambell auctioned two freehold cottages in Tickford Street. These were numbers 65 and 65a, respectively in the occupation of Mr. T. Meadows and Nurse Eastwood, and having commenced at £300 the bidding increased to £350, at which price they were purchased by Mr. F. W. Bull for Major Doyne Ditmas, of Great Linford.

Convened by the U.D.C., a preliminary meeting was held on Friday evening, February 21st 1919, to consider the question of a permanent memorial for the fallen from the town. Supported by Mr. A. Inwood, of the Foresters' Society, Dr. H. Wickham proposed a Cottage Hospital for minor medical and surgical cases, and in pursuance Dr. Digby White said that the cost of the upkeep would be about £500 p.a. The meeting then resolved that the doctors of the town should confer with Mr. E. Ward, Clerk to the Urban Council, to obtain all the necessary financial information, which would then be put to a public meeting at an early date. Mr. Bullard announced that the Electric Theatre would be available as the venue and thus it was here that with a large attendance the meeting took place on Tuesday evening, March 11th 1919. The general view was that the scheme would involve a heavy expense, which the locality couldn't hope to meet, and 'it was regrettable that the discussion towards the end of the proceedings developed into personalities and into remarks which lacked common sense and were not in good taste.' With no definite figures on finance available the meeting was therefore adjourned for more detailed information, with Mr. Bullard suggesting that the town should be canvassed to see if residents were in favour of a Cottage Hospital, and how much they would be prepared to subscribe annually. Subsequently at a meeting of the War Memorial Committee, held on Friday, May 23rd 1919, Mr. Ward reported on the response from those village authorities who it was thought would like to join. However, only eight replies to the letters had been received and in consequence a decision to abandon the idea was carried by eight votes to four. Two alternatives were suggested. These were a fund to assist both disabled soldiers and the dependants of those who had fallen in the war, and the provision of a motor ambulance for the district, and on the suggestion of the Reverend Gunnery it was agreed that the sponsors should prepare details for a future meeting. On Saturday afternoon, June 28th 1919, just as the townspeople were holding their annual effort for Northampton Hospital, news arrived that the Peace Treaty had been signed. Thus at the fete on Bury Field a telegram announcing the news was handed to Mr. J. Short, chairman of the U.D.C., who from a lorry then announced the welcome news to loud cheering from the large attendance.

BUCKS V.A.D. 48 & TICKFORD ABBEY V.A.D. HOSPITAL

Organised through the Red Cross and the Order of St. John, Voluntary Aid Detachments had been established in 1910 to supplement the established nursing services and by July 1914, 47,000 women had enlisted into the 2,500 V.A.D. branches throughout the country. Primarily from middle class, wealthy backgrounds, with the outbreak of war many more would enlist and speaking in November 1914, Mr. Tonman Mosley, the Chairman of the Bucks Territorial Force Association, made reference to the position regarding those Voluntary Aid Detachments in the county. (The following year he would be sadly bereaved, when on April 20th whilst serving as Adjutant to the 5th Sherwood Foresters his only son, Captain Nicholas Mosley, died from wounds.) Attached to a Central Hospital in Oxford there were five base hospitals in Bucks and these were organised under the Southern Command, the headquarters of which was in Salisbury. Wounded men would be initially sent to the Central Hospital but should this become overcrowded they would be dispersed to the base hospitals. The Voluntary Aid Detachments were expected to keep themselves in readiness for 48 hours notice and any that were mobilised and called up would become military units.

At Tyringham, for the village and the communities in the local district in April 1915, Miss Helen McFerran and Miss Annie Wood established a Voluntary Aid Detachment at their home of Tyringham Cottage, with the former being the Lady Superintendent and Commandant, and the latter the Quartermaster. In fact they were no doubt well qualified for these roles, since for some while they had respectively been the honorary secretary and treasurer of the Tyringham branch of the Gayhurst Habitation of the Primrose League. Amongst the many ladies from the local district who would join the V.A.D. section were Mrs. Trevor and Miss Trevor of Lathbury

Park, Mrs. Bowyer of Weston Manor, Miss Rickards of Filgrave Rectory, Mrs. Lawrence, Mrs. Brett, Mrs. Reeks, Mrs. Clarke, Mrs. Philpott, Mrs. Waine, Miss Church, Miss Burgess, Miss Owen and Mrs. Baldwin of Newport Pagnell. Dr. C. Bailey, of Newport Pagnell, was the surgeon and, having just completed 21 years in the St. John Ambulance Brigade, Mr. William Thomas Dawes Knight, the superintendent of the Olney Ambulance Division, gave his services as instructor for the weekly classes, which were held every Tuesday evening at Emberton. As for Tyringham, Superintendent Knight was not unfamiliar with the village, for he had freely given of his expertise when, around the beginning of 1914, a section of the St. John Ambulance was formed there with Dr. Bailey of Newport Pagnell as the class instructor. In fact at the first examination all the members had gained their St. John certificates, which were presented at a gathering in the village school by Mr. F. Konig, who had not only financed the initial cost of the doctor's lectures but had also kindly equipped the section with a stretcher, bandages and everything else that was needed.

A native of Olney, William was the son of Mr. and Mrs. Thomas Knight, whose family had lived in the town since the 17th century, and he became associated with ambulance work in 1894, by assisting in the formation of the Olney Division. Then on its reformation in 1902 he was appointed sergeant and within a year first officer, to be shortly afterwards made Superintendent. During the early 1900s he formed the local section of the Royal Naval Auxiliary Sick Berth Reserve and when the First World War broke out 11 trained members were mobilised for service. As for the Tyringham V.A.D., by the end of May 1915, all the members had passed the two exams and gained their certificates, and - with these being the necessary qualification for recognition by the War Office and the Red Cross - in consequence Miss Rickards was awaiting orders to take up duty in one of the field hospitals in France. Apart from help to humans, Miss Wood also took a keen and active interest in the work of 'Our Dumb Friends' League' and at Filgrave school on the afternoon of Wednesday, June 9th 1915, many distinguished people gathered for a charming concert that she had arranged in aid of the Blue Cross Fund. A festoon of flags of the Allies occupied a prominent position, and the stage was decorated with a profusion of choice flowering and foliage plants from the Tyringham House conservatories, arranged by Mr. E. Golding, the head gardener. Master David Price and Miss Vera Price sold programmes and Mrs. Slater Harrison, of Shelswell Park, Bicester, received hearty applause for her piano solos which, including compositions by Debussy, were played without any reference to music sheets. Mrs. Troyte, accompanied by her sister, Mrs. Alston, of Harrold Hall, enjoyed much praise for her violin playing, and Mrs. Alston rendered her songs so agreeably that in the second part she had to return and acknowledge a well-deserved encore.

Songs by Miss Marjory Wood, who was locally renowned as a vocalist, were also much appreciated. Being in excellent voice Mr. Ernest Groom responded to a recall by singing 'On the road to Mandalay' and the humorous side of the programme was provided by Mr. Arthur Moss. In fact his 'When father tried to put the twins to bed' caused particular mirth and his encore of 'When I was a single man' convulsed the audience. After the concert the audience were kindly entertained to tea by Miss Wood, with the event raising the useful sum of £12 10s. For the Voluntary Aid Detachment, by courtesy of Miss McFerran and Miss Wood this was again an entertainment on Thursday evening, July 1st 1915, when at Tyringham Cottage, in recognition of his services, a presentation was made to Superintendent Knight. This was a malacca cane, upon the solid silver mount of which were engraved the arms of the Order of St. John and the words; 'Presented to Supt. Knight by the Tyringham V.A.D., 1915, in recognition of his valuable help.' Expressing the thanks of the Voluntary Aid Detachment, Miss McFerran made the presentation and in reply Superintendent Knight said that he hadn't expected any reward, since in the present crisis it was the duty of everyone to do all that they could for their country. After the presentation the members gathered on the lawn, to be given a useful lesson in drill formations and stretcher work.

Again at Tyringham, despite the rain on Saturday, August 7th 1915, a drill for instruction in field work and hospital training was held by Superintendent Knight, with the men of the Olney Division forming a stretcher bearer party. Boy Scouts, labelled with their pretend injuries, played the role of patients and with the men having rendered first aid the patients were brought into a collecting station, to be provided with cups of hot soup by the lady cooks of the V.A.D. At this 'field hospital,' under the superintendent, Miss McFerran, the ladies of the Detachment then redressed the patients injuries under the eye of Dr. C. Bailey, the divisional surgeon, who gave valuable instruction. Before the class dispersed, as the commanding officer Captain Stevens kindly allowed the party to inspect the military convalescent home at Tyringham House, after which the members were conducted around the beautiful gardens by Mr. E. Golding. In October 1915, those ladies from Olney who had been associated with the Tyringham V.A.D. now transferred to a nursing division which, with Mrs. How, of Emberton, as Divisional Superintendent, Miss Fryer as Lady Secretary and Mrs. Clifton as Inspector of Stores, had been formed in the town. As for the members of the Tyringham Voluntary Aid Detachment, after a month's service at the 1st Eastern General Hospital, Cambridge, Edith Bull, the eldest daughter of Mrs. W. Bull, of Ouse Bank, Newport Pagnell, signed on for a further six months. (After three years in the nursing service she would be demobilised in June 1919, with her name brought to the notice of the Secretary of State for War for her valuable nursing services during the conflict. The outbreak of World War Two would then find her in India performing valuable work in the Wardlaw Thompson Hospital at Chikka Ballapena, Mysore State, from where on the completion of her six months work she would leave on Monday, August 27th 1939, for a C.M.S. Hospital in Kashmir, prior to returning to Newport Pagnell.)

Inscription on the grave of Edith Bull in Newport Pagnell churchyard.

At the quarterly meeting of the Berks and Bucks Needlework Guild, held at Gayhurst on Monday, April 9th 1917, Mrs. Carlile, the president, said she had received an appeal from Miss McFerran, who was to be the commandant of the soon to be established Auxiliary Hospital at Tickford Abbey. This was for sheets, blankets and pillow slips and stating these requirements Mrs. Carlile had consequently sent a notice to each Working Party and Vice President. In fact it was hoped that the hospital would be opened at the beginning of May 1917, to be staffed by the Tyringham Voluntary Aid Detachment Bucks 48. In fact towards raising finance for the Equipment Fund, and also for the North Bucks War Hospital Depot (situated at 36, High Street, Newport Pagnell), a concert had been held at the Electric Theatre, Newport Pagnell, on the evening of Sunday April 1st 1917. Under the auspices of the P.S.A. Brotherhood £10 4s 6d was raised and also during the month on the evening of Wednesday 18th members of the Newport Pagnell Parish Church Girls' Club, in the formation and development of which Mrs. Mitchison, the wife of the Reverend R. Mitchison, had taken an active role, provided one of the best entertainments to have ever been held at the Electric Theatre. This was to raise money to purchase equipment for the hospital and proved so popular that many people had to be turned away. The girls had been instructed by Mr. C. Kenneth Garratt, who acted as the accompanist, and, with members of the Royal Engineers performing the role of concert stewards, the programme opened with the descriptive tableau

'Spring & Winter,' which, being rapturously received, had to be repeated. The song 'England,' by Cecil R. Line, aroused immense patriotism and the enthusiasm was intense as a party of young ladies marched onto the stage carrying flags of the United Kingdom. Towards the close of the song the lady performers then grouped themselves on the stage, to be greeted by loud cheering as Union Jacks dropped from the 'flies.'

As one of the performers Miss Bertha Richens, from Emberton, sang beautifully and following many other excellent performances and sketches the programme concluded with a tableau of 'Empire,' representing England, Scotland, Ireland, Wales and the overseas dominions. The girls taking part wore the costumes of the country, or dependency, which they represented and then onto the stage came khaki clad soldiers from New Zealand and South Africa. Towards the close of one item Miss Elsie Brooks appeared and unfurled the Stars and Stripes, whereupon the enthusiasm of the audience knew no bounds. Over £40 would be raised by the impressive event with all the expenses, amounting to about £10, being defrayed by the Reverend and Mrs. Mitchison. Organised by the ladies' committee of the Newport Pagnell Red Cross, an 'American Party' was held on Saturday, April 21st 1917, to raise money for their 'Newport Pagnell Ward' at the forthcoming hospital. During the afternoon many guests attended the Girls' Council School, where on arrival they handed over gifts of a value each of not less than 2s 6d. Afternoon tea was then handed round with the occasion additionally enhanced by songs from Miss Webster and also Sapper Cahill, of the Royal Engineers. They were accompanied by Mrs. P. Gambell, an accomplished pianist and also performing was Miss Gillespie, who performed a violin solo accompanied by her mother. The gifts were subsequently sold to the guests for funds and then in the evening there was a large attendance at the school from 6.30 p.m. to 8.30 p.m., with, being expected 'to buy one of the treasures brought in by the rest,' each guest bringing a parcel to the value of 6d.

Appearing in fancy dress the girls of the school gave a charming concert under the personal direction of Miss James, the popular headmistress, and during the event Winnie Rout, one of the most promising of the musical scholars, sang the 'Slumber Song' beautifully, to which she played her own accompaniment. She also accompanied the Japanese dance and also the 'Fairy Ring' dance, for which performance the girls, appearing in Greek costume, were emphatically encored. For selecting a parcel, to obviate confusion the guests were marshalled into line by Miss James and at a given signal marched up in 'a frontal attack' on the items, some of which were extremely good value. With each guest having selected a parcel Mr. A. Bullard, who had given his services as auctioneer, then sold those gifts which had been left over from the afternoon, or had been given up for resale. On the afternoon of Saturday, May 12th 1917, the V.A.D. Auxiliary Hospital at Tickford Abbey was officially opened by the Right Honourable the Marquis of Lincolnshire, K.G., the Lord Lieutenant of Bucks, and present was Colonel Ranking, the Administrator of the 3rd Southern General Hospital, Oxford, to which it was affiliated. Miss McFerran was the Lady Commandant with Miss Wood as Quartermaster, and under a fully qualified Matron the Abbey would accommodate wounded soldiers who had reached the convalescent stage. All being skilled in their duties the 51 ladies of the V.A.D. Bucks 48, which had been organised at Tyringham in April 1915, would tend the patients and as well as the provision of staff quarters and domestic offices there were facilities for the recreation and amusement of the patients. Through the generosity and kindness of the town's residents, and also those of the district, the premises had been equipped on the most modern scientific principles and accommodating a total of 40 beds the nine wards were the Bucks V.A.D. 48 (equipped by members of that organisation), Newport Pagnell (by the Newport Pagnell Red Cross Committee), Newport Pagnell (by the Parish Church Girls' Club), Wolverton (by the Wolverton Red Cross Committee), Village (five beds given by Emberton, Great Linford, North Crawley, Haversham, Broughton), a ward equipped by Mrs. Gunnery, Mrs. Symonds, and Miss Allfrey (Newport Pagnell), a ward equipped by the Misses Taylor (Lovat Bank, Newport Pagnell), a ward equipped by Stantonbury Mothers' Meeting, Stantonbury Girls' Club and Stantonbury Infants' School, and a ward equipped by the teaching staffs of the Wolverton Secondary, Stantonbury Council (Girls) and Old Bradwell Schools.

> **V. A. D. Auxiliary Hospital,**
> **TICKFORD ABBEY, NEWPORT PAGNELL.**
>
> **Opening Ceremony**
> BY THE
> **MARQUIS OF LINCOLNSHIRE, K.G.,**
> ON
> **Saturday, May 12, 1917,**
> At 3 p.m.
>
> *Admission, from Three to Four o'clock 1s. Four to Six 6d.*

Included in the V.A.D. Bucks 48 nursing staff were many ladies from the local district with those on duty in the week preceding the official opening being Mrs. Trevor of Lathbury Park, Mrs. St. John Mildmay, Old Wolverton, Miss W. Butler, Newport Pagnell, Miss Walpole Simmons, Newport Pagnell, Mrs. Williams, Emberton, Miss Walker, Stoke Goldington, Mrs. E. Baldwin, Miss Weeks, Miss Powell, Newport Pagnell, Miss Jordan, Wolverton and Mrs. Wain (cook) of Tyringham Cottage. Others who would undertake alternate duty would be Miss D. Saunders, Mrs. J. Dove, Miss D. Jarvis, Miss Bessie Brandon, Miss Annie Brandon, (North Crawley), Miss

Allfrey, Miss Owen, Miss Burgess, (Newport Pagnell,) Miss I. Walker, (Stoke Goldington), Miss Winifred Clarke, (North Crawley), Miss Daphne Trevor, (Lathbury Park) and Mrs. Starling, (Moulsoe). However, some members were presently unable to give their services and ten others were serving abroad or in hospitals in various parts of the country. For the opening ceremony, despite the prospect of rain the weather remained fine throughout the afternoon and it was shortly before 3 p.m. that on his approach to the Abbey the Marquis passed along the drive to the main entrance, between the lines of a guard of honour. This comprised the Special Constables as well as three troops of Boy Scouts who, including the buglers, numbered 80 of all ranks and came from Wolverton, Stony Stratford and Lathbury. All were under the command of Scoutmaster Percy Sharpe and Assistant Scoutmasters Ricketts and Chapman, whilst in command of the 36 Special Constables were Captain C. Wilford and Lieutenant F. O.Butler. Immediately in front of the hospital the V.A.D. nurses were lined up in two ranks and behind them waited a large number of the public from Newport Pagnell and the neighbouring towns and villages. Upon his arrival the Marquis was introduced by Mr. Carlile to Miss McFerran, Miss Wood and other leading officers of the hospital. As for others who were taking part these included, clad in his official robes, the Vicar of Newport Pagnell, the Reverend F. Gunnery, Dr. H. Wickham and Mr. Joseph Short, J.P., who, wearing the King Edward Medal presented to him on his retirement from the postal service, was the chairman of the Newport Pagnell Urban District Council.

Having offered prayers for God's blessing on the hospital the Vicar then said that as the deputy president for Newport Pagnell on the County Red Cross and St. John Ambulance Council he had the honour to ask the Marquis to open the premises. For all their skill in bringing the premises to its state of readiness he next expressed gratitude to the Commandant, Miss McFerran, and the Quartermaster, Miss Wood, and also to Mrs. Knapp for her able financial management of the institution. Yet there was still a need for money and, with the wish for a continuing support from the people in the district, it was hoped that during the afternoon contributions might be made. Expressing his regret that his wife, Lady Carrington, who was President of the Red Cross for the county, was unable to attend, the Marquis in reply congratulated everyone involved with the hospital and spoke of the county's noble response to its duties in war, the heroic stand of the soldiers and the voluntary work of the women of Bucks. With the hospital then declared open the Red Cross flag was hoisted on the flagpole in front of the building and, on behalf of the town and neighbourhood, Mr. Short said that he had been asked to propose a vote of thanks to the Marquis, as his first public duty since being appointed chairman of the Council. On behalf of the hospital staff Dr. H. Wickham seconded the proposition and affirmed that he and the nursing staff would do all that they could to restore the convalescent patients to health. Cheers for the Marquis were then given, followed by the National Anthem played by the Newport Pagnell Band. Miss McFerran then presented the Marquis to each member of the V.A.D. nursing staff, after which he and those who had been present at the opening ceremony were given the opportunity to view the premises.

The uniform of a Red Cross nurse.

In consequence the Marquis expressed high praise for the hospital and, personally thanking them for coming out on parade, inspected the Special Constables. Passing down the lines he was then introduced to Scoutmaster Percy Sharp through whom he complimented the Boy Scouts on "a very good turn out." Superintendent E. Dibben was in charge of a posse of police on special duty in the grounds and under Lance Corporal G. Keay, junior Royal Engineers Smith, Flitcroft, Varley, Cresswell, O'Donnell, Chilford, Hoyland, Batchelor, Larry, Saunders and Renton undertook duty at various points in the immediate vicinity of the hospital.

£17 8s 6d would be taken at the gate in entrance monies and the occasion would benefit the hospital funds by £20 10s, which included the money collected in the boxes. On Thursday, May 17th 1917, the first convoy of wounded soldiers then arrived at the hospital followed by another ten on Friday, May 18th 1917. Gifts of vegetables, eggs, cake and walking sticks were always welcome and in addition during May 1917, 201 items would be sent to the hospital from the Newport Pagnell

Group of the Berks and Bucks Needlework Guild. From other sources, up to June 30th 1918, the following goods would be received: Mr. Boswell, four armchairs and four screens, Mrs. Boswell, games for garden, the Reverend Canon Harnett, a piano, Miss French, three small tables, Miss Jordan, two trays, Mrs. Knapp, mats and clothes baskets, 'Granny,' (Stantonbury) kettle holders, the Misses Taylor, 12 bath towels and four cushions, Miss Allfrey two tables, Miss Shakeshaft, puzzles, Mr. Bullard, burgundy and champagne, Mrs. Douglas Fraser four pairs pyjamas, Mr. Line 20 walking sticks, Mrs. St. John Mildmay garden chairs and various gifts, the children of Emberton school comfort bags, spills, and kettle holders, the children of Wolverton Secondary School covers for milk and Newport Pagnell Girls' Club five cushions and 'Narcissus,' stout and burgundy. Gifts were also received from the North Bucks War Hospital Supply Depot, The Bletchley War Rooms, The Order of St. John and the Red Cross, Queen Mary's Needlework Guild, The Stantonbury Red Cross Work Party, The Wolverton Congregational Red Cross Work Party, The Wimbledon War Hospital Supply Depot, The Woman's War Dressing Association and The Soldiers' and Sailors' Smokes. Amongst the many who had sent vegetables were Mrs. Dove, Mrs. Vaughan Harley, Mrs. Sams and Lady Farrar (who had also sent fruit) and whilst many other people had sent occasional quantities the children of Little Linford and Haversham were sending a weekly supply of eggs.

Those persons supplying books and magazines included Mrs. Carlile

Looking smart in their uniforms, these Scouts are members of their Rifle Club.

and also Mrs. Trevor, who further supplied butter and a weekly quota of cakes. Thanks were additionally due to Mr. N. Cole for his weekly delivery of buns. As for the patients' entertainment, the first concert at the hospital took place on Saturday, May 26th 1917, with Mr. C. Kenneth Garratt as the honorary secretary for the entertainment and recreation of the wounded soldiers. As an accomplished artiste Miss Bertha Richens performed many songs, as also the Reverend Father Walker, of Wolverton, whilst Miss Mabel Wilford caused much laughter with her recitations. Lance Corporal George Keay gave a clever demonstration of club swinging and also performing was an instrumental quartet from Wolverton. Then, consisting of about 11 performers, on the evening of Saturday, June 9th 1917, the Pom Pom Concert Party from Wolverton gave a well received concert, with Mr. W. Branton as the stage manager. Yet apart from entertainments staged on the premises the patients also enjoyed local outings with, through the invitation of Sir Herbert and Lady Leon, one occasion being on the afternoon of Tuesday, June 12th 1917, at Bletchley Park. Albeit in some cases with the aid of crutches, here a party of 20 firstly visited the private gardens and lawns, with one surprise being the absence of flowers, since all the beds in the gardens and grounds had been planted with vegetables. Also visited were the conservatories, vineries and greenhouses, of which, with girl labour now almost exclusively employed, was included the famous orchid house. Of other activities a punt on the lake proved popular and towards the end of the visit afternoon tea was enjoyed in the large dining room of the mansion. Mrs. P. C. Lovett had taken charge of a musical and social entertainment and before the soldiers left they were each presented with cigarettes by Lady Leon.

A meeting of the management committee of the hospital was held on the afternoon of Saturday, June 16th 1917. Mr. J. Boswell, of Crawley Grange, presided and among those present were Miss McFerran, the Commandant, Miss Wood, Quartermaster, Dr. H. Wickham, the Reverend F. Gunnery, Mrs. Knapp and Mr. J. Short who, at the unanimous request of the meeting, agreed to be the honorary secretary. Amongst others, delegates from the local Red Cross organisation and other associations were appointed to serve on the committee, with Mrs. Knapp and Mr. F. Littleboy appointed as the honorary treasurers. The Commandant then gave an interesting report on the work of the hospital since its recent opening, saying that 25 beds had been occupied for three weeks and five of the patients had left. Therefore 20 beds were presently occupied. In other matters the Quartermaster reported that £56 was due from the War Office for maintenance. The subscriptions received had amounted to £407 1s 9d and after payments of £334 5s 1½d this left a balance of £72 16s 7½d. During the month, as the Commandant of the hospital Miss McFerran would express thanks for the many gifts received, which included vegetables from Mrs. Dove, of Tyringham Cottage, Mrs. Williams, of Emberton, and Mrs. Trevor, of Lathbury Park and for visitors the hospital would be open on Thursdays and Saturdays between 2 p.m. and 5 p.m. During June 1917, the Reverend Gunnery wrote to the Council asking if the town could provide a few public seats where the convalescents could sit and read. Presently there was no place to rest except on window sills and low walls and since other towns had provided seats he thought that the Council at Newport Pagnell had the power to do the same.

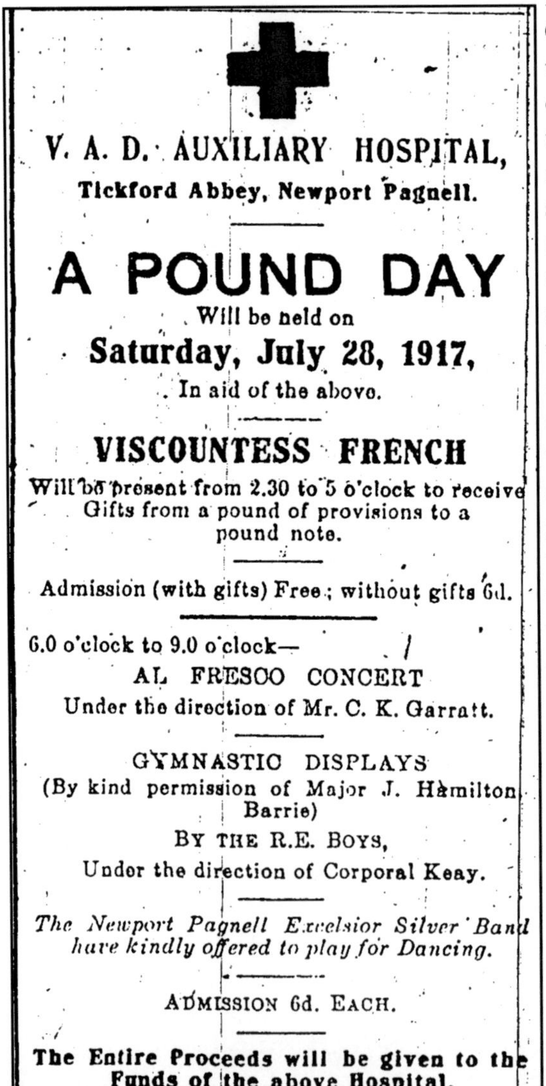

In reply the chairman of the Council said he thought two seats had been placed outside the entrance to the market, whilst another member said they had been sent by Mrs. Taylor. Another member had noticed men outside the Abbey grounds sitting on the pavement and window sills and in further discussion another member said that, since some patients were not able to go far, there should be one or two seats just outside the hospital. As for another contribution it was remarked, "I don't think you can expect these men to go in Bury Field. There was not much to look at there, although it was very nice." It was decided to leave the matter in the hands of the chairman and a Council member. However, the town would come to benefit by a number of seats placed through the kind offices of Miss A. M.Coales. Voluntary kitchen workers were now urgently needed at the hospital but plenty of produce was being regularly received and in July 1917, the Commandant thanked the many donors. Eggs were being sent from the C. of E. Schools, Stony Stratford, whilst of other sources vegetables and fruit had been received from Tyringham Cottage, for where the need for a 'good, single handed gardener. No glass. Good 5 bed roomed cottage. Wages 30s. Apply Miss Wood,' had been recently advertised.

For the benefit of the hospital on Saturday, July 28th 1917, Lady French attended a 'Pound Day.' Appeals had been made to the residents in the town and the district for gifts - from a pound note to a pound of provisions - and the weight of the parcels handed in to Lady French would total a pleasing 530 lbs. There were also cheques and notes to the value of £24 and the proceeds from all sources, excepting the value of the parcels but including competitions, entertainments and teas, would reach £67 10s. Being met by Miss McFerran and Miss Wood, in ideal summer weather Lady French had arrived shortly after 2.30 p.m. with her sister, Mrs. Thornton, of Bedford, Mrs. Mark Poore and Mr. and Mrs. J. Knapp, of Linford Hall. On entering the grounds the party was met by a smart guard of honour of the Bucks Volunteers from the Newport Pagnell Company, which, under the command of 2nd Lieutenant H. Middleton, paraded with arms at the salute. Nearby stood a section of the Boy Scouts and after being introduced to the hospital's nursing staff Lady French was later shown over the premises, for which she expressed her admiration. Amongst the large gathering in the grounds were many local notables, including Major W. Trevor, Mrs. Vaughan Harley, Mr. J. Boswell and Mrs. Savory, and it was whilst seated at a table under the shade of the large pine tree that Lady French received the gifts from the visitors. Early in the proceedings Private J. Ross, of the Cameron Highlanders, had presented her with a bouquet of sweet peas, whilst similar gifts of appreciation were received by Miss McFerran from Private J. Hatch, of the Loyal North Lancs. Regiment, Miss Wood, from Private Renham, R.F.A., and the Matron from Private H. Chalton, of the Liverpool Scottish. In the charge of Miss Mabel Holland, Miss Sharp and Private Ross, amongst the afternoon's events were guessing competitions and hoop la (lent by Mr. J. Short) as well as clock golf, superintended by Nurse Coales, and, chaperoned by Nurse Mildmay, Aunt Sally. Flowers were sold by Nurse Walker and Nurse Robinson and, with the tickets for tea being issued by Mrs. A. J. Simpson, teas and refreshments were served by Nurses Allfrey, Williams, Brandon, Jarvis, Simmons, Butler, Powell and Jordan, plus Cooks Warren and Priddle. As for the Boy Scouts, they had charge of the croquet and additionally assisted Private Renham with the bowls.

Of the other competitions Sergeant Flat, Royal Engineers, correctly guessed how many times an egg cup could be filled from a bottle of lime juice. As a further contribution towards the hospital's funds, in August 1917, Lieutenant Middleton and the N.C.O.s and men of C Company, 3rd Battalion Bucks Volunteers, sent £5 to the hospital. On the instructions of Miss McFerran and Miss Wood, who were now leaving the district, on Thursday, September 20th 1917, a sale of antique and modern furniture took place at Tyringham Cottage. This was conducted by Messrs. Wigley Sons and Gambell and amongst the lots was an Axminster carpet, £5, a brass bedstead and mattress, £6, a Chippendale chest, £13, a portable hen house, £2 5s, and a mowing machine, £5. In fact Miss McFerran now announced that the hospital was to close on March 25th 1918, when the tenancy expired, and, with the opening scheduled for April 15th 1918, it was proposed that a transfer should be made to Westbury House. This, free of charge, would be let to the management until the end of the year and then for a year by the owner, Mr. Shaw, of Haversham, but for the meanwhile the Consulting Surgeon for the Auxiliary Hospitals in Southern Command, Colonel Mayo Robson, R.A.M.C., paid a visit to the hospital on August 30th 1917, and finding all in order fully commended all the aspects. In September 1917, the hospital had the need for three or four extra Night Orderlies and also required were men who were willing to help by sitting up for one night in fourteen from 10 p.m. to 6 a.m. and thus relieving the nurses. Persons interested were to contact the Reverend Gunnery at the Vicarage, Newport Pagnell. In fact if any of the applicants had to go to work, it could be arranged for them to leave earlier.

After a stay of two years in the town the Signal Section of the Royal Engineers would leave Newport Pagnell for new quarters at Bedford on Sunday, 28th October 1917. They had willingly assisted in many of the town's social functions and war charities, and to show the town's appreciation Mr. C. Kenneth Garratt organised a farewell concert at the Electric Theatre on Monday evening, October 15th 1917, with the soldiers and nurses from the hospital amongst the attendance. Then on Saturday evening, November 3rd a concert was given at the hospital by the Wolverton Pom Pom Concert Party, with Miss Connie Banton as the accompanist. By the beginning of November 1917, for the past two months the hospital had been averaging over 30 patients a week. Many gifts from local people were being regularly received, including a weekly supply of eggs from the children of Little Linford, and 12 boys from the town had also been helping by collecting 12s on Guy Fawkes Day. The money would be spent on buying tobacco for the men. On Wednesday, November 7th 1917, the first soldier patient from Newport Pagnell was admitted to the hospital. Having worked in the office of the Bucks Standard newspaper before joining up he was Private David Hackett, of the 4th Bedfords, whose father lived at an address in the High Street. Also in November 1917, certificates and badges for the voluntary work performed during the past six months at the hospital laundry, accommodated at Abbey End School, Newport Pagnell, were awarded to Mrs. L. Eaton (who had entire charge of the laundry) and also the Mrs. Waine, Watts, Mawby, Griffin, Smith, Stowe, Eaton, junior, Flavel and Brown, all of whom were registered under the North Bucks War Hospital Supply Depot No 1531.

His wife being responsible for the organisation the Reverend Gunnery had kindly allowed the use of the premises, where among the people voluntarily spending many hours each week were Mrs. Harrison, Mrs. Holland, Mrs.

Tickford Abbey was used as a hospital during World War I. It is now a care home.

Glidewell and Mrs. Markham. Through the kindness of Mr. C. Kenneth Garratt, on the evening of Saturday, November 17th 1917, the patients at the hospital were entertained to a concert of vocal and instrumental music. Throughout the performance there were frequent encores and as one of the highlights Mr. Garratt performed the piano solo, 'Ah! I have sighed.' Mr. O Critchard contributed 'Roses of Picardy' and Miss Eva Garratt played the violin solo 'Air de Ballet.' The event then concluded with the National Anthem but - again arranged by Mr. Garratt - the hospital patients enjoyed further entertainment on the evening of Saturday, December 1st 1917, when a whist drive took place. About 25 ladies attended and, with several members of staff acting as partners for the men, 16 tables were occupied and 16 games played. The patients had subscribed amongst themselves for three handsome prizes for the ladies, with the soldiers' prizes provided by the visitors. First prize for the ladies was won by Mrs. C. K. Garratt and for the soldiers by Private Hurst. Afterwards the tables were cleared away and Mr. Garratt played the piano for a short programme of dances. The evening then concluded with Auld Lang Syne and the National Anthem, followed by hearty cheers for the Matron, Mr. Garratt and the visitors.

On the evening of Wednesday, December 5th 1917, many residents from the town and district attended a concert given at the hospital by a small company of professionals from London who, by arrangement with the headquarters of the Red Cross Society, were making a tour of the military hospitals. During the afternoon the party had given an entertainment at the V.A.D. Hospital at Winslow but due to the limited railway services their arrival at Newport Pagnell would be subject to a short delay. However, during the interval the audience was entertained with piano selections by Lance Corporal Semple, who was a patient at the hospital, and songs were performed by the Quartermaster, Miss Wood, and also Miss K. Powell and Mr. Cecil R. Line. Christmas Day 1917, saw the hospital decorated with flags, holly, evergreens etc. and a sumptuous dinner was provided of turkey, plum pudding, fruit and other seasonal fare. The vegetables were gifts from the children of Wolverton and Emberton, the plum puddings had been presented by a member of the nursing staff, and the fruit was from the Reverend R. and Mrs. Mitchison. Of Gayhurst House, Mr. and Mrs. W. Carlile had presented a splendid Christmas tree from which in the afternoon each patient received a gift, with both Mr. and Mrs. W. Carlile being present at the occasion accompanied by Mrs. Slater Harrison and Miss Eda Wake. Every member of staff received a calendar and at 5.30 p.m. an enjoyable entertainment was given by Captain Stephen Trevor and Miss Daphne Trevor, of Lathbury Park. In addition two of the patients contributed to the programme - Sergeant Scobell giving a recitation and Lance Corporal Semple performing piano selections. Then at 10 p.m., just as the patients were retiring to rest in their wards the strains of a well known song, 'The end of a perfect day,' could faintly be heard, played on the piano in the entrance hall by Lance Corporal Semple.

Concluding the entertainments for the year, on Thursday, December 27th 1917, 37 patients from the hospital were entertained by Lady Farrar at Chicheley Hall, where, following an excellent tea, games and other amusements were much enjoyed. Of the many people who had kindly given Christmas gifts to the hospital the Reverend U. J. Easson had donated £1 from the Village Children's Concert at Chicheley, cakes had been donated by, amongst others, Mrs. Trevor, Mrs. Boswell had given eggs, Mrs. Harley, vegetables, and Mrs. Boswell, Nurse Wright and Mrs. Symons had contributed crackers. New Year's Day 1918, proved to be very pleasant for the convalescent soldiers. A bran pie was prepared and through the auspices of Miss McFerran and Miss Wood each patient received a suitable present. Tea was enjoyed at 4 p.m. and afterwards came an entertainment by Miss Gillespie and Mrs. Hillyard, who played guitar selections. Both ladies then joined in an amusing dialogue entitled 'Geese.' Another amusing sketch was entitled 'A brown paper parcel,' performed by the Misses Ella and I. Allfrey. On Saturday, January 5th 1918, the patients were entertained for the fifth time by a party from Wolverton, who were conveyed to and from the hospital by motor bus. However, the patients sometimes created their own amusement for, being surrounded by a 12 foot high wall and featuring an inscribed 25 foot high stone obelisk, within the Abbey grounds lay the private burial vault of the Hooton family. In the roof of this some of the soldiers had made a large hole and so exposed to view, at least by the light of a torch, the coffins which were ranged around the circular confines.

With the continuing need for fresh produce at the hospital, on Saturday, January 26th 1918, the First Wolverton Troop of Boy Scouts, under Acting Scoutmaster C. Axby and Senior Patrol Leader J. Carter, toured the Wolverton allotments to collect vegetables. Filling two handcarts the produce was then conveyed to the hospital on Sunday morning in a float, which had been kindly lent by Mr. E. Norman of Stacey Hill Farm. In fact in some quarters there seemed to be an opinion that the convalescents were being too well fed, in response to which the Medical Officer in charge, Dr. H. Wickham, wrote an open letter to the local press;

> "Dear Sir.
>
> It has come to the knowledge of those responsible for the management of the Auxiliary Hospital, Tickford Abbey, Newport Pagnell, that there is a feeling abroad that the patients are being fed extravagantly. They are well fed, and I know that they appreciate the fact, but from the first the Quartermaster has kept within the allowance laid down by the army authorities, both as regards quantity and cost, in spite of the difficulties of the times.
>
> The diet sheets are checked every month by the Administrator from Oxford, and Mr. T.S. Mason has devoted considerable time to auditing the accounts every week.
>
> Since they have been fortunate enough to obtain the services of the present cook waste in the kitchen has been reduced to the vanishing point.
>
> I do not believe that anyone would be mean enough to grudge these men all they need to restore them to health, even though we have to deny ourselves many of the things we have been used to, for, after all,

what is our sacrifice compared with theirs?"

Organised by Mr. A. Bullard, a concert in aid of funds for the hospital took place at the Electric Theatre on Wednesday, January 30th 1918. As part of a tour of military hospitals the artistes, a company of London professionals, had visited Tickford Abbey the previous year, and the programme commenced with a piano solo by Miss Adeline Jones who provided the accompaniment throughout. Miss Norah Newport, soprano, 'was heard to distinct advantage' in Arditi's 'Il Bacio,' and for an encore she gave 'Down Vauxhall way.' Miss Dora Delise, mezzo soprano, made a most successful first appearance in the district and received several encores, whilst Miss Phyllis Allan, who on the previous Saturday had given a highly successful recital at Steinway Hall, London, was encored several times for her brilliant performances. In fine baritone voice Leader D. Ashton Davies (of the Y.M.C.A. Hut at Newport Pagnell) rendered 'The Windmill.' This he encored with 'The Glory of the Sea' and his later performance was also encored. Also greatly appreciated was John E Nester, 'The modern jester.' He performed funny stories, recitations, jokes and impersonations and on his second appearance included a clever demonstration of 'chapeau-graphy,' with all his performances receiving loud applause and double encores. On Saturday evening, February 9th the patients enjoyed a whist drive arranged by Mr. C. K. Garratt. A party of about 24 persons arrived to play with the prizes, subscribed for by the visitors, being won by Private Grieg, Gunner Davenport and Private McMillan. Again organised by Mr. C. K. Garratt, a concert on the premises was given to the patients on the evening of Saturday, February 23rd.

Songs were by Mr. D. Ashton Davies, Miss Bertha Richens, Sid Cook, Mr. C. K. Garratt and, performing 'The Gay Cavalier,' Mr. C.R. Line. Sapper Fuller played violin solos and Mr. Garratt accompanied on the piano. With the hospital having been scheduled for closure on March 25th 1918, this being the date that the lease ran out, at Tickford Abbey Mr. Alfred Bullard, 'auctioneer etc.,' of Newport Pagnell, offered the remainder of the furniture for sale at the premises on the afternoon of Thursday, May 8th 1918. This was per the instructions of General Butler and in the presence of a large attendance the items included a billiard table and fittings by Thurston, £55, a grandfather clock, £16, a lawn mower, £5 15s, and a book case, £14 10s. Also included was a 20h.p Panhard motor lorry and a 16h.p Clement car, both to be sold without reserve. Then at the Hanover Square Estate Room, on Tuesday, May 28th 1918, at 2.30 p.m. Tickford Abbey, 'a freehold residential estate, including a picturesque old fashioned stone built residence (14 bed and dressing rooms)', plus a finely timbered park and pleasure grounds, garage and stabling, and farm and several cottages, the whole being an extent of 340 acres,' was to be sold by auction either as a whole or in two lots However, it seems that this was postponed until further notice and Mr. Bullard became the owner. The premises then continued to accommodate the hospital, where the clothes posts and lines had been wilfully damaged on May 17th by two boys aged 7 and 13. When summoned at the Divisional Petty Sessions on Wednesday, May 29th 1918, they pleaded guilty, the damage being proved by the Quartermaster, Miss Wood. The offenders were bound over for good behaviour for six months for £5.

Organised by the Committee of the P.S.A. Brotherhood, and with the piano accompaniments played by Mr. C. K. Garratt and Mrs. P. C. Gambell, an open air sacred concert was given in the grounds of the hospital on Sunday evening, June 2nd 1918. Dr. H.T. Wickham presided and apologised for the absence of the Commandant, Miss McFerran, who being indisposed had gone away for a few days' rest. That afternoon Miss Beatrice Ashton L.R.A.M., contralto soloist at the City Temple, London, had been paying her first visit to the town and her performance of 'Sink Red Sun' received an encore. Miss Margaret Webster, soprano, was also encored and Corporal Fuller displayed his excellence on the violin. Private Turnbull, tenor, was in excellent voice and Mr. A. Bullard, bass, was greatly appreciated for 'When the Ebb-tide Flows.' The artistes were equally applauded in the second part and at the close after the National Anthem Dr. Wickham proposed a vote of thanks to the performers, which was heartily accorded. A visit to the hospital was made on Wednesday, June 26th 1918, by Major General Sir Francis Treherne, the Inspector General of the Southern Command. Accompanied by Sir Frederick Bradshaw, the Hospital Consulting Physician, and Lieutenant Colonel Rankin, Administrator of the 3rd Southern General Hospital, Oxford, after his inspection he congratulated the Commandant, Miss McFerran, on the efficiency of the staff and the general management of the hospital. In connection with a march of women war workers to Buckingham Palace, scheduled to take place on Saturday, June 29th 1918, Nurses A. Walker and A. Whiting were chosen to be the representatives of the local Volunteer Aid Detachment, Bucks 48, with the purpose of the event being to present an address of loyalty to the King and Queen on the occasion of their approaching silver wedding, on July 6th.

In July 1918, a list was published in the local press of all those persons Miss McFerran wished to thank for providing support to the hospital, from the opening 14 months ago up to June 30th 1918. Especial thanks were due to Mr. T. Mason, who spent many hours each month keeping the hospital accounts, Mr. L Salmons and the proprietors of the Electric Theatre, Mrs. Wickham, who arranged daily papers to be sent to the patients, and Mr. Cecil R. Line, for allowing a fortnightly notice of gift acknowledgments to be printed in the Bucks Standard. Boy Scouts had given help whenever needed, Mr. C. K. Garratt had arranged concerts and whist drives during the winter and Mr. A. Bullard had arranged three concerts for hospital funds. Especial thanks were also expressed to the V.A.D. members of Bucks 48 for their loyal service and help during the year, namely the Misses Allfrey, W. Butler, D. Trevor, K. Powell, A. Walker, D. Jordan, E. Hulton Sams, A. Whiting, L. Lambert, E. Brandon and Mrs. St. John Mildmay. Also to those workers who had given their services when able; these being the Misses Burgess, Owen, D. Odell, B. Brandon, M. Smith and Mrs. Dove and Mrs. Agnew. Also to those who had helped in nursing, in the kitchen and the pantry; ie. the Misses I. Allfrey, D. Fairey, D. Peabody, J. Mead, Robinson, Gillespie, Phyllis Taylor and Mrs. Mead and Mrs. Adams. The Mesdames Glanley, Cooke Yarborough, Maugham, Gray and the Misses Nunn and Brandon had mended the patients' clothes and others who had greatly assisted the hospital were the Night Orderlies, who since the opening were the Reverends F. Gunnery and R. Mitchison, and Messrs. A. Simpson, W.Ellis, A. Fairweather, C. Wilford, C.R. Line, W. Line, C. K. Garratt, F. Bell, A. Phillips, D. Reynolds, E. Glanley, T. Williams, A. Lott, J. West, A. Higgins, H. Brown, W. Carr, J. Thickpenny, J. Clare, R. Odell, W. Willis, L. Rose, H. Thickpenny, W. Cole, J. Bolton, F. Foster, C. Ratcliffe, J. Sargent and A. Balls.

With the United States now participating in the war it seems that at least one of their soldiers made the acquaintance of Newport Pagnell, for having been lost on Sunday, August 4th 1918, between Tickford Abbey Hospital and Bury Field, a black leather pocket book containing six or seven £1 Treasury Notes, plus cheques payable to C. H. O'Rourke, was the property of a wounded American soldier. A reward was advertised for anyone returning these belongings to Newport Pagnell police station. At the meeting of the U.D.C. at the Council Chamber, High Street, on Tuesday evening, September 3rd 1918, a letter was read from Lieutenant Mittell complaining that the seats for the wounded soldiers at the entrance to Tickford Abbey park only attracted children. As a result several panes of glass had been broken in the cottage that he occupied just outside the gates and since children and older girls congregated in this area it was decided to remove the seats. Also it had been decided to close the hospital from August 30th to September 20th 1918, and in consequence a farewell concert for the patients took place on the evening of Thursday, August 29th 1918. The excellent programme featured contributions by Mrs. P. C. Gambell and her sister, Miss M. Webster, the Misses Reading and Sheppeard (members of the Land Army working in the district), Sapper Bentley, a Canadian stationed with the Royal Engineers at Newport Pagnell Wireless Depot, Mr. and Mrs.

A. Bullard and Mr. C.R. Line. Also Corporals Hodge and Norris and Private Dixon, who were patients at the premises. All the acts received enthusiastic applause and many encores, and, saying that they were all sorry to leave, at the conclusion Corporal Hodge proposed a hearty vote of thanks to the visitors for their contributions, as well as to the Commandant, Quartermaster, Sister and Nurses. As for Dr. Wickham, he received three extra cheers. Having performed at this farewell concert, following the reopening of the hospital it was therefore appropriate that one of the performers at a concert on Thursday, October 3rd 1918, was Private Dixon, who played the piano.

During October a large supply of vegetables was received at the hospital from the girls of the Council School, Wolverton, and in addition the Reverend Guest had sent the Harvest Festival offerings from Stantonbury. Nevertheless, at the end of the month Miss McFerran earnestly appealed for more vegetables, which due to the reduced meat ration were becoming more necessary than ever. With the hospital full 'every cabbage, or greens of any description, will be most gratefully received and acknowledged,' and they could also be left at the 'Red Cross Depot,' 36, High Street, Newport Pagnell. In addition to a shortage of vegetables Miss McFerran now had other worries for in early November 1918, at the Law Courts, in London, in a case which lasted five days Mr. F.A. Konig, of Tyringham House, brought a claim against her and Miss Wood as his late tenants at Tyringham Cottage. This was for dilapidations at the property and breach of contract although the claimed amount had been reduced from £365 to £333 2s 2d. Judgement was deferred for a week but was then given with costs in favour of the defendants, who afforded Mr. Konig the £185 which they had already paid into court. Yet such matters paled into insignificance when news arrived that an Armistice had been signed and in consequence on Sunday, November 17th a special thanksgiving service was held at Newport Pagnell Parish Church. The staff and wounded soldiers from the hospital were amongst those attending and after the service the convalescent patients proudly joined a procession of Royal Engineers, Volunteers and Special Constables which, having been formed on North Square, marched behind the town band to Market Hill where they were dismissed. However, despite the end of the hostilities there was still a continuing need for produce at the hospital, especially potatoes. The stocks had been completely exhausted but at least 'smokes' were being sent by Miss Ward from the Inland Revenue Office of McCorquodales, at Wolverton, and various monetary gifts had also been made. In December Miss McFerran thanked all the people who had continued their support including Mrs. Trevor for a weekly supply of cakes, Mr. N. Cole for a weekly supply of buns, Mrs. Vaughan Harley, Mrs. Boswell and Mrs. Taylor for a weekly supply of vegetables and potatoes and the Girls' School, Wolverton, via Miss Townsend, for a sack of potatoes.

Since the war was now at an end a rumour began that the patients were leaving the hospital but this proved incorrect and on Wednesday, December 18th 1918, the funds came to benefit by £3, as the proceeds from the raffle of a doll. This had been appropriately dressed in a St. John's V.A.D. uniform by Miss A. Cattall, of Walton Manor, and the lucky winner was Mrs. Ditmas, of Great Linford. Then on Monday evening, December 23rd the Parish Church carol singers visited the hospital and on the following evening Captain Stephen Trevor and party gave a special entertainment. In fact the convalescent patients would spend Christmas 1918, at the hospital and during the evening of Christmas Day a fancy dress dance was greatly enjoyed by the patients and staff. On the Friday a conjuror, provided by Mrs. Boswell of Crawley Grange, gave a fine show and on Sunday evening, December 29th after the service at the Congregational Church members of the choir paid a visit to the hospital to sing a selection of carols. As for the many people who had sent seasonal gifts, Miss A.E. Hatch, the late Matron, forwarded £1. On Tuesday evening, January 14th 1919, by invitation the wounded soldiers from the hospital contributed to a concert for the inmates at the Workhouse with one of their number, Sergeant Brazier, in the chair. Of the performances Private Brennand sang 'When you are a long, long way from home,' Sapper Nichols sang 'Old folks at home' and afterwards the hospital contingent were handed cigars by the Master of the Workhouse. Then on Saturday, January 18th 1919, it was their turn to be entertained, when Mrs. Power and 24 ladies of the Lavender Day Committee came over from Wolverton for a whist drive. Then on the following Saturday, Miss Ward and Miss Wilks, of the Inland Revenue Office at McCorquodale's Printing Works brought a party of 20 for another whist drive and also during the month the patients were entertained to a concert and supper at the Workhouse organised by Mr. Bullard. Additionally the Y.M.C.A. invited the patients and staff to their weekly concerts. As for the directors of the Electric Theatre they 'franked' (sic) the men to all the entertainments there and on Thursday, January 23rd 1919, Lady Farrar invited 25 of the patients to tea and games at Chicheley Hall.

Being much enjoyed by the patients and staff, on Thursday, February 27th 1919, a farewell social evening and whist drive took place at the hospital. For the whist drive the prizes had been given by the Commandant and Quartermaster, Miss McFerran and Miss Wood, who during the evening presented the Medical Officer, Dr. Wickham, with a silver tea caddy engraved; 'Presented to the Commandant and Quartermaster by the medical officers and staff of the Auxiliary Hospital, March 1919.' The doctor was also presented with a handsome leather blotter and case of books by Nurses

Worker, Mumby and McDonald, the Quartermaster and Commandant and also Sister Wigley, who herself was presented on behalf of the hospital staff with a set of silver brushes. The proceedings continued until long after midnight, to finally conclude with the singing of 'Auld Lang Syne' and 'God Save the King.' Then on Saturday, March 1st 1919, the Bucks County Director of the Order of St. John and the Red Cross visited the hospital and after his inspection thanked all the staff, saying that a total of 413 men had passed through the facility. It would then be on Saturday, March 8th 1919, that the hospital finally closed and on March 22nd a sale of beds and general effects took place on the premises. Subsequently in June 1919, for their wartime work at the hospital Voluntary Aid Certificates of Merit from the Bucks Territorial Force Association were awarded to Mrs. Fitzgeorge, Mrs. M. Wain, Miss E. Brandon, Miss D. Jordan, Miss W.E. Butler, Miss K.P. Powell, Miss A. Whiting and Miss E. Allfrey, and the month would also witness another recognition when the former Commandant, Miss Helen McFerran, received this letter from the Right Honourable Evelyn Cecil, M.P., Secretary General of the Order of the Hospital of St. John of Jerusalem in England:

> "I desire to convey to you, and through you to the officers and members of your detachment, the cordial appreciation and thanks of the Chapter-General of the Order of St. John of Jerusalem in England for the admirable services rendered to the sick and wounded of His Majesty's Forces during the War. You yourself, and the officers and members have, by your self-denial, zeal, and devotion to duties so willingly and efficiently undertaken, earned high praise; and in no uncertain way you have fulfilled the mottoes of the Order, 'Pro Fide' and 'Pro Utilitate Hominum.'"

It seems that having purchased the Abbey some time in 1918, Mr. Alfred Bullard had sold it shortly afterwards, with six acres of garden, to Mr. William Ward. As the International Secretary of the Brotherhood Movement, in December 1918, he had been in Lille distributing food and clothing supplies but on Thursday, July 24th 1919, Tickford Abbey was dedicated to the Brotherhood Cause forever by the Reverend Dr. John Clifford (the National Brotherhood President) as the freewill offering of Mr. William Ward. It was the intention of the Abbey Committee of the National Brotherhood Council to not only use the premises as a Holiday Home but to also organise a Speakers' School, where the young men of the Brotherhood could be trained to become efficient platform workers. In fact the premises would serve as a religious and social centre for conferences, a summer school and a fellowship home and here any members could spend a week at an all inclusive charge of £2 10s. With the closure of the hospital, as a balance of the funds in July 1919, Miss McFerran sent £200 to the County

Director Red Cross. In view of the excellent work performed during the war by the county's V.A.D.s, in November 1919, an important and well attended meeting of Deputy Presidents of the County Branch, the British Red Cross Society and St. John, and Commandants of the V.A.D. Establishments in the county was held at 53, Princes Gate, London, the intention being to hear from the new County Director, Colonel Bull, V.D., K.H.S., D.L., how he proposed to establish a post war organisation by which the V.A.D. work of Bucks could be kept at the fore. Introducing Colonel Bull, Lady Lincolnshire briefly alluded to his wartime work, with Mr. Eyre, the honorary treasurer and secretary, then reporting on the conference which had taken place at St. James' Palace on the 23rd of the month.

Comprised of the representatives of the Joint Societies of the Counties of Great Britain, this had been to consider the future organisation of V.A.D. work and having revealed the details of the scheme Colonel Bull then invited the Deputy Presidents to transfer themselves to his staff. Also, he was anxious for fully certificated V.A.D. Nurses to offer their services to the Village and District Nurses and after some discussion and questions the following resolution was carried:

'That this meeting of Deputy Presidents B.R.C.S. and St. John, and Commandants of V.A.D. Establishments in the County of Bucks, being desirous of continuing their voluntary work in Peace time, and preserving the continuity between the War and Peace organisation in the county, agrees to place their services at the disposal of the County Director for such work as may hereafter be decided will best promote the improvement of health, the prevention of disease, and the mitigation of suffering throughout the county.' (In fact the V.A.D. Bucks 48 lapsed after the war but was later revived and with 12 mobile and six 'demobile' members was inspected by the War Office in October 1930, together with members of the V.A.D .from Olney and Buckingham.) In September 1920, a meeting of the Hospital Committee of the late V.A.D. Auxiliary Hospital at Tickford Abbey was held in the Urban Council Chamber, Newport Pagnell with those present being Mr. Boswell, chairman, Dr. Wickham, Miss Wood, Miss McFerran and Mr. T. Sibley Mason, the honorary accountant. Letters of apology were received from Mrs. Knapp and the Reverend Gunnery. The accounts were put to the meeting and passed and the chairman then proposed a vote of thanks to Miss McFerran and Miss Wood. This was for everything they had done and it was also decided at the meeting to hand the balance of £36 3s 0½d with the thanks of the committee to Mr. Sibley Mason, in recognition of his services. As for those who had performed nursing duties at the hospital during the war, as a masseuse Amy Holland, whose only son lost a leg in the conflict, had often been in demand there and at other institutions. She was the wife of Albert Holland, a foreman carriage finisher at Wolverton Works, of 32, Wolverton Road, Stony Stratford, but tragically she died one Friday evening in January 1925, aged 47. Having felt ill earlier in the day she retired to bed and her death was caused by a burst blood vessel. Some of those who had performed wartime nursing duties at the hospital would later return to the profession including, after the death of her husband in 1928, Mrs. Ada Buckingham. Born at Yarnton, Oxfordshire, she had come to Newport Pagnell shortly after her marriage to Henry Buckingham, who was employed as a wheelwright at Salmons and Sons, and aged 83 she would die after an illness of some seven weeks on Sunday, March 30th 1952, at 172, Tickford Street, Newport Pagnell.

THE ROYAL ENGINEERS HOSPITAL

32, High Street, now T.T. Photo. On December 4th 1916 the premises opened as a hospital for the Royal Engineers in the town, dealing with minor cases.

With nearly 800 men billeted in Newport Pagnell, the Medical Officer, Dr. Digby White, found there was a need for a facility in the town to treat those men whose condition did not warrant a transfer to Aylesbury Hospital. Therefore with the approval of Major Hamilton Barrie, the commanding officer of the Royal Engineers in the town, for minor cases two wards with the provision of 12 beds (lent by Mrs. Trevor, Mrs. Mead, Mrs. Symons, Mrs. Fairweather, Miss F. Taylor and Miss Smith) were opened at 32, High Street, on December 4th 1916. Four ladies - Mrs. Digby White, Miss Smith, Miss Walpole Simmons and Miss L. Gillespie - would voluntarily look after the

GREAT LINFORD.

A Whist Drive and Danc

Will be held in the Schoolrooms,

ON THURSDAY, JANUARY 3, 1918,

Commencing at 7 p.m.

PRIZES WILL BE GIVEN.

Proceeds will be given to the R.E. Hospit 32, High Street, Newport Pagnell.

Tickets 2s. each, which may be obtained fro Mrs. Hedges, Mrs. Powell, and Mr. Whittake Linford, and from Mrs. C. Wilford and Mi Powell, Newport Pagnell.

Light Refreshments at moderate charges.

patients and since the facility was self supporting there would be no need for funds. However, gifts of eggs, books and magazines etc. would be welcomed. In the following months the wards were full and after a brief closure the hospital again opened on Wednesday, December 5th 1917, now classed as an official centre under Eastern Command. Organised by Mr. C. K. Garratt, a concert in aid of the hospital was given at the Electric Theatre on Monday evening, March 11th 1918. The venue was packed and Mr. Garratt apologised at the outset for the absence of George Baker, the eminent baritone 'of Queen's Hall Concerts etc.' Due to an outbreak of measles, at the military camp where he was stationed, he was unable to attend and Frederick Taylor, a baritone of the Royal Choral Society, London, appeared instead.

As a pupil of Mr. Garratt, Miss Olive Sarrington, of Stoke Goldington, opened the programme with a piano solo by Chopin, with her tutor playing the accompaniments throughout the concert. Frederick Taylor's first song was a Russian composition, 'When the King Went Forth to War,' which, causing rapturous applause, was encored with 'King Charles.' In the second half he then performed Elgar's 'Fringes of the Fleet,' encored with 'The Long Shore.' Paying a return visit to the town Miss Beatrice Walley, 'the popular North country soprano from Crewe,' sang 'The Pipes of Pan are Calling,' encored with 'Coming Home,' and later favoured with 'The Dancing Lesson,' encored with 'The Songs my Mother Sang' and 'The Moorish Maid.' As her initial contribution Miss Bertha Richens performed the aria 'Softly awakes my heart,' from 'Samson and Delilah, and as her second number gave 'The Home Flag,' encored with 'Soldier, I wish you well.' The violin obligato had been provided by Sapper Fuller, who for his performance played a number of solos, all of which were encored. Father Walker, bass, of Wolverton, was encored for 'The Ballad Monger' and the amusing selections of Ben Lawes kept the audience convulsed with laughter. Programmes had been sold at the concert by the Misses Ella Goodman, Marjorie Line, Ivy Sully and Eileen Tandy, whilst before the performance programmes had been sold around the town by the senior girls of the Council Schools. The seating arrangements had been carried out by Royal Engineers, under the superintendence of Colour Sergeant Major Harrod. As the troops were shortly going into camp the hospital closed on April 6th 1918, 251 men having passed through the wards since the re-opening in December 1917.

Dr. Harry Townshend Wickham

Born in 1866, a son of the Reverend Latham Wickham, of Twyford School, Hants., Harry Townshend Wickham graduated as a Bachelor of Medicine at Edinburgh in 1888, taking his M.D. degree six years later. In

1890 he came to Newport Pagnell as assistant to Dr. H. C. Rogers and later practising on his own would then go into partnership with Dr. Bailey and Dr. Morris. He married in 1895 and becoming much involved in public life would occupy positions to include that of public vaccinator under the Board of Guardians and district medical officer of health and medical officer to the Post Office and the Northern Division of the Bucks Constabulary. Also for several years he would be a member of the board of Council School managers and as a staunch churchman was a valued friend of the British and Foreign Bible Society. His daughter, Dorothy Elaine Wickham, was juvenile secretary of the Newport Pagnell Habitation of the Primrose League, which with the outbreak of war refrained from all political work to instead concentrate on charitable causes. These included the St. John Ambulance and the Red Cross and in other medical matters Dorothy began organising a special course of nursing lectures for the women of Newport Pagnell. Her father and Dr. C. Bailey were to give their services as the class instructors with persons interested to contact Miss Wickham at The Close, Newport Pagnell. Towards raising funds for the plight of Belgian refugees, an enthusiastic public meeting was held in the Electric Theatre on Sunday evening, September 6th 1914. Among the many notables on the platform was Dr. Wickham whilst as for Dorothy on Wednesday, December 15th 1915, at an agricultural jumble sale she presented a bouquet of red and white carnations and ferns to Lady Farrar, who had opened the event.

In late January 1916 Dr. C. Bailey wrote to the Council saying that he had joined the R.A.M.C. He therefore asked for leave of absence for the duration of the war and with this readily granted Dr. Wickham was appointed to act in his place. Two grand concerts in aid of the Serbian Relief

Fund were held in the Electric Theatre on Tuesday, February 1st 1916. At the crowded afternoon performance among the programme sellers was Dorothy, but it was the medical skills of her father that were urgently needed on Friday, May 12th 1916, in consequence of an Army biplane having landed in Bury Field. On his way to dinner, Mr. F. W. Saunders had taken a work colleague in the sidecar of his motorcycle to see the aircraft but on the return journey a dog suddenly ran into their machine. However, Mr. Saunders' injuries were swiftly treated by Dr. Wickham who subsequently took his patient to the man's home in Wolverton Road. Then on Saturday, November 4th 1916, Dr. Wickham attended another accident when, at the junction of Hill Street and Station Road, a horse pulling a cart was suddenly startled by some pigs and bolting down Station Road collided violently with a traction engine. Having been aboard the cart a boy was taken unconscious to a nearby house from where, after attention by Dr. Wickham, he was conveyed to his home at Moulsoe. On a central site in the High Street on January 20th 1917, a Y.M.C.A. Hut was opened. Miss Dorothy Wickham would be one of the volunteers at the canteen although not on Tuesday, March 27th 1917, when in the afternoon in a full choral service at the parish church she married Lieutenant Temple George Hillyard, of the Devon Regiment. He was the only son of the Reverend A. Hillyard and Mrs. Hillyard, of The Parsonage, Upton Pyne, Exeter, and the large attendance included a number of soldiers.

With the opening of the Tickford Abbey V.A.D. Hospital, Dr. Wickham would act as the Medical Officer and on behalf of the hospital staff affirmed that he and the nursing staff would do all that they could to restore the convalescent patients to health. As for Mrs. Wickham she would arrange for daily papers to be sent to the patients. In other matters, on the evening of Wednesday, July 25th 1917, a meeting was held regarding the formation of a Town Institute and as an interested party Dr. Wickham would be amongst those present. During the late afternoon of Saturday, August 18th 1917, there was great excitement when an aeroplane crashed at Lathbury. Dr. Wickham was quickly summoned by telephone and with the assistance of Nurse Dorothy Odell attended to the injured pilot who, following the arrival of an ambulance from Newport Pagnell Fire Station, was taken to the Newport Pagnell home of his father in law. Then on the evening of Thursday, February 21st 1918, Mr. J.J. Marshall required Dr. Wickham's medical expertise when, tripping over a bicycle at the Unionist Club, he fractured his knee cap. However, there was a more serious misfortune the following month when on Thursday, March 21st 1918, at Salmons motor carriage works Percy Taylor, the younger son of the late Mr. W. Taylor and Mrs. Taylor, of 42, High Street, was struck on the head and knocked unconscious by a piece of timber flung from a circular saw. Diagnosing concussion Dr.

Wickham was summoned and although the patient was later transferred to Northampton Hospital he died after an operation for a fractured skull. On Sunday evening, June 2nd 1918, Dr. Wickham presided at an open air sacred concert given in the grounds of Tickford Abbey hospital for the benefit of the patients. However, in some quarters there seemed to be an opinion that the convalescents were being too well fed, to which as the Medical Officer in charge Dr. Wickham wrote an open letter to the local press;

> "Dear Sir. It has come to the knowledge of those responsible for the management of the Auxiliary Hospital, Tickford Abbey, Newport Pagnell, that there is a feeling abroad that the patients are being fed extravagantly. They are well fed, and I know that they appreciate the fact, but from the first the Quartermaster has kept within the allowance laid down by the army authorities, both as regards quantity and cost, in spite of the difficulties of the times. The diet sheets are checked every month by the Administrator from Oxford, and Mr. T.S. Mason has devoted considerable time to auditing the accounts every week. Since they have been fortunate enough to obtain the services of the present cook waste in the kitchen has been reduced to the vanishing point. I do not believe that anyone would be mean enough to grudge these men all they need to restore them to health, even though we have to deny ourselves many of the things we have been used to, for, after all, what is our sacrifice compared with theirs?"

Apart from the medical welfare of the convalescents, Dr. Wickham also dealt with the everyday matters of the local population, of which one of the more unusual was that in July 1918 when a 21 year old married woman, from Moulsoe, pleaded not guilty to a charge brought under D.O.R.A. Regulation 40D. This concerned a member of the Forces who was suffering from venereal disease but on examining the woman at her home he found absolutely no sign of the alleged complaint and the case was ultimately dismissed. It had now been decided to close the hospital at Tickford from August 30th to September 20th 1918, and at the consequent farewell concert Dr. Wickham received three extra cheers, in appreciation of his medical services There was even more cheering in November with the signing of the Armistice and Dr. Wickham was amongst those attending the special thanksgiving services on Sunday, November 17th 1918. In the aftermath of the war, at a meeting convened by the U.D.C. on Friday evening, February 21st 1919, the question of a permanent memorial for the fallen from the town was considered and, supported by Mr. A. Inwood, of the Foresters' Society, Dr. Wickham proposed a Cottage Hospital for minor medical and surgical cases. However, the expense was consequently be found to be too great.

Much enjoyed by the patients and staff, on Thursday, February 27th 1919, a farewell social evening and whist drive took place at the Tickford Abbey hospital, where during the evening Miss Wood presented Dr. Wickham, as the Medical Officer, with a silver tea caddy. This was engraved: 'Presented to the Commandant and Quartermaster by the medical officers and staff of the Auxiliary Hospital, March 1919,' and he also received a handsome leather blotter and case of books from Nurses Worker, Mumby and McDonald, and also the Quartermaster, Commandant and Sister Wigley. Medical experience gained during the war would be put to good use by several local people when, in June 1922, the Newport Pagnell Orthopaedic Clinic was founded by Miss G. Savory, of Emberton. Dr. Wickham was appointed as the chairman but in 1929 he relinquished all his medical appointments upon his impending retirement. In fact it would be at the meeting of the Newport Pagnell Board of Guardians that on the morning of Wednesday, March 27th 1929, he tendered his resignation and in tribute the chairman, George Tayler, said that by his kindness and sympathy he had endeared himself to everyone, remarks which were readily affirmed by Mrs. O. H. Bull. Prior to his departure a town's testimonial fund was opened by the U.D.C. and in the Vicarage garden on July 9th 1929, a well deserved recognition was made with a cash gift of £95. Then in mid July Dr. Wickham and his wife left to live at Bubnell Hall, Baslow, Derbyshire. There they would be near their only child, Dorothy, the wife of Mr. Temple George Hillyard, who was the principal of St. Anson's School at Bakewell, and it would be at Bubnell that Dr. Wickham died on Monday, August 1st 1931, having suffered a relapse after a serious operation. He was 65. The funeral took place at St. Anne's Church, Baslow, on the Thursday morning and of the floral tributes many were sent from people in the Newport Pagnell district, including from the Reverend Easson and family and a sheaf from Miss Dorothy Odell. Dr. Wickham had been a Freemason and Worshipful Master of SS Peter & Paul Craft and Mark Lodges and St. George's (Wolverton) Royal Arch Chapter, and to his memory there was also a floral tribute with a Masonic emblem from the brethren of SS Peter and Paul Lodge No. 1410 and SS Peter and Paul Mark Lodge No. 163. Among the mourners was Mr. Albert Edward Goodman. For the whole of his time in Newport Pagnell he had been a servant of Dr. Wickham after whose departure he then worked for a time at the North Bucks Supply Stores for Messrs. Hayllar and Sons, with his son, George, being in business in the town as a hairdresser and tobacconist. Having had to keep to his bed for the previous three months, Albert died on September 20th 1939 at The Rockery, Lakes Lane, having been greatly affected by the death of his wife two years earlier. A native of Newport Pagnell he had lived in the town all his life and as a great lover of dogs was well known as a breeder of spaniels. As for other interests he was an excellent gardener and also practised poultry keeping.

In the year after Dr. Wickham's death, a former resident of Newport Pagnell suggested that a memorial to him should be made, writing; 'I noticed in a Sussex village churchyard an inscribed memorial stone seat, placed in a sunny position and commanding a fine view. The thought struck me how suitable some such erection would be to commemorate Dr. Wickham's life of service, in that it would accord with his own views.'

NATIONAL EGG COLLECTION

As the local representative for the town, as a result of her appeal for gifts of eggs for wounded soldiers during the last week of August 1915 Miss Allfrey, of Bury Lawn, sent a consignment of 444 to the National Egg Collection, whose headquarters were situated in Fleet Street, London. Then in 1916 the last week of February was declared Children's Week in connection with the scheme, and to the Council Schools on Wednesday, February 23rd the pupils brought 405 eggs. These comprised 180 from the girls, 145 from the boys, and 80 from the infants, and all were handed over to Miss Allfrey for despatch to the headquarters. Between May and late December 1916 the girls of the Council Schools would collect 1,217 eggs for the cause, and with the eggs to be taken to the school a special Christmas effort was made on Wednesday, December 20th 1916. Organised by Miss Allfrey and Mr. C. K. Garratt, a sacred concert for the National Egg Collection was given on Sunday evening, January 28th 1917 at the Electric Theatre. The scheduled artistes included Miss Gwendoline Farrar, L.R.A.M., cellist, Miss Muriel Farrar, Miss Hilda Mynard, of Emberton, Sapper Victor Earl, Sapper J.P. Kellet, and Lance Corporal Jerry O'Connor. However, on the night Miss Muriel Farrar was indisposed, as well as Lance Corporal O'Connor, although despite having met with an accident earlier that day, necessitating two stitches for a cut above his right eye, Sapper Victor Earl still managed to perform his songs. Making her first public appearance since her recent success at the Royal Academy of Music, Miss Gwendoline Farrar was rapturously encored for her contribution, and during an interval Mrs. Wellesley Taylor, of Sherington Manor, thanked the audience for their attendance, and said that one million eggs a week were needed for the big hospitals in England and overseas. Men from the Royal Engineers acted as stewards, and as programme sellers Miss James, the headmistress of the Girls' School, had organised a party from among the older girls, who were each allocated certain districts of the town to canvass. Just over £7 was raised, and on Wednesday, April 4th 1917, on the eve of breaking up for the Easter holidays, the girls of the Council School contributed 119 eggs (and 2s 6d in cash) to the National Egg Collection. Having been requested to arrange for a collection in the town of 500 pennies a week, in November 1917 Miss Allfrey asked the Parish Church Girls' Club to undertake this task, and in consequence the honorary secretary, Mrs. Mitchison, divided the town into districts, with several girls having volunteered to make the collections each week. In fact by late December 1917 the appeal would exceed the amount required for the four collections so far. A final effort for the National Egg Collection was then made in the town on Saturday, March 1st 1919. Organised by Miss Allfrey this was a flag day which raised £15 13s 0½d, whilst as for the town's contribution during the whole of the period 16, 873 eggs had been collected, with in addition over £96 having been subscribed for the purchase of eggs.

The collection in Newport Pagnell during the scheme;

Newport Pagnell - 3,777 eggs, money subscribed £6 6s 11½d.
Girls' Council School - 2,013 eggs, cash £9 17s 1½d.
Boys' Council School - 202 eggs, cash 8s 3d.
Infant School - 16 eggs, cash 10s.
Flag Day - Cash £15 13s 0½d.
Girls' Club Collection - Cash £55 17s 11½d.

NEWPORT PAGNELL BREWERY

The Newport Pagnell Brewery had been started in the 1780s and with the associated public houses was purchased in 1875 by Messrs. Allfrey and Lovell, becoming in 1899 a limited company known as the Newport Pagnell Brewery Co. The Newport Pagnell partner was Mr. Francis Allfrey, who as a young man had joined a brewery firm in Monmouthshire, and when the Lovell family ceased their interest in the business he, being resident at Lovat Bank, carried on the enterprise. On coming to Newport Pagnell he held the rank of Major in the Volunteer Corps and his eldest son Frank, who for many years would be in partnership with his father, also had military associations, having been educated at Sandhurst. Thus following the outbreak of war, having taken a commissioned rank he went as a colonel to France and subsequently saw active service in the fighting around Arras. Many employees of the brewery would also see active service and following the declaration of war the chief clerk, Thomas Attkins, having passed the medical and other tests enlisted in the Bucks Territorials. As a member of the Newport Pagnell Rifle Club he was an excellent shot but the perils of active service were brought home when in November 1914 news arrived that, having been seriously wounded in an engagement near Ypres, Corporal F. Burgess, the brother of Arthur Burgess, manager of the Newport Pagnell branch of the Aylesbury Brewery Company, was in hospital in North Staffordshire Infirmary, Hartshill, Stoke on Trent. Two employees of the Newport Pagnell Brewery had been on active service with the Navy when the war began. They were Robert Moulton and Sidney Hall, with the latter undergoing annual training with the Special Naval Reserve. However, with the sinking of the 'Good Hope' he became an early casualty, leaving a widow and two small daughters in the town. Thus for their benefit, and also that of the family of Able Seaman Fred French, who had been a member of the crew, the Newport Pagnell Autos Football Club and the local P.S.A. Brotherhood staged a sacred concert at the Electric Theatre on Sunday

evening, December 6th 1914.

During the morning of Monday, February 1st 1915, a tragic accident occurred after Job Griffin, the driver, and Henry Stanton, the drayman, left the Newport Pagnell Brewery in a steam lorry loaded with barrels of beer. These were for delivery in New Bradwell, Wolverton and Stony Stratford from where, with the outward journey accomplished, the two employees left to return home around 1.30 p.m., reaching Wolverton just as the railway workers were going back after their midday meal. For conveying railway carriages from one department to another the road at the entrance to the offices of the Works spanned a wide track of metals and as the lorry reached the summit of the slight rise the back wheels skidded on the greasy surface sending the vehicle into the corrugated iron fence to the right, before crashing 20 feet to land upside down on the railway below. With both men buried beneath the wreckage the steam crane was hurriedly fetched to raise the lorry and extricate the men but Mr. Stanton was already dead, and, although conscious, Mr. Griffin was in great pain, having sustained a compound fracture of the thigh, a compound fracture of one arm and the other arm broken. Yet there were no internal or head injuries and after treatment by two doctors he was taken to Northampton Hospital. Aged 52, Mr. Stanton had been employed by the brewery for 21 years and left a widow, four daughters and also three sons, one of whom was serving in France with the Royal Irish Dragoon Guards with another in training with the 6th Oxon and Bucks Light Infantry. Single, a native of Woburn Sands, Mr. Griffin was an experienced and careful driver and before the war had been employed by Mr. F. Allfrey, the head of the firm, as his chauffeur. Aged 35 he lived at 73, Tickford Street, and although at the outbreak of war he had volunteered for military service, in the mechanical transport section of the Army Service Corps, an injury to his thigh in an accident three years before had prevented this. He died in Northampton hospital on Friday evening, February 5th 1915, with an inquest into the accident held at the North Western Hotel, Wolverton. Then on Thursday morning, July 29th 1915, there was another sad fatality, when shortly after 9 a.m. as part of his duties William Sawbridge, a married man with two daughters, was preparing to empty the refuse from the brewery copper work. From an upper story of the building this was tipped some 20 feet into the yard below through a trap door but through this, despite having performed the task many times, William fell, heavily striking the base of his skull on the sill of a window immediately beneath. Practically unconscious he landed on a heap of ashes in the yard at the entrance to the engine house, where he was picked up by his fellow workmen. After his injuries had been bound by Dr. C. Bailey he was conveyed on the ambulance litter to his home at Hill View, Wolverton

Road, but died at 2 p.m. An employee of the firm for 24 years his duties had been to look after the boilers and engines and at the time of the accident one of his sons was also working at the brewery.

As for his eldest son, having enlisted in the Royal Engineers he was in hospital from wounds received in action in Flanders. William's funeral took place in the local cemetery on Saturday, July 31st 1915, with Mr. J. Day, the manager, and several workmates among the mourners. Under the Workmen's Compensation Act, from the award paid into the court, of £214 17s 2d, in September Mrs. Sawbridge applied at Newport Pagnell County Court to determine the amount to be set aside for her dependent children. She also asked to be paid the sum of £14 17s 2d to meet immediate needs and in consequence the judge allowed £15 to each of the two dependent children, granted her request for immediate needs and made an order for her to receive 10s a week from the compensation fund. By November 1915 every eligible man employed by the Newport Pagnell Brewery Company had enlisted, which perhaps explained why on three Wednesdays at the end of the month and the beginning of December drovers, having brought cattle into the town, saw fit to pitch the young stock in front of the brewery for several hours on the footpath, blocking the thoroughfare and 'leaving behind them reminiscences which were odorous and not pleasant.' The cattle were apparently from Ireland and the Council decreed that if there was a reoccurrence a heavy toll would be imposed. Due to the shortage of manpower, in April 1916 there was an immediate need for two men to work at the brewery. This was followed the next month by the requirement for a labourer at 23s per week and a strong lad for cask scrubbing in July. 'Good wages' were offered, whilst in November women aged over 22 were needed. With Salmons having given up their largest building to the Royal Engineers as a mess room, by March 1917 the brewery had placed at the firm's disposal their principal malting in the High Street, which, with suitable adaptations, provided accommodation for the motor chassis as they arrived from the works. The brewery premises were also being used by the Royal Engineers as accommodation for instructional purposes and here, whilst about his usual duties as an instructor in the workshops, Lance Corporal F. Davies suddenly died on Wednesday afternoon, January 9th 1918. When taken ill he was given immediate assistance and conveyed outside the building but while sitting on a chair he collapsed and despite the swift arrival of Dr. Digby White was unable to be revived. Aged 40 the deceased had lived at Cardiff and left a widow and two children. Apart from the use by the Royal Engineers, on Friday, June 21st 1918, for the Newport Pagnell and District Committee the brewery would also accommodate a stall for the sale of surplus fruit and vegetables. This would be open every Friday and purchasers were requested to bring their own receptacles, due to a shortage of paper. As for those donating produce they would receive the full retail price less a commission of 2d in the 1s, for working expenses.

After the war, in 1919 Charles Wells and Co. Ltd., of Bedford, took over the business and although the premises were closed some of the tied houses were retained. These included the nearby Dolphin, aptly named since the son of the landlady in 1915, Engine Room Artificer Reginald Levin, had served aboard H.M.S. Albion in the Dardanelles. For the manufacture and supply of farm machinery, after the war Mr. W. J. Cooper would occupy the brewery premises, with which he had first become acquainted in 1915 when sent there as a motorcycle despatch rider with the Royal Engineers. As for 'The Brewery House,' occupying a central and detached position in the High Street, adjoining the former brewery premises, on the instructions of Messrs. Charles Wells Ltd. this, excepting the large garden at the back, was auctioned in 1928 by Messrs. Stafford, Rogers and A.W. Merry Ltd. It had been formerly occupied by Mr. J.A. Price and was purchased for £820 by Mr. J.J. (Johnny) Wagstaff, a local antique dealer.

NEWPORT PAGNELL UNION WORKHOUSE

The Workhouse. In later years the premises became a hospital catering mainly for the elderly. It closed in 1992 and the building was demolished in August 1994.

Having begun as a porter at Woolwich, and subsequently holding similar positions at Aylesbury and Headington, William Chapman became assistant master of the Abingdon Union, and in October 1901 he and his wife secured the appointment of Master and Matron of the Newport Pagnell Union Workhouse, built in 1836. Here at the outbreak of the war 100 persons were accommodated, and for their benefit the Newport Pagnell manager of the Aylesbury Brewery Company had supplied books and magazines. However, there had been no applications for the position of Nurse, and so it had been decided to seek the consent of the Local Government Board to employ a person who was not certificated. As for the position of Assistant Nurse there had been two applicants. They were Florence Leeks, aged 21, a domestic servant of North Crawley, and Eva Cook, aged 23, a machinist of Newport Pagnell, and both would be asked to attend the next meeting of the Committee. On the afternoon of Sunday, August 23rd 1914 the local members of the P.S.A. Brotherhood held an open air service in the grounds of the Workhouse which was much appreciated by the inmates, as also the books and magazines which had been sent for their enjoyment by Dr. Buxton of Fenny Stratford. Meanwhile an advert would be placed for a Nurse at £40 p.a., although regarding the two applicants for Assistant Nurse whilst both had been interviewed no appointment was yet made, as the post of Nurse was still vacant. Towards the end of August 1914 a letter from Mr. C.

Glanville, Clerk to the Board of Guardians, called attention to the nuisance caused adjoining the Workhouse by rubbish being tipped into a field. He asked if it could be disinfected since the flies were a great nuisance, especially in the infirmary, but the Surveyor to the Council said that the rubbish was levelled down by the workmen after tipping, and that the problem was due to it being turned over afterwards by people picking in it. By mid September 1914 42 applications for the position of Nurse at the Workhouse had been received, and from this number the following candidates would be asked to attend for interview on the 30th of the month; Miss Eleanor Glynn, of East Grinstead, Miss Sarah Foat, of Hanwell, and Miss Lavinia Wilson, of Birmingham.

ASSISTANT NURSE WANTED at the Newport Pagnell Union Workhouse Infirmary. Salary £20 per annum with board, lodging and washing in the Workhouse.—Application on or before Monday, 17th August, ON FORMS TO BE OBTAINED FROM

C. H. GLANVILLE,
Clerk to the Guardians.

60, High Street,
Newport Pagnell,
22nd July, 1914.

As with many men from the town, following the outbreak of war the Master of the Workhouse, Mr. Chapman, had enrolled as a special constable, and he would employ both of his duties on September 16th 1914, when at 4 p.m. a 27 year old man from Chester called on him at the Workhouse, and asked for assistance. Enlisting in the Cheshire Regiment, he had joined Kitchener's Army on September 1st, but had deserted on the following Saturday. When questioned by Mr. Chapman he admitted that he was a deserter, and said "Me and a pal left together. We have been sleeping under hayricks." Being very cold and hungry the man was given some tea by Mr. Chapman and then temporarily put in the cells, prior to being taken to the police station. In court the following day the man denied having asked to be put up for four nights, and said that he had told the porter he wanted to obtain some money to get back to barracks. Superintendent Pearce then asked that the man be sent back on a warrant, unaccompanied, to his depot at Chester, and with the Bench agreeing to this the chairman said "Remember this, that at this time every young man is wanted to serve his country, and the Bench hope you will go and be a useful soldier in Lord Kitchener's Army." Having been a founder member of the town's club, during his leisure time Mr. Chapman, who was also a prominent Freemason, enjoyed playing bowls, and on the afternoon of Thursday, October 15th 1914 beat Mr. G. Chasty by 15 shots to nine. This was in the competition for the Championship Cup given by Mr. F. J. Taylor, which he could now keep for 12 months.

As for the Workhouse, at the end of the month the tender of John Odell of 12s 6d each for 12 bedsteads was accepted, whilst of the applicants for the post of Nurse, Miss Sarah Foat had been engaged. However, with the position of Assistant Nurse still vacant she wrote to the Board of Guardians;

'Gentlemen. I find I cannot do the work in the infirmary properly without an assistant and I should be grateful if you will allow me to have one. The night attendant is absolutely no help to me except for relieving me of responsibility for the night. I find she does not even wash a patient. I cannot go out and have my mind at ease, and I feel I do not like leaving the building without someone in charge. Mrs. Jennings is properly in charge, but the work is at a standstill when I am out. Yours faithfully, S. FOAT. Nurse.'

It was consequently proposed that the House Committee should interview the two applicants for the post of Assistant Nurse at the next committee meeting, with it being recommended that in the meantime Mrs. Haynes should be engaged as temporary nurse, for duty in the isolation ward of the Workhouse. Following the interviews Miss Cook was duly recommended for the post at £20 p.a. and although this included apartments, rations, and washing in the Workhouse, there would be no provision for uniform or beer. Then in other matters, in late November 1914 it was suggested that the pigs at the Workhouse should be given more straw. This would not only provide more manure for the farm, but also be cheaper than that bought in the town. For the male inmates of the Workhouse a usual task was breaking stones, but for refusing to perform his allotted duty, saying that he was unable to break the stones, a homeless man at the vagrant ward was sentenced to 10 days in prison. As for Ernest Miller, a crippled inmate of the Workhouse, at an agricultural jumble sale, held by the Newport Pagnell Branch of the National Farmers' Union on Wednesday, November 25th, the model of a church that he made was sold for 2s, with this sum being added to the fund for Belgian refugees. Despite it now being winter, during the first week of December 1914 Mr. Chapman had gathered some fine strawberries in the open. However, less pleasing was a warning issued by the public auditor that beer served on Christmas Day to the inmates could not be charged on the public funds. This was despite the decrease of 252 quarts of beer drunk in the House during the year, showing a saving of £2 14s 1½d, but fortunately the Aylesbury Brewery Company, and Mr. W. Uthwatt, of Great Linford, came to the rescue by providing a quantity free. Thus on the festive day this greatly enhanced the enjoyment at the Workhouse, which had been profusely decorated with holly and evergreens sent by the Duke of Bedford, as also decorations provided by Colonel A. Finlay, the Reverend R. and Mrs. Mitchinson, Mr. J.C. Hipwell, and Mr. J.W. Mann, J.P.

In fact with the predominance of the national emblems the dining hall was a blaze of colour. Streamers of coloured paper completely hid the ceiling from view, whilst on the walls were hung seasonable mottoes and the patriotic message 'God bless our brave Soldiers and Sailors and our Allies.' For breakfast the inmates were served tea, coffee, and bread and butter, whilst for dinner the fare comprised over 200 lbs. of English beef, served with roast potatoes and boiled parsnips, and plum pudding then followed. Beer and mineral water were provided for refreshment, and those of the inmates too sick or infirm had their fare taken to them. The Master and Matron acted as carvers and waiters, and assistance throughout the festivities was given by the officers of the House. After dinner Mr. Chapman then proposed a hearty vote of thanks to the Guardians for providing the extra fare, and also to all the people who had sent gifts including Mr. F.A. Konig, of Tyringham House, who had sent tobacco for all the old men, Mr. Lewis Thompson, a grocer of Olney, who had sent oranges, and Dr. and Mrs. Sheppard, of Newport Pagnell, by whom presents had been forwarded for all the old women, and those in the infirmary. Cake was a welcome introduction for tea, and at a concert held in the evening in the dining hall Miss Laura Thorn, the niece of the Master and Matron, presided at the piano and performed several songs. There was also a domino tournament, for which the prizes were presented by Mrs. Chapman, and when the festivities concluded around midnight cheers rang throughout the building for Mr. and Mrs. Chapman and the Guardians. For the men's new dormitory at the Workhouse, in the New Year 12 mattresses would be purchased for the 12 bedsteads that had been recently bought, and for associated comfort the purchase was also made of 1 cwt. of flocks. Also for the benefit of the inmates concerts were regularly provided, and particularly enjoyed was that on Friday evening, January 15th, at which, organised by the Matron, amongst the many talented local artistes was Mr. Alfred Bullard, with Mrs. Bullard providing the piano accompaniments.

On Wednesday, February 3rd 1915 at the fortnightly meeting of the Rural District Council and the Board of Guardians, held in the Boardroom of the Workhouse, the Local Government Board had written to sanction the appointment of Nurse Foat and Assistant Nurse Cook. In other business the matter of provisions for the Workhouse was considered, and amongst the tenders accepted would be those of fresh butter, from the Duchess of Devonshire Dairy Co., clothing, from Mr. J. Berwick of Fenny Stratford, and tobacco and snuff from Mr. A. Marshall, of Newport Pagnell. As for seed potatoes since there was only 7s 6d difference between John Odell and Messrs. Perkins and Sons, the former was favoured, since he was a large ratepayer in the Union. At the A.G.M. of the Newport Pagnell Bowling Club, held on Tuesday evening, March 30th in the Urban Council Chamber, at the conclusion of business Mr. Chapman was presented with the championship cup by Mr. C. Branford, the captain, who had been unanimously voted to the chair. Normally the trophy would have been presented at an annual dinner, but this had not been held due to the war. Then in other matters, during the meeting it was reported that the £30 cost of the new pavilion had been paid for, with the money having been raised through whist drives, shares taken up by members, a donation, and a grant from club funds. During the first week of June 1915 several swarms of bees had been taken in the district, and in the Workhouse garden the fine swarm that settled on a rose standard were dealt with by Mr. E. F. Dant, who was well known locally as a bee expert.

Hatt House. In the later 19th century this was a doctor's residence, the house at the front and the surgery at the rear. It later became a boarding house.

Flies were also a problem, and it was now recommended that two meat safes should be purchased for the Workhouse, for the use of the Master and

Nurse. As for additional expenditure a new leg was required for the wooden washing tray, and £13 8s 6d would be paid as the tender of Mr. H. Rose for the wood block floor in the receiving ward and porter's lodge. With there now being four young children in the Workhouse, in early July the Matron would be grateful if anyone could donate a perambulator, whilst as for the Master, during the month he received a letter from one of his 'old boys' who was serving in the Navy on the North Sea. This former inmate had expressed a wish to spend his 10 days' leave at the Workhouse, and this was unanimously agreed.

At the invitation of Miss Littleboy, on Thursday, July 29th 1915 some 30 elderly inmates of the Workhouse spent a happy afternoon in the gardens of Hatt House. Following tea, games were enjoyed and then on August 24th the old and young women of the Workhouse were entertained to tea at The Croft by Mrs. F. Littleboy. At the end of September 1915 a recommendation was accepted that electric bells should be fixed from the Nurse's to the Master's room, as also from the Master's room to the porter's room, and in other matters a payment of £33 11s 6d had been made to Mr. Stanley Brandon's account for painting and other work in the infirmary, less 5s 6d for painting the wall of the men's staircase. Due to the high price of butter it was now decided to substitute margarine at the Workhouse, with the recommendation being worded 'That margarine be given to the inmates, and fresh butter to the officers and inmates of the infirmary.' About 18 lbs. of fresh butter and 32 lbs. of margarine would be required weekly, realising a saving of about £50 for the half year. During October 1915 the Master reported that an able bodied tramp, aged 42, had been sentenced to prison for refusing to perform his allotted task whilst an inmate of the casual ward. The man had also refused to join the Army, and Mr. Chapman said "It is the worst case I have ever had. He ought to have been given three months." More agreeable were those inmates of the Workhouse who celebrated the safe gathering in of the harvest on Thursday, October 28th. As in past years the vicar and Union Chaplain, the Reverend F. Gunnery, entertained all the old and infirm people to tea, served in the dining hall by Mr. and Mrs. Chapman, and not forgotten were those who were unable to get downstairs and join in. Apart from the Reverend and his wife, also assisting the Master and Matron were the Reverend R. Mitchison and his wife, and after tea on behalf of the inmates Mr. Chapman gave thanks to the vicar, who suitably replied. Subsequently a thanksgiving service was held in the Workhouse chapel, which had been especially decorated by Mrs. Chapman with flowers, vegetables and corn. November 1915 was the month in which Mr. G. Chasty exacted his revenge on Mr. Chapman, who had previously beaten him in the bowls competition for the silver cup.

This had been donated to the club by Mr. F. J. Taylor, of Lovat Bank, and also now highly appreciated was the work of Miss Cook, the Assistant Nurse at the Workhouse, who in December applied for a salary increase. Since the Nurse spoke highly of her work, and the Ladies Committee regarded her services as invaluable, this was agreed. The amount would be increased by £5 to £25 from January 1st 1916, and in other expenditure for the six cases of measles which had broken out a temporary nurse had to be engaged by the Master, who also during the month would send three bags of potatoes for the agricultural jumble sale to be held for Red Cross Funds. As for other provisions, having been the supplier for many years, and having always given satisfaction, Mr. Eles, of North Crawley was given the contract (in fact the only tender to be received) for flour, dan (sic), and also bread which, at 7¼d per 4 lb. loaf, formed, along with butter, coffee and tea, the breakfast for the inmates on Christmas Day 1915. Following this, in the chapel, which had been especially decorated by Mrs. Chapman, a service was then conducted by the curate, the Reverend R. Mitchison. Having spent the morning in games and leisure, at midday the old people then gathered in the festively decorated dining hall for a repast of roast beef, baked and boiled potatoes, boiled parsnips, and plum pudding. Not forgotten were the sick and infirm, and, with tobacco having been distributed to the men, after dinner a vote of thanks to the Guardians and donors of gifts was proposed by the Master, for whom cheers were then given, as also for his wife. The tea at 5.30 p.m. consisted of bread, butter and cake, and then during the evening some of the inmates contributed old time songs at a capital entertainment at which Miss Thorn not only presided at the piano, but also rendered several songs. The event had been arranged by the Matron and also the Master, on whose polyphone musical selections were played, and with other contributions performed by Mr. Alfred Bullard and his brother cheers were given at the close for the Guardians, and the Master and Matron. Following a verse of the National Anthem the inmates then retired to rest.

With the Christmas decorations still in place, on Wednesday evening, January 5th the dining hall accommodated Mrs. Chapman's concert for the inmates, who assembled at 7.30 p.m. No doubt she had been aided by Mrs. R. Jennings, her assistant, whilst the pot plants and flowers that adorned a platform at the far end had been grown by Mr. Chapman in his conservatory. As one of the Guardians Mr. F. W. Coales, of Lathbury, presided, and the programme comprised such well known local artistes as Mrs. A. Bullard, Miss Laura Thorn, Messrs. O. Critchard, L. Salmons, J. Winton, A. Bullard, C.R. Line, and Ernest Platt, who performed humorous songs. Two patriotic songs were given by Dora Judge, a tiny girl inmate, and during an interval gifts of oranges, sweets, buns and tobacco were distributed to the inmates. During the event the artistes and visitors were entertained to light refreshments by Mr. and Mrs. Chapman, to whom towards the close the chairman proposed a vote of thanks as also to the artistes, for whom the accompaniments had been played by Miss Thorn. The concert then concluded with the singing of a verse of the National Anthem. For soldiers suffering from scabies, in January 1916 the Medical Officer in charge of the troops in the town asked if accommodation could be found at the Workhouse, and in reply Dr. Sheppard advised that three cases could be accommodated in the receiving ward, where there was a good bath. However, this would be only on condition that the military sent an orderly, and paid all expenses. At the Divisional Petty Sessions, on Wednesday, January 26th 1916 two tramps, aged 41 and 44, were charged with having refused to perform their task of stone breaking whilst in the casual wards of the Workhouse. One was further charged with destroying his clothes, and giving evidence Mr. Chapman said they had both been admitted to the wards on Sunday evening. On the following morning they were given a task of stone breaking, suitable to their age, but instead, except for one having broken only about half a pound of stone, they 'stood in the wards all day.' Mr. Chapman had visited the cells several times during the day, and when he asked if there was any reason why they should be excused from work they asked to see a doctor. The medical officer was duly called, but one of the men then tore up his own clothes to avoid any work. After considering the evidence the Bench sentenced one of the pair to 14 days imprisonment, and the other to two consecutive terms of 14 days.

In early February 1916 the Council agreed to seek tenders for seeds for the Workhouse garden and farm. With his chief hobby being floriculture, during the summer the garden fronting the Workhouse testified to the skills of Mr. Chapman, and before the war he had won many prizes with flowers, fruit and vegetables at local shows. However, although last year the Master had asked for 24 kinds of flower seeds, this year he requested only eight, with potatoes as a special item. The tenders were to be received by February 16th, and would then be opened by the Farm Committee which had been assigned the power to accept or otherwise. Following Miss Cook's recent salary increase, the House Committee had now considered the application from Nurse Foat for an increase, and it was decided that she should be paid £45 p.a. instead of £40 p.a. Mrs. Jennings, the Matron's help, would be paid £25 p.a., an increase of £2, but although the decisions had not been unanimous 'they felt discretion was the better part of valour,' in view of the difficulty of getting good nursing staff. At the Divisional Petty Sessions on Wednesday, February 23rd 1916 a woman of Old Bradwell appeared on remand on a summons, charged with having neglected to provide for her illegitimate child. The offspring had thus become chargeable to the common fund of the Newport Pagnell Union, and Mr. C. Glanville, the Clerk to the Board of Guardians, asked for two weeks further remand. Meanwhile, as a possible solution the Guardians had received an offer from the St. Albans Diocesan Union to find a home for the woman for two years, if they would keep the child for that time. Additionally, the Secretary of a Refuge at Bedford had offered to take the woman back with her, but Mr. Chapman said her proper place was in the Workhouse to look after her children. Not least in fact since they already had two of them there, one having been accommodated since February 9th 1915, and then, following the woman's arrest two weeks ago, another had been 'foisted' on them. He was therefore of the opinion that she should be in the Workhouse, where she would at least be doing something to support her offspring, and with this being also the view of the Bench she was remanded to the Workhouse for a fortnight.

Under the Derby Scheme, the last day on which application could be made for military exemption by attested men was February 26th 1916, and in consequence the House Committee had sent an application to the U.D.C. Tribunal of Newport Pagnell for conditional exemption for Owen Thorn, the Workhouse porter. Being the son of Mr. Chapman's married sister, Mrs. R. Thorn, at Bierton, he was the nephew of Mr. Chapman, who had another sister in the same village, Mrs. Watts. The question as to whether to proceed with the application was then considered on Wednesday, March 1st by the Board of Guardians at their monthly meeting, where the House Committee recommended that they should go ahead. This was because the man had only been rated for garrison duty, and based upon this the recommendation was adopted. With the increasing threat of enemy attacks from the air, for a premium of £12 3s the chairman and vice chairman of the R.D.C. had now insured the Workhouse against air raids. This was with the County Fire Office, at a sum insured of £12,137. Regarding seeds for the Workhouse farm and garden only two tenders had now been received. Of these that of John Odell for potatoes at £18 5s, and garden seeds at £5 8s 6d, was chosen, whilst of other tenders that of £13 from Mr. A.G. Ellingham, of Newport Pagnell, for haircutting and shaving was accepted. At the Military Tribunal for the Newport Pagnell urban area, on Wednesday evening, March 15th 1916 Mr. Alfred Bullard, as chairman of the House Committee, appealed for the porter at the Workhouse to be exempted from military service. Having already tried to enlist the man had been initially rejected, and under the Derby Scheme had only been accepted for home service. Thus it was the opinion of the Guardians that he would serve the country better in his present position, for only an active man could deal with the pauper lunatics. In addition the many bedridden cases in the Workhouse were his responsibility, and with it being said that the Workhouse was now more like a hospital, he regularly had to bathe the 79 male inmates, aged from 65 to 92. As for other duties, not only did he superintend the work in the garden, but he also acted as undertaker and had charge of the tramp wards.

Additionally, from the military depot at Bletchley blankets and clothing were being sent for treatment and disinfection, as also soldiers, who could not be bathed by a woman. Then as a possible solution a member of the Tribunal suggested that an ex policeman in the town could perform the duties, but to this Mr. Bullard reiterated the nature of the work and the case was adjourned, to enable the military representative to study the man's medical sheet. For the inmates, on Sunday evening, March 19th 1916 members of the P.S.A. Brotherhood held a service at the Workhouse, with Mr. F. Sharp presiding, and Sapper Watson offering prayer. Mr. Stone gave an address on the 'Parable of the Prodigal Son,' and with the accompaniments played by Miss Amy Harris solos were given by Sapper Baird and Mr. Bullard. Towards the end of the month the Master reported that those male inmates who had assisted at funerals were now too old and infirm. Fearing some accident he therefore asked permission to obtain help from outside in heavy cases, and this was granted. In other matters the tenders for snuff and tobacco from Mr. A. Marshall, of Newport Pagnell were accepted, and that for butter from Mr. Lewis Thompson of Olney. Held at the Urban Council Offices, at a meeting of the Newport Pagnell Urban Tribunal one of the 15 cases on the evening of Wednesday, March 29th was that of the Workhouse porter. The military representative said that the man had been passed for garrison duty at 'home and abroad,' and it was the opinion of the Advisory Committee that he could better serve the country in the Army. As for disinfecting Army clothing there was no reason why a man from the Bletchley depot couldn't do the work, but in reply Mr. Chapman said that, with an average of between 100 and 180 Army blankets coming straight through from France, all the disinfecting was done by the porter, whose work load was additionally increased by such incidents as that which had occurred during the previous week, when a patient with scarlet fever was brought in by the Red Cross.

In all, regarding the 48 parishes of the Union only the Workhouse had the facilities to disinfect the man's bed and field kit, and apart from such duties the porter had to assist the elderly male inmates to dress, and cut up their food. Additionally, to keep the rates down there were 14 acres of land attached to the Workhouse for growing vegetables, plus 48 pigs to look after, but nevertheless the Tribunal only granted a month's exemption, to enable the Guardians to find a replacement. A concert was given at the Workhouse on the evening of Friday, March 31st 1916 by members of the Royal Engineers and friends. Lieutenant Moreton occupied the chair, and amongst the artistes were included Miss G. Middleton, contralto, Miss K.

Powell, soprano, Mr. A. Bullard, bass, Lieutenant Moreton, baritone, and Sappers Sharp, tenor, Lucas, baritone, Hanlan, bass, and Jackson, who performed a musical sketch. As for Mr. and Mrs. W. Charlton and Sapper Manson, they performed instrumental trios. On the evening of Wednesday, April 26th the question of military exemption for the Workhouse porter was again a subject at the Tribunal for the Newport Pagnell Urban area, held at the Council Offices. This was because despite having advertised the position in three newspapers, stating a salary of £28 p.a. all found, the Guardians had received no applications. However, the Military Representative saw this as no reason for further exemption, which prompted a member of the Tribunal to remark that it would be hard for the man if he came back from military service to find that his place had not been kept open. Praising the qualities of the man, and his kindness to the old people, Mr. Bullard said that the porter did a tremendous amount of work, and in further evidence the Master intimated that the man was indispensable, and would be of little use to the Army since he had a flat foot and suffered from rheumatism. Continuing, he said that the Workhouse now had a lot of chronic old cases, and that five of the men who were old soldiers had joined the National Reserve. After due consideration the Tribunal then gave three months, although it was made clear that an indefinite period could not be granted. In their view the man was single and active, and therefore the Army wanted him.

Apart from such concerns Mr. Chapman still had the duties of a special constable, and on May 2nd 1916 apprehended a man who had been hawking postcards around the town without a license. The miscreant was duly taken to the police station, and sentenced the following day to seven days in prison. When finding time for leisure pursuits Mr. Chapman greatly enjoyed a game of bowls, and at the A.G.M. of the Newport Pagnell Bowling Club, held in the Urban Council Chamber on Monday evening, May 1st 1916, he was elected as vice captain, with Mr. C. Branford being again elected as captain. In fact this would be the first occasion that a treasurer was appointed, Mr. W. J. Line, and amongst other matters it was decided to admit up to 20 soldiers to the club at a charge of 3s a month. By late June 1916 no applications had been received regarding the advert for a temporary porter at the Workhouse, and so another application would be made to the Tribunal for an extension of the exemption. Meanwhile the tenders of Messrs. Bramley for 100 tons of coal at 25s a ton, and 30 tons of house coal at 26s 6d per ton, had been accepted, and Mr. F. Eles, of North Crawley, was again successful in his tender for bread at 7½ d per 4 lb. loaf, flour at 46s a sack, and dan at 11s 6d per cwt. Well wishers in the town and district often gave gifts for the inmates of the Workhouse, and in July the Master acknowledged the presentation of books and magazines from the manager of the Newport Pagnell branch of the Aylesbury Brewery Company, as also flowers for the sick from the flower service at the parish church, and toys for the children from the Reverend F. Gunnery and the Ladies' Committee. A little later thanks were then expressed to Mrs. T. Robinson of the High Street for books, and also a doll for the children. With Mr. O. H. Bull in the chair, and Donald Fraser as the Military Representative, at the Urban Tribunal on Wednesday evening August 9th 1916 the porter at the Workhouse was again given temporary exemption. This was because his medical sheet was marked only for sedentary work, which was hardly the case for an energetic company of Royal Engineers who, on the evening of Wednesday, October 4th 1916 appeared behind the footlights at the Electric Theatre. Under the patronage of Lieutenant Colonel J. F. Lister, and held for the benefit of regimental charities, the concert opened with the chorus 'Cheereo,' and in typical pierrot dress the troupe performed under the name of 'The Quaints.' In her first visit to the town Miss Choules, L.R.A.M., was deservedly encored for her brilliant violin playing, and Miss Kathleen Fleet, soprano, was heard to excellent advantage in the Japanese song 'Butterfly Land,' as also, amongst other numbers, 'If you were the only girl.' This she sang as a duet with Sapper R. Hector,' tenor, who also performed 'They wouldn't believe me' as a duet with Miss Grace Middleton, contralto.

Other artistes were Corporal J. Cahill, tenor, Sapper T. Steven, baritone, Sapper J. O'Connor, bass, Sapper W. Elmes, humorist, and Sapper A. Hyde, pianist. All the performances were greatly appreciated, and the concert ended with the Good Night chorus performed by the whole troupe. Then on the following evening 'The Quaints' visited the Workhouse and repeated the programme. At a special police court, held in the town on Tuesday, October 17th, a man aged 47 'of the tramping class' was sentenced to 14 days hard labour, this being for having refused to perform his allotted task of stone breaking whilst an inmate of the casual ward at the Workhouse. The Master said that not only had he refused to do the work but he had used disgusting language towards the men serving their country in the war, and was therefore liable to prosecution under D.O.R.A. The little chapel of the Workhouse had been especially decorated by Mrs. Chapman, Nurse Foat, and Nurse Cook, for the services of harvest thanksgiving held on the evening of Thursday, October 12th 1916. The old folk joined in with reverent heartiness, and with Mr. W. Willis at the organ the service was conducted by the Reverend F. Gunnery, vicar of the parish and chaplain of the Workhouse, by whose kindness, and that of his wife, the inmates enjoyed extra fare in the dining hall. During November 1916 Mrs. Jennings, the Matron's help at the Workhouse, wrote to tender her resignation, and it was agreed that in her testimonial it should be noted that she had been 'a capable and painstaking officer.' Miss Richardson, of Northampton, would be her successor, at a salary of £20 p.a. Continuing his responsibilities as a special constable, whilst on duty at Cannon Corner at 5.45 p.m. on October 31st Mr. Chapman saw a man riding his bicycle without a white light at the front, and with no red light at the rear. This was of especial concern because wounded soldiers were about, having attended a concert at the Electric Theatre, and in court the defendant, a student at Lathbury Park, was fined £2, plus 2s 6d expenses for Mr. Chapman.

With the festive season now approaching, for those receiving out relief the Board of Guardians had decided to grant an extra shilling for each adult, and sixpence per child for Christmas week, whilst for the Workhouse the only additional expenditure would be for roast beef and plum pudding on Christmas Day, and cake for tea. But tragically this would not be enjoyed by one of the inmates, for he met with a fatal accident at the Workhouse on the afternoon of Saturday, November 25th 1916. Running an errand for the Master, on returning from the town Joseph Keeves, aged 66, duly delivered the required articles, but on returning to the men's day quarters he suddenly remembered that he had forgotten to deliver up the death register book, which he had taken to Dr. J. Sheppard, the Medical Officer of Health, for his signature. At once he proceeded to the Master's office, but with this being approached by a flight of stairs he missed his footing and, having only one arm, was unable to prevent his fall to the bottom. No one else was around, and so it would be just after 4 p.m. that a young woman taking milk to the Workhouse discovered him lying unconscious, with blood issuing from his nose. The Master and Nurse Foat were soon on the scene, but before Dr. Sheppard could arrive the man had died. A native of Stoke Goldington, he had lost his right arm some years ago in an accident on the Great Central Railway, and having been an inmate of the Workhouse for about four years was well known for his kind and obliging manner. On Christmas day 1916 breakfast was served at the Workhouse at 8 a.m., consisting of bread and butter, coffee and tea. Then at 9.30 a.m. the Reverend R. Mitchison, curate of Newport Pagnell, conducted a service in the Union Chapel which, with the white flowers adorning the altar table as a gift from him and his wife, had been decorated with evergreens and flowers by Mrs. Chapman. The inmates then spent the morning in leisure, and at 1 p.m. assembled for dinner in the dining hall, where seasonable mottos hung on the walls, and chains of coloured paper masked the ceiling. Plus baked and boiled potatoes parsnips, plum pudding, beer and mineral waters, huge joints of prime English beef provided the fare, and Mr. and Mrs. Chapman were assisted in the carving by Mr. Bullard, a member of the Board of Guardians.

The officers of the House attended the welfare of the inmates, and a distribution of oranges, sweets and tobacco was made after dinner. The Master next proposed a vote of thanks to the Guardians and also to the donors of the fare, who included Mr. F. Konig for tobacco for the men, Lewis Thompson, of Olney, for sweets and oranges, and the Aylesbury Brewery Co. for 18 gallons of ale. At 5 p.m. a tea of bread, butter and cake was served, and an hour later a concert was given by the Royal Engineers, assisted by Miss Laura Thorn and Mr. Bullard. With the chair occupied by the Master the varied programme was greatly enjoyed, and the proceedings were brought to a close by the singing of the National Anthem. Arranged by Miss Allfrey, the annual New Year's treat for the inmates of the Workhouse took place on Tuesday, January 9th 1917. A meat tea was served to the old people in the dining hall, and among those assisting the Master and Matron were the Reverend F. Gunnery, the Reverend R. Mitchison, Miss and Master Gunnery, the Misses Allfrey, Mrs. F. Littleboy, and Mr. and Mrs. Bullard. After tea a distribution of suitable and seasonal gifts took place, followed by a concert arranged by Mr. C. K. Garratt. With Mr. Chapman occupying the chair the artistes included members of the Royal Engineers, and the Misses Grace Middleton, Laura Thorn, Dorothy Pettit, Kathleen Powell, Hilda Branford, and Winnie Cotton, who performed a piano duet with Mr. C. K. Garratt, gave an amusing musical sketch, and played the accompaniments. At the conclusion light refreshments were then served. For absenting himself under the Military Service Act, describing himself as 'The King of the Mint' a rag and bone collector, of no fixed abode, was charged at a special police court at Newport Pagnell on Wednesday, January 17th 1917. Giving evidence police sergeant Roberts said that on visiting the Workhouse on January 16th he had arrested the prisoner, who gave his age as 40. He then failed to produce any exemption papers, but in court documents were produced to show that he was born in 1877, and should have reported to the military authorities on March 16th 1916. From the Recruiting Office at Bletchley, Lieutenant McFarlane said that the prisoner by his own statement was liable for military service, and that he had asked to be handed over to the military. According to Superintendent Dibben the man had been originally detained at Bletchley, and by describing himself as 'The King of the Mint' had displayed signs of insanity. He had therefore been handed over to the relieving officer for admission to the Workhouse, to be kept under observation. For his part the prisoner said that some time ago he had applied to the recruiting officer at Spalding, but was told that because he had lost his right thumb he was no good for the Army. Since then he had been examined by an Army doctor but rejected, and when asked by the Magistrates' Clerk where this had been he said, to loud laughter, "In gaol." Being latterly with the steam roundabouts the man had led a roving life, and by the verdict of the court he was fined £2 with 5s 9d costs, and handed over to a military escort to be taken to Oxford.

Another criminal case was dealt with at the Divisional Petty Sessions on Wednesday, January 24th 1917, when, describing himself as a labourer, an able bodied man was charged with having refused to perform his allotted task whilst a casual inmate at the Workhouse. Mr. Chapman said that when admitted the previous day the man had been set the customary task of stone breaking. However, following an application from Messrs. Coales and Sons for a labourer, to assist in unloading coal, he asked the prisoner if he'd be willing to perform this task, but the man said that he would need a lot of money for any work that he did. Having supposedly misunderstood the Master's question, in court the man pleaded not guilty to refusing his task, but he was nevertheless sentenced to prison for 14 days' hard labour. On Wednesday evening, February 14th 1917, at the Newport Pagnell Urban Tribunal six months' military exemption was granted to the porter at the Workhouse, where during the month 24 pairs of trousers at 7s 9d per pair, and 24 waistcoats, at 1s 6d each, were to be purchased for the inmates from Mr. Berwick of Fenny Stratford. In March 1917 it was announced that Dr. Digby White, resident at Cedar Lodge, Union Street, had agreed to act as temporary Medical Officer at the Workhouse where, due to the landlord of the town's lodging house now taking in soldiers, there was presently a problem in accommodating tramps. Private residents would not take them, and further compounding the problem the Board of Guardians was making an application to close the casual wards. Thus a committee would be set up regarding the matter, and not least because - with tramps upon admission receiving 3 lbs. of food above the scale laid down by the Food Controller - the amount of bread and cheese being consumed at the Workhouse was becoming a concern. With increased shipping losses due to U boat activity there was a growing shortage of food, and it had even been decided to purchase a potato sprayer and chemicals for use on the crops on the Union garden. As for additional expenditure, with the Master having been empowered to purchase, if possible, wood from the camp at Woburn, by the end of April 1917 one of the two floors in the Workhouse had been repaired. Also, alterations had been made to provide accommodation for the 20 inmates of the Potterspury Union Workhouse, which had now closed, and in view of this new influx it was not surprising that the Master and Matron now asked for a salary increase. This would be referred to the House Committee, but despite these workaday concerns Mr. Chapman was still fulfilling his role as a special constable, and on the morning of Friday, May 4th 1917 apprehended a drunk in the town. In consequence, the following day at a special police court the man was fined 10s with 2s 6d costs.

For another case, a man was charged at Newport Pagnell on Thursday morning, June 28th 1917 with having on September 30th 1916 deserted from the 238th Forestry Battalion of the Canadian Infantry Force. Bronzed and fit, and stating his Army age as 45, in the dock he indicated that he had served in the Afghan and Egyptian campaigns, and when not in military service had experienced 33 years of bush life in the wilds of Canada. Lately he had been roaming about the country, until obliged to seek shelter in the casual wards of the Newport Pagnell Workhouse, where he told Mr. Chapman that he yearned for a more active life. The Bench remanded him in custody to await an escort. At their meeting on Wednesday, July 18th 1917, held in the boardroom of the Workhouse, the Board of Guardians confirmed the action of the House Emergency Committee in purchasing goods to the value of £102 from the Potterspury Union Workhouse. In other business, with regard to the request for a salary increase by the Master and Matron, that of the former would remain the same but the Matron's remuneration would be raised from £35 to £40 p.a. Also at the meeting it was announced that due to her approaching marriage Nurse Cook had resigned as Assistant Nurse. Having carried out her duties admirably she would be wished well for the future, whilst as for a replacement an advertisement would be posted for 'single or widow without children,' at a salary of £20 p.a. inclusive of apartments, rations and washing. However, there would be no allowance for uniform or beer, and applicants were to apply to Mr. C. H. Glanville, the Clerk to the Guardians. The visiting committee of the Potterspury Union reported in September that they had found their inmates at the Workhouse comfortable and satisfied, and in the temporary absence of the Master and Matron, who were now taking their well deserved annual holiday, the porter would be in charge. Also during the month Miss Bearman, of Buckingham, applied for the post of Assistant Nurse, but on learning that the salary was £20 p.a., and had no uniform, she wrote to withdraw her interest, since her present position paid £26. However, in view of her experience, and the difficulty of finding other applicants, the House Committee recommended that £30 should be offered, and this was adopted.

With the food shortage now becoming serious, two youths of the town could hardly expect lenient treatment when on Sunday, September 16th they were caught stealing plums from the garden at the back of the Workhouse. At a Special Petty Sessions, held on Wednesday, September 26th 1917, Mr. Chapman said that around 7.45 p.m. he had seen the two lads in the garden, to which they had probably gained access by scaling the 10 foot wall. On being asked what they were doing they replied "We have come to get some plums," and asked to be given a chance. Yet because so much fruit had recently gone missing he suspected that they had been the culprits, and their claim to innocence was hardly helped when they gave false names and addresses. In fact they had been discovered with greengages to the value of 1s, and in court Mr. Chapman said "bushels of the best plums grown in the Union gardens had been missed." Having nothing else to say both the defendants pleaded guilty, and it transpired that soon after the offence they had absconded to Luton, where they obtained work in a munitions factory. Not that their wages seemed to have lasted long, for having no money they were unable to buy food and so returned to their homes at Newport Pagnell. One, who had a conviction for a previous and similar offence, was sent to prison for 21 days, whilst for the other a fine of 10s was imposed, which his sister promised to pay on the following Monday. There was another court appearance regarding the Workhouse in the last week of September 1917, when a 46 year old man, of no fixed abode, was charged for not having performed his allotted task. Giving evidence the Master said that it had been on Sunday evening that he admitted the accused, who said that his last work had been in Scotland, and that he had been tramping for two months. On Monday he was then given the job of breaking stones, but on Tuesday he flatly refused to complete the task. In court he pleaded guilty, and was sent to prison for 14 days with hard labour.

As chairman of the House Committee, in October 1917 Mr. Alfred Bullard reported that there were still drugs in the now disused Workhouse surgery. They had been accumulating for probably 50 years, and since many were valuable, and practically unobtainable at this time, with the sanction of the Committee he had asked for the stock to be examined by Dr. White. His consequent medical opinion was that some should be used, and these Mr. Bullard suggested should be given to Northampton Hospital, or a similar institute. With this agreed it was decided to leave the question of the best means of disposal to the House Emergency Committee. On Wednesday, November 7th 1917 at the monthly meeting of the Board of Guardians, and the Rural District Council, an application was received from Mr. and Mrs. L. Barker of Wolverton, in which they asked if, since they had no children of their own, there might be a child in the Workhouse that they could bring up. Age would not be a concern, and they would raise the child as their own, at no cost to the Guardians. In response the chairman said that it was very good of them, and the letter was referred to the Children's Committee. On Wednesday evening November 14th 1917, at the Newport Pagnell Urban District Appeal Tribunal conditional exemption was given to the Workhouse porter, a C3 man. In fact he was ill in bed, but despite this staff shortage Mr. Chapman was still pursuing his duties as a special constable, and on the same day attended the Divisional Petty Sessions regarding a Lathbury student, whom he had cautioned at 6 p.m. in London Road on November

9th. This was for riding a bicycle without lights, but despite Mr. Chapman's initial leniency after a little way the lad mounted the bicycle and rode off. This he denied in court, but nevertheless a fine of 13s was imposed. On Christmas Day 1917, for breakfast the inmates of the Workhouse enjoyed bread, butter, and coffee which, for reasons of economy, and no signs of complaint, had now been substituted for tea. Then at 9.30 a.m. a service was held by the Reverend Mitchison in the Union Chapel, which, with the white flowers adorning the altar table as a gift from him and his wife, had been decorated with evergreens by the Matron.

Also gaily decorated was the dining hall, where at 1 p.m. the old people assembled for a dinner of roast beef, parsnips and mashed potatoes. The Master and Matron carved the joints, and following a dessert of apple pie and custard a distribution of oranges, sweets, dates, and biscuits took place. At 5 p.m. tea was taken, consisting of bread, butter and cake, and afterwards the dining hall was cleared for the inmates to hold a sing song, with Mrs. Chapman presiding at the piano. Throughout the day the officers of the Workhouse had attentively looked after the comfort and wellbeing of the inmates, and amongst those who had sent presents were Mr. F. Konig (tobacco for the men), the Duke of Bedford (holly and evergreens), Mr. R. Bason, of Indianapolis, U.S.A. (sweets), Dr. and Mrs. Sheppard (presents for the women in the infirmary), and the Reverend Mitchison (a donation of 10s.) Continuing the festivities, by the kind invitation of Messrs. Bullard and Salmons the following day the inmates then attended the matinee at the Electric Theatre. Organised by Miss Allfrey, on Thursday, January 24th 1918 the annual treat for the inmates was held. After tea the usual distribution of presents took place, and arranged by Mr. C. K. Garratt in the entertainment that followed songs were given by the Misses Bailey, E. Garratt, K. Fleet, and West, and also Mr. Ashton Davies, Pioneer Rogers and Mr. Garratt. Several carols were rendered by the Carol League, Miss Wilford gave recitations, and Sapper Fuller performed violin solos. On Wednesday, January 30th 1918 at the meeting of the Board of Guardians, held in the Boardroom of the Workhouse, Mr. Bullard read the report of the House Emergency Committee at the meeting of which, on January 10th, the resignation of Nurse Foat had been accepted. She would be given a testimonial, and subsequent to the advertisement placed by the Clerk for a successor 11 applications had been received, with the appointment to be left to the House Emergency Committee. As for another vacancy, the resignation of Miss Bearman as Assistant Nurse had been accepted, and would take effect from February 28th. Sadly there was another departure from the Workhouse on February 12th 1918, when Elizabeth Huckle died. She was aged 82, and had been admitted in 1846. At the meeting of the Board of Guardians, on Wednesday,

February 27th 1918 it was reported that the vice chairman, Mr. J. Sutton, and Mr. F. J. Sharp, had met with the representatives of the Potterspury Board, Messrs. A. Sharp and A. Elmes, regarding the increased cost of the maintenance of the inmates from the Potterspury Union. In consequence a sum of 12s 3d per head from January 1st 1918 had been duly agreed, and also at the meeting an application from Mr. and Mrs. Beesley, who resided near Kenilworth, was agreed, this being for their adoption of a three year old child from the Workhouse.

In other matters Mr. F. W. Coales read the report from the meeting of the House Emergency Committee which, on February 6th, had interviewed the three selected candidates for the post of Nurse for the Infirmary. They were Mrs. Nicoll, of Hatfield, Miss Bennett, of Chester, and Miss M. Blower, of Knutsford, and the recommendation of the Committee was that Mrs. Nicoll should be appointed. As for the drugs in the dispensary of the Workhouse, a letter was read from Dr. Easte, to whom thanks would be expressed, with Dr. White to be asked to go through the medicines. Those needed at the Workhouse were to be retained with the rest to be given to Tickford Hospital, the Commandant of which, Miss McFerran, had only that morning thanked the Guardians for their gift at the meeting of the House Committee. A sale of the bottles would be made, with the redundant cupboard to be used in the storeroom. The three applicants for the post of Assistant Nurse at the Workhouse Infirmary had now been considered and with the recommendation being that Miss L.M. Clark, of Weston Underwood, should be appointed, Nurse Bearman would be asked to remain until March 31st. On Sunday, February 17th 1918 there was high praise for the Workhouse from overseas, when in the company of Mr. William Ward, the Honorary International Secretary of the Brotherhood Movement, Mr. George W. Coleman, President of the Northern Baptist Convention, Massachusetts, U.S.A., paid a visit and consequently reported; "This institution, like every other public institution I have, so far, visited in England, impressed me as wonderfully well managed, both from the point of view of good method and human consideration of the feelings of the inmates. It is far above my preconception of an English Workhouse." At the Divisional Petty Sessions on Wednesday, March 20th a member of the Royal Engineers in the town pleaded guilty to having ridden a bicycle without lights in the town on February 27th. Waiving his claim to expenses, the case had been brought by special constable Chapman, who at the A.G.M. of the Bowling Club, held at the Urban Council Chamber on Tuesday evening May 14th 1918, was elected to the chair. The finances were reported to be in the black, and there was also good news for the officers and committee members, for they were all re-elected.

In May 1918, subsequent to a letter from the National Poor Law Officers' Association the House Committee recommended paying weekly bonuses, for the duration of the war, of 3s 6d to the Master, 2s 6d to the Matron and Nurse, and 2s to the Assistant Nurse, Matron's Help, Porter, and Cook. The payments would commence on June 3rd, although perhaps Mr. Chapman had little need of the money for, at an auction held at 6 p.m. at the Swan Hotel on Wednesday, June 26th, he purchased the freehold property of 24, St. John Street for £200. On Saturday, July 6th 1918, by kind permission of Messrs. Bullard and Salmons the inmates of the Workhouse enjoyed a matinee at the Electric Theatre. However, there was no cause for joy on Wednesday afternoon, August 28th, when Mr. H. Webber, the Deputy Coroner for the Honour of Ampthill, held an inquest at the Sugar Loaf, Wroxhill, Marston Moretaine, regarding the tragic circumstances regarding the demise of an inmate, Alfred Bone. Aged 74, he had been found dead in a field the previous day, and was said by Mr. Chapman to have been an agricultural labourer and a native of Wavendon, who had been admitted to the Workhouse in August 1917. Subsequently he had absconded on several occasions, but on Sunday morning August 25th he seemed all right when seen by Mr. Chapman in the men's dayroom, having eaten a good breakfast at 7.30 a.m. Then at 9.30 a.m., this being church time, he went missing, and during a search the porter even cycled to North Crawley, then to Cranfield, and then to the home of the man's daughter at Woburn Sands, but all to no avail. Mr. Chapman consequently phoned the police at Newport Pagnell, and then on Monday 26th the police at Ampthill, giving a description of the man who, despite suffering from senile dementia, was very much liked. As to the finding of the body, police constable Herbert Taylor said that on Tuesday 27th at 9 a.m. he was told by a man named Holman that a man's corpse was lying on its back in a field, with the head resting on a piece of wood. One boot and the cap were off, and in the pockets were only a few loose beans. The hands were folded over the stomach, and it appeared that the man had died in his sleep. In the afternoon Dr. A. Street, of Cranfield, was asked to examine the body, and although he found no signs of injury the Workhouse clothing was very wet underneath. Mrs. Lily Annie Mann, of Woburn Sands, duly identified the man as her father who, having lived with her until his affliction, she had not seen since last July. The cause was stated to be heart failure accelerated by exposure, and this was the verdict that the jury returned.

On happier matters, in September toys for the children at the Workhouse were given by Mrs. Doyne Ditmas, of Ivy House, Great Linford, and following an application by Assistant Nurse Miss L.M. Clark a salary increase of £5 was recommended, bringing her remuneration to £30 p.a. Yet although welcome this amount was insignificant to that awarded to the porter, Owen Thorn. He had written to the Guardians tendering his resignation, but, having at the request of the chairman been interviewed by the House Committee, it was unanimously recommended that his resignation should not be accepted, and that his salary should be increased from £28 p.a. to £40 p.a. from October 1st 1918. As for the inmates of the Workhouse, during October their weekly allowance of bread would be increased from 64 ozs to 84 ozs. The annual harvest thanksgiving service at the Workhouse was held on Thursday evening, October 10th and with the chapel having been suitably decorated the chaplain, the Reverend Gunnery, conducted the service, with the Reverend Dove, the rector of North Crawley, preaching a sermon. Additionally, a special choir had been arranged for the occasion by the organist, Mr. Willis, which comprised Messrs. F. Bell, O. Critchard, L. Salmons, Mechanist Sergeant Major Price, and Mr. C. R. Line, with Mrs. Bell, Mrs. Willis, Miss I. Allfrey, Miss Mills, Miss West. Also participating was Miss E. Allfrey, of Bury Lawn, who with her customary benevolence would now be pleased to receive subscriptions towards the fund for the annual treat for the inmates. On Christmas Day, breakfast at the Workhouse consisted of tea, coffee, bread and butter. This was followed by a short service in the chapel, which had been decorated by Mrs. Chapman, and then at 1 p.m. dinner was served in the brightly decorated dining hall, where Mr. and Mrs. Chapman discharged the duties of caterers. With games being played afterwards, for tea there was bread, butter and cake, and at entertainment staged in the dining hall Miss Thorn, Nurse Clarke, Mr. Thorn and Mrs. Chapman all contributed to the harmony. Despite their age many of the inmates danced and sang until the conclusion of the festivities at 11.30 p.m. On the first day of the New Year, at the meeting of the Board of Guardians a subscription list was passed round for the annual New Year's treat for the Workhouse inmates. £5 12s was raised from those Guardians present, and the chairman said that this would be handed to Miss Allfrey, who organised these treats. There was also a treat on Tuesday evening, January 14th 1919, when at a concert held in the dining hall Miss Laura Thorn, from Aylesbury, displayed her considerable musical ability with songs to include a 'A perfect day,' a duet performed with Mr. Hamilton, a coloured gentleman.

In consideration for the kindness that his mother had received from the Master and Matron, and for the attention given by the Nurse, in March 1919 a man forwarded a cheque for £10 to the Board of Guardians. This was for her nursing attendance and maintenance during a temporary stay, and a member said that it was nice to receive such a testimonial, since there was so much prejudice against the Workhouse. For the celebrations on Peace Tuesday, in July 1919 the old people at the Workhouse were treated through

The grave of William Coverley and his wife in Newport Pagnell churchyard.

the kindness of the Guardians to a dinner at midday of roast leg of mutton, potatoes, broad beans, batter pudding, stewed gooseberries, jellies, and blanc mange. There was a choice of beer or mineral waters, and after the singing of a verse of the National Anthem cheers were given for the Guardians and Master and Matron. Bread, butter and cake was served for tea, and arranged by Mr. Chapman in the evening a concert in the dining hall took place, with Mr. J. Short presiding over the first part, and Mr. F. J. Sharp over the second. Mr. Alfred Bullard and Mr. William Coverley were other Guardians present, and with selections on the gramophone being given by Mr. J. West, others who contributed to the programme were Mrs. Shedd at the piano, and Miss Ellingham and Messrs. A. Bullard, E. Platt, L. Tibbetts, J.West, all of whom performed songs. Mr. H. Clayton Jones performed violin solos, Mr. Hopper told interesting stories, and during the evening a distribution of beer, mineral waters and cake was made. With similar gifts having been distributed earlier in the day, the old men received packets of tobacco, and after a short speech by Mr. Short cheers were given for the Guardians, the entertainers, and for the Master and Matron. The artistes and visitors were then entertained to light refreshments. Intending to improve her position, in September 1919 Miss Lucy N. Clarke, the Assistant Nurse at the Workhouse, wrote tendering her resignation. In consequence she would be given a testimonial, whilst as a testimonial for the town's returning soldiers a 'welcome home' was given on Saturday, January 24th 1920, at which for a company of about 500 the joints for a hot dinner were prepared by Mr. Chapman and the staff at the Workhouse.

In August 1920 Miss Fielding, the Assistant Nurse at the Workhouse, resigned, and with only one application being received the post, offering a salary of £40 pa., with no war bonus, was re-advertised, to be subsequently offered to Miss Bertha Jenkins. Addressed to Mr. Chapman, in April 1921 a letter was read by the Guardians from Kate Butt, a former inmate of the

Workhouse, who was now living at North Crawley. This was with regard to the recent allegations made by a man against the officers of the institution, and the treatment received by an inmate, and in her letter she said that she felt deeply hurt by the remarks made against the Master and Matron. In fact "If she had heard the man she would have struck him." For three months she had been under the care of the Master and Matron and could not have received better or kinder treatment. The food was good, and all the officers had been considerate and kind. Indeed, her brother who was now in the Workhouse also spoke with respect of the Master and Matron. "I never spent an unhappy moment in the House, and when I read that wicked man's lies I thought I must write and thank you for your kindness to me." After an investigation the man who had made the accusations, about the alleged mistreatment of an inmate, signed an unreserved apology. However, such insinuations could hardly have been of benefit to Mr. Chapman, who during the month was admitted to Northampton Hospital to undergo a serious operation. By now the soldiers who were returning to civilian life were finding that far from being a land fit for heroes the country was not fit for employment, and 20 unemployed from the town were engaged in October 1921 in hand digging the garden ground of the Workhouse.

Despite his recent operation, after a long and painful illness William Chapman died aged 54 on the night of Tuesday, January 10th 1922. Often complimented by Government officials on his management and excellent supervision, he had been a man of high character, and being cheerful and honest had been well respected by all. As a Nonconformist his place of worship was the Congregational Church, and up to the time of his illness he was connected with the Brotherhood movement in the town. Following his death 53 applications would be received for the vacant positions of Master and Matron, and in April a shortlist of those candidates with excellent testimonials was drawn up. However, one couple from Kettering had secured another post and withdrew their application, leaving the other candidates as Mr. C. Mitchell, aged 29, the Assistant Master for the last three years at Northampton Workhouse, Miss Gertrude Hoxley, aged 31, Assistant Matron at Northampton Workhouse, and Mr. and Mrs. Thomas Eden, respectively aged 34 and 41, who were Master and Matron at Towcester Workhouse. Mr. Mitchell had served four years with the Sherwood Foresters during the war whilst as for Mr. Eden he had volunteered three times for active service, but was debarred from joining the Army because the Doncaster workhouse, where he was employed, had been converted into a military hospital. After deliberations, by a unanimous vote Mr. Eden and his wife were appointed. At the end of April 1922, due to a breakdown in health Nurse Nicholls was to be granted 28 days leave, with Nurse Amos, of unfortunate marital problems, to be appointed Assistant Nurse at £35 p.a. As for a Miss Page she would be appointed Matron's help at £30 p.a. However, the career of Mr. Owen Thorn, the porter, seemed in doubt, for he had not returned from the 14 days' leave of absence granted following an accident. In fact if he did not return by the next Monday his office would be determined, although this seemed superfluous for in late May he wrote to tender his resignation, and, having asked for a testimonial, a good reference would be supplied.

***

A letter written by a 'casual' at the Workhouse in November 1914

On the last day of October 1914 bread and water as a diet for casual paupers in the casual wards of workhouses. Under the new regulations of the Local Government Board the diet for vagrants must consist of 8 ozs of bread and an ounce of dripping or margarine with porridge, shell cocoa or broth for the morning and evening meals, and ½lb of bread, 4 ozs of potatoes and 2 oz cheese for dinner. Up to recently breakfast and supper at the Newport casual ward comprised 6 oz of bread and a pint of gruel. "However, if you should at any time desire to take yourself to a casual ward don't fall into the error of thinking you are off to a convalescent home. Otherwise you will soon find that a very rude awakening awaits you in the discovery that it is a place where there is a wealth of work and a paucity of food. But let me commence my rigmarole from the beginning. Casuals are taken in at six o'clock, and the Guardians dislike turning away any tired and hungry mortal on account of the lateness of the application and therefore admissions are sometimes made quite late. The first item on the programme on entering is making a record of the usual personal details - name, age, occupation, where from and to where going, and so on. Then comes the search of pockets for hidden treasure - lucre, tobacco, matches, and other things barred in such establishments. A usually by no means unwelcome bath follows, and then a newcomer gets outside his supper, after which he may adjourn to his bed and slumber away the hours of darkness in the sure and certain knowledge that on the morrow he is in for nine hours work at wood sawing, scrubbing, stone breaking, oakum picking, cleaning up, garden labour, or any general employment on hand. The dinner hour is from twelve to one, when work is resumed and continued till 4.30, supper being served soon after, and then follows a general turn-in for the night, so that while tarrying at the expense of the Newport ratepayers a vagrant's life is all work and bed. Those due for discharge are not eligible for readmission till they have "tried their luck" for work elsewhere, and if they apply again within a month they are liable to three days' detention, although with the more costly dietary under the new regulations the Guardians are by no means anxious for more detentions than necessary. On leaving each casual receives half-a-pound of bread and two ounces of cheese." "Poor as is the hospitality at the Newport casual ward, those who are compelled to take advantage of it may derive some consolation from the more or less comforting reflection that hard as life is there it is harder in some similar establishments. For instance, in some places a wood bed and wood pillow is the order, with as much as 13cwt. of stones to break up; the men being detained on the second day till the task is completed, in addition to which the work is done under the superintendence of officers who are mere bullies, whereas at Newport one does fall in for a little more reasonable treatment at the hands of the Master and his subordinates if one makes a proper attack on the work. It seems hard that our Poor Law system should compel a man to be absolutely destitute before he can take advantage of the casual ward, and then when he does so afford him no chance of earning so much as a copper with the result that he comes out as hard up as he goes in, although this is no fault of the Guardians, but a system over which they have no control. It means, however, that on quitting the establishment he must break the law to live. If he does so by begging he is liable of course to be prosecuted, as he is if caught stealing, and if he attempts suicide he may be indicted. Verily our Poor Law system as it touches casual paupers is a fearful and wonderful one."

NORTH BUCKS WAR HOSPITAL SUPPLY DEPOT

Tyringham Cottage, now a care home. Here a Voluntary Aid Detachment was started by Miss Helen McFerran, being approved by the War Office and designated as the Bucks/48 in October 1915.

In the early days of the war, Miss Helen McFerran and Miss Annie M. Wood organised a Voluntary Aid Detachment, and gave the use of their home at Tyringham Cottage, Tyringham (which they rented from Mr. Frederick Konig, of Tyringham House) for the making of medical and other comforts. Having subscribed for the supply of the materials, here, at this 'War Hospital Supply Depot,' Regd. no. 1531, from November 16th 1915, ladies from the local area voluntarily worked two days a week from 10 a.m.& to 3.30 p.m., and, with the items to include surgical swabs, roller bandages, pneumonia jackets etc., by the end of May 1916, 5,599 items had been sent to the Red Cross at Pall Mall, 2,074 to the Bucks and Berks Needlework Guild, Newport Pagnell Group, 580 to Lady French's Fund, 81 to the V.A.D. Bucks 48 Dressing Station, Newport Pagnell, and eight bandages had been sold. Even in inclement weather many of the ladies attended every week, and in view of the volume of work enquiries were made about the possibility of transferring the depot to larger and more convenient accommodation at Newport Pagnell. In consequence Mr. F. Taylor offered his premises at 36, High Street, Newport Pagnell, rent free, and, with the facility having been opened on Tuesday, May 30th 1916, on Monday, October 16th 1916, a meeting of all the subscribers and workers of the 'North Bucks War Hospital Supply Depot,' 'registered under the Red Cross for making hospital appliances for the wounded,' was held at the Urban Council Chamber in

Newport Pagnell.

36, High Street, now the Willen Hospice shop. In 1916 Mr. F. Taylor granted the use of the premises rent free to accommodate the war hospital supply depot.

Amongst those present were Mrs. Vaughan Harley, Mrs. Good, Mrs. Mead, Miss Allfrey, Mrs. Gunnery, Miss Helen Farrar, Mrs. Carlile, Mrs. Salmons, Mrs. St. John Mildmay, Miss D. Odell, Miss Wood, Miss McFerran and the Reverend F. Gunnery, whilst of those unable to attend letters of apology had been received, amongst others, from Lady Farrar, Mrs. Trevor and Mrs. G. Uthwatt. However, despite her absence through illness Lady Farrar was elected president, with Mrs. Vaughan Harley, Mrs. Knapp, Lady Leon, Mrs. Trevor, Mrs. G. Uthwatt and Miss Wood as vice presidents. As for the committee, this would comprise Miss Allen, Miss Allfrey, Miss I. Allfrey, Miss French, Mrs. Gunnery, Mrs. Good, Mrs. Mead, Mrs. A. St. John Mildmay, Miss E. Savory, Miss Turnbull, Miss C. Turnbull, Mrs. Wellesley Taylor, and Mrs. Traill. Miss McFerran was elected honorary secretary, Mr. Edmund B. Traill (of the Manor House, Newport Pagnell) honorary treasurer and Mr. F. O.Butler honorary auditor. Miss McFerran and Miss Wood were elected as the managers of the depot and the meeting then adopted the

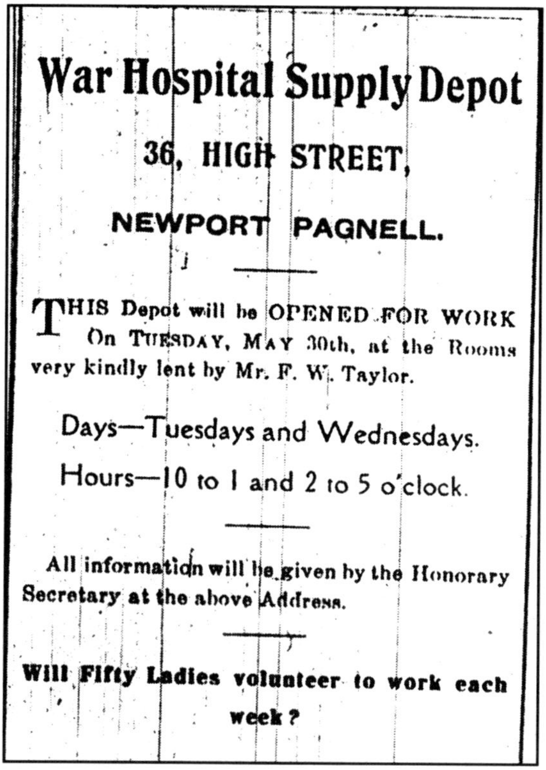

War Hospital Supply Depot

36, HIGH STREET,

NEWPORT PAGNELL.

THIS Depot will be OPENED FOR WORK On TUESDAY, MAY 30th, at the Rooms very kindly lent by Mr. F. W. Taylor.

Days—Tuesdays and Wednesdays.

Hours—10 to 1 and 2 to 5 o'clock.

All information will be given by the Honorary Secretary at the above Address.

Will Fifty Ladies volunteer to work each week?

Bucks Standard May 27th, 1916

following standing orders;

1) The Depot shall be called "The North Bucks War Hospital Supply Depot."

2) The management of the business and funds of the depot shall be in the hands of a committee elected every year by the workers and subscribers to the depot.

3) The President, Vice President, Hon. Secretary, and Hon. Treasurer shall be elected at the annual meeting, and shall be ex-officio members of the committee.

4) The committee shall meet at least once a quarter and no business shall be transacted unless at least five members be present.

5) The committee shall elect its own chairman at the first meeting in each financial year.

6) The Chairman or Secretary may at any time convene a meeting. The Secretary must do so on the requisition of five members of the committee in writing, but seven clear days notice must be given of such a meeting.

7) The committee shall at each quarterly meeting delegate to certain of its members the duty of buying such material for work as may be necessary.

8) No article of the constitution shall be revoked or altered unless carried by two thirds majority of those present at the annual meeting, seven days notice of such alteration having been sent to each worker and subscriber, or at a special general meeting called for the purpose; of which three weeks notice must be sent to all workers and subscribers.

9) The financial year shall commence on January 1st.

From the time that the depot had commenced, at Tyringham Cottage, the total output of work had been surgical swabs 15,146, bandages (roller) 2,418, bandages (many tail) 383, pneumonia jackets 639, shrapnel pads 293, and slippers 48 pairs, whilst of those who received the goods the following letter of thanks had been sent from Lady Jekyll, St. John Ambulance Warehouse:

"On behalf of the Ladies' Committee of the Order of St. John, of which Her Majesty the Queen is President, I write to acknowledge and thank you most warmly for the useful contribution you have so kindly sent. The calls for hospital requirements, clothing, and comforts for the sick and wounded at home and abroad, are so numerous and urgent that all gifts are most gratefully received. We are so very grateful for your prompt and excellent response to our request, all bandages sent are very nice."

A letter had also been received from No. 26 General Hospital, France:

"Thank you very much for the chest and abdominal bandages which arrived a few days ago, they are such nice ones and will be extremely useful. It is most kind of you to offer us swabs, we shall be delighted to have them." Lady French wrote: "I am indeed most grateful," and from the French Wounded Emergency Fund was received: "Please express to your workers our most sincere thanks for the excellent consignment of hospital supplies which you have sent us. You will see from the piteous appeals of our delegates in France, which we enclose, with the official receipt, how terrible are the needs of the French Hospitals, and can imagine with what joy your gifts will be received."

Presenting the report of the provisional committee, Mrs. Knapp said that the work of the depot had increased to such an extent that Mrs. St. John Mildmay, the wife of the Reverend Arundell St. John Mildmay, of Old Wolverton Vicarage, had even begun an operation to make slippers in a room at her home, and continuing the report she said that the thanks of the workers were due to Miss McFerran and Miss Wood, for the patriotic spirit in which they had started and carried on the enterprise. The honorary treasurer's report showed an increase of £55 5s 1d, and after the payment for material this left a balance of £6 0s 10d. Then in conclusion a hearty vote of thanks was passed to Mr. Taylor for his generosity in having allowed the use of the rooms. Thus at 36, High Street, Newport Pagnell, during the following month the depot began. Meanwhile, Tyringham Cottage continued to be the home of Miss McFerran and also Miss Wood, who was summoned at the Newport Pagnell Divisional Petty Sessions on Wednesday, January 10th 1917, for having used electric headlights on her motor car without the necessary sidelights. She pleaded not guilty but giving evidence Police Constable Bonner said that on December 20th 1916, he, in company with Superintendent Dibben and Police Sergeant Roberts, was on duty at Cannon Corner when at 7.25p.m. he saw the defendant driving the car. The lamps were giving a brilliant light which could be seen for a considerable distance and when stopped, and told that she could not use headlights without sidelights, she replied; "I've been running about for six weeks and have not been stopped." Police Sergeant Roberts said that electric sidelights were on the car but were not lit. As for his evidence, Superintendent Dibben said that the lamps were insufficiently screened. Saying she was under the impression that the new order would not apply until January 1st, Miss Wood apologised to the Bench and a fine of 10s was imposed.

During the first week of March 1917, on the Tuesday and Wednesday an exhibition of the work carried out at the Newport Pagnell depot was held. On the ground floor a host of articles for despatch to war hospitals was displayed, whilst in the upper rooms the ladies could be seen busy with fabric and needle. In fact with a need for more voluntary ladies the Committee hoped to secure 50 workers a day, and indeed since moving into the Newport Pagnell premises it had been possible to forward 25,200 articles to various hospitals, with, additional to the branch at Old Wolverton, a depot having now been established at Addington, to make many tail bandages. The quarterly meeting of the North Bucks War Hospital Supply Depot was held on Tuesday, March 27th 1917, at the Newport Pagnell headquarters, where the superintendents of the workrooms gave the following returns; pneumonia jackets 177, many tail bandages 517, roller bandages 2167, swabs 7524, shrapnel pads 30, slippers 70, Old Wolverton Branch slippers 47½(sic) Addington Branch many tail bandages 40. These had been sent to Northampton General Hospital, Endell Street Military Hospital, the V.A.D. Hospital at Winslow, the Royal Engineer Sick Billet Wards at Newport Pagnell, the Red Cross, 83, Pall Mall, and to Lady Jekyll at the St. John Warehouse, St John's Gate. It was also pleasing that there was much local support for the depot and in fact in aid of the funds two excellent concerts were given at the Electric Theatre, Newport Pagnell, on Tuesday afternoon and evening May 1st 1917. The advertised artistes were Mr. Gervase Elwes, 'the squire of Billing,' who was a tenor of world repute, Miss Gwendoline Farrar L.R.A.M., cellist, Mr. Philip Cathie, solo violinist of the principal London concerts, and Joseph Farrington, bass soloist of St. Paul's Cathedral. Also billed to appear was Miss Louise Dale, the popular English soprano, but since she was indisposed her place was taken at the last minute by Miss Jane Croft. Providing the accompaniment throughout was Fred Kiddle, of London, and appearing at the evening performance was Ben Lawes, 'the mirth maker.'

At both the concerts members of the Royal Engineers would act as stewards and the audience enthusiastically greeted Joseph Farrington when, wearing the King's uniform, he opened the afternoon's programme. The quarterly meeting of the North Bucks War Hospital Supply Depot was held at the headquarters, 36, High Street, Newport Pagnell, on Tuesday, July 3rd 1917, where the superintendents of the workrooms gave the following returns; swabs 4147, slippers 55½ pairs, many tail bandages 580, pneumonia jackets 125, square surgical swabs 50, shrapnel pads 12, arm slings 12, roller bandages 983, comfort bags 90. Also given was the quota from the branches at Old Wolverton, and Addington, as well as the Wolverton branch which, operating from 'delightful rooms,' had only been open for two weeks. In fact the premises had been secured by Mrs. F. O.Harvey, who apart from her Red Cross work was the secretary and organiser of the Wolverton Soldiers' and Sailors' Christmas Presents Fund. Hospital requisites had been sent to Northampton Hospital, Endell Street Military Hospital, the V.A.D. Auxiliary Hospital at Newport Pagnell, plus four consignments to Lady Jekyll at the St. John's Warehouse, but with attendances at the Newport Pagnell Branch having fallen greatly during the last three months, in view of the decreased output more workers were urgently needed. Yet there was still local support and to raise funds for the depot on Thursday, July 26th 1917, a whist drive 'in Mrs. Hedges' Garden,' Linford House, Great Linford, took place at 6.45p.m. 'prompt.' Tickets were priced at 1s and the billing included; 'Do please come along and bring your friends.' In fact they could also enjoy a short concert, for with the musical programme having been organised by Dudley Gardner, through the generosity of his friend Mr. C. Kenneth Garratt, a party of first class entertainers gave an al fresco performance which included songs rendered both by themselves and by several soldiers. Bowls and other attractions were featured and under the old apple trees refreshments were available at moderate prices.

The chief part of the event was a 16 game whist drive, the prizes for which were distributed by Mrs. Mead, of Great Linford Manor. As for the prizes of the other entertainments, in the putting competition Mr. Pebody, of Olney, won a framed water colour by Miss Dorothy Hedges which he then entered it into an auction, conducted by Mr. Gambell, and duly kept bidding to win it back. Given by Miss Hedges, the second prize, of a Bucks lace handkerchief, was won by a wounded Scots soldier, Private Ross, and he also correctly guessed 310 as being the exact number of sweets in a bottle. The whole occasion proved very successful and after expenses Mrs. Hedges would be able to hand over £16 4s. Then providing an additional £3 13s 6d, also in July the doll to be raffled for the depot funds, which had been presented by Miss Fanny Taylor, was won by Mr. T. Lineham. There was more fund raising for the depot later in the year, when in ideal weather a grand fete and bazaar took place in the grounds of Chicheley Hall on Thursday, September 6th 1917. As the President, Lady Farrar opened the occasion, and, with the mansion being open to the public, throughout the afternoon and evening she and her daughters helped to make the event a great success. In November 1917, at the quarterly meeting of the depot, no returns were produced from the Old Wolverton or Addington branches since both had been closed during the summer months. In fact for six weeks the Newport Pagnell depot had also been closed, but by the end of the year it was business as usual, and, with Lady Farrar in the chair, the annual meeting of the subscribers and members of the 'North Bucks War Hospital Supply Depot, Newport Pagnell' was held in the Urban Council Chamber on Monday afternoon, December 31st 1917. The election of the officers included Lady Farrar as president and Lady Leon as vice president, and also appointed were Mrs. Vaughan Harley, Mrs. Knapp, Mrs. Trevor, Mrs. G Uthwatt and Miss Wood, with Miss McFerran as the honorary secretary.

The total output of the depot from October 1916 to December 31st 1917 had included 28,680 surgical swabs, 15 pairs of pyjamas for the Newport Pagnell V.A.D. Hospital and 40 pairs of collars for the same. With the accounts having been given it was then stated that the Red Cross H.Q. had advised that one special badge was to be awarded to the Newport Pagnell depot. In unanimous agreement with the committee the meeting recommended that this should be received by Miss McFerran, who in reply said that although she was honoured all the heads of the workrooms deserved one. The next quarterly meeting was held at the depot on Wednesday, March 20th 1918, where details were given of the work output from Newport Pagnell, Wolverton and the home workers. However, not from the Old Wolverton or Addington Branches, since no reports had been received. The Newport Pagnell Branch was closed from Wednesday, March 27th 1918, to Tuesday, April 16th 1918, but on Wednesday, July 10th 1918, provided the venue for the quarterly meeting, at which the superintendents of the workrooms gave their returns. Amongst the items from the Wolverton Branch were nine limb pillows and 4,000 surgical dressings and from the Newport Pagnell Branch 100 eye shades and 13 pairs of pyjamas, with some requisites having been sent to the V.A.D. Auxiliary Hospital at Tickford Abbey. For a summer break the Newport Pagnell depot closed from July 24th to September 10th, yet local fund-raising events continued with the annual fete at Chicheley Hall on August Bank Holiday raising over £200.

Indeed, this was due to the efforts of many people and as the chairman of the Depot Committee from Linford Hall Mrs. Katherine Knapp would consequently write to a local newspaper:

"Dear Sir. May I take this opportunity of thanking on the behalf of my Committee, all those who so very kindly helped to make the Fete at Chicheley Hall the great success that it has been. Where so many gave time and trouble it seems almost invidious to specify, but I should like to thank, first of all, Lady Farrar for all she did, and also to mention the names of Messrs. H. C. Cummings, A. Fairweather, P. Flemons, F.T.W. Litchfield, A. J. Simpson, T. and C. Shelton, and C. M. Wilford, without whom it would have been impossible to carry out the admirable arrangements which conduced so much to the success of the afternoon. May I say that I hope the Fete will show a profit of over £2."

The quarterly meeting of the North Bucks War Hospital Supply Depot was held at 36, High Street, Newport Pagnell on October 16th 1918, but due to the Newport Pagnell Branch having been closed for six weeks' holiday, and the Wolverton Branch for a month's holiday, the returns of work were not as large as usual. In fact the attendance at Newport Pagnell had proved very small and of the returns from the superintendents of the workrooms that of the Newport Pagnell Branch, from July 5th to September 25th, was surgical dressings 1,984, roller bandages 519; many tail bandages 107, pneumonia jackets 21, slippers 68½ pairs. Sundries included 40 pairs of pyjamas, 10 pairs of socks, eight pairs of bed socks, eight pairs of operation stockings, two mufflers, two pairs of mittens, and six knitted swabs. Many of these items had been made by those who could not attend the workroom. As for the Wolverton Branch, from July 5th to October 8th the number of surgical dressings numbered 3,000; roller bandages 100; many tail bandages 336, knitted swabs one; pillows two. From the Old Wolverton Branch 20 pairs of slippers had been sent, whilst of the hospitals supplied from July to September these were Northampton Hospital, the V.A.D. Hospital, Newport Pagnell, Lady Jekyll (St. John's Warehouse) and Hospital Luxembourg, Meaux, France, from where the following letter had been received:

> "Dear Miss McFerran. The Newport Pagnell War Depot Cases arrived yesterday. I simply cannot express how grateful we all are. They arrived at a moment when I, personally, was absolutely through my last bandage. I can honestly say I have been at an immense number of war depots and I have never seen any dressings or bandages better made (or as well made) as the ones you have sent to the Hospital Luxembourg, (which is now Hospital of Evacuation 18). The packing was so splendidly done they might have been in the boxes five minutes only. I went straight over to the Bureau of the Medecin Chef to tell him about them, and he was radiantly pleased. You cannot think how the French doctors and surgeons appreciate the well made English dressings - just exactly the right size, etc. Of course, the abdominals I have not touched, they look just perfect, but some of the roller bandages and dressings went straight into use. You will have seen by the papers that the tide of battle (which was very near us when I came

out the last weeks in May) has now gone splendidly away from us, owing to all our grand victories, but our Hospital continues very busy. As well as our French wounded, I have had a good deal of first aid work to do among the American soldiers. A few days ago one fell from a train going at 20 miles an hour close to me - he had a terrible hole in his head (fractured skull), but is going to get well. I had to do the best I could. Now, I feel I am well set up, too. Please convey my warmest thanks and admiration to your workers - you have been so generous to our Hospital, and it is impossible for me to thank you sufficiently. The milk covers all went into instant use, and are not only greatly admired, but worth their weight in gold, as flies are appalling, and we simply have not a minute to do anything in the work line. When I am next in England I hope you will allow me to write you more fully of how we used your dressings, and some of the exciting days here.

Yours sincerely,
MILDRED WHATMAN."
Directrice.

I was so interested, when reading "Dauntless France," to see the Newport Pagnell War Supply Depot was mentioned, among others, which had assisted French war Hospitals.

Directrice des Cantines,
Anglaise Hospital Luxembourg,
Meaux."

With the depot now in need of more voluntary workers this was no doubt a boost to morale. However, there would soon be an even greater lift with the signing of the Armistice and with the war at an end at the quarterly committee meeting on Tuesday, December 18th it was decided to close the Depot, due to the diminished demand for hospital requirements. The reports from the workrooms of Newport Pagnell and Wolverton from October to December were given, and for having lent 36, High Street, Newport Pagnell for the past two years and seven months a hearty vote of thanks would be passed to Mr. F. W. Taylor. Yet there was still some unfinished work and with a need for pneumonia jackets it was decided to work from a room in the Auxiliary Hospital, Tickford Abbey, for a few hours from 11 a.m. on Tuesdays. This would open on Tuesday, January 14th 1919, but was intended to run for only a few weeks. All accounts due from the North Bucks War Hospital Supply Depot were to be sent in before Wednesday, February 12th 1919, and on Saturday, February 22nd 1919, the general meeting was held at 3p.m. in the Urban District Council Offices, High Street, Newport Pagnell.

Here there was a large attendance of the voluntary workers and with Lady Farrar in the chair also present were Mrs. Knapp, the chairman, Miss Wood, the manager of the depot, Miss McFerran, the honorary secretary, and Mr. Allfrey, the honorary treasurer, who told the crowded meeting that there was a balance of £280.

After the minutes of the last general meeting were read, confirmed and signed, the following annual report of the Committee was then read:

> 'The Committee have pleasure in presenting their annual report for 1918 with statement of accounts. The past year has been a heavy and anxious time for all workers. Not only have the demands for surgical dressings increased but material has been expensive and hard to procure. The regular workers in the Newport Pagnell rooms have done much useful service to the wounded in the hospitals, and the Wolverton workroom has not only turned out splendid work but the members have increased again during the year. The thanks of the committee are again due to Miss McFerran and Miss Wood for their management of the Newport Pagnell depot, and to Mrs. Harvey for her untiring energy at Wolverton. The time has now come when surgical dressings are not so much needed as convalescent clothes, so it has been decided to stop the work unless necessity again arises. May the committee take this opportunity of thanking Mr. Taylor for his hospitality and the public for all their kind help which has enabled the depot to be supported entirely by local contributions.' Following applause, Mrs. Knapp then read the report of the honorary secretary and the manager for the year ending December 31st 1918:
>
> 'The output for the year is not so large as the previous year. The following are details and numbers of work made at the depot and branches:- Surgical dressings 15,103, surgical swabs 5,220, pneumonia jackets 222, roller bandages 4,451, many tail bandages 2,637, capeline bandages 233, eye shades 102, slippers 416, operation stockings 62 pairs, operation socks 70 pairs, bed socks 72 pairs, mufflers 24, mittens 8 pairs, pyjamas 40 pairs, night shirts 24, pillows 38, treasure bags 82, milk covers 40, vermin vests 20, knitted swabs 36, letter cases 10, total 28,910....'

During the operation of the depot those hospitals supplied had been Northampton, the Royal Buckinghamshire Infirmary, Meaux Hospital, Luxembourg, France, the V.A.D. Auxiliary Hospital, Newport Pagnell, the Sick Billet Wards, R.E., Newport Pagnell, St. John Warehouse (Lady Jekyll), and the British Red Cross, Pall Mall, and supplies had also been forwarded to the Reverend H. Blomefield, B.E.F. On behalf of the Committee, Lady Farrar thanked everyone who had taken part in the work of the depot throughout the past three years and two months, and especial thanks were due to Mr. F. Taylor, who had allowed the use of the accommodation rent free. Thanks were also expressed to Mrs. Wright for painting and cleaning the premises free of charge, to Mr. Burgess and Mr. Cotton, of the High Street, for pressing and cutting cloth and soles for the slipper workers, and to all those who had given cloth, carpet etc. for use in the slipper rooms. Next, Lady Farrar referred to the balance in hand and after a lengthy discussion as to how to employ the money it was decided to make an investment in War Bonds, with a committee of Lady Farrar, Miss McFerran, Miss Wood, Mrs. Vaughan Harley, Mrs. G. Uthwatt, Mrs. A. Cook and Mr. F. Allfrey being formed for the purpose. As for the ultimate use, it was the expressed opinion of the meeting that the finance should be applied to the Newport Pagnell Cottage Hospital, should that scheme be carried through as a War Memorial. Then at the close of the ordinary business Mrs. Knapp rose to present a silver afternoon tea tray to Miss McFerran and Miss Wood. They were the real founders of the depot and in appreciation the engraved inscription read;

'Presented by the Workers of the North Bucks War Hospital Supply Depot to Miss McFerran and Miss Wood in recognition of their able management and organisation, 1915 - 1919.' Both ladies expressed their gratitude and with a hearty vote of thanks to Lady Farrar the meeting came to a close. However, for another who had played an important role there would be recognition on the evening of Tuesday, October 21st 1919, when in the large hall of the Science and Art Institute, Wolverton, Mrs. J. O. Harvey was presented with a gold wristlet watch, set with diamonds. Contributed to by 'all classes of residents,' this was in recognition of her wartime work, with the presentation being made by Mrs. J. Strachan.

St. John Street in days gone by. The Admiral Hood first building on the right.

It was demolished, with the adjacent shops and houses, in 1958 for the widening of St. John Street, as seen in the present day photograph.

PUBLIC HOUSES

ADMIRAL HOOD

Aged 59, William Heritage, the landlord of the pub, died at the Admiral Hood on August 21st 1915, and the licence was next granted to Edwin Lucas, a relative. Then at the Divisional Petty Sessions, Mr. J. Day, manager of the Newport Pagnell Brewery Co., applied for a temporary holdover of the premises on Wednesday, October 6th 1915. On this date there should have been an application by Henry Lucas for permanent transfer but Superintendent Pearce said that if the application had come forward then, "I should have had something serious to say on the matter. For the moment Mr. Day is applying to hold this licence pro tem., which I think is the right course, and I have no objection." The application was granted with the Bench intimating that the full transfer of the licence would not be sanctioned to Henry Lucas. Not that matters progressed smoothly, for on Wednesday, October 20th 1915, before Colonel W. J. Levi and other magistrates Edwin Lucas, 'the former holder of the licence of the Admiral Hood public house, Newport Pagnell,' was summoned at the Petty Sessions for having on September 26th 1915, allowed certain members of the Forces to be on licensed premises after 9 p.m., contrary to an order issued by a competent military authority. His wife, Lucy, now living at Ecton, Northants., was also summoned for aiding and abetting him. In contrast to her husband she pleaded guilty and for the prosecution Superintendent Pearce intimated that the proceedings were taken under the Defence of the Realm Consolidation Regulations.

Giving evidence, police sergeant Roberts said that on August 28th 1915, he received instructions from Superintendent Pearce to visit all the licence holders in Newport Pagnell, to inform them that the Army Council had issued certain instructions forbidding a publican to serve soldiers any drink except during certain hours. Also they were debarred from serving wounded soldiers at any time and a copy of the notice was served at the Admiral Hood on August 20th, being displayed in the pub. Continuing, police sergeant Roberts told the court that at the time William Heritage was the holder of the licence, keeping house for him, as well as being in charge, was Mrs. Lucas, who was told by the witness that any contravention of the new instructions would be severely dealt with under D.O.R.A. Evidence was then given that on September 27th Mr. Lucas went to Newport Pagnell police station and made a statement, which included that about 7.30 p.m. on September 26th three soldiers went into the pub. With the others apparently in khaki one was wearing a Scotch cap and, having told Mrs. Lucas that they were wounded soldiers from Tyringham House, they went into the parlour, where she and the servant girl, Daisy Osborne, from Milton Keynes, attended to them. Stating that he knew nothing about the instruction regarding wounded soldiers, Mr. Lucas said that he stayed in the tap room and could not see how they were dressed. He didn't know what they had to drink but saw some bottles of stout taken in. At 9 p.m. he then knocked on the door saying it was time, at which his wife said that she had also told them. Leaving his wife downstairs at 10 p.m. he went to bed and having at about 10.30 p.m. heard her coming up to her bedroom he went to sleep. However, around midnight he was awoken by voices in his wife's room, where on striking a match he saw a pair of 'khaki knickers' on the floor. Striking another match he then saw a man crouching by the side of the bed and looking under the bed he saw another. Exclaiming "Is this your game?" he rushed back to his own room to put some clothes on and when his wife called out "Alf, I want some water!" he retorted "You get it then."

He then left to fetch help and on his return saw two soldiers leaving the house with their boots off. They didn't look like the two from Tyringham and his wife later denied that there were any soldiers, saying, when told that he was going for the police, "find the soldiers." At 10.30 a.m. the next morning he reported the facts to Superintendent Pearce, explaining that having left the house he had parted from his wife and instructed the brewers to take the beer away. As for allowing beer to the soldiers, he said he wasn't informed they were wounded until they had been served two or three times. On the same day Mrs. Lucas was summoned to the police station, where, before making a statement, she was warned that under D.O.R.A. she would have to answer any questions under penalty of £100, or six months prison. She duly made a somewhat ambiguous statement that no soldiers had been in the house on Sunday evening, or if they had they left before 9 p.m. In her evidence, Daisy Muriel Osborne, a domestic servant of Milton Keynes, said that on Sunday, September 26th at 7.30 p.m. three soldiers went into the pub in the company of George Roberts and Arthur 'Dot' French, a 29 year old rag and bone collector of Baker Street, Leighton Buzzard. The soldiers and Roberts went into the bar parlour, whilst French stood outside in the passage. Two of the soldiers wore khaki coats and hats and one had a khaki coat and Scotch cap. They were wearing blue trousers but she didn't notice their jackets until they left. In answer to Superintendent Pearce she confirmed that one of the jackets had been left behind in the lavatory and that they left at 9 p.m., having since 7.30 p.m. been served two bottles of beer between the three of them by Mrs. Lucas. When Mr. Lucas had gone to bed, two of the soldiers returned at 10.15 p.m. and were allowed into the parlour, where one sat in the big chair and the other on the sofa. Daisy went to bed and slept with Mrs. Lucas but about 11.30 p.m. two of the soldiers came into the bedroom, where they were found by Mr. Lucas. George Roberts, of Newport Pagnell, who had joined the army the previous day, told the Bench that he and French had met three soldiers at Cannon Corner at about 7.30 p.m. and he had no knowledge until the following day that they were patients from Tyringham.

After French had given them a light the soldiers asked if they would like a drink, and, because French wouldn't be served at the Plough, they went to the Admiral Hood, where the landlady served them beer. At 9 p.m. the soldiers departed and taking them 'down river side' French left two on the iron bridge but went further along the street with the third. However, on returning they found that the other two had gone and when they passed the Admiral Hood Mrs. Lucas said, "They are gone Dot, and are looking for you." Then at the Admiral Hood the next day, Monday September 27th, Mrs. Lucas confided to Roberts that her husband had been knocking her about. Stationed at Tyringham Military Hospital, Private Harry Whatmough, R.A.M.C., said that on September 27th he had been asked by a soldier patient to fetch his coat from the Admiral Hood, the garment being a blue hospital coat. Sergeant Millican, R.A.M.C., next gave evidence about search parties being sent out late on Sunday night. This was to find three patients who had broken bounds from Tyringham Hospital and between 1 a.m. and 2 a.m. he met the three patients, dressed in hospital uniform, coming from Newport Pagnell. All were under the influence of drink and Captain N.W. Stevens, the officer in charge at Tyringham, said that when brought in the condition of the men lead him to think they had been drinking. In fact as a result of drink one had to have medical treatment. During the hearing it was stated that Mrs. Lucas had kept house for William Heritage, the licensee of the Admiral Hood, and when she married Mr. Lucas about four years ago he went to live with her at the pub. Following the death of Mr. Heritage, Mr. Lucas then took the licence of the house but only intended to live there until Mr. Heritage's affairs had been cleared up. He said he worked at Salmons, did not cohabit with his wife and had no intention of ever living with her again. For her part Mrs. Lucas said she gave the soldiers a night's lodging and they had no right to enter her bedroom.

As for her husband, she said that he had left her seven times because he couldn't afford to keep her. After 20 minutes the Bench found the case against the male defendant proved, being liable to a fine of £100 or six month's hard labour in prison. However, they were going to impose a fine of £10, at 10s a week, or in default one month's prison. Mrs. Lucas was sentenced to six weeks hard labour in each case, to run consecutively. In consequence Mr. Glanley, a solicitor, applied for the transfer of the Admiral Hood to

Mr. J. Day, the manager of the brewery, and since a temporary holdover had been granted a month ago he now asked for the permanent transfer. This was such that Mr. Day could hold the licence until a suitable tenant was found and the request was granted. Then on behalf of the Newport Pagnell Brewery Co., in February 1917 Mr. Day applied for the renewal of the licence of the Admiral Hood and this was granted, on condition that Mr. Day promised, in writing, not to reopen the premises before the next annual licensing meeting. Then in 1918 on behalf of the Bucks Brewers' Association Mr. F. Allfrey, of the Newport Pagnell Brewery Company, sought permission to voluntarily surrender the licence and this was accepted.

Railway Tavern

It would be in one of the brakes of Mr. R.J. Layton, the landlord of the Railway Tavern, that, having received their mobilisation papers before midnight on Tuesday, August 4th 1914, the Newport Pagnell members of the Wolverton Companies of the Bucks Battalion (Territorials) travelled to Wolverton, needing to be at their new drill hall headquarters before 8 a.m. Wednesday. With them they carried a large Union Jack, and a large crowd vociferously cheered their departure. On Saturday, September 12th 1914 Mr. R. Layton had an unusual customer when, shortly after midday, a noise was heard in the smoke room. Bernard Maag, who assisted with the bar duties, went to investigate and was startled to find a bullock, which then left as quietly as it had arrived. The Railway Tavern was often chosen as a venue for those wishing to celebrate special occasions, and after his marriage at the parish church of Hampstead, London, to Miss Helen Whiting, of Caldecote House, it was there that on the evening of Thursday, October 29th 1914, John Price, a corn and coal merchant of Newport Pagnell, entertained all his workmen to supper. 18 sat down to partake of an excellent hot spread of English fare that, they having also prepared the food, was served by Mr. and Mrs. Layton. Then one Monday evening in late January 1915 the officers and a few members of Court 'Unity,' Ancient Order of Foresters, met for a convivial evening at the Railway Tavern. This was on the occasion of the transfer of their Court from the Masonic Hall to The Poplars, and after a hot supper the loyal toasts were proposed. Mr. J. Short, the secretary, next gave a speech on the progress of the Court, and the sound financial position, and amongst those contributing to the evening's harmony were Miss N. Layton and also Miss K. Layton, who presided at the piano. Apart from being the landlord of the Railway Tavern, from April 10th 1915 Mr. Layton took over the Swan Hotel Yard for the hire of conveyances of all kind at short notice. Also acquired was the hostelry's associated bus business, and a special conveyance would meet the last train from London on Sunday nights at Wolverton, for the convenience of passengers to Newport Pagnell - 'Telephone No. 33.'

Given by the customers of the pub, on Saturday, April 17th 1915 a box of cigarettes, tobacco etc. was sent to the wounded soldiers at Northampton Hospital, at the annual fete for which, held in the town on Saturday, June 21st 1916, cycles were stored at the Railway Tavern. As told in the relevant chapter, at the Divisional Petty Sessions on Wednesday, October 4th 1916 Mr. Layton was summoned for not having extinguished lights in his house when Zeppelins were over the country. A fine was imposed, but by the opinion of the Bench the offence had been caused by an oversight of his daughters. However, they would soon redeem themselves, for after an auction sale to provide Christmas comforts for the town's soldiers, held in the Girls' Council School on Saturday evening, November 18th 1916, by offering two buttonholes for sale one of the daughters 7s 6d. Then at the annual fete to raise funds for Northampton Hospital , on Saturday, July 21st 1917 they, together with their mother, both before and during the day sold buttonholes and scented cards, the latter of which Miss K. Layton sold a record number of 29 dozen. As for Mr. Layton, he donated the money raised by storing cycles at the Railway Tavern to the fund, and the following year for the Red Cross Sale, held on Wednesday, April 24th 1918, provided brakes to fetch those members of the band employed at Wolverton Works. In late August 1915 Mr. Layton had advertised the need for a man to look after horses and 'do driving' at the Swan Hotel Yard, and in April 1918 the same requirement arose. However, Alfred Childs would be unable to apply. He had been ill for many months, and at a whist drive and dance, held for his benefit at the Council Schools on Friday evening, October 18th, Miss K. Layton was the winner for the first prize for ladies. On September 29th 1920, Mr. Layton transferred his posting business to the Anchor Hotel Stables, from where the bus would run to meet trains. Special orders could be given at the Railway Tavern or the Anchor Yard, although in the case of the latter this would be only until February 28th, 1926, when Mr. Layton relinquished his tenancy. All orders for horsed vehicles for weddings private parties etc would then have to be directed to the Railway Tavern, High Street.

The Anchor

The Anchor Inn, a military scene. This closed in 1963 and with the porch removed the premises became divided into three shops. Photo courtesy of Ken & Joyce Graham

The Swan

Miss Mary Jane (Minnie) Howard, the daughter of the late Mr. and Mrs. Robert Howard, formerly of Wavendon, came to the Swan Hotel as manageress in 1914, having been with Mr. and Mrs. Gardner at the Rose Hotel, Bedford, for five years. The Swan would be the venue for many of the local social and business events and with the consequent need for staff in January 1915 there was an immediate requirement for a kitchen maid, especially since on the 27th of the month the annual meeting of the Newport Pagnell branch of the National Farmers' Union was held, followed on Wednesday, February 10th by the 20th annual meeting of the Newport Pagnell Shire Horse Society. April saw the need for a 'boots' whilst from the 10th of the month Mr. R.J. Layton, 'job master,' who kept the Railway Tavern, took over the Swan Hotel Yard (and the bus business connected with the hostelry) from where conveyances of all kinds could be hired at short notice. Additionally, for the convenience of passengers to Newport Pagnell a special conveyance met the last train from London at Wolverton on Sunday nights, 'Telephone No. 33.' Business flourished and in August 1915 a man was needed 'to look after horses and do driving, apply R.J. Layton, Swan Hotel Yard.' The Swan was also doing a good trade, including

on the afternoon of Wednesday, August 18th 1915, serving a 'capital tea' after a friendly match between the town and two rinks of bowlers from the Beech Hill Club, Luton. The latter proved the winners by four shots. Recruited by Superintendent Pearce in October 1915 the 'boots' at the hotel, John Bagshaw, of Union Street, aged about 43, joined the Army Veterinary Corps and there was another loss on October 14th 1916, when a fine of 2s 6d, plus the same in expenses, was imposed on the manageress, 'Minnie' Howard, for 'allowing a chimney to be on fire.' The case had been brought by special constable Chapman who at the hotel on Wednesday, June 26th 1918, purchased the freehold of 24, St. John Street for £200. Conducted by Alfred Bullard the auction had commenced at 6 p.m. and also on offer was 'Cedar Lodge' in Union Street. Having three reception rooms, five bedrooms, a veranda and gardens which overlooked Bury Field, to which it had a private entrance, this at £45 p.a. was in the occupation on a short let to Dr. Digby White and although bidding rose from £500 to £700 it was then withdrawn, to be available for private sale. By now it seemed that Mr. Layton had at last engaged a man 'ineligible for the army' for duties at the Swan Hotel Stables, for no doubt due to the shortage of manpower he had been advertising the position for a couple of months. In March 1920 the manageress of the hotel, Miss 'Minnie' Howard, fell ill and aged 41 died a week later of double pneumonia on Sunday, March 28th. The funeral was held on the Wednesday with the burial in Newport Pagnell Cemetery. As for the hotel, having disposed of his hairdressing and tobacconist business at 58, High Street, which until recently had been the Food Control Office, by late October 1920 the new proprietor was Mr. A.G. Ellingham.

The Dolphin

The Dolphin After the war, in 1919 Charles Wells and Co. Ltd., of Bedford, took over the business of the Newport Pagnell Brewery and although the premises were closed some of the tied houses were retained, including the nearby Dolphin. In 1915 Engine Room Artificer Reginald Levin, the son of the landlady, Mrs. Levin, widow of Frederick Levin, was serving

aboard H.M.S. Albion in the Dardanelles whilst at the parish church on the morning of Tuesday, April 27th 1915, his only sister, Eva, in a semi military ceremony Sergeant Percy Coddington, of the Lincolnshire Yeomanry, who had formerly been employed by John Odell.

Pig & Whistle Cottage, Mill Street

On Sunday afternoon, October 11th 1914, Mr. and Mrs. H. Harris, of the Pig and Whistle Inn, Mill Street, were driving with other friends along the Watling Street when, near the Brickhills, the horse stepped on a stone and stumbled. The shafts of the cart were smashed and with all the occupants thrown onto the road a baby boy, the nephew of Mr. Harris, was pitched between the legs of the horse, which was uninjured. Fortunately the boy only received a severe shaking but Mrs. Harris suffered bruising and a bad cut on the head and Mr. Harris had a cut face. After assistance they secured another trap and then drove home to Newport Pagnell. An engineer by profession, during the war Mr. Harris would work on munitions at Newcastle and Coventry. His father having kept the pub before him, he held the licence of the Pig and Whistle for 24 years and, aged 51, died on the night of March 3rd 1922, leaving a widow and a married daughter.

RAILWAY STATION

On the morning of Monday, August 3rd 1914, there were touching scenes on Newport Pagnell railway station when the ex-servicemen left to take part in the war. However, there were scenes of the light-fingered touch at Newport Pagnell Police Court on Wednesday, January 20th 1915, when a soldier was charged with having stolen certain property from a woman of 11, Paggs' Court, Silver Street, with whom he had lodged. Giving evidence, Charles Ratcliffe, the stationmaster at Newport Pagnell, said that on calling at the booking office the man had enquired about the time of the next train to London, but, carrying his collar and tie in his hand, he seemed to be under the influence of drink. Despite saying that he was going away for a weekend he only purchased a single 3rd class ticket, and the reason, and the details of the case, are given in the chapter on 'Crimes and Punishment.' On Saturday, April 24th 1915, at about 4 p.m. a fire broke out in the smoke shaft of the engine shed at Newport Pagnell railway station, and it was only due to the prompt action of two Wolverton Works employees, Harry Cowley and G. Meadows, who were tending their allotments nearby, that the incident did not become more serious. A spark from an engine had apparently lodged in the soot of the smoke shaft in the roof of the building, and on seeing a huge tongue of flame the two men hurriedly fetched a ladder and poured buckets of water onto the burning woodwork, so preventing the blaze from spreading.

Help was also rendered by Mr. Ratcliffe, the stationmaster, and two porters, and on the arrival of the train from Wolverton the locomotive engine fire hose, a new and very useful fire fighting device, which had recently been provided for all the North Western stations, was brought into use, and soon proved its worth. With the war having reached stalemate, in the ensuing attrition there was now an increasing need for additional men at the Front, and one of those to respond was Joseph Sturgess, despite this meaning that he would have to leave his employment in an important railway position at Buenos Ayres. Previously he had been booking clerk at Newport Pagnell station, where in May 1915, the present booking clerk, as also an employee in the goods office - Messrs. Stacey and Bonfield - were about to enlist. They were waiting to be relieved from their railway duties, with a Miss Warwick being instructed in the role of booking clerk. In fact in August, Jack Bonfield, a married man, who for a while had been employed as accounts clerk in the goods office, would join the motor machine gun detachment with his wife moving to stay with her parents at Northampton. Yet despite the gloom of the war situation, during the same month the station staff would be very pleased if anyone could spare plants to brighten up the station flower beds. Shortly after mid day on Monday, July 19th 1915, there was an accident in the High Street, when two farm carts, belonging to Mr. Lawrence, of Rectory Farm, Filgrave, were proceeding to the goods station. Just past Cannon Corner the shafts of the rear cart came into contact with the leading cart, and, with this causing the horse to rear and kick, the cart collided with a gas standard directly outside Mr. William Fleet's butcher's shop, almost wrecking the premises.

Fortunately there were no injuries, but tragically this would not be the case on Friday evening, August 27th 1915, when Thomas Williams, of 'The Nook,' Spring Gardens, suffered an accident whilst returning home on his bicycle from Wolverton Works. He had finished his working day in the electrical department at 5.30 p.m., but whilst cycling home the head stay of his machine snapped as he was descending the hill into Stantonbury, and he fell heavily onto the road. Rushing to his aid railway workers found him unconscious, bleeding from facial wounds, and with two of his teeth knocked out he was put on the workmen's train to Newport Pagnell, to be attended at his home by Dr. Digby White. Without any mishap he had been cycling to and from Wolverton for 14 years, and would happily make a speedy recovery. Corporal Leo Tompkins, of the Northants. Regiment, had formerly been a booking clerk at Newport Pagnell railway station, but in October 1915, it was announced that he had received a commission as second lieutenant in the Oxon and Bucks Light Infantry. As for those about to join the Army, in late October 1916, Mr. Charles Ratcliffe, the stationmaster, acquired possession of an unclaimed parcel of Army recruit's clothing. This had been despatched from Bury St. Edmunds on November 12th, and being addressed to 'T.H. West, near Newport Pagnell, Bucks.,' attempts were being made to try and trace the intended recipient. Opposite The Poplars, at the junction of Hill Street and Station Road, on Saturday, November 4th 1916, a collision occurred between a motorcycle and sidecar and an approaching motorcar.

The car was being driven by Mr. Pebody junior, of Olney, whilst astride the motorcycle was Mr. Tracy Higgins, an assistant master at the Council School. The frame of the motorcycle buckled in the collision, but the sidecar in which Mrs. Higgins was travelling was practically wrecked, and having suffered a badly cut leg, bruises, and a cut on her face, she was taken to The Poplars, being returned to her home in Lovat Street after treatment by Dr. White. Badly shaken, Mr. Higgins had suffered a cut about the mouth, and incredibly about 90 minutes later a second accident occurred, within 200 yards from the site of the first.

This involved Edward Keys, an employee of the local horse breeder Donald Fraser, who was driving a horse and cart to the railway station accompanied by seven year old Joseph Hart, a boy who was never happier than when spending time among the horses on Mr. Fraser's farm. Approaching the Town Hall the horse was suddenly startled by some pigs, and bolting down Station Road collided violently with a traction engine negotiating the corner opposite Coales' wharf. The shafts of the cart snapped and both the occupants were thrown into the road, but apart from a shaking Keys escaped serious injury. However, the boy was taken unconscious to a nearby house from where, after attention by Dr. Wickham, he was conveyed to his home at Moulsoe. The horse escaped injury, but the collision had not only bent the front axle but also caused other damage to the traction engine. In January 1917, a strong youth, aged about 16, was required as a porter at the railway station, and would perhaps porter the two consignments which, on the afternoon of Friday, March 30th 1917, featured as evidence at Newport Pagnell Police Court. The case involved the theft of Army food, and in court Superintendent E. Dibben said that on Wednesday, March 28th on visiting the railway station, to where the two consignments had been taken by a boy and the female prisoner, he found a leather case consigned to an address at Manor Park, Essex, and also a trunk destined for a Bournemouth address. On taking possession of both he found the leather case contained various Army provisions valued at 16s 8d, and the full story is told in the chapter on 'Crimes and Punishment.' In May 1917, there was again the need for a strong youth, aged about 16, to work as a porter at the station, where on May 13th between 8 a.m. and 9 a.m. two horses pulling carts, which had been sent to fetch coal by Len Roberts, of North Crawley, bolted when startled by the noise of the shunting engine. Dashing from the goods yard the first horse passed the slight turn into the High Street, but was soon stopped by police constable Bonner. However, unable to make this turn the second horse dashed into Mrs. Higgs' cottage opposite, and on colliding with the iron fence was freed from its harness by the impact. The animal was not seriously hurt, but the heavy cart broke the fence, dislodged some brickwork and slightly damaged a window frame. Changes to the times of trains by the London and North Western Railway took place from Monday, October 1st 1917, and these would include those of the Newport Pagnell branch line, where, instead of 9.10 a.m., it would now be 9.20 a.m. when the Wolverton train left for Newport Pagnell station.

With conscription now in force, in November 1917, there was once again the need for a strong youth to act as a porter at the station, where there was much concern on Tuesday, February 12th 1918, when 'Dolly,' a black spaniel bitch belonging to the stationmaster, Mr. Ratcliffe, went missing. Yet it seems that she didn't go far, for having been seen several times in the town Mr. Ratcliffe requested her return from whoever was providing her with food. On Wednesday evening, April 10th 1918, presentations were made to Mr. Henry Charles Cummings, who at the end of 1917 had retired on a pension from the post of Chief Goods Clerk at Newport Pagnell Railway Station. On behalf of the subscribers, at the Swan Hotel, Mr. J. A. Price presented him with a purse of Treasury notes, and both by him and Mr. H. Whiting speeches of appreciation were made, in which was mentioned his 45 years of service with the London and North Western Railway. In fact having come to the town in 1880, 36 of these had been at Newport Pagnell, where he had served under at least 10 stationmasters. As for some of the youths that he trained, they had gone on to responsible positions across the globe. During his leisure time, for some years Mr. Cummings had given his services as a teacher in the Church of England Schools, whilst in other pursuits he had many years ago earned considerable notoriety for his Shakespearian recitations at the old Penny Readings, given in the Masonic Hall. Indeed, delighting his present company it was a characteristic recitation that he gave when responding in suitable words to his retirement presentation. On the following evening, in the Railway Tavern Mr. Ratcliffe presented him on behalf of the station staff with a silver mounted umbrella. This had been suitably inscribed, and Mr. Ratcliffe's father, who had been in charge of the station for eight years, then added his testimony to the worth of Mr. Cummings, who gave a brief response before the rest of the evening was pleasantly indulged, to include contributions to an enjoyable programme by Miss Sargent, the booking clerk and Mrs. C. Ratcliffe. A keen swimmer, in retirement Mr. Cummings would often spend his leisure in making daily trips to the Willen Road bathing place, where on many occasions he would even break the ice to take his dip. He would die at his home in Priory Street in January 1936.

At the Petty Sessions, on May 1st 1918, Wilfred Green, the clerk at the station's Goods Office, was summoned for having failed to screen the inside office light on April 17th. Giving evidence, police constable Nicholls said that he saw a bright light shining from the Goods Office at 10.25 p.m., and on investigation found an incandescent burner alight, devoid of any form of shade. When questioned Mr. Green said "I went off and forgot it," and in court Mr. Ratcliffe said that the office was a dark one, and they had to have the lights on all day. A fine of 2s 6d was imposed. There was an unusual shipment from the station on Whit Monday 1918, for having force-landed during the Red Cross Gala day, held at Woad Field, an Army Observation Balloon had to be deflated and taken aboard a lorry to Newport Pagnell railway station, from where, with its complement of five officers, to begin a return journey to London on the 5.20 p.m. train. In October 1918 the need had again arisen for a railway porter, but for Mr. J. Tattam, the secretary of the Newport Pagnell Co-operative Society, his concern was the weakened state of the former P.O.W.s who were now beginning to arrive at the station. There were no arrangements to take them to their homes, which could be many miles away, and so instead of them having to walk he said that his Society would be pleased to subscribe to a fund for their conveyance. Then at the A.G.M. of the Newport Pagnell Naval and Military War Pensions Sub Committee, held on Friday, December 20th 1918, it was reported that the return of the P.O.W.s had now been addressed by the local representatives, and in consequence the stationmasters, who were to deal with each case on its merits, would assist in the special arrangements to deal with their transport. No notification of arrival was sent, but there was provision to cover the cost of conveyance. It was because men were now being released from the Forces that Miss Marie Sargent, the third daughter of Mr. and Mrs. J. Sargent, of St. John Street, had to relinquish her employment as booking clerk at the station, a position which she had held for the last 4½ years.

With the railway company now replacing the lady clerks with the former employees, her position would be filled by re-engaging the man who had been on active service with the London Scottish for four years. Yet no doubt Miss Sargent didn't mind, for at the parish church on Tuesday, August 12th 1919, she married George Fitt, the son of Mr. and Mrs. Fitt of King's Lynn, who had been severely wounded whilst serving with the Norfolk Regiment in Palestine. With one of her bridesmaids being her sister, and her brother as best man, she was given away by her father, and following the ceremony a reception was held at the bride's home, with the honeymoon being spent in Hunstanton. Of the station employees who would return from the war Jack Bonfield had distinguished himself on active service. Having voluntarily enlisted in August 1915 in the Motor Machine Gun Section he was attached to a light armoured motor battery and went to France in March 1916. Within a year he had been promoted to corporal and from November 1917 would serve in Mesopotamia, where in recognition of his abilities he was promoted to sergeant and then acting sergeant major, being awarded the Military Medal for bravery in 1918. Since there was no longer a need for Army accommodation, at 3.30 p.m. on Wednesday, June 8th 1921, Wigley, Sons and Gambell, on the instructions of E. Patton and Co., Government contractors of Blanford and Luton, auctioned at the station yard a 25,000 foot run of second-hand sawn timber, glazed windows, clothes hooks etc., which, being no doubt of great interest to the local builders, had accumulated through the dismantling of Army hutting. As for Mr. Charles Ratcliffe, in 1926 he left the town to take up duty on April 5th as stationmaster at Loughborough main line station (Midland section), also having charge of the London and North Western section station and would later be appointed to an important position on the railway at Redditch. Succeeding his late father, Silas Ratcliffe, who had previously held the job for eight years, he had been at the Newport Pagnell station since 1912 and was lately also in charge of the station at Great Linford. Silas died in 1923 and after his death his widow, Mrs. Mary Ann Ratcliffe, continued to live in the town until moving to live with her daughter, Mrs. Richmond, at Sheffield where after a short illness she died aged 84 in 1937. Her body was then brought to Newport Pagnell for burial in the same brick grave as her husband.

SALMONS & SONS' MOTOR CARRIAGE WORKS

Despite the declaration of war domestic life still had to go on, and in late August 1914 at the family home Mrs. Lucas Salmons, the wife of the head of the firm, had the need for a good general servant. Meanwhile, over 40 employees at 'Messrs. Salmons and Sons' Motor Carriage Works' had volunteered for military service, and the firm had agreed to keep their places open. As for the works, in September a letter from the Home Office stated that the provision for the means of escape from fire at the paint shop was unsatisfactory, and in consequence the letter was referred to the Council's Surveyor. For potential customers the firm could offer, 'at a special price,' a Swift Cycle Car, complete with lamps and accessories which, having a list price of £140, had only been used for a few trials. However, for persons wishing to hire vehicles, open and closed cars were additionally available. On the employment scene several smart lads were now needed, but the German mechanic Otto Schonebrook, who for a while had been employed at Salmons, was re-arrested one Tuesday morning in September 1914, and on the following day conveyed as a prisoner of war to the compound at Newbury, Berks. Police constable Miles was his escort, and this was the first time that a police officer had been noticed to be armed with a rifle, and wearing the regulation military bandolier.

Many local worthies were anxious to help the war effort, and Walter Carlile, of Gayhurst House, had asked the firm to design and build, at his own expense, an ambulance body to be fitted to his Rolls Royce chassis. For use at the Front this would be able to accommodate four persons lying down, or two lying down and six sitting, or 12 sitting, and orders for ambulances had also been placed by others of wealthy means including Mrs. Boswell, of Crawley Grange, Mr. and Mrs. Konig, of Tyringham House, Miss Maxine Elliott, the famous actress, and Bernard Morice, the brother in law of Colonel Good, of Broughton. In fact such was the firm's reputation that a special feature appeared in the Daily Telegraph of Monday, October 5th 1914. With patriotic fervour still running high more employees were now joining up, and in October 1914 ex Colour Sergeant J. Rich, of Priory Street, re-enlisted in his old regiment, the Suffolks. Presently stationed at Bury St. Edmunds he had been appointed as an instructor in the new army, with the rank of Colour Sergeant, and his two sons were also in the Forces - Private J. Rich in the Bedfordshire Regiment, and Private G. Rich in training at Chelmsford with the Wolverton Detachment of the Bucks Territorials. But inevitably news of casualties was being received, and during October 1914 it was learned that among the officers missing on H.M.S. Hawke was Engineer Lieutenant Commander D.J. McGregor who, having married a daughter of the late Mr. Gaius Hillyard, of Newport Pagnell, had for some considerable time been employed at Salmons.

In evidence of the type's important role in the war effort, one Monday in late November a motor ambulance built and supplied by Salmons, and designed to the order of the London Panel Doctors Committee, headed the City of London Red Cross Detachment in the Lord Mayor's procession through London. Meanwhile, on the local scene later in the month between Newport Pagnell and Sandy the firm managed to lose a spare tyre fitted on a detachable rim. This had been wrapped in a black waterproof cover, and upon its return a reward would be paid to the finder. However there was a more tragic loss when during a naval engagement off the coast of Chile the 'Good Hope' was sunk. The entire crew perished, and amongst the victims was Able Seaman Fred French, of the Special Naval Reserve. Employed at Salmons, he had been undergoing his annual training when the war broke out, and his loss bereaved a wife and four young children. For several seasons he had been the trainer for the Newport Pagnell Autos Football Club, and on the evening of Sunday, December 6th 1914 they, in combination with the local P.S.A. Brotherhood, staged a sacred concert at the Electric Theatre for the benefit of his widow and family, as also for another seaman from the town who had perished. 900 people packed the venue, and with the party of performers being from Luton they were conveyed to the theatre in a car lent by Salmons at nominal expense. Especially for the event Mr. Thickpenny had provided a fine upright piano free of charge, and the success of the occasion was greatly due to Mr. C. K. Garratt, who acted as pianist. Amongst others the concert had been held under the patronage of Lady Farrar, who contributed to the patriotic speeches, and with the sum of £19 being raised the fund would be kept open until the evening of Monday 14th.

Despite news of the increasing casualties more employees from the firm were joining up, including by early December Messrs. G. Rout, C. Dicker and G. Tofts, all of whom had volunteered for Kitchener's Army. As the head of the firm Mr. Lucas Salmons was also doing his bit, as one of a party of local vocalists who visited the town and surrounding villages at Christmas to sing carols. However, the festive joy was sadly tempered on February 23rd 1915, when at London Road his seven day old son, Geoffrey, died. As a gift to Russia, and built to order by Salmons, on Friday, March 5th 1915 a fleet of 10 motor ambulances was inspected in the grounds of Marlborough House by Queen Alexandra, accompanied by Princess Victoria and Sir Dighton Probyn. Yet there was also an increasing need for ambulances in France, where, near Armentiers, Sapper Leonard Knight, of the 12th Company Royal

Engineers, was severely wounded on March 11th 1915. Shot by a Maxim gun he was suffering from a badly fractured arm and shoulder, and would subsequently undergo hospital treatment at Southsea. He was the youngest son of the late James Knight, a bootmaker of the town, and before the war had been employed at Salmons for some eight years. Having last September produced the best type of motor ambulance on the market, from the ideas of Colonel P.B. Giles, of Holne Chase, Bletchley, Salmons were now building a motor field kitchen, and in two editions of the Daily Graphic in March 1915 photos were shown of the type in use cooking and travelling. In fact the motor kitchen had recently formed up with the Transport Column of the City of London Red Cross in front of the Guildhall, London, and, with the fire having been lit at 1.30 p.m., during the route march to Hyde Park a meal was cooked aboard the vehicle for 300 people. Consisting of roast meat, baked potatoes, soup and tea, this was then distributed with rolls and butter in Hyde Park at 3.30 p.m. Of Wigmore Street, Messrs. Benham and Son were the manufacturers of the stove range, and with this being an improvement on the type they had manufactured for Captain Scott, for use on his Antarctic Expedition, the special and ingenious flue draught was so arranged that practically any heat could be obtained. Similar to that of the kitchen type, the draught could be diminished whenever there was a need for only a portion of the range, which, burning any kind of fuel, was accommodated in a specially designed body. This was well ventilated, with windows opening each side, and a raised double louvered top lined with asbestos, and additional features were the numerous cupboards and storage facilities, and, on one of the rear doors, a large panel which could be let down to provide a metal covered carving and serving table.

Being presented to the City of London Red Cross, and duly posted by Colonel Broome Giles to the Transport Column, this particular 'Motor Field Kitchen' had been purchased by Mr. A. Hill, of Upper Norford, S.E., and with it being his intention to drive the vehicle his friend, Mr. Kirkby, would act as orderly to superintend the cooking and the distribution of rations. In fact the vehicle would be used at the rail head in London where the ambulance trains arrived from the Front, and parading with the Transport Column would be the vehicle from where those personnel, as also the wounded, would receive their food. Salmons were now providing motor ambulances weekly to enable Colonel Broome Giles to instruct his personnel, whilst at Newport Pagnell the firm was experimenting with a new type of motor ambulance, with a view to securing a prize offered by Messrs. Burrows and Wellcome. Regarding an appeal for the ladies of the county to purchase an ambulance, for use on the battlefront by the British Red Cross, on November 16th 1914, from Daws Hill, High Wycombe, Lady Lincolnshire had written to Mr. O. H. Bull, J.P., the chairman of the Newport Pagnell Urban District Council:

> "Dear Sir. I have been asked to raise the sum of £400 to buy a motor ambulance as a gift to the Red Cross Society from the ladies of Bucks for our wounded soldiers at the front. Two subscriptions of £25 each have already been promised. I shall keep the list open to collect, if possible, another £400 for the maintenance of a Buckinghamshire car, and I will gladly receive and acknowledge the smallest sum. Every ambulance sent up to the fighting line means the saving of many precious lives, and to be able to help in such a definite way must appeal to us all.
>
> Yours sincerely,
>
> LADY LINCOLNSHIRE."

In Newport Pagnell subscriptions were gratefully received by Mrs. Eva Mitchison, The Green, and Miss Bailey, The Elms, High Street, who on November 19th wrote:

> "In order to assist in raising the £400 from the women of Bucks to present a Motor Ambulance for the front, members of the Newport Pagnell Girls' Club and St. Agnes Guild will make a house to house collection during the early part of next week, and it is hoped that all will put some contribution, however small, into the bags."

The monies were then forwarded by Mr. Bull to Lady Lincolnshire and in the first week of April 1915 the ambulance, which had been built by Salmons, was displayed in the showrooms of the firm at Newport Pagnell. In fact £25 had been contributed to this 'Bucks Ladies' Ambulance Car' by the town and district, and it was hoped to later exhibit the vehicle in London, so as to be viewed by other subscribers from the county. In fact being moved to Messrs. Salmons and Sons' London showrooms at 6,7, and 8, Upper Saint Martin's Lane, this would take place on Monday, April 26th 1915, and with £515 as the cost of the vehicle, the total subscriptions to date, to include its maintenance, had amounted to £659 15s 6d. Then, with 'Buckinghamshire' written in large letters on the side, around the beginning of June 1915 the vehicle was accepted by the War Office, with a Mr. Barnard enlisted as the driver. With all the wartime contracts the firm now had the need for several 'good, strong lads' as apprentices, and not least since some 60 of the 80 employees who had volunteered were now in the Forces. But apart from personnel there was another loss on Friday, June 4th 1915, when carrying a dozen eight cylinder King cars, consigned to the firm, the S.S. Inkum was sunk by a German submarine off the Scilly Isles. Having volunteered his services, an employee of the firm, Mr. A. Appleton, had now been accepted as a viceman (sic) in a Government munition factory, whilst on June 19th

1915 eight employees of the firm, one being a widower with three children, enlisted at Bedford in the East Anglian Division of the Royal Engineers. Complete with military outfits they then returned to Newport Pagnell in the evening, having been motored that morning to Woburn Sands station in a motor bus lent by Salmons. However, it was horses and trolleys that the firm lent on Saturday, June 26th 1915, for the annual special effort to raise funds for Northampton Hospital. Elsewhere, on the same day the first 10 of the cavalry ambulance cars, which had been provided by subscriptions raised in London, and duly inspected by Queen Alexandra, were handed over in Russia in a special ceremony at Tsarskoe Selo, where Sir Robert Buchanan, the British Ambassador, introduced Messrs. Firebrace and Holmwood, who were in charge of the cars, and Mr. Hall, the organising secretary. Accompanied by the Grand Duchesses Olga and Tatiana, the Czaritsa (sic) thanked the donors for the gift, and as one who now drove his own little car the Czarevitch (sic) was a most interested spectator. The vehicles were fitted with the popular Salmons ambulance bodies, yet apart from vehicles the firm was also engaged in making toys, for which they now had the need for smart lads who might later be apprenticed to the motor trade, if recommended by the foreman.

News was now being received of former employees who had joined up, including in July 1915 Sapper W. Daniells, of the Royal Engineers. The son of Edward Daniells, of Greenfield Road, he had taken part in a great military sports meeting at Brightlingsea, Essex, and in the 100 yards had lost by only a few inches to the renowned runner A. Moncrieff, who, having competed against the cream of English runners, now held a commission in the London Company of Royal Engineers. Nevertheless, as a prize Edward received a silver handled hand-painted cake stand, as also a silver topped pickle stand and fork for coming second in the 220 yards. As for another former employee, Alfred Tofts, a brass cleaner, leaving a wife at 3, St. Paul's Terrace he had enlisted on the last day of November 1914, and as a private serving in the 6th Oxon and Bucks Light Infantry was wounded on the Western Front on September 25th 1915. He would be subsequently treated in a nursing home in Folkestone. Meanwhile, for the war effort in Newport Pagnell Mr. Lucas Salmons was one of the stewards at two grand concerts held in aid of the Serbian Relief Fund. These took place at the Electric Theatre on Tuesday, the first of February, during which month the firm completed four Rolls Royce cars to the special order of the War Office. These, fitted with landaulet bodies, were for the use of the General Staff in France, and the feature of folding tables and other accessories was to enable British officers, directing operations on the Western Front, to transact map work etc. whilst on the move. In fact one had already been used by General Sir Douglas Haig, the Commander in Chief. As for other work, the firm was continuing to make toys, for which two smart boys were presently needed. With the blackout now in effect, for a contravention of the regulations George Salmons was summoned at the Divisional Petty Sessions on Wednesday, May 3rd 1916. He chose not to appear in court, but made an apology through Superintendent Pearce. Giving evidence, police constable Bonner said that around 10 p.m. on April 27th he had seen, whilst on duty in Tickford Street, a large gleam of light showing from the side of the house. Upon investigation he found the source to be an electric light showing down the passage, and with the door being open he pointed out the transgression to the defendant, who said that the girl had gone to bed and forgotten to extinguish the light. When told that the offence would have to be reported he replied "Certainly," and a fine of 10s was imposed. On behalf of the Russian Government, at the end of May 1916 the War Office placed a contract with the firm for fifty of the seven seat motor car bodies.

An advert from 1916.

For use in the field these were to be fitted to Clement-Talbot and Austin chassis, and not surprisingly a labourer was now needed in the smith's shop. In addition, at the Local Appeal Tribunal for the Newport Pagnell Urban Area, held on Friday evening, June 16th, the firm sought military exemption for 25 employees, and all but one, for whom the firm withdrew their application, were granted an exemption of three months, with six months being allowed for a partner in the firm. The question of exemption from military service then arose again on the evening of Wednesday, August 9th

'Olympia.'

1916, when a costing clerk, aged 25 and single, a manager, and a painter, married with one child, were, despite a previous exemption, challenged by the Recruiting Officer. However, he had been made aware of the importance of their work that very day, for whilst visiting the works he had met the Russian War Office representative who told him; "We have sent a lot of Russians to fight your battles in France and you must not have these men, because it is necessary we should have these cars." Nevertheless it was thought that a woman could replace the costing clerk, who it was mentioned had been passed at Oxford for general service. But countering this a member of the firm pointed out that they had already provided 120 men for the Army, and each of the contested men was indispensable for the completion of the Russian orders. Thus after consideration all three were granted exemption for three months, albeit conditional on joining the Bucks Volunteer Regiment. In fact this was just as well, for the firm had now received a further contract from the War Office to build and supply 40 War Department motor lorry bodies. By now good progress was being made with the previous War Office order for 50 touring motor car bodies for the Russian Government, and, with the firm also making the transit cases, the first shipment of the vehicles had already been made to Russia. Thus with the military now fully aware of this importance, at a later Tribunal the Chief Recruiting Officer for the county, Captain L. Green, gave a long report regarding the firm, which he now conceded was seriously understaffed. Of the employees 50 men were of military age, four were badged men, seven were apprentices aged 18, whilst of the 20 single men eight were fit for general service. Except for the latter, who would be given a temporary exemption of three months, he recommended conditional exemption for the duration of the Government contracts, and with this the Tribunal agreed. As for the costing clerk he had written to say that he intended to join up, and the military would be asked not to call him before September 30th.

(Captain Green would remain as Recruiting Organiser for the county until the control of recruiting was assumed by the Ministry of National Service. In a letter read at the Newport Pagnell Rural District Tribunal on January 21st 1918, he therefore severed his connection with the county. A proposal was then passed "That this local Tribunal have heard with deep regret of the removal of Capt. Green from this area, and desire to place on record their appreciation of his work in so far as it applied to this Tribunal where his advice, always so freely given, has been found to be sound, and his treatment of the many complicated cases has been fair and just.")

For some months the Signal Section of the Royal Engineers had been present in the town, but during September 1916 it was made known that they would soon have to move to another centre for training. However, since in terms of trading and behaviour they had been of great benefit to the town, representations to keep them in Newport Pagnell were made to the military authorities, and to overcome the difficulty of 'messing' accommodation Salmons had offered a portion of their large motor garage. Here the soldiers could be fed in two relays, although this was provided that the firm could find storage elsewhere for their vehicles. Regarding the number of available billets in the town a canvass was duly made, and with the accommodation exceeding all expectations the military agreed to remain in the town for the winter months. However, although staying in billets the men would take their meals together, for, as promised, Salmons had given up the major portion of their building known locally as 'Olympia.' Measuring 110 feet by 50 feet this would be the mess room, where between 800 and 900 men would take their meals at one sitting. Apart from the coming and goings of the Royal Engineers, from the end of October 1916 there would be additional activities at the works, for a further order was then received from the War Office for a large number of W.D. motor lorries, this being the fourth such order since the beginning of the war. Then in the first week of November 1916 instructions were received to build an additional 25 motor car bodies for use by Russian Headquarters Staff, and this was swiftly followed by a further order from the War Office for 100 ambulance cars. In fact these orders were even additional to the ongoing Government contract for 10 three ton W.D. lorries per week, and it was therefore not surprising that on Wednesday, December 13th 1916 the firm lodged six appeals to retain skilled men. Five had been passed for general service, and one B1, and a representative of the firm said that if they had to go then the firm would be unable to continue the contract for not only the W.D. motor lorries but also the motor ambulances. The present output was 15 vehicles a week, but the War Office now wished to increase this rate, and, although substitution was suggested as a remedy, it was emphasised that the men were indispensable. Three months was accordingly allowed in each case, to be revised at the end of that period if the contract had not been completed. As for those employees who had joined the Forces, it was with pride that in January 1917 the firm received news that Sapper Albert Weston, whose wife lived at 51, Greenfield Road, had been awarded the Military Medal.

The question of exemption for the employees again arose at the Urban Area Tribunal on Wednesday evening, January 17th 1917, when an appeal was made for a single man, a sawyer, whose name had been omitted by mistake from the list of those employees put back until April 1st. A representative said that the firm was fully engaged on important war contracts, and with no private work being undertaken they had a War Office order to turn out three ton lorries at a rate of 10 per week for as long as the war lasted. 150 had already been delivered, and in addition they had just commenced an order for 100 motor ambulances for the British Government. With the interior being finished in white enamel, and the exterior painted in service green, with the Red Cross on both sides and on the top, these would each carry four stretchers, and with a weekly output of eight having to be delivered by road to London for final inspection, the first had now been passed by the Inspector. He therefore stressed the need to retain all the employees to achieve this output, and in consequence the man, who had been passed A1, was exempted until April 1st, this being the date on which the case of all the other men would come up for revision. By the end of March 1917 222 three ton W.D. lorries had been delivered by the firm, with a guaranteed output of 10 per week, whilst as for their construction the necessary timber was sawn up and prepared at the Newport Pagnell works, and then sent by motor lorry to the London workshops for the final build. Apart from this, 54 of the 75 bodies for use by the Headquarters Staff of the Russian Army had now been packed and despatched to Petrograd. Having given up 'Olympia' to the Royal Engineers as a mess room, for storing the motor chassis as they arrived from the works the firm had accepted the Newport Pagnell Brewery Company's offer to adapt their principal malting in the High Street, and perhaps here would also be stored the 600 iron bound trench boards, and 20,000 timbers for shell carrying, for which the firm had received a contract from the War Office during the third week of March 1917. As for the firm's ambulances, persons wishing to inspect these vehicles, both finished and in construction, could view them on the Saturday afternoon between 2 p.m. and 6 p.m. Yet despite all this work Salmons was continuing with toy making, and for a large agricultural and general auction sale, held in the town on Wednesday, March 21st 1917, Mrs. G. Salmons and Mrs. L. Salmons gave 12 of the firm's beautifully made English toy ambulances and wagons, which raised a total of £2 18s 6d.

At the Local Appeal Tribunal for the Urban District, held at the Council Chamber on Wednesday evening, March 28th, considerable time was spent considering the position of those Salmons employees who were of military age. 28 had been passed for general service, five were B1, five were B2, four were C1, six were C2, seven were C3, and 11 had been rejected by the Medical Board. However, when asked by the chairman, the Chief Recruiting Officer for Bucks, Captain L.H. Green, agreed that the work on the Government contracts was of the utmost importance, and the only point in contention was the number of so many single men. In fact he was very impressed by the company, for no private work was being undertaken, and the portions of timber that could not be turned into motor bodies were being turned into toys. Therefore no waste was involved, and it was his opinion that certain men in the toy factory could be replaced by women and put on motor work, so releasing some of the single men for the Army. However, from a staff of 240 men in July 1914 the firm now employed 140, the others being in the Army, and the senior partner said that he hardly knew of any man who could be spared. Ultimately, having gone through the list of medical categories, it was decided to dismiss the application regarding an engineer's apprentice, aged 18, A1, as also a panel beater, aged 21, B1, and a day book and wages clerk, aged 22, B1. But in the case of the latter the military would promise not to call him up until June 8th. Seven apprentices passed for general service were granted three months' exemption, and also exempted were all the other employees, on condition that they continued on Government work. A pleasing point of the proceedings was the expression by Captain Green of the fair and straightforward way in which the firm had met the military, and of the facilities which had been offered for a full inspection of the works. As for the manpower shortage, several young girls were now required to assist in light work in connection with box making etc., and also possibly stretchers, for at a meeting of the U.D.C. in June 1917 the following letter was read;

> "The Lamblies, Newport Pagnell.
> Dear Sir,
> When the Emergency Hospital at the schools was started to deal with possible air raid casualties, two stretchers were purchased from Messrs. Salmons and Sons for £4 4s. These have recently been paid for, and as officer in charge, after consultation with Dr. Wickham, the medical

officer, I wish to hand them over to the Urban District Council for the use of the town. If the Council accept the offer I would suggest that for the duration of the war one of the stretchers be kept at the V.A.D. Hospital. At the present time one is kept at the Fire Station and the other at the Police Station.

Yours truly,

H. I. MIDDLETON."

The Council accepted the offer, and a vote of thanks was passed. At the Swan Hotel, under instructions from the executors of the late Mrs. Ann Buxton a sale of business and residential accommodation in the town, and also Stantonbury, took place on Wednesday evening, June 27th 1917. Lot 2, the brick and slated residence of 72, London Road, was in the occupation of Messrs. Salmons and Sons, or their under tenant, with the purchase being made for £230 by Mr. J. Short, J.P. For the Newport Pagnell Habitation of the Young Helpers' League, this being a branch of Dr. Barnardo's Homes, a sale of work took place in the Masonic Hall on Thursday, August 30th 1917. Margaret Salmons was among those selling buttonholes, and the name of Salmons was again associated with good works in the town on Wednesday, October 17th 1917, when, in connection with the 'Our Day' celebration, to raise money for the Red Cross Society, the firm made an advertisement board for a Red Cross shop in the High Street.

On the evening of Wednesday, March 20th 1918, Mr. Lucas Salmons was amongst those taking the quartets at the parish church, when to a good attendance Harold Moore's Cantata 'The Darkest Hour' was sung by the choir. The members were augmented by several lady residents and also a number of Royal Engineers stationed in the town, with the principal soloists being Miss Bertha Richens, from Emberton, and Graham Smart, baritone, of Westminster Abbey and Southwark Cathedral Choirs. Parts were sung by Mr. C. R. Line, while apart from Mr. Lucas the others participating in the quartets were Messrs. O. Critchard, C.R. Line and D. Ashton Davies, with Mr. C. K. Garratt, the organist and choirmaster of the church, presiding at the organ. Prayers were read by the Reverend Gunnery before and after the performance, and by the offertory £5 was raised to defray expenses. The following morning there was a tragic accident at Salmons when, having gone to the sawmill to fetch some wood, Percy Taylor, the younger son of the late Mr. W. Taylor and Mrs. Taylor, of 42, High Street, was struck on the head and knocked unconscious by a piece of timber flung from one of the circular saws. Diagnosing concussion Dr. Wickham was summoned, and although the patient was later transferred to Northampton Hospital he died after an operation for a fractured skull, performed on the evening of Good Friday. At the inquest, held at Northampton Hospital on Monday morning, April

1st, Walter James Line, of 105, London Road, identified the body and said that the deceased was the nephew of his wife. As for William Rogerson, of 159, Tickford Street, he was a metal worker employed by Salmons, and said that on Thursday, March 21st he noticed, whilst cutting slabs of wood on a circular saw, the deceased walk in front of the machine carrying some scrap boards to be cut up. These he then put down but as he was walking away a piece of wood being removed by William was flung out when caught by the teeth of the circular saw, striking Percy on the head. Revolving at 1,000 r.p.m., at the time the saw blade was not protected by a guard, and in answer to the Coroner the Inspector of Factories, Mr. J. H. Nicholls, said that dangerous machines had to be guarded. In evidence William said the machine was now protected by a steel bar at the back of the saw, and this would have prevented the accident. Dr. Madan, the house surgeon, said that when admitted to the Hospital the deceased was suffering from a fractured skull, and although a piece of bone was removed during an operation the patient succumbed to the injuries.

As to why he had not been admitted until eight days after the accident, Walter Line said that during that time the man had been attended by a doctor who, having expected him to regain consciousness any day, had assured them that the patient's life was not in danger. In conclusion the jury returned a verdict of accidental death, and the funeral took place quietly on Tuesday afternoon, April 2nd in Newport Pagnell Cemetery, conducted by the Reverend J. Craig Kelly, a former pastor of the Congregational Church. At the monthly meeting of the U.D.C., held in the Council Chamber, High Street, on Tuesday evening May 7th the report of the Fire Brigade Committee was studied, regarding a report that the fire engine had not been able to attend a recent fire because horses were unavailable. It had been consequently agreed to ask Salmons for the trial of a motor vehicle, and the rest of this story is told in the chapter on the Fire Brigade. At the Divisional Petty Sessions on Wednesday, May 15th 1918, Mr. Lucas Salmons appeared for the firm, when Salmons were summoned for having failed to fence a circular saw at their Newport Pagnell works. Mr. J.H. Nicholls, Inspector of Factories and Workshops, of Northampton, prosecuted, and said that when he inspected the works on July 6th 1917 he had found among other things an unguarded circular saw. He duly pointed this out, and a notice was sent to London. The accident to Percy Taylor had occurred on March 21st 1918, and replying to the Inspector the operator, William Rogerson, agreed that the machine was dangerous. In explanation Mr. Salmons said that all the saws were guarded except that one, and this was because it had been the last to be installed in the saw mill, and was used only for occasional work. Due to the labour shortage they could not get skilled operators, and had a skilled man been using it then the accident might not have occurred. Also it was impossible to do certain work with a guard on, to which the Inspector said that a special guard could be fitted for cross-cutting work. On behalf of the firm Mr. Salmons pleaded guilty, and after consideration the Bench imposed a fine of £5.

For raising monies to purchase a military aircraft, an 'Aeroplane Week' would be held in the town during June 1918, and Mr. Lucas Salmons, as a member of the appointed sub committee, said that he would allow speeches to be introduced in the programmes at the Electric Theatre. Then also regarding the Electric Theatre, by his kind permission, and that of Mr. Bullard, on Saturday, July 6th 1918 the inmates of the Workhouse greatly enjoyed a matinee performance at the cinema. As for Salmons, during September 1918 the firm would require carpenters for making cases for Government work, and this would be at a wage of 10½d per hour plus bonus. For the inmates of the Workhouse, at the annual harvest thanksgiving service, held on Thursday evening, October 10th 1918, Mr. Lucas Salmons was among the members of a special choir, but he would also be present at an even more special evening on Monday, November 12th 1918, when at the Electric Theatre a public meeting was held following news that the Armistice had been signed. However, there was sad news the following month when, after a short illness, Bertram Reynolds died on Friday, December 15th 1918 at 15, Wolverton Road. He was aged 33, and had been employed as a painter and decorator at Salmons, where regarding the need for painting toys two girls were needed in March 1919. On Saturday, July 19th 1919 the Peace Day rejoicings took place in the town, with Mr. Lucas Salmons as the chairman of the committee of the most interesting programme of sports ever to be witnessed in the town. Then in business matters, with there no longer being a need to concentrate on military vehicles a 25-30 h.p. Crossley, with a smart four seat coupe body, was exhibited on their stand at the London motor show in 1919. Also displayed was a 30 h.p. six cylinder Daimler, and regarding the Salmons all weather body much favourable comment was caused by the ease with which the hood could be opened and closed. Also on view were two standard King touring cars, both of which were fitted with three-quarter coupe bodies built at the Newport Pagnell works. Following demobilisation many of the former employees were now re-adjusting to civilian life, and for those attending a 'welcome home' in the town, held on Saturday, January 24th 1920, it was perhaps fitting that Mrs. L. Salmons and Mrs. G. Salmons were amongst the waitresses, attending to a company of some 500.

SCHOOLTEACHERS

Orson Henry Bull

Orson Bull (Photo courtesy of Don Hurst.)

On Tuesday afternoon, May 18th 1937, Orson Henry Bull died at his home, Colville House. He was aged 82 and left effects to the value of £4094 16s 10d. He had been ill for about four years but had been able to take fresh air in his bath chair until about three weeks before. Attended by many prominent mourners the funeral took place on Friday, May 21st at the Parish Church and with the service being semi choral Mr. C. K. Garratt presided at the organ. The only son of Henry Bull, a lime and cement manufacturer, he was born at Oulton Broad near Lowestoft, in which town he received his early education. He then trained as a pupil teacher at Carlton Colville, a suburb of Lowestoft, and on going to Culham College, Oxford, academically distinguished himself by taking Honours not only in science and English but also in other subjects. Indeed he came top of his College for a year and later took his B.A. at London University, with refresher courses at Oxford. Attracted to the town by the fine parish church and organ, at the age of 20 he was appointed headmaster of the National School at Newport Pagnell and when the Riverside schools were condemned he continued as headmaster at the schools under firstly the School Board and, when this was abolished, the Council. Additionally he would frequently teach at Colonel Trevor's school at Lathbury Park, as well as instructing for many years at the evening classes of the Wolverton Science and Art Institute, specialising in science. Mr. Bull was also very active in the civic life of Newport Pagnell and as a young man gained election to the Parish Council in 1904.

Colville House

Subsequently he was successful at the first election for representatives for the Urban Council and, always being first in the poll, would retain his seat until he resigned for health reasons in April 1933, including in his letter: " I carry with me one disappointment - the failure of the Council to purchase Bury Field and the market rights in perpetuity." He had also served on the County Council for six years. In sporting matters in his younger days he was a keen footballer, being president of the old Town Club and the Autos, and having been a founder member of the Bowling Club he sometimes played for the county, even engaging in match play at the age of 79. Backed by Frederick Taylor, it was due to him that the Bathing Place was established and opened as a Jubilee Memorial in 1887, despite this being a time when swimming was unknown in the town. Yet despite the scepticism he remained very enthusiastic and for many years gave a three penny piece to boys from his school whenever they swam across the River Lovat. In fact in total he would teach about 2,000 people to swim - the record being kept on the boards of the huts at the bathing place - and swimmers from Newport Pagnell would twice reach the final in the Midland Counties 100 yards championship. As the founder of the Swimming Club he was president for many years and the winner of many trophies. In 1890 George and James Pike began to sell the land they bought at an auction the previous year at the

Swan Hotel and of the extent six plots opposite Lovat Bank were purchased by a consortium which included Thomas George Harris, a butcher of the High Street. Having previously lived at 49, High Street, with his wife Harriet (a sister of Thomas) and daughter, Ethel, Mr. Bull built Colville House on two of the plots and would also construct the two adjoining villas as well as a number of working class homes, the last of which would be the row in Tickford Street near the new cemetery. Following the outbreak of war, on Thursday night, September 3rd 1914, he organised a recruiting meeting held on the Market Hill.

This was in his capacity as chairman of the U.D.C., and then the following year after the nominations for candidates closed on Thursday, March 11th he retained his seat on Newport Pagnell R.D.C. In fact with no opposition offered the three retiring members, which included himself, would retain their seats for another three years without going to the poll. Mr. Bull was a founder and director of the Newport Pagnell, Olney and District Permanent Building Society. This held its first annual meeting at the Urban Council Chamber at Newport Pagnell on Friday, March 26th 1915, whilst later in the year in the second week of November his married son, Lorenzo Orson Bull (born 1882) enlisted under the Derby Scheme in the Army Reserve (Section B). He was an assistant master at Wolverton Council School and would be called up when required. As an Oddfellow, Mr. Bull was for several years secretary of the Loyal Chandos Lodge, in which capacity at the meeting of the Council School Managers on Tuesday evening, January 25th 1916, he wrote to ask for the terms to use a room for Lodge meetings every fortnight. Also for meetings of the juvenile branch monthly, when the sole business would be to collect the members' contributions. The meetings of the Society had previously been held in the Masonic Hall but this had now been converted into a reading and recreation room for the troops billeted in the town. The application was duly granted, on the same terms as paid to the Masonic Hall. The second annual meeting of the Newport Pagnell, Olney and District Permanent Building Society took place in the Urban Council Chambers in March 1916, with Mr. Bull, the president, in the chair. Here the accounts were passed and Mr. W. Littleboy, of 44, Waterloo Street, Birmingham, eulogised upon the manner in which the books had been kept by the secretary, Mr. Nicholson.

Having been approached in the street, at the Newport Pagnell Urban Area Tribunal on Wednesday evening, January 17th 1917, Mr. Bull, the chairman, made a statement before the proceedings. Since the last meeting a disappointed applicant, who failed to secure exemption from military service, apprehended him and alleged that none of his relatives were taking part in the war. In response Mr. Bull made clear that he didn't mind slurs against himself but he would not tolerate those against his family and to put the record straight he had one son in South Africa who had sold his business and been in the Army for some time, and another son, a teacher, who had attested at the start of the Derby Scheme and been graded B1. He was then sent back to his duties under the Education Committee but had been told to be ready to be called up, which now he had been. Ten of his nephews had joined up and three had been killed. On Tuesday, March 27th 1917, the third annual meeting of the Newport Pagnell, Olney and District Permanent Building Society was held at the Urban Council Chamber where, with Mr. Bull presiding, it was announced that the membership had increased to 53 and the assets totalled over £2,000. (In 1925 Mr. Bull would sell sold Merton Villa, which was once the chief office of the Newport Pagnell, Olney and District Permanent Building Society, to Mr. Arthur Higgins, a university lecturer.) On the domestic scene, at Colville House in October 1917 Mr. Bull's wife, Harriet, had the need for a strong girl as a 'general.' The need again arose in March 1918 but on the afternoon of April 1st Mrs. Bull sadly died at her home after an illness of only a few hours. Born on January 26th 1858, she was aged 60. It had been during the previous morning while getting dressed that she suddenly became unwell and falling unconscious she so remained despite every medical attention. The funeral took place in Newport Pagnell Cemetery on Saturday afternoon, April 6th and as the cortege passed from Colville House all the business establishments were closed and the blinds of the private houses drawn. For the prizes presented by the Misses Taylor of Lovat Bank, on the afternoon of Tuesday, July 23rd 1918, the annual swimming tests for the boys of the Council School took place at the Bathing Place. Present were Mr. C.G. Watkins, the Education Secretary, and Miss Dunn, Inspectress (sic) of Physical Exercises for the County, and having been in charge of the proceedings Mr. Bull subsequently received a complimentary letter from Mr. Watkins:

> "Dear Mr. Bull. I should like to say how heartily I congratulate you upon the prowess of your scholars in the art of swimming. It was a real pleasure to see them disport so ably in the water.
>
> With all good wishes for the holidays, yours faithfully,
>
> C.G. WATKINS, Secretary."

At the Petty Sessions on Wednesday, January 9th 1919, Mr. Bull was congratulated on being made a permanent Magistrate, his name having been recommended by the Oddfellows. In fact he previously sat on the Bench for three years but had then retired. However, on August 31st after 44 years he retired on a pension as headmaster of the Boys' Council School. Yet he would now become more acquainted with the Girls' Council School for the following month he married the headmistress, Miss Catherine James. The ceremony took place at the Parish Church at 8 a.m. on Tuesday, September 2nd 1919, but the date had been kept a comparative secret and consequently only a few people attended. With the Reverend R. Mitchison, the curate, officiating the bride was given away by Mr. W.H. Smith, of Sherington, and the couple would spend their honeymoon at Scarborough. In her married life Mrs. Bull would perform valuable work on the Newport Pagnell Board of Guardians, being in 1929 appointed to represent the National Council of the Association of Poor law Unions on the Central Committee for Mental Welfare. As for the children of Mr. Bull's first marriage, his daughter would become Mrs. Potts, resident at Harrow, his second son, Edward, a qualified chemist who had trained at T. & F. J. Taylor's in Newport Pagnell, would become an executive of the Pharmaceutical Society for the Transvaal, in South Africa, whilst having taken a degree the eldest son, Lorenzo, would become a member of the teaching staff of the Council School at Wolverton, where the plans for his six new subsidy houses, to be built on the new building estate at Radcliffe Street, were passed with a subsidy of £50 for each property endorsed. In 1942 Mrs. Bull sold Colville House to James and Richard Hayfield and in 1955 it was sold to George Mazzone. Lorenzo ('Lorrie') was resident at 37, Cambridge Street, Wolverton, and having been elected a member of the first Wolverton U.D.C. in 1919 he served as County Alderman from 1952 until his retirement in 1964. He had been a teacher for 33 years at Wolverton where he played a major role in establishing the College of Further Education. After an illness of a week he died in early 1965 aged 83 at Northampton General Hospital.

Tracy Higgins

An assistant master at the Council School, Mr. Tracy Higgins was also active in the social life of the town. As on Saturday, June 21st 1916, when at the annual fete for the Northampton Hospital he and his wife introduced the new feature of the sale of natural roses, this being instead of artificial ones as in previous fetes. However on Saturday, November 4th 1916, the couple met with a thornier situation at the junction of Hill Street and Station Road when, with Mr. Tracy driving and his wife in the sidecar, their motorcycle collided opposite The Poplars with a car driven by Mr. Pebody, junior, of Olney. The sidecar was practically wrecked and the frame of the machine buckled and suffering a badly cut leg, bruises and a cut on her face Mrs. Higgins was taken to The Poplars. There she was treated by Dr. White before being conveyed to her home in Lovat Street. As for Mr. Higgins he was cut about the mouth and badly shaken.

CATHERINE JAMES

At the Town Hall on Thursday evening, September 24th 1914, there was a large audience for the first of four performances of the Japanese operetta 'Princess Ju Ju.' This was performed by the girls of the Council Schools and although the performances incurred a loss of £6 7s 0½d Miss James, the headmistress, had last Spring promised to pay from the proceeds an account for infants' prizes incurred by the late Miss Jupp. This was duly fulfilled. Prior to the breaking up of the schools for the Easter holidays, the prize giving at the Council Schools took place on Tuesday afternoon, March 30th 1915. Despite having been in charge of the Infants' School for only a short while the efficiency of the headmistress, Miss E.S. Mills, had come to the notice of the County Education Authority and School Managers whilst for the Girls' School the excellent standard achieved by Miss James was also recognised. However after Easter she would be absent from duty for a while with Miss Amos, an 'unattached trained certificate mistress,' to temporarily assume her position. Also absent would be Miss Kemp, who had tendered her resignation as monitress (sic) in the Infants' Department from March 31st. By the beginning of May 1915 the return of Miss James was imminent for, with Miss Amos coping admirably in the interim, she was making good progress having successfully undergone an operation at Chelsea Hospital. In March 1916 a depot for the collection of eggs for the National Egg Collection was started in the town. With the other head teachers Miss James was tasked with collecting in the schools and in other activities at the annual fete for the Northampton Hospital on Saturday, June 21st 1916, she supervised the dances performed by the Council School girls. Then on the evening of Thursday, July 13th she supervised their costume dances performed at the annual garden party of the Congregational Church in the grounds of The Lodge.

On Tuesday, September 26th 1916, at the monthly meeting of the Council School Managers it was stated that Miss E. Bailey, of the girl's department, was resigning and as headmistress Miss James was asked to rearrange the teaching appointments to obviate the need for a replacement. As for Miss Mills, head teacher of the infants, she was instructed to obtain birth certificates before admitting children to her school. For the National Egg Collection, for a sacred concert Miss James organised a party of programme sellers from among the older girls. The event would be held at the Electric Theatre on Sunday evening, January 28th 1917, and in order to canvass the whole town they were allocated certain districts. In other fund raising matters on Friday evening, May 18th 1917, at a general meeting of the Christmas presents fund committee, for men from the town on active service, appreciation was expressed to Miss James and the ladies' committee for their efforts in raising £25. In the grounds of Green Lodge on Thursday afternoon, June 14th 1917, a sale of work and a garden party in aid of the Newport Pagnell Church Institute and the Melanesian Mission was held. Miss James directed the picturesque dances performed by the Council School girls whilst for a garden fete and sale of work for the Congregational Church, held in the grounds of Ouse Bank on Thursday, July 12th 1917, she and her assistants undertook the training of a party of school children for Old English and character songs, dances and a tableau. Then on Saturday, July 21st 1917, at the annual fete to raise funds for Northampton Hospital, held in Bury Field, the first item, repeated later in the afternoon, consisted of character dances by girls of the Council Schools who had been trained by Miss James and her staff. Apart from school activities Miss James was also involved in town ventures and on Thursday evening, July 26th 1917, on the proposition of the Vicar was unanimously chosen as secretary for a War Savings Association for the town and district. Then at a farewell concert to mark the departure of the Royal Engineers from the town, staged at the Electric Theatre on Monday evening, November 15th 1917, she arranged the light refreshments for the artistes. The venue being the Central Hall of the Girls' School, she also arranged the second of a series of whist drives and dances for the Soldiers' and Sailors' Christmas Presents Fund. This took place on Friday evening, November 16th 1917, and the following month Miss James organised a house to house collection in the town on behalf of Lord Roberts' Memorial Workshops, to be carried out by her regular authorised band of senior scholars.

In glorious summer weather, on Whit Monday 1918 the Red Cross Gala Day and Gymkhana proved a great success and not least since under Miss James the girls of the Council Schools, each carrying a flag, gave a display of marching on the lines of a military tattoo, accompanied by the band. This was followed by Old English dances and folk songs with Mrs. Gillam as one of the helpers. For an 'Aeroplane Week' commencing Monday, July 8th 1918, the person chosen to be the honorary organising secretary was Miss James who for a flag day for the war work of the Salvation Army, held in the town on Saturday, June 8th 1918, undertook a collection in the Council Schools. Then on Saturday, July 20th 1918, on Bury Field at the annual fete in aid of the Northampton Hospital it was under her direction and with Miss Winnie Rout at the piano that the spectacle was repeated, followed by several Old English dances and folk songs. Later in the afternoon Maypole dances were performed by children of the Infants' Department under the supervision of the headmistress, Miss Mills, who also played the piano accompaniments. Regarding Aeroplane Week, at the final committee meeting, held at the Girls' Council School on Tuesday evening,

July 23rd 1918, the question of forming a Town War Savings Association was discussed and it was unanimously agreed that Miss James should be the honorary secretary. With the first item being a Maypole dance by the infants, who were directed by their headmistress, Miss Mills, an autumn fair and 'razzle dazzle' for the Town Christmas Presents Fund took place in the Council School playgrounds on Saturday, October 12th 1918. Under the supervision of Miss James the event came to a close with an illuminated marching display by the girls of the Council School and on the following Wednesday for the 'Our Day' effort in the town one of the helpers, at the shop in St. John Street, would be their headmistress. However Miss James would soon relinquish the teaching profession for on Tuesday morning, September 2nd 1919, at the parish church she married Mr. Orson Henry Bull, who had recently retired as headmaster of the Boys' School.

Dorothy Juffs

She being in the teaching profession, Miss Dorothy Juffs, the only child of Mr. and Mrs. Arthur Juffs, of Bury Street, Newport Pagnell, married Jack Gillam whilst he was training to be a teacher. The son of Mr. J. Gillam, formerly stud groom at Lathbury Park and then the licensee of The Black Horse Inn at Winslow, as a Rugby footballer he had gained distinction in the East Midlands and at the outbreak of war was employed on the teaching staff of the Fenny Stratford Council School. When Captain Mobbs raised the football company of the 7th Northants. he readily volunteered and was accepted for service. Then on the morning of October 14th 1915 Mrs. Gillam received official news that her husband, Sergeant J. Gillam, of the 7th Northants. Regiment, had been killed in action. Captain Edgar Mobbs wrote;

> " 7th Northants Regiment, B.E.F.
> France.
> Dear Mrs. Gillam,
> I am sorry to say your husband was killed in the great fight on September 26. I am so sorry for you all. He was such a man in every sense of the word. He was wounded on the Sunday, and as he passed me in the trenches said, "I shall soon be back - it is only a slight wound." He came back shortly afterwards and started fighting again, but got killed on the following day. I managed to get his disc, which I have sent you. You must bear up and be brave; I know it would be his wish. He died a hero. Yours very truly,
> EDGAR MOBBS."

Dorothy later remarried and she and her husband, Mr. B.J. de Villiers, on Friday, July 7th 1919, attended the funeral of her mother, Mrs. Laura Juffs, who aged 58 had suffered a protracted illness.

Herbert Ingle Middleton

Mr. Herbert Ingle Middleton came to Newport Pagnell around 1892 and for a while was assistant master at the old National Schools, before becoming assistant master at the Council Schools. As a night school he also took 'Continuation Classes' and for the boys attending these he provided an annual supper, with himself and his wife playing host. As secretary of the Newport Pagnell Association, of teachers, it was Mr. Middleton that suggested at one of the meetings that a County Association should be formed. In consequence the Bucks County Teachers' Association was set up in 1903 with in 1908 Mr. Middleton being County President and first Secretary of the Association. Following the outbreak of World War One Mr. Middleton was amongst those at a meeting on Wednesday evening, August 26th 1914, to consider restarting the Rifle Club and reopening the range. This was held at the Town Hall and he asked if an appeal could be made for employers in the district to allow their men to go to the range and practice shooting. Mr. Middleton's daughter, Grace, was also keen to support the war effort and, with a collection taken for the Belgian Relief Fund, in October 1914 she sang at a musical afternoon of the Newport Pagnell P.S.A. Brotherhood. This took place at the Electric Theatre, where for publicity in November 1914 the proprietors offered postal orders of various values in a competition. One name and address would be selected from each of the 13 sheets of the Newport Pagnell voters' lists which,

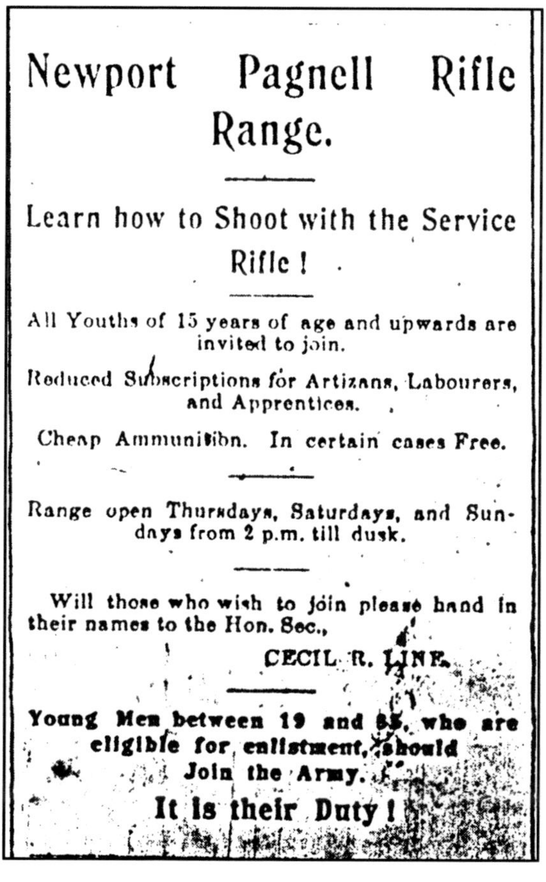

at the selection on Saturday evening, November 21st 1914, were placed on a table in full view of the audience. A lad was then blindfolded and given a lady's hat pin by which to prick out the names of 13 persons. These were written on slips of paper to be placed in a box and shuffled and although no one was present to claim the first three prizes, of 10s, 7s 6d, and 6s, the fourth name was Mr. Middleton. Amid much applause his daughter duly stepped forward to receive the prize of 5s 6d value. In March 1915 Mr. Middleton joined the Newport Pagnell Company of the County Volunteer Defence Corps. By his abilities he would soon become a section commander and he also performed valuable service as a special constable. As for his daughter, Grace, she would serve on the nursing staff of Bedford Military Hospital.

In other activities in June 1915 Mr. Middleton would be the organiser when the Higher Education Committee proposed holding a class in Home Nursing. He was also the honorary secretary of the St. Luke's Committee of St. Luke's Church and on Sunday evening, December 26th 1916, made the presentation of a handsome stole to the Reverend W. St. John Lindars, on the occasion of his farewell sermon. As for Mr. Middleton's daughter, she sang at the Masonic Hall on Wednesday evening, January 5th 1916, and was a performer at a musical pleasant evening at the Wesleyan Schoolroom on Thursday, February 17th 1916. Then on Monday evening, February 21st 1916, she sang at a smoking concert arranged by the Royal Engineers in the Masonic Hall and also at a repeat occasion a week later. Continuing her performances she took part in a concert by members of the Royal Engineers and friends at the Workhouse on the evening of Friday, March 31st 1916, and also at a musical programme arranged by the Royal Engineers on Thursday evening, April 6th 1916. This was held in the Wesleyan Schoolroom where having recited a poem of her own composition, entitled 'To His Mother,' she afterwards raised £1 15s for the British Red Cross by selling copies. She then sang at a concert for the Royal Engineers in the Soldiers' Recreation Room on Monday evening, May 8th 1916, and again at a smoking concert at the Unionist Club on Thursday evening, May 18th. Here as an encore she repeated her original poem, raising 13s 7d for the Red Cross by again selling copies. In the grounds of Green Lodge, at the annual sale of work, staged to raise funds for the Newport Pagnell Church Institute and the Melanesian Mission, on Thursday, June 15th 1916, Mrs. Middleton and Grace ran a fancy rummage stall whilst Mr. Middleton, as the honorary secretary of the Parochial Church Council, conducted a rummage sale in the evening. For the benefit of the London Missionary Society the annual garden party of the Congregational Church took place, despite unfavourable weather, in the grounds of The Lodge on Thursday, July 13th 1916, with Miss Middleton's singing heard to fine advantage. Then on Wednesday evening October 4th 1916, at an event for the benefit of regimental charities she was a member of a troupe which performed under the name of 'The Quaints.' With the assistance of talented local lady vocalists, this was a company of Royal Engineers who appeared as pierrots and amongst the performances she sang 'They wouldn't believe me' as a duet with Sapper Hector. Apart from being a member of the Volunteers her father was also a special constable and had charge of the patrols on October 1st 1916, when the town was the subject of an air raid alert. On Tuesday, January 9th 1917, Miss Middleton was amongst the performers at the annual New Year's treat to the inmates of the Workhouse and also at a concert given at the Y.M.C.A. Hut on Saturday evening, January 27th 1917.

Her mother was also involved in the social life of the town and had charge of the rummage stall when, on Thursday afternoon, June 14th 1917, the grounds of Green Lodge were the venue for a sale of work and garden party in aid of the Newport Pagnell Church Institute and the Melanesian Mission. A meeting representing the various religious bodies in the town was held on Wednesday evening, July 25th 1917. This was to announce that on the present lines the Church Institute could not be continued and, having been the secretary from 1902, Mr. Middleton gave details of the finance, management and membership. At the Y.M.C.A. Hut on Thursday evening, December 6th 1917, a concert included songs sung by Grace but there was family sadness on Christmas Eve when after a long illness Mrs. Middleton died at her home 'The Lamblies,' in Wolverton Road. She had been an assiduous church worker and a district visitor for many years and since the opening of the St. Luke's Mission Church, and the transfer of her residence to that part of town, she had taken a keen interest in the services held there. In addition she superintended and kept the books of the Mothers' Meeting associated with the Church. Her funeral took place on Friday afternoon, December 28th 1917. Mr. Middleton and his daughter continued their activities in the war effort and whilst in July 1918 he would be appointed on the committee for 'Aeroplane Week,' the previous month at the annual 'Sale of Work and Rummage Sale,' in connection with the parish church, Grace would be one of the young ladies in 'The Merry Magnets.' They also performed at the Electric Theatre on Wednesday evening, September 25th 1918, in an event to raise funds for Christmas presents for those men from the town serving in the Forces. In October 1918 the Newport Pagnell Higher Education Committee arranged classes for the coming season. Mr. Middleton was the organising secretary and also during the month on the evening of the 17th his daughter took part in a concert for the Town Christmas Presents Fund for Soldiers and Sailors. This was held at the Y.M.C.A. Hut where as an encore she sang 'Write to me Dear.' At the meeting of the U.D.C. on Wednesday evening, October 30th 1918, Mr. Middleton, in his capacity as Lieutenant, spoke on the question of Volunteer training conditions, saying a number of the men who had been granted exemption had never carried out their duties. However, such matters became irrelevant following the Armistice and he and the Newport Pagnell Company of Volunteers attended the thanksgiving service at 11 a.m. at the parish church on Sunday, November 17th 1918.

With the welcome return of peace, in aid of the Christmas presents fund at the Electric Theatre on Monday evening, December 16th 1918, the 'The Merry Magnets' gave a performance in which Grace was encored for 'Comrade.' However, the town would soon lose her talents and those of her father who at the annual meeting of the Unionist Working Men's Club, held on Tuesday evening, February 18th 1919, resigned as auditor, since he was shortly to leave the country. In fact he had instructed Wigley, Sons and Gambell to auction his freehold residence 'The Lamblies,' situated on the main road from Newport Pagnell to Wolverton, together with a good garden, well stocked with fruit trees, and a tennis lawn. The premises featured a large entrance hall, reception rooms, five bedrooms, bathroom, domestic offices and outbuildings and with vacant possession on completion was auctioned at the Swan Hotel on Wednesday, March 19th 1919, at 4.30 p.m. The bidding opened at £500 but swiftly advanced to £800, with the purchaser being Mr. A. J. Simpson of Newport Pagnell. In the wake of the sale, in April 1919 at the quarterly meeting of the Newport Pagnell, Stony Stratford and District Teachers' Association, Mr. Middleton was presented with a cabin trunk, since he was shortly to leave the teaching profession and go to Rhodesia. Grace was also going abroad, for now as Mrs. Lionel Noble on Friday, July 5th 1919, she and her husband sailed from Tilbury aboard the 'Durham Castle' for South Africa, with their permanent address to be Salisbury, Rhodesia. At a meeting of the Newport Pagnell Conservative and Unionist Association on Wednesday evening, August 13th 1919, a presentation was made to Mr. Middleton who for a long while had been the chairman. He would also leave for South Africa and, with a testimonial fund having been organised by the committee, in recognition of his services Mr. G. Tayler made the presentation of a gold mounted cigarette case and also a solid silver wristlet watch with illuminated dial, inscribed, 'H. I. Middleton. An appreciation for services rendered, from the Conservative Association, Newport Pagnell.' On his return to England he became headmaster of St. Leonard's School and President of the Chesham Association in 1930. He died in late 1956 aged 87.

George Page

As a wedding present, on the morning of Wednesday, July 29th 1914, Mr. George William Page, one of the assistants at the Newport Pagnell Council Schools, was presented by the headmaster with a silver teapot, sugar basin and set of carvers. These had been subscribed for by the headmaster and boys plus a donation from Mr. F. J. Taylor, the late chairman of the managers. George was the younger son of Charles Page, of Newport Pagnell, and as an old pupil of the school had gained a minor scholarship in 1905, later passing the examination for the certificate for his present position. The second daughter of Mr. and Mrs. William Cowley, of Newport Pagnell, his bride was Miss Florence Edith Emily Cowley, who for the past six years had been an assistant teacher in the girls' department. She would be presented with a tea service and china centre vase, subscribed for by the children and teachers plus again a donation from Mr. F. J. Taylor. The wedding took place on Wednesday, August 12th 1914, at the Newport Pagnell Congregational Church of which her father was one of the deacons. For the past 45 years he had run a successful business as a parchment manufacturer but being indisposed for the wedding the bride was given away by her brother. A reception took place at the Town Hall and in the afternoon the newly weds drove to Wolverton, to continue by train to Llandudno for the honeymoon. Resident in Wolverton Road in November 1915 George applied to enlist in the Royal Flying Corps whilst as for his wife she was president of the Congregational Church Girls Club. In this capacity on Saturday, July 21st 1917, at the annual fete to raise funds for Northampton Hospital she and Miss A. M. Coales superintended a flower and vegetable stall, which did excellent business. On October 5th 1918, at 'Abervale,' Wolverton Road, a daughter was born to Mr. and Mrs. Page, with Mr. Page now being an air mechanic in the R.A.F.

Thomas Sim

A native of Whitehaven, in Cumberland, as his first teaching appointment Thomas Sim came to the Newport Pagnell Council Schools in 1899. He also became much involved in public life and being a member of the U.D.C. for six years was appointed as vice chairman. He also served on the local Hospital Week Committee, was secretary of the Good Samaritan Society, the Unionist Club and the Newport Pagnell and Olney District Building Society, and in other duties fulfilled the post of clerk to the North Crawley Parish Council, of which village he had at one time been the rate collector. During the war Mr. Sim served as a special constable and with his efforts being energetic in connection with the Christmas Presents' Fund, to which he devoted much of his spare time, he greatly cherished the hundreds of letters of appreciation which he received from the men on active service. In sporting activities he was a keen billiard player, being one of the founders of the North Bucks Amateur Billiards Association and for seven years captain of the Social Club team. Also for many years he was honorary secretary of the Town Football Club, the North Bucks representative on the Berks and Bucks F.A. Council and a member of the referees' examining board. Mr. Sim retired from teaching in 1932 and was presented by the staff, managers and pupils with an easy chair and a fountain pen. Nevertheless he would still lead a busy life in the town as secretary of the Loyal Chandos Lodge of Oddfellows Manchester Unity, for which he had performed much valuable work.

SHOPKEEPERS

Ernest Dant

Around 1908, Mr. Ernest Frederick Dant and his wife, Florence Louisa, moved from Cambridge to Newport Pagnell. There Mr. Dant began in business as a fruiterer at 65, High Street, next to the Post Office, where, being an expert bee keeper, in October 1914, he advertised 'Honey, in Comb and Glass Jar, gathered by our own Bees.' The business expanded and as a 'wholesale and retail confectioner, fruiterer, and greengrocer' in April 1915, he advertised for 'a clean and respectable youth' to work as an assistant, aged 16 to 17. Despite being British born of British parents the following month a malicious rumour began that he was of alien extraction, claimed initially to be German but then Austrian. In fact one Saturday night there was common talk that a raid was about to be made on his shop but fortunately this did not materialise and, with the matter brought to the attention of the police, Mr. Dant took prompt measures to deal with any further gossip. Indeed there was no questioning his loyalty nor that of his son, Albert, who in the last week of June 1916, went before the Army Medical Board at Oxford. However, he failed to pass for any branch of military service, either at home or abroad. Also on health matters, in February 1917, Mr. Dant advertised that he was 'a Special agent' for 'Mother Michell's Cough Tablets' whilst with rationing in force in June 1917, he could offer 'Turban Dates,' 'a perfect substitute for sugar.' Apart from his daily employment Mr. Dant served as a special constable and took part in the arrest of two escaped German prisoners of war in December 1917. By now his shop also stocked poultry food and 'molassine dog cakes' and in July 1918 could even offer a good, sound, spring trap, built by Hunneybun and Son, of Cambridge. Tragically in April 1919, his eldest daughter, Miss Mabel Dant, died in the influenza epidemic aged 17. Of a bright and cheerful disposition she had only been ill for a few days and her death greatly affected the family. However, with, in May 1920, Canadian canoes 'paddles and cushions complete' offered for sale, the business carried on although the trauma undoubtedly contributed to Mr. Dant's suicide, aged 50, in October of that year. The inquest was held on the afternoon of Wednesday, October 13th 1920, at the police station where, as the first witness, his widow said that because he had been greatly suffering from stomach trouble she and her eldest son, Bert, had managed the shop of late. His first attack of gastritis had occurred about 14 years ago and although last year he was very bad for some time he wouldn't heed her advice to have Dr. Bailey. Instead he would lie in bed in the morning and have bread and milk when he came down, which suited him best. She said he had recently been very depressed and although he never mentioned money worries; "he has been worried about business, but he didn't confide in me nor in my son. He was very reserved." On the morning of Monday, October 11th she said she came down stairs at 6.30 to get her second son off to work at Wolverton by the 7.20 train. She then took a cup of tea up to her husband and was just getting her daughter ready for school when her eldest son came downstairs and said; "Will you call Dr. Bailey. I believe Dad has taken some carbolic." Used for his bee keeping, this was kept in the storeroom connected by a short passage to his bedroom and at the inquest Mrs. Dant said she didn't remember seeing the bottle since they moved from Cambridge. She immediately went to the bedroom where her son was trying to rouse his unconscious father and although Mr. Burridge, a neighbour, was called their efforts proved in vain and the doctor was sent for. Giving evidence, Albert George Dant said he heard a loud gurgling sound whilst he was dressing in his bedroom. This was immediately above that of his father, and on investigation he found Mr. Dant lying in bed in his night attire, unconscious and with a strong smell of carbolic. Continuing, he said that having been pressed for money writs had been issued against his father and although the books of the business had been well kept until about 12 months ago, since then Mr. Dant had taken little interest in the business, leaving the financial side to him. Concluding the case the Coroner returned a verdict; "That deceased came to his death by suicide, and that he was not of sound mind when he committed the act." The funeral took place at Newport Pagnell on Friday, October 15th 1920.

ARTHUR ELLINGHAM

Late of Woburn Sands and resident in Park Avenue, Newport Pagnell, Mr. Arthur George Ellingham was in business at 55, High Street, as a hairdresser in the town and in the last week of May 1915 his son, Stanley Ellingham, enlisted in the Royal Engineers as a motor cycle despatch rider. However, on Sunday, August 22nd 1915, when riding with a party of 80 motorcyclists - 'somewhere in France' - the dust clouds thrown up by the bikes meant that he failed to notice a sharp turn in the road. Running into the bank he was thrown off his machine, which was a total write off, and having sustained serious injuries to his head, back and leg he was picked up unconscious and received subsequent treatment in the 3rd British Red Cross Hospital in France. Subsequently on the morning of Thursday, September 2nd 1915, Mr. Ellingham received official information from the War Office regarding his son, from whom several cheery letters would be scent in due course. In fact Corporal Ellingham would delight the audience with his violin solos at the Soldiers' Institute, Newport Pagnell, on Monday evening, February 14th

1916, where the fine singing of his sister, Miss Olive Ellingham, resulted in encores, her performance having also been much appreciated at a concert at the same venue in the previous month. In fact as 'Miss O.K. Ellingham, A.T.C.L., Medallist of L.C.M.,' in May 1916 she advertised for pupils for piano and organ playing, 'Various exams prepared for. Concert, evening parties, and dances attended as pianist. Park Avenue, Newport Pagnell.' However, there were other matters to attend to on Tuesday, June 6th 1916, when by special licence she married Sapper Frederick Westlake of the Royal Engineers. He was the fifth son of Mrs. and the late Mr. W. Westlake of Plymouth, Devon, with the ceremony being of a quiet nature since he was to be immediately called away on military service abroad. In February 1916 Mr. Ellingham's tender of £13 for haircutting and shaving at the Workhouse had been accepted but his main business was still his hairdressing shop in the High Street, which on the night of November 12th 1916, attracted the unwelcome attention of a youth. Mr. Ellingham had retired to bed but at about 11 p.m. he heard footsteps on the path of his house in Park Avenue and on opening the window he asked a young lad what he wanted. The lad said, "Do you know there is a key in your shop door in the High Street?" but having visited his premises on Sunday evening, and having locked the door on leaving at about 6 p.m., he told the youth he must be mistaken. Nevertheless he got dressed and went with him to the shop, where he found that a key had been jammed in the lock. The lad explained that he had been to a party and on walking past the shop had noticed the key whilst lighting a cigarette. However the circumstances seemed suspicious and with the matter going to court Gertrude Roberts, a shop assistant, said at 9.45 p.m. she was standing near Mrs. Phillips' shop in the High Street when she heard someone trying a key in the lock of Mr. Ellingham's shop. She saw the boy but didn't know him. Police sergeant Roberts said that on Tuesday 14th he questioned the defendant who at first denied trying to enter Mr. Ellingham's premises. Yet afterwards he said, "I put the key in the lock and could not get it out again. I saw a man and asked him where Mr. Ellingham lived. I went to him and told him there was a key in the lock of his shop door. I took the key from Mr. Gibson's stables about 8.15, and I went up the street." Police sergeant Roberts then charged and cautioned the lad who replied, "I have been reading Nelson Lee's book and that is the cause of this. I have told the truth." Asking the boy what the book was about the chairman learned that it was a detective story about a robbery. "Breaking into somebody's house?" asked the chairman, to which the boy replied, "Yes." 16 years and 9 months old the boy had been in a reformatory school, to a representative of which he was then handed over. Concluding the case the chairman told the boy that they were treating him kindly because they wanted to give him a chance.

He must go back to school and "be a good boy and get some better books to read." Under the directions of Mr. Ellingham, on Wednesday evening, April 11th 1917, at a sale of property conducted at the Swan Hotel by Alfred Bullard, 'auctioneer and valuer,' a newly built four bed roomed detached freehold residence known as 'The Ark,' in Park Avenue, was purchased for £425 by Mr. G. Burgess of the town. Yet the family was still resident in the town and at a garden fete and sale of work for the Congregational Church, held on Thursday, July 12th 1917, the many stalls included hoop la under the charge of Miss Maisey Ellingham, who was amongst those selling buttonholes on Saturday, July 21st 1917, at the annual fete to raise funds for Northampton Hospital. As for her brother, William Ellingham, at a grand water carnival, organised by the Newport Pagnell Hospital Week Committee on Thursday afternoon, August 23rd 1917, in the schoolboys' swimming tests he won the championship of the school, despite having only recently learnt to swim. Also regarding sports, the return billiards match between the Woburn Sands Men's Club team and Mr. Ellingham's team was played at the Unionist Club on Wednesday, December 12th 1917. Owing to army duties the visiting team was not as strong as before and being a player short Sergeant Speller, a well known 'cuist', was invited to play as a substitute. This he did and secured the only win for the team, which was defeated by 239 points. As with many of the town's business people Mr. Ellingham had joined the Special Constables and was amongst those who one Friday night in late December 1917 apprehended two escaped German P.O.W.s. His daughters were also assisting the war effort and at the festivities at the Y.M.C.A. Hut on Christmas Day 1917 Miss Ellingham was amongst those giving assistance 'at the tea tables and otherwise.' Then at an entertainment at the premises on Wednesday evening January 9th 1918, she presided at the piano. Later in the year, on Sunday evening, July 7th 1918, she was amongst the performers at a sacred concert arranged by the committee of the P.S.A. Brotherhood, whilst at Christmas 1918 at the festivities at the Y.M.C.A. Hut her brother, now Sergeant Ellingham of the Royal Engineers, gave a violin solo. In February 1919 it was announced that the younger brother of Mrs. Ellingham, Company Sergeant Major C. Green, had been awarded the D.C.M. for gallantry. A native of Linslade he went to Canada about 1902 and enlisting at the outbreak of war came over with the 18th Canadian Division in 1915. The award was for bravery during an attack at Marceleave on August 8th, when the company was held up by a strong point. He organised a party and made a feint on the left flank and, despite being surrounded, by daring and skill cut a way through with his party and, sustaining only a few casualties, captured the strong point consisting of five machine guns. The old people at the Workhouse celebrated a 'Peace' on Tuesday, July 22nd 1919, with

Miss Ellingham amongst those who contributed to the entertainment. In October 1920 Mr. Ellingham disposed of his hairdressing and tobacconist business at 58, High Street (until recently the Food Control Office) and since he was now the proprietor of the Swan Hotel it was there on Thursday, October 21st 1920, that, for some 50 guests, a reception was held following the marriage at the parish church of his youngest daughter, Miss Joan A. Ellingham. The bride was well known in musical circles and the groom, Horace Badham, the only son of Mr. and Mrs. F. Badham, of Forest Gate, London, had for a time been attached to the Royal Engineers at Newport Pagnell. The following morning the couple then left for London.

William Fleet

Having a shop in the High Street, William Fleet was a butcher who also rented property in Union Street from the Council. In the last week of May 1915 his son joined the Royal Bucks Hussars but in September of that year he sent a letter to his father saying he was a prisoner of war at Constantinople. As for Mr. Fleet's daughters, one at the setting up in March 1916 of a depot for the collection of eggs, for the National Egg Collection, would be designated to receive the eggs each week. The daughters also performed at charity concerts throughout the war with Miss Kathleen Fleet, the fifth daughter, being associated with 'The Quaints' and also 'The Merry Magnets' concert parties. She was also a tennis player and with Mrs. Norris was triumphant in one of the sections of a tournament played on behalf of the Y.M.C.A. Huts Fund in August 1918. At Newport Pagnell parish church on Monday, December 1st 1919, she married Arthur Leafe, of Boston, Lincolnshire, and after a reception at the Swan Hotel the couple left by car for Bletchley Station, to board a train for the honeymoon in Brighton. Among the wedding gifts had been those from the young ladies associated with the bride in 'The Merry Magnets' concert party.

Foll & Bawden

With business continuing almost as usual, in September 1914, a 'very cheap' 6 h.p. De Dion car was offered for sale by Foll and Bawden, auctioneers at 58, High Street, Newport Pagnell. However, once it became clear that the war was going to be a protracted conflict there was a continuing need for men for the Army and in the last week of October 1915, Vivian Gardner, a clerk in the offices, was accepted for the Army Ordnance Corps. He had previously tried to enlist five times, including at Dunstable and Finsbury Barracks, but had been rejected on each occasion. In early 1916 it was announced that the business carried on in the town for the last six years by Foll and Bawden would shortly pass to Geo. Wigley and Sons. This was principally because Lieutenant T. Bawden, who was in partnership with Mr.

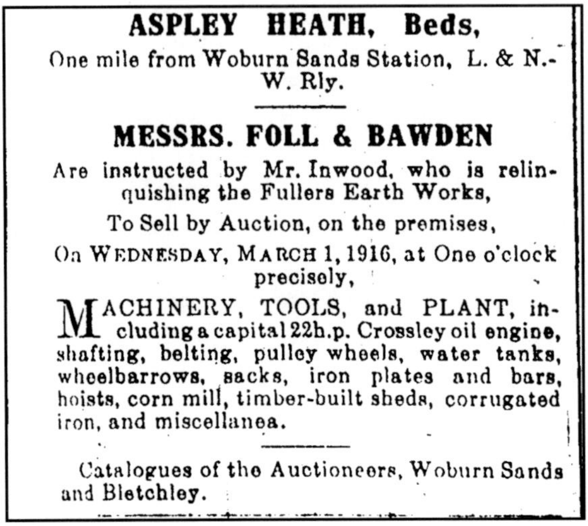

ASPLEY HEATH, Beds,

One mile from Woburn Sands Station, L. & N.-W. Rly.

MESSRS. FOLL & BAWDEN

Are instructed by Mr. Inwood, who is relinquishing the Fullers Earth Works,

To Sell by Auction, on the premises,

On WEDNESDAY, MARCH 1, 1916, at One o'clock precisely,

MACHINERY, TOOLS, and PLANT, including a capital 22h.p. Crossley oil engine, shafting, belting, pulley wheels, water tanks, wheelbarrows, sacks, iron plates and bars, hoists, corn mill, timber-built sheds, corrugated iron, and miscellanea.

Catalogues of the Auctioneers, Woburn Sands and Bletchley.

Bucks Standard February 1916

W.A. Foll, was expected to soon leave for foreign service, since he had accepted a commission in the Army Service Corps in the autumn of 1915. In fact it was perhaps in consequence of this that on April 24th 1916, at the Swan Hotel a daughter was born to his wife, who in January 1917 required a young girl as a general servant at 'Ingleside,' Wolverton Road. A year later it was announced that Lieutenant Bawden, who for some months had been commanding a Horse Transport Company in France, had been promoted and it was thus as Captain T. Bawden that he sent a cheque for £1 1s for the funds of the new Town Institute. This had been inaugurated on Monday evening January 7th 1918, and in the letter he said; "I have been a member of the Church Institute for some years and I think, even in these times, it would be a great pity if the old Institute had to shut up altogether." Before enlisting Captain Bawden had been a special constable in the town and at a supper to mark the winding up of the movement, held at the Swan Hotel on Thursday evening, February 6th 1919, he was amongst those who spoke of how valuable this training had been for his subsequent Army service.

Raffaele Mazzone

A native of Italy, in 1900 Raffaele Mazzone came to Bicester where during the next year he was joined by his wife and two young children. In the town he began a fish merchant's business but in 1908, supposedly playing a barrel organ, he came to Newport Pagnell to become the proprietor of a lodging house at 22, Silver Street, which he had bought from Mr. C. Kenneth Garratt, of local musical fame. From the premises he also ran a fish and chip saloon and traded as a general fish merchant, supplying the town and local villages. Also he introduced ice cream to the district, selling his product from a horse drawn cart with bells on the harness. At ½d and 1d he sold his ice cream in small glasses but some adults were unimpressed saying, "you will freeze our children on cold days." Nevertheless the children loved the new introduction and Mr. Mazzone further endeared himself with his broken English. Following the outbreak of the First World War he readily became involved in charitable events and in 1916 at the annual fete for Northampton Hospital, held on Bury Field on Saturday, June 21st, despite the heavy rainstorms raised £1 6s from his fruit and ice cream stall, having towards the raising of further funds lent two barrel organs, one of which, mounted on a horse and trolley, was paraded around Bradwell, Wolverton and the neighbouring villages. However there was no charitable outcome for contravening the lighting restrictions and at the Divisional Petty Sessions on Wednesday, October 4th 1916, Mr. Mazzone was summoned for not screening the inside lights of his shop on September 26th. Giving evidence Police Sergeant Roberts said that in company with Superintendent Pearce he had been on duty that night and at 8.50 p.m. he saw a light shining across the road from the defendant's open door. When questioned Mr. Mazzone said he had screened the gas jet with a piece of cardboard but customers were

Raffaele Mazzone

continually opening the door to enter the shop. Nevertheless, Superintendent Pearce said that many cautions had been issued to Mr. Mazzone who, pleading not guilty, was told to attend to the problem by the Bench, which imposed a lenient fine of 10s. On Saturday, July 21st 1917, the annual fete to raise funds for Northampton Hospital took place. This was again held on Bury Field and of the barrel organs lent by Mr. Mazzone for the occasion one was taken around the villages on a horse drawn trolley, provided by George Taylor, a shoeing smith. Then on Wednesday, April 24th 1918, on Market Hill at a sale held under the auspices of the Newport Pagnell Branch of the

The two shops (now demolished) owned by the Mazzone family in St. John's Street. Photo courtesy of Don Hurst.

N.F.U. and the Newport Pagnell Red Cross Committee the sum of £14 6s 6d was collected by Mrs. Durrant and the Misses U. and K. Easson. They were the daughters of the Vicar of Chicheley and attired in their Women's Land Army uniforms toured the town with a barrel organ lent by Mr. Mazzone. As for the fete in 1918 for Northampton Hospital, on Saturday, July 20th one of the two piano organs lent by Mr. Mazzone was taken around Willen, Woolstone, Woughton, Simpson, Walton, Milton Keynes and Broughton. This was in the charge of Messrs. S. Brown, A. Hammond, F. Rainbow and J. Richardson whilst the other, in the charge of the Misses Harris and Mills, went to Wolverton, Stantonbury, around the town and then onto the venue. A total of £21 16s 5d was raised and in addition Mr. Mazzone made £1 5s for the funds by selling ice cream in the field. As a loyal subject Mr. Mazzone was naturalised during the war and his eldest son, Michael, saw much active service with the 1/6 Gloucester Regiment on the Western Front and with the 1/7th Worcesters and other units on the Italian Front. In fact after the war he served for a while with General Watson in Egypt but then returned to Newport Pagnell where he went into business with his father at 7, St John Street, which the latter bought in 1920.

Sometime before 1907 here Joseph Bosworth had set up as a fishmonger, with the subsequent occupiers being Ernest Turner and then the Nicholls family, from whom the purchase was made by Mr. Mazzone. Here was built up a successful business as a purveyor of fish, a green grocer, fruiterer and confectioner whilst as for his social life he would be a member of the Chamber of Trade, the Town Bowling Club and the Working Men's Social Club. In December 1926 Michael married Miss Antonette Secondine, the eldest daughter of Dominic Secondine, of 4, Duddlestone Road, Birmingham, and his sister Mary would be one of the bridesmaids at the wedding, held at St. Michael's Roman Catholic Church in Birmingham. The honeymoon would be spent at Southsea. Another of his sisters was Adeline, who being a talented pianist often played at local concerts. In fact at her home in Silver Street she gave music lessons and at the end of 1926 two of her pupils were successful in piano examinations held by the Associated Board of the Royal Academy of Music and the Royal College of Music. Phyllis Millard won the Elementary Division certificate, 'with honourable mention,' and Dorothy Toffs passed in the Primary Division. With a passageway in between, in 1927 Mr. Mazzone acquired the premises adjoining his own in St. John Street, which had been previously owned by Mr. Kempster, a boot repairer, and then a Miss Mason, who sold hats. Thus from 22, Silver Street (of which they retained ownership), in January 1928 a move was made to St. John Street by the Mazzone family consisting of Raffaele, his wife, their sons, Michael and George, and, with her young son Anthony, Mrs. Giovanne 'Ginny' Valente. She was one of the five daughters and sadly a widow for her husband, Stefan, whom she had married during the First World War, had died in 1920. Sadly in the month of the family's move there was another bereavement when Raffaele's wife, Andoniella, died, being buried in the London Road cemetery. George and Ginny would now live at no. 5, selling fruit, vegetables and sweets, whilst Michael and his father occupied no. 7, where they sold fruit, vegetables, fresh fish and fish and chips. Produce was also loaded onto their horse and carts for sale in the town and local district. As for Adeline, the third daughter, in January 1931 at the Roman Catholic Church in Wolverton she married Leslie Griffin. He was the only son of Mr. and Mrs. Harry Griffin, of Spring Gardens, and was in business with his father as a painter and decorator. Adeline was given away by her brother, Michael, and at the Town Hall in Newport Pagnell one of the 70 guests at the reception would be Toni Arpino, a boxer who had recently fought Desmond Jeans, 'the actor pugilist,' at the Albert Hall. Tragically in 1932 Raffaele suffered a seizure. This left him unable to take any further part in managing the business and for his occasional short walks from his house he had to be accompanied by family members, of which he gained much comfort from one of his daughters, 'Ginny,' who was a member of the Newport Pagnell Nursing Division of the St. John Ambulance Brigade and for many years would undertake nursing at Renny Lodge Hospital. At 5, St. John Street, aged 70 Raffaele died on June 9th 1942. He was buried in the grave of his wife and at the funeral, held at the Church of St. Francis de Sales, Wolverton, where the family had always worshipped, the salute was given by his younger son, George, who was serving as a driver in the Royal Army Service Corps. After the war, in 1946 Ginny married Mr. Nicky Pelle and with her son, Anthony, moved to 8, Silver Street, to begin a general stores. Unfortunately she would develop a serious illness but was making a good recovery until in late 1955 she broke her thigh in a fall. At the beginning of December she returned to hospital for a minor operation but died in Northampton General Hospital aged 59. As for George Mazzone, in 1955 he bought Colville House, in Silver Street, whilst as for the shops in St. John Street they were scheduled for demolition for road widening at the end of November 1956. However deliveries of vegetables and fruit would be made from 5, Wolverton Road, whilst as for the trademark ice cream, in a contemporary competition Peter Mazzone would beat his father, Michael, to take the accolade of champion ice cream maker.

John Odell

Born in 1849 into the ironmongery and agricultural implement business, John Odell was the eldest son of John Odell. After a period working in his father's establishment in the High Street, Newport Pagnell, he completed his apprenticeship in Banbury with John Barford and at his father's death in 1896 he then took over the Newport Pagnell business, which he built up into one of the largest in that part of the county. In other activities in his younger days he served in the Bucks Regiment of Volunteers and for many years would be a member of the Volunteer Fire Brigade. He married the eldest daughter of Thomas Shakeshaft, of Ravenstone, and within an hour of the outbreak of war on August 4th 1914 their eldest son, Percy, volunteered for active service saying, "I am prepared to do anything." He would be subsequently stationed with the Territorials at Cosham whilst at Newport Pagnell his father was amongst those at an adjourned meeting in the Town Hall which, held on the evening of Wednesday, August 26th 1914, had been convened to consider restarting the Rifle Club and reopening the range. In fact with many men now volunteering for Kitchener's Army the need for replacement staff would increase and in September he had the need for an active man as a porter and also an errand boy. Of his staff who joined up at the outbreak of war Herbert Dowling would serve with the Herts. Territorials and Ernest Omans as a driver with the Royal Field Artillery. However, tragically one of the early casualties would be Harry Bunker who, serving with the Coldstream Guards, was killed in action at Mons.

Commencing at 8 p.m. a special benefit night was held on Wednesday, November 4th 1914, to provide money for his family and also that of Private Edward Lake, of the 1st Bedfordshire Regiment. Edward had been the

Bucks Standard, November 13th 1915

attendant at the Electric Theatre, which being the venue for the occasion was packed for a programme which, raising £30 10s, consisted entirely of the latest war films. In business matters the tender of John Odell of 12s 6d each for 12 bedsteads for the Workhouse would be accepted whilst in military matters as a member of the Bucks National Reserve in December 1914 Reginald Odell, John's second son, volunteered for active service. He was a member of the town's fire brigade but by the end of the month was in training with the Oxon and Bucks Light Infantry. On New Year's Eve 1914, as the forty eighth occasion the members of the Newport Pagnell Church Institute were entertained to a supper by Mr. F. J. Taylor at Lovat Bank. Amongst the many present were John Odell, as vice president of the Institute. and his son Private Percy Odell who, being afforded a cordial reception, said it was a privilege to appear in uniform. During the past few weeks many of them had been preparing themselves and getting fit and he hoped that when the hour came they would be a credit to the town. As for Reginald, under the command of Lieutenant Colonel F.T.H. Bernard by January 1915 he was serving in the 3rd (Reserve) Battalion of the Oxon and Bucks Light Infantry, stationed at Portsmouth. Meanwhile at Newport Pagnell his place in the fire brigade was a subject at the fortnightly meeting of the Rural District Council and the Board of Guardians. This was held in the Board Room of the Workhouse on Wednesday, February 3rd 1915, where it was decided that until their return from the war the replacements for himself and another member would be Frederick Platt and Frederick Moore. For supplying seed potatoes to the Workhouse, during the month there was only 7s 6d difference between the tenders of John Odell and Messrs. Perkins and Sons and since Mr. Odell was a large ratepayer in the Union it was decided that his should be favoured.

By March 1915 Private Reginald Odell was on active service in the trenches. Percy was serving with the Bucks Territorials at Chelmsford and the third son, Cecil, was serving in Egypt, having been in Australia when the war broke out. As for a former employee of the firm, in a semi military ceremony the wedding took place on the morning of April 27th 1915, at Newport Pagnell Parish Church of Sergeant Percy Coddington, of the Lincolnshire Yeomanry, and Miss Eva Levin, the only daughter of the late Frederick Levin and of Mrs. Levin, of the Dolphin Inn, Newport Pagnell. Having been a clerk for John Odell another employee was Sergeant Bert Dowling who, subsequent to being shot through the left elbow and the back at the Dardanelles on August 19th 1915, was transferred to a London hospital. He had joined the regiment at the beginning of the war and went to the Front about two months ago. Elsewhere, in France also on active service were Private Percy Odell, of the Bucks Territorials, and Private Reginald

The memorial in the parish church to Corporal Percy Odell, killed in action on the Somme aged 37.

Odell, of the Oxon and Bucks Light Infantry, both of whose photos would feature during August 1915 in the Hardware Journal's Roll of Honour. At Newport Pagnell the following month their father had the need for a man - 'used to horses' - for delivery work but apart from business matters there were other concerns to occupy him in September 1915, when news arrived that Private Reginald Odell had been wounded for the second time in Flanders. However in a subsequent letter to his parents he wrote that it was only a slight shrapnel wound in the knee and after four days in a rest camp he was able to rejoin his regiment. This was welcome news to his father who as churchwarden at the annual social gathering in connection with the dedication festival of St. Luke's Mission Building, held on the evening of Monday, October 18th 1915, presented the accounts. Having for the past five years been one of Mr. Odell's assistants, on Christmas morning 1915 Mr. F. Shedd married Miss Dorothy Higgins. A member of the teaching staff of the Sherington Day Schools, a position which she had occupied for eight years, as an accomplished musician she had for some time been organist at the Wesleyan Church and also presided at the piano at the Senior Sunday School Class of the Congregational Church.

With the rank of corporal, on December 31st 1915 Reginald Odell became a casualty for the third time when, in Flanders, a bullet smashed his rifle and caused a wound in his side, which occasioned his treatment in Boulogne Base Hospital. During February 1916 only two tenders were received regarding seeds for the Workhouse farm and garden, these being £18 5s for potatoes and £5 8s 6d for garden seeds. Both were from John Odell who the following month had the need for a carter for delivering goods and looking after horses. In May 1916 news arrived that whilst serving with the Bucks Battalion, Oxon and Bucks Light Infantry, Lance Corporal Percy Odell had been slightly wounded by a bursting shrapnel shell, which fractured his right thumb. He was being treated in a French hospital and the news had been conveyed in a letter, sent to his parents by a friend who was with him at the time. As for his brother, Corporal Reginald Odell, he had been wounded for the fourth time and was presently in Chelsea Hospital with serious shoulder injuries. In June 1916 a collector/salesperson, being an ineligible man, or a woman, was needed by John Odell for country journeys, 'Must cycle,' whilst as for his only daughter, Dorothy, at the annual sale of work to aid the funds of the Newport Pagnell Church Institute and the Melanesian Mission, held by permission of the Reverend R. S. and Mrs. Mitchison in the grounds of Green Lodge on Thursday, June 15th 1916, she was in charge of the hoop la together with Miss Connie Saunders. Her father was also assisting in the town's charitable events and lent weighing machines for the Northampton Hospital annual fete on Saturday, June 21st

1916.

Then came the tragic news that Corporal Percy Odell had been killed in action on the Somme, and on Thursday, October 19th 1916, his parents received the following letter from the Reverend C. H. Hadfield, chaplain of the Forces;

> "Dear Mr. Odell, - I deeply regret to have to tell you that your son, Corpl. Odell, has been reported killed in the recent fighting. Our men showed great bravery and attacked with complete success, but unfortunately not a few were called upon to make the supreme sacrifice for their country. We shall miss your son. May I offer you our sincere sympathy for you in your loss. May God give comfort to you and yours."

The eldest of the three sons of Mr. and Mrs. John Odell, of Newport Pagnell, Percy was educated at the town's National Schools and then Bedford Grammar School. Being for some years with Mr. Thomas at Windsor he then returned to Newport Pagnell, to assist in his father's extensive ironmongery and seedsman business. In his earlier years Percy had been a member of the Bucks Volunteer Corps and being a first-class rifle shot took a great interest in the formation of the Newport Pagnell Rifle Club, initially occupying the position of assistant secretary and then, on the retirement of Sergeant Major G. F. Trimmer, secretary. Included several times in the team which shot for the Astor Cup, he also took part in competitions on the Bisley ranges, and, as an aid to marksmanship, apart from shooting with the service rifle he recognised the importance of the miniature weapon. Thus when Mr. Walter Carlile, of Gayhurst House, presented a miniature range in the grounds of the Unionist Club it was he who designed and superintended the construction of the facility. An excellent shot with both versions he won several prizes when representing the Newport Pagnell Club on the North Crawley range, and following the outbreak of war within an hour volunteered for the Bucks Territorial Battalion. Subsequently taking part in much of the heavy fighting, after training at Chelmsford he went with his regiment to France where as one of the most popular and well liked members of the Battalion he was soon marked out for promotion. However, he was content to stay in the company of 'the boys' - as he was proud to call his comrades - and it would be only after much persuasion that he agreed to accept his corporal's stripes. Wounded in action, after a brief leave at home he then returned to the Western Front with a draft of the Oxford and Bucks Light Infantry, with which he was serving when killed in action. A staunch churchman, at Newport Pagnell he had been a sidesman of the parish church, a member of the C.E.M.S. and frequently helped as a teacher in the Sunday School. He was also a Past Master of the SS. Peter and Paul

Lodge of Freemasons and being a Conservative took a prominent role in establishing the Unionist Working Men's Club.

As for Reginald, after being wounded four times he would be discharged from the army. Regarding those who were seeking military exemption, at the Local Tribunal for the Newport Pagnell urban area, on Wednesday evening, January 3rd 1917, Mr. Odell appealed on behalf of his clerk and also for his seedsman, the former having been passed C1 and the latter for general service. Mr. Odell had already supplied the army with 15 of his staff and after consideration six months was granted in each case. On a central site in the High Street a Y.M.C.A. hut, erected for the recreation of soldiers billeted in the town, was opened on Sunday, January 20th 1917. Among the voluntary helpers in the canteen would be Miss Dorothy Odell, for the death of whose brother Percy regrets were expressed on Friday evening, March 2nd 1917, at the annual meeting of the Unionist Working Men's Club, of which committee he had been a member. On Wednesday, March 21st 1917, at a large agricultural and general auction jumble sale Miss Odell was one of ladies carrying trays of flags and the £36 18s thus raised would be divided between the British Farmers' Red Cross Fund and the Bucks Branch of the Red Cross Society. For the first 12 pig keepers who called at his shop, in June 1917 Mr. Odell offered a valuable booklet about pigs plus a packet of Karswood Pig Powder. Hopefully this would prove as productive as his seed potatoes for during the last week of July a crop of potatoes dug by George Moseley, on his allotment at Fox Gate Piece, yielded nine bushels from a peck of Sir John Llewellyn seed which had been bought from Mr. Odell's shop.

There was great excitement during the late afternoon of Saturday, August 18th 1917, when flying extremely low over Newport Pagnell an aeroplane seemed to be experiencing difficulties. Eventually the pilot turned towards Lathbury but hitting an air pocket lost control and, to the horror of the hundreds of spectators, spun from 400 feet to crash into a large elm tree in a field. Sustaining a bad cut on the jaw the pilot was rendered unconscious although apart from a severe shaking and a small cut on the head the observer escaped unhurt. Dr. Wickham was quickly summoned by telephone and with the assistance of Nurse Dorothy Odell attended to the pilot

The grave of John Odell and his wife, Newport Pagnell churchyard.

who, following the arrival of an ambulance from Newport Pagnell Fire Station, was taken to the Newport Pagnell home of his father in law. There on several occasions he regained consciousness during the night and for three nights Nurse Odell would sit up with him. As told in the relevant chapter, later in the year Mr. Odell played a role in establishing the Town Institute at the inauguration of which he was present on Monday evening, January 7th 1918. Then on Thursday evening, January 24th 1918, at the first general meeting Reginald Odell would be a member of the committee.

In glorious summer weather the town's Red Cross Gala Day and Gymkhana took place on Whit Monday 1918. Of the procession of adorned cars which commenced the proceedings amongst those who had decorated the four vehicles from Newport Pagnell was Dorothy Odell, whose brother Reginald would be kept busy during the festivities with the popular swings. By now no less than 17 of Mr. Odell's employees were, or had, been on military service and at the meeting of the Urban District Tribunal on Wednesday evening, May 29th 1918, amongst those applying for military exemption was his 36 year old manager. Married and classed as Grade 2 he was described as a specialist in agricultural machinery etc. and six months open was given although without being excused Volunteer drills. The annual Sale of Work and Rummage Sale in connection with the parish church took place on Thursday afternoon, June 13th 1918, in the grounds of The Green Lodge, where of the many stalls and amusements hoop la was the province of the Misses E. West and also Dorothy Odell. In the local press the following month a list was published of those people Miss McFerran, the Commandant of Tickford V.A.D. Hospital, wished to thank for providing support to the hospital. As one of the Night Orderlies mention was made of Reginald Odell who at the first half yearly meeting of the members of the Town Institute, held on Wednesday evening, August 7th 1918, offered to give prizes for a billiard tournament. As for his father he presently had the need for an errand boy, 'able to ride a bike,' whilst at 25, Beaconsfield Place, Mrs. Odell had resumed dressmaking and was able to accept work from August 19th.

On January 13th 1920, Mrs. Elizabeth Annie Odell, the wife of John Odell, died, the funeral taking place on the Friday in Newport Pagnell Cemetery. She was born on January 30th 1850 and among the mourners were her husband with Dorothy and Reginald and her sister, Mrs. York, and her brother, Mr. W. Shakeshaft. With the help of his sons Mr. Odell carried on the business whilst as for Dorothy she was a pioneer of the Girl Guide movement in the town, being captain of the Parish Church Company. Also she taught in the Sunday School, of which in 1927 she became superintendent. Apart from involvement with his business at Newport Pagnell her father was a Freemason and also served as a Governor of Northampton Hospital, of the Board of which he was a member when aged 83 he died on Friday, January 9th 1932, at his home, Blair House, High Street. He had been ill for a while but was still able to get about fairly regularly until he suffered a seizure on the Tuesday from which he didn't recover. Including many persons of prominence, on the Monday there was a large attendance at his funeral which being one of the most impressive seen in the town was attended by a former curate of the parish, the Reverend R. S. Mitchison, who came down from his parish of Barby, in Leicestershire, and by special request read the lesson. Mr. Odell was buried in the grave of his wife and, having been the churchwarden for 20 years, in the evening as a mark of respect a half muffled peal of Gandshire Triples was rung on the church bells. In the wake of their father's death Reginald and Cecil now took over the business as Odell Brothers but on Saturday, April 16th 1932, Dorothy left Newport Pagnell to begin a training course in religious and social work at St. Andrew's House, Portsmouth Training College. As an appreciation of her good work the girls of the Sunday school presented her with an inscribed silver pencil case and from the members of the church she received an inscribed silver Crucifix, with the money left over from the subscriptions to be spent as she wished. Consequently in a letter of thanks she wrote, 'If I pass my exams I shall be sent to some overcrowded parish where the clergy need help in Sunday school work, infant welfare, Girl guides, Mothers' Meetings, etc. Thanking everyone so much for their kindness.' Cecil Odell died in 1970 aged 85 and Reginald in 1976 aged 93 and it would be in December 1991 that the Odell's shop at Newport Pagnell finally closed.

RICHARD PETTIT

Owning a butcher's shop in Tickford Street, well known in the town was Richard Pettit and his family of which his eldest daughter, Miss Dorothy Pettit, suffered an unnerving accident on Friday, January 1st 1915. Whilst returning from Wolverton with her sister in a pony and trap, on the steep hill from the station to Stantonbury the back strap of the harness broke and immediately falling to the ground the shafts snapped in two parts. Despite being thrown onto the pony's back Miss Nancy Pettit suffered only a severe shaking but having bravely held onto the reins her sister was pulled from her seat and dragged under a wheel of the trap by the terrified pony. One of her legs was badly bruised and the flesh shredded and after prompt assistance from men who were passing she was taken to Stonebridge Farm, where Mrs. Norman skilfully dressed her injuries. She was then conveyed to Newport Pagnell, to make a steady recovery. In April 1915 her brother, William, was appointed as a member of the Fire Brigade but in June he then applied to join the Royal Naval Air Service. Dorothy, a soprano, was also helping the war effort by performing in local concerts and most notably with a group of local young ladies who would term themselves The Merry Magnets. In December 1916 Mr. Pettit had the need for 'a respectable lad, just left school' for pie making, and hopefully the successful applicant was of a more honest disposition than the two miscreants who, at the Newport Pagnell Divisional Petty Sessions on Wednesday, February 21st 1917, were charged with theft from his shop. They were a schoolboy of 28, Priory Street, who was charged with stealing about £1 in money on February 10th, and a boy of 4, River Side, who was charged with having received 3s from him, knowing it to be stolen. Giving evidence, police sergeant Roberts said that on the 14th he saw the accused and told them he was making enquiries about money stolen from Mr. Pettit's shop in Tickford Street. At this the boy said, "I took it and I suppose I shall have to tell the truth now." It then transpired that in the evening his mother had sent him to get 2d of suet from the shop but the manager, John Read, said he didn't have any. Leaving his ten year old daughter in charge he then told the boy to wait but when the girl's back was turned the boy put his hand in the drawer and took out a note and some silver. Then on Monday evening when he saw the other boy he told him he had some money and together they bought two flashlights, went for tea, bought a pocket book, two oranges, two jellies, two packets of chocolate, half pound of cheese, some bread and also some biscuits. The latter he bought from the shop of Mrs. Betsy Tooth at 79, Tickford Street, and on spreading a pound note on the counter in reply to the woman's enquiry he said his mother wanted it changing to send some money to his uncle in France. In court the parents of the boys asked for the case to be dealt with by the Bench and with the boys pleading guilty the one who had taken the money was sentenced to eight strokes of the birch and the other to four. As a responsible member of the community, in August 1917 Mr. Pettit was amongst those appointed for food control by the U.D.C. but in November his reputation was slightly tarnished when at the Divisional Petty Sessions he was summoned on the 28th for having on November 19th driven a horsed vehicle without white lights at the front and a red light at the rear. Police constable Nicholls said that at 5.05 p.m. he saw the defendant drive a pony and trap through the town and when questioned Mr. Pettit said he had been delayed at his farm feeding cattle and didn't realise it was so late. Lighting up time that day was 4.37 p.m. and although he had been only 200 yards from home a fine of 10s was imposed. In his defence he said he thought that the law made allowances for farmers. Mr. Pettit remained in business in the town until November 1922, when it was taken over by William Hall. He was the son of the late Mr. John and Mrs. Hall of Wisbech and for 12 years had been living in British Columbia, having previously been associated with his brothers in their butchering businesses at Manchester. In February 1923 at Newport Pagnell parish church he married Dora, widow of Lieutenant Albert Thorpe, of Wisbech.

Arthur John Simpson

Arthur John Simpson was the grandson of John Simpson, who from offices in the High Street ran a printing business and established and ran the 'Newport Pagnell Gazette' (sometimes referred to as the 'Newport Pagnell Gazette, Wolverton Times and Olney Free Press.' He was succeeded in the business by his son, Alfred, who as a journalist, and for a long time a correspondent to the contemporaries circulating in Bucks and neighbouring counties, continued to be the proprietor of the newspaper until around June 1915. Then on Sunday, August 29th 1915 whilst attending Evensong at the Parish Church at the age of 64 he suddenly died. As a chorister he had occupied his customary seat in the choir stalls and having read the second lesson returned to his place just as his fellow choristers began to lead the chanting of the Nunc Dimittis. However, scarcely had he got there than he collapsed and fell into the arms of Mr. Cecil R. Line who, with others, carried him into the vestry. Despite the assistance given by Nurse Foat he died and having been summoned by telephone Dr. Bailey, Dr. Digby White and Dr. Wickham could do nothing despite their swift arrival. The body was placed on an ambulance litter and with the assistance of Sergeant Dolan and Corporal Millican of the R.A.M.C., who were on the staff at Tyringham House Convalescent Home, taken to the deceased's home in the High Street. From 1916 to 1920 the stationery shop and printing business would be owned by Mr. Arthur Fairweather, who in his old age made his home at Southwold, Suffolk, and the last owner of the printing works would be Arthur Canning. As for the premises, on the site would later stand a branch of Woolworths. At 24, High Street, a millinery business was run by Alfred's only son, Arthur John Simpson, and his wife and it was by her organisation that on Saturday, July 17th 1915, a penny house to house collection in the town made £15 8s 2d for the British Red Cross Society and St. John Ambulance Association. In March 1916 Miss Phyllis Simpson, the daughter of Mr. and Mrs. A. J. Simpson, passed with honours the junior division piano playing at the Trinity College exam held recently at Bedford. A pupil of Mr. C. K. Garratt she was aged 12 and in two previous exams had gained 90 marks out of 100. The annual meeting of the Newport Pagnell Diamond Jubilee Nursing and Good Samaritan Society was held in the Vicarage on Saturday evening, April 1st 1916 and with the Reverend F. Gunnery presiding amongst those present was Mr. A. J. Simpson, the secretary. Since the outbreak of the war the Newport Pagnell Habitation of the Primrose League had refrained from all political work and had assisted in charitable causes. The Dame president was Mrs. Wellesley Taylor who at a whist drive held at the Unionist Club on Thursday evening May 4th 1916 presented to Mr. and Mrs. Arthur J. Simpson, the Habitation's late secretary and treasurer, a pair of handsome silver candlesticks, and a list of the subscribers. The address read;

> 'Primrose League, Newport Pagnell Habitation, No. 624
> Presentation made on May 4, 1916, to Mr. and Mrs. Arthur Simpson in token of their valuable services as hon. secretary 1913-1916, and hon. treasurer, 1914-1916.'

As Mrs. Simpson stepped forward to receive the gift there was hearty applause. Mr. Simpson gave thanks for the gift, sorry that they had to sever their official connection but hoped to do their best for the work in the future. For the men from the town in the Forces, towards providing Christmas comforts an auction sale was held in the Girls' Council School on Saturday evening, November 18th 1916. Among the items were a brooch made from a piece of the Zeppelin brought down at Cuffley which having been contributed by Mrs. A. J. Simpson. This found a ready sale and also regarding Zeppelins: 'Suitable for lighting restrictions,' in February 1917 green paper blinds, available in all widths from 36" to 72", were available from Arthur J. Simpson. On Saturday evening, March 24th 1917, the annual meeting of the Newport Pagnell Diamond Jubilee Nursing and Good Samaritan Society was held at the Vicarage. The Reverend F. Gunnery occupied the chair and also present were Mrs. Gunnery, Mrs. F. Littleboy, Mr. and Mrs. W.R. Chantler, Miss A. M.Coales, Mr. T. Meadows and also Mr. T. Sim, the secretary, who was assuming the double office of Mr. A. J. Simpson, secretary, and Mr. A. Ablett, collector, both of whom were resigning. For the benefit of the Tickford Abbey V.A.D. Hospital on Saturday, July 28th 1917, Lady French attended a 'Pound Day' and for tea and refreshments tickets were issued by Mrs. A. J. Simpson, whose husband did duty at the hospital as a night orderly. As for their daughter, Phyllis, at a farewell concert for the Signal Section of the Royal Engineers, after their two years' stay in the town, at the Electric Theatre on the evening of Monday, October 15th 1917 she presented Mrs. Hamilton Barrie, the wife of Major Hamilton Barrie, with a beautiful bouquet. The annual meeting of the Newport Pagnell Nursing and Good Samaritan Society was held at the Vicarage on Saturday evening, March 23rd 1918 with the President, the Rev. Gunnery, in the chair. He was re-elected as president and of the other offices amongst those re-elected on the committee was Mr. A. J. Simpson. Held under the auspices of the N.F.U. and the Town Red Cross Committee, and in conjunction with the Royal Engineers Wireless Depot in the town, the Red Cross Gala Day and Gymkhana took place at Newport Pagnell on Whit Monday 1918, with of the displays the prize of £2 2s, presented by Messrs. C. Coales, W. Cotton, and A. J. Simpson going to the 'Agriculture (Present)' car. Then on Saturday, October 12th 1918, an autumn fair and 'razzle dazzle' took place in the Council School playgrounds with the tea and refreshments being the province of amongst others Mrs. A. J. Simpson. At the annual meeting of the Unionist Working Men's Club, held on Tuesday evening, February 18th 1919, Mr. Herbert Middleton resigned as auditor and since he was shortly to leave the country he had instructed Wigley, Sons and Gambell to auction his freehold residence 'The Lamblies.' This was situated on the main road from Newport Pagnell to Wolverton and featured a large entrance hall, reception rooms, five bedrooms, bathroom, domestic offices and outbuildings. There was also a good garden, well stocked with fruit trees, and a tennis lawn and with vacant possession on completion the premises were auctioned at the Swan Hotel on Wednesday, March 19th 1919, at 4.30 p.m. Opening at £500 the bidding swiftly advanced to £800 with the purchaser being Mr. A. J. Simpson. In 1927 he and his wife sold 24 High Streetand retired that year to Hove. There he died at his home 14, Portland Avenue, in November 1955 aged 80.

Henry Walton

A native of Worcestershire, around 1895 Henry Walton came to Newport Pagnell where he commenced a successful grocery and provision business. In his social life although actively associated with the Primitive Methodist cause he would later worship at the Congregational Chapel whilst as for recreational pursuits he would be a member of the Golf Club, the links of which were on Bury Field, and of the Newport Pagnell Bowling Club. Indeed, on one occasion he would beat an English international in a tournament at Wellingborough. During the First World War the Government appointed him as wholesale food distributor for a large portion of North Bucks and in August 1917 he was nominated by the U.D.C. as a member of the Food Control Committee. Following the outbreak of war with the shortage of men on the home front boys, girls and women were increasingly needed to fill the vacancies and in November 1915 came the need at Walton's Stores for a boy to work in the office and 'to make himself useful.' As well as a strong boy for deliveries in January 1917 the need again arose for a young lady to fulfil this role, which a year later was advertised with a stipulation that applicants, either boy or girl school leavers, 'Must be neat writer and correct at figures.' Then in May 1918 two young girls were required, one for the office and one for the counter, as well as two boys. Being a man of enterprise

and initiative, when during the railway strike of 1919 Mr. Walton had five tons of mostly perishable goods on the railways he, since there was no hope of it being delivered on the required Wednesday, hired a motor lorry and went to London where from the West India Docks he acquired a supply of sugar, tea from the tea centres and from Smithfield the provisions of bacon, tinned meats etc. In all this amounted to some two tons of produce and within 12 hours he was back at Newport Pagnell to supply his local demand. Having for some years been plagued with ill health, in 1923 he suffered a serious illness and although he made a good recovery he later suffered a relapse and died in January 1928 at his home, 21, High Street, Newport Pagnell. He was aged 65 and left a widow and two sons. The burial would be in the family vault at the cemetery at Handsworth, Birmingham, but on the morning of the funeral his staff arranged with the vicar to hold a memorial service at Newport Pagnell Parish Church from 8.30 am to 8.50 a.m. Then after leaving the church they formed up outside the house of the deceased such that the coffin, which was not taken into the church, should pass between them to the hearse which as a further mark of respect they followed in coaches as far as the turn to Great Linford.

SOLDIERS' & SAILORS' CHRISTMAS PRESENTS FUND

For monies to buy Christmas presents for the townsmen on active service, on Wednesday evening, November 17th 1915 the P.S.A. Brotherhood held a concert at the Electric Theatre. The programme, for which Mr. C. K. Garratt provided the piano accompaniments, was excellent, and Miss Beatrice Walley of Crewe, the winner of the Crewe and Chester Eisteddfod, proved a popular favourite at her first appearance in the town. Sung in a pleasing soprano voice her songs were rapturously received, and also encored for her fine singing was Miss Bertha Richens, of Emberton, who was pursuing her professional studies in London. Mr. Oliver Critchard and the Reverend Father Walker sang both individually and as a duet, and humour and ventriloquism were the province of Charles Conyers. He hailed from the Queen's Hall, London, and his amusing stories and jokes, and his comic songs at the piano, were loudly re-demanded. Making only about £3, unfortunately the event was not as successful as their first effort, which had raised upwards of £18, but nevertheless in September 1916 the formation of a Town Christmas Presents Committee was announced, with the Reverend F. Gunnery as chairman, and Mr. T. Sim, of 4a, Beaconsfield Place, as the secretary. Comprised of people from the town, and representatives from the corporate bodies, the aim was to raise a 'Town Fund' to send a Christmas present to every man from the town in the Forces, and, with the need to raise about £150, authorised canvassers would call at every house during October 1916, although cheques could be paid direct to 'The Town Xmas Presents Fund' at Barclay and Co's Bank. Local events were also staged to raise money, such as a whist drive and dance attended by about 170 people on Tuesday evening, October 24th 1916 in the Girls' Council School.

A fine programme of dance music was provided by the Excelsior Silver Band in the Central Hall, but it was the Electric Theatre that on Sunday evening, November 12th provided the venue for a sacred concert organised largely by Mr. C. K. Garratt, who, opening the concert with the National Anthem, played all the accompaniments. Pupils of the Girls' Council School had sold the programmes, and the performance featured Miss Gune Atkinson, soprano, of Cosgrove Priory, Mr. W. Charlton, solo violin, Sapper V. Earl, tenor, Pioneer W. Huggins, baritone, Sapper C. Watson, bass, and Miss Bertha Richens, who was rapturously encored on each of her three appearances. The event proved a great success, to which Corporal Peet and other members of the Royal Engineers had contributed by providing much help as stewards. Then in other monies at the Girls' Council School the pupils collected £1 15s. The following year, on Friday evening, May 18th 1917 a general meeting of the fund's organising committee was held at the

Urban Council Offices where, with the Reverend F. Gunnery presiding, to a large attendance Mr. T. Sim presented the balance sheet This revealed that of the total income of £162 18s 6d, £130 10s 2d had been spent on sending out 431 parcels, and in consequence 300 replies had been received, with other expressions of thanks having been made to the vicar. Those parcels sent to the men training at home were sent through the Co-op Society, whilst those wholly containing tobacco were despatched through Messrs. A. Marshall, H. Watson, and A.G. Ellingham. all of whom were local tradesmen. Parcels to men abroad and on the seas went via Harrod's Stores, per Mr. F. Bettle. Also at the meeting appreciation was expressed to the headmistress of the Council School, Miss James, as also the ladies' committee, by whose efforts £25 had been raised, Mr. C. K. Garratt, for organising a sacred concert which raised £16 10s 3d, Mr. P. C. Gambell, for his services as auctioneer at a jumble sale that raised £59 6s 3d, and to four working men of the town who, by going around the town with an organ, raised £4 17s 3½d. In October 1917 the committee then made an appeal for a sum in excess of £200 for that year's Christmas gifts. A house to house collection would be made, and at a meeting on Tuesday evening, November 13th 1917 it was decided to send by registered mail a postal order for 7s to each of the men, whose names, rank and full address should be sent to Mr. T.H. Sim, the honorary secretary, at 4a, Beaconsfield Place.

The second of a series of whist drives and dances for the 'Soldiers' and Sailors' Christmas Presents Fund' took place in the Central Hall of the Girls' School on Friday evening, November 16th 1917. This had been arranged by Miss James, and with 116 persons competing the first prize for ladies was a piece of sirloin, presented by Mr. J. Sawbridge. Mrs. Read was the winner, whilst for gentlemen the first prize was a note case presented by Mr. Geo. Tayler, for which after a cut Sapper Bunker was declared the victor. As for a guessing competition, for which the prize was an order on a local tradesman, this was won by Mrs. Holland, and for the subsequent dance the music was provided by the Excelsior Silver Band. In fact they, as well as the Workmen's Social Club, had lent the cards for the whist drive, with the Women's Liberal Association having lent the crockery for the refreshments. The event raised a profit of £16 2s 5d, and on Friday evening, November 30th 1917 by the last of the three such events, again held in the Council Schools, £12 11s 4½d was made. 23 tables were played, and for the first prize for the ladies a bracelet, given by Miss Payne, was won by Mrs. Read. For the men the first prize of a cigarette case, given by Mr. Jesse Adams, was secured by Pioneer Hose, with Pioneer Homans being the winner of a guessing competition, for which the prize had been given by Miss Payne. As in the previous events refreshments were available, and the Excelsior Silver

Band played for dancing. In total the three functions raised £38 8s 8½d, and to further benefit the fund an auction sale took place at the Council Schools on the Saturday, raising about £63. Playing various selections, during the afternoon the Excelsior Silver Band paraded the town, and the sale was further advertised by a hand drawn trolley which, having been lent by Mr. J. Clare, had been prepared by Messrs. Meadows and Bell, and Salmons motor works. Mr. T.H. Sim was the honorary secretary, and with a horse and trolley lent by the U.D.C. Messrs. J. Parrott, W. Read and J. Short collected the goods, which included bunches of grapes from Mr. F.A. Konig, choice specimens of Bucks point lace, a quantity of special quality flour, given by Francis Coales and Son, fruit, plants and vegetables, and, from the farmers, a large consignment of rabbits. Then shortly after 5 p.m. the sale was opened by Mrs. Symons, of Brooklands, to whom after her suitable address Mr. J. Short presented a bouquet of roses and carnations, a donation that he had secured from Mr. Alfred Cockerill, the well known Northampton florist and seedsman.

Accepting this with gratitude, to applause Mrs. Symonds then handed the bouquet back for sale, and asked Mr. Gambell to offer it for the funds since he, as also Arthur Bullard, was an honorary auctioneer. In fact Mr. Gambell was the first purchaser at the sum of a guinea, and after this a sale of the individual blooms was made. Apart from the sale there were attractions to include searching for a hidden treasure in a patch of turf, houp la, guessing the weight of a cake, and, in the charge of Mr. F. Bell, a flag competition, with 18 flags painted on sheets accompanied by a list of the countries they represented. Correctly identifying 10, the winner was Sapper Adams, and also of the Royal Engineers later in the evening Sapper Collett gave a clever acrobatic display, which by the subsequent collection added 15s to the funds. On Sunday evening, November 25th 1917 there was a packed audience at the Electric Theatre for a sacred concert. This had been organised by Mr. A. Bullard and the P.S.A. Committee, and the proceeds from a silver collection at the door raised £9 for the Christmas presents fund, which now totalled about £180. Assisted by a few local musicians the orchestra of the Royal Engineers Wireless Section played three selections, Miss Bertha Richens performed two songs, as also Miss M. Webster, and contributions were also made by Miss Eva Garratt, Oliver Critchard and Mr. D. Ashton Davies (bass). Violin solos were played brilliantly by Sapper Fuller, and the piano accompaniments were by Mr. C. K. Garratt and Mr. P. C. Gambell. Commanding the Wireless Section of the Royal Engineers, as the chairman of the concert Captain J.B. Mowatt said in his address that he had twice spent Christmas at the Front, and sometimes not arriving until April the Christmas puddings were often smashed up, and the sweets stuck together in a gluey mess. The event raised about £60, whilst as for further monies the committee of the Christmas presents fund organised a competition for a lady's keyless watch, with the box in which it was sealed to be opened on Thursday, November 29th 1917. The holder of the winning ticket was to contact the honorary secretary, Mr. T.H. Sim. Concluding the fund raising for that year, in December the collection in the Council Schools raised 30s in the girls' department and 15s in the boys.' For the members of the Unionist Club, on Saturday, September 7th 1918 the 7th annual flower and vegetable show took place in the building's concert hall, and practically all the exhibits, plus the 'not for competition' fruit and vegetables, given by other members, were auctioned afterwards, with the £5 raised being forwarded to the fund to provide Christmas presents for the members in the Forces. As for the town's general fund, with members of the Royal Engineers as stewards the Merry Magnets Concert Party organised an entertainment at the Electric Theatre on Wednesday evening, September 25th 1918. The theatre was crowded, and with songs given by the Misses Cameron, K. Powell, Middleton, Pettit, and K. and N. Fleet, the characteristic costumes added greatly to the effect. In the K-nut song 'Top-hole' the male impersonations of Miss K. Powell and Miss Pettit were cleverly performed, and a decided success was their duet 'Flirting.'

Another popular item was the dancing of the Misses Marjorie and Kathleen Reynolds, who were two little girls who had been trained by Miss Minnie Knott, who played all the piano accompaniments. Having been used in one of the numbers, a bouquet when sold by auction raised £2, and overall the event made £20. At a committee meeting of the 'Newport Pagnell Soldiers' and Sailors' Christmas Presents Fund,' on Thursday evening September 26th 1918 it was resolved to make a house to house collection, and in addition a whist drive and dance, for which the music was provided by the Excelsior Silver Band, was held in the Council Schools on Friday evening, October 4th. Then on Saturday, October 12th 1918 an autumn fair and 'razzle dazzle' took place in the Council School playgrounds. Under the direction of the headmistress, Miss Mills, the first item was a Maypole dance by the infants, and with Superintendent Dibben as the referee during the afternoon a tug of war for men was won by the Royal Engineers team, with that for ladies, for which five teams competed, won by the W.A.A.C.s from Fenny Stratford. The numerous side shows included a hidden treasure and doll competition, organised by the Misses I. and K. Powell and G. Middleton, a 'Fairy well,' in which the Misses Gunnery assisted, a shooting gallery, under the charge of Mr. H. Thickpenny, weighing machines, lent by Mr. F. W. Taylor and John Odell, 'nailing the Kaiser's coffin,' by Mr. C. K. Garratt and Mr. C. R. Line, and skittles, lent by the Unionist Club.

The latter also provided cigarettes, as well as the crockery for the tea and refreshments, which were the province of amongst others Mrs. Gunnery, Mrs. G. Tayler, Mrs. A. J. Simpson, Mrs. C. M. Wilford, the Misses A. M. Coales, A. Gunnery, K. Powell, and Mr. T. Shelton. For dancing the Excelsior Silver Band played from 4 p.m. to 6 p.m., and the event came to a close soon after 6 p.m. with an illuminated marching display by the Council School girls, under the supervision of Miss James.

On the following Thursday, organised by Leader T.W. Allen a concert to raise money for the town's Christmas presents fund was held at the Y.M.C.A. Hut, which was crowded with Royal Engineers and friends. Among the artistes were Miss Wilford, Miss Platt, Mr. C. R. Line, and also Miss G. Middleton, who as an encore gave 'Write to me dear.' Mrs. Thomas and Miss Minnie Knott A.L.C.M. acted as the accompanists, and under the conductorship of Leader Allen a well received feature was the singing of several glees by a chorus of 20 voices. Proposing a vote of thanks to Mr. Allen and the contributors, during an interval Mr. O. H. Bull made appropriate remarks, and a collection for the Fund made just over £3. On Monday evening, December 16th, despite the end of the war the troops had yet to be demobilised, and in aid of the town's fund for Christmas presents the Merry Magnets performed at the Electric Theatre, with Miss Minnie Knott A.L.C.M. presiding at the piano. The performance opened with 'Some Show,' and among the contributions were 'We ain't half proud of Dad,' by Miss Mabel Wilford, 'Catch me,' (encored), by Miss Violet Cameron, 'Flattering,' also encored, by the Misses Kathleen and Helen Fleet, Dorothy Pettit and Mabel Wilford, 'Comrade,' encored, by Miss Grace Middleton, a duet 'A Fickle Maid,' encored, by Misses K. Powell and V. Cameron, the song 'In my Old Fashioned Way,' by Miss D. Pettit, the recitation 'Algy's awfully good at algebra,' by Miss M. Wilford, and 'What a naughty old gentleman,' encored, by the trio of Misses D. Pettit, H. Fleet, V. Cameron. In the second part many of the items were also encored, and acting as the stewards for the concert were Messrs. C. M. Wilford, H. I. Middleton, W. Lineham and Sapper McLean. In January 1919, as secretary of the fund for Christmas presents Mr. H.T. Sim reported that 12 of the letters containing the town's gifts have been returned for insufficient address, or other reasons. Measures would be taken to resolve this issue, and with no further need for a fund there would be no reoccurrence. In fact convened by Mr. J. Short, chairman of the U.D.C., at a meeting representative of the corporate bodies of the town, held on Tuesday evening, December 9th 1919, there was unanimous agreement that a 'welcome home' should be arranged for those men from the town who had served during the war. Presiding, Mr. Short said that several of his friends had promised to liberally subscribe to a fund which, it not being intended to make a general appeal, would be financed, it was hoped, by the corporate bodies and residents in the town. In addition the Town Christmas Presents Fund Committee would be asked if their balance of over £60 could be used, and in consequence their contribution of £67 would help to make the event possible.

SPECIAL CONSTABLES

The local 'Specials,' (with armbands) seen on parade at a Red Cross sale in the town in 1918

In August 1914 it was announced that a Special Reserve of police constables was to be formed in Buckinghamshire. The purpose was to fill the vacancies of those service men who had been summoned to join their regiments, or report to their Naval depots, and on the evening of Monday, August 10th at Newport Pagnell police station the first detachment of North Bucks Special Constables, numbering 113, was sworn in by Colonel W. Bowyer, late of the Royal Engineers. Mr. Gerard Uthwatt, of Great Linford, was appointed to command the detachment, with the squad leaders being Mr. G. Trimmer, No. 1, Mr. E. Saner (late lieutenant in the 1st North Staffs.), No. 2, Mr. P. C. Gambell, No. 3, and Mr. Percy Sharp, No. 4. The bailiff of the Newport Pagnell County Court, ex Colour Sergeant Thomas Lucas, of the Northants. Regiment, had offered to be the instructor, and in consequence would put the detachment through a preliminary drill at a parade on the following Wednesday night. Thus by mid August including an ironmonger's assistant and a motor carriage builder three 'specials' were on duty at Newport Pagnell. However, Thomas Lucas had received a telegram from the War Office ordering him to report as soon as possible to his old regiment, and having therefore resigned as instructor he was presented at the Anchor Hotel on Thursday evening, October 15th with a purse of gold, to which practically all the members had subscribed. Mr. P. C. Gambell made the presentation, and accompanying the purse was a written list of subscribers, given 'in recognition of his services in converting an awkward into an orderly squad.' He would leave to rejoin his regiment on October 17th. Including Mr. W.C. Chapman, the Master of the Workhouse, despite the onerous duties of their normal employment many men of the town applied to be special constables, and special constable Ernest Platt had an unusual case to deal with on the night of Wednesday, November 11th, when he encountered a hopelessly drunk middle aged woman in Station Road. In fact he had to take her to the police station in a wheelbarrow, and the following morning, now respectably dressed, she pleaded not guilty when charged, saying that she only had some drink when forced to shelter from the rain.

Giving evidence, police sergeant Bryant said that about 9 p.m. she had been brought hopelessly drunk to the police station in a wheelbarrow, of which conveyance she complained "of course a special constable would do a thing like that, but an ordinary constable would not think of it." Regarding the circumstances, she explained that on Wednesday she had gone to Stony Stratford to try and get enough money from a friend for her train fare; "He gave me 3s 9d and said he would draw some money from the bank today to take me to Reading. I came by bus to Newport Pagnell and was going to the lodging house. I was not drunk. Let me get away from this and I won't trouble you again." However, the magistrate remarked that she had been in court only seven days ago, when the chairman had given her a caution, and replying to this she admitted that only the previous morning she had been released from Northampton gaol. Concluding the case the magistrate imposed a fine of 10s and costs, or in default a prison term of 14 days. However, if she came up again she would probably be sent to an inebriates' home, which would mean a term of three years. Unable to pay the fine, the woman opted for gaol. On Wednesday, December 9th 1914, Mr. Cecil Line was amongst those sworn in as a special constable, and others who would join were Mr. F. W. Taylor and Mr. W. J. Hobbs, who both had sons in the Army who were expecting to be shortly sent to the Front. As for others volunteering for military service, having been one of the original special constables on Monday, February 1st 1915, Mr. George Marshall, the manager of the town's branch of the Empire Meat Company, went to Oxford to offer his services.

Nearly 200 special constables assembled in the Girls' School on Thursday evening, February 11th 1915, when Mr. W. Marsh gave a lecture on 'Identification of Aircraft.' This was illustrated by lantern slides, and with the importance of their role being heightened by the prospect of air raids, at their drill on Monday evening, March 13th 1915 the Newport Pagnell special constables were issued with a new and much more dignified badge which, made of bronze, featured the county arms in the centre, with around the

The Coachmakers Arms.

The licensee since 1899 was Mrs. Amelia Franklin. Born in Newport Pagnell she was a daughter of Mr. and Mrs. Knowles the previous licensees. In fact the family had held the licence for about 100 years. Her husband was on the engineering staff of the National Mint and when she died, aged 67, she would be buried in the same grave.

outer circle the inscription 'Bucks Special Constabulary, 1914.' One duty of the special constables was to assist Superintendent Pearce and the men of his police force in finding billets for the military, and this was required on the night of Wednesday, March 24th 1915 when, whilst in training in the districts of Wing and Leighton Buzzard, a section of troops took part in a staff ride through North Bucks. Those troops duly accommodated overnight in the town then continued the ride the following morning. As another of their duties, special constables were present at an open air recruiting meeting in the town on Saturday evening, April 24th 1915, and with age being no barrier to their own recruitment during July 71 year-old Albert Stone, of 34, Tickford Street, was enrolled and given the post of messenger at the headquarters of the Special Constabulary. Generally the duties of the special constables involved upholding the law in the town, such as the instance on the night of June 5th 1915 when, at about 10 p.m., special constable Joseph West whilst in the High Street saw a man trying to persuade a soldier to go into the Coachmakers Arms. However, the man was unwilling, and in the ensuing intervention the antagonist squared up to fight the special constable. As for the soldier, he fell off his bike and with injuries to his face had to be taken home in a trap. Subsequently at the Divisional Petty Sessions on Wednesday, June 16th Ernest Goodman, of Broad Street, was summoned for threatening conduct, although the case was dealt with in his absence since he was employed on building an ambulance train at Wolverton Works. A fine of 12s 6d was imposed. For a lecture on 'Police Duties,' on Wednesday evening, July 14th 1915, almost 150 special constables, from Newport Pagnell and the surrounding district, attended the Central Hall of the Council Schools, where Superintendent Pearce dealt lucidly with the subject for almost an hour. Colonel Bowyer, the Divisional Commandant, presided, supported by Mr. W. Carlile and Mr. J. Knapp, and also present were the captain of the Newport Pagnell Special Constabulary, Mr. W. Uthwatt, as well as Mr. William Trevor and Mr. George Tayler. Afterwards the members were inspected in the parade ground by the Divisional Commandant.

Numbering about 1,200, on Wednesday evening, August 4th 1915, a patriotic crowd gathered on Market Hill, where they pledged to see the war carried through to a victorious conclusion. The meeting emphatically endorsed the action of the British Government, and present in force were the special constables, who formed a smart guard of honour around the waggons which served as a platform for the speakers. Having earlier in the war been invaluable in the instruction of the special constables, Thomas Lucas was now on active service as a sergeant major in France with the 16th Battalion Royal Irish Rifles. As for those he had trained, on the night of April 2nd 1916 at 8.30 p.m. special constable J. Thickpenny had to charge William Powell, a vet, with a contravention of the Lighting Order. Then on Tuesday afternoon, May 2nd 1916 whilst on duty in Tickford Street special constable W.C. Chapman arrested a man for hawking without a licence. In yet another court case, on Wednesday, May 31st 1916, a foreign governess of the town was summoned for having unlawfully taken a photograph of an army aeroplane in Bury Field. The case had been brought by special constable Sayle, and she pleaded 'guilty in ignorance.' As stated in June 1916 by the military representative at the Military Tribunal, the War Office had now instructed that the place of those men called up from volunteer fire brigades could be taken by special constables, the local detachment of which was on parade at a large patriotic meeting held on Market Hill on Friday, August 4th. Then during the following month George Taylor, a shoeing smith of the town, who was one of the founders of the district Farriers' Association, was sworn in as a special constable, and was perhaps one of those who, under orders from Superintendent Pearce, carried out an urgent canvass of the town to find sufficient winter billets for the Royal Engineers. Due to the apparent lack of housing accommodation, on leaving their tented summer camp they were scheduled to move to Leighton Buzzard, but greatly helped by the efforts of the special constables sufficient billets were duly found, and the town could thankfully continue to benefit from the trade brought by the military influx. With the increased danger of Zeppelin raids it was essential that there was compliance with the lighting restrictions, and the special constables were instrumental in reporting any contraventions. Thus at the Divisional Petty Sessions on Wednesday, October 4th 1916 a case brought by special constable Higgins was heard. This regarded Robert Layton, a licensed victualler of the town, and in a later case brought by special constable W.C. Chapman a summons was issued to Minnie Howard, a hotel manageress, for 'allowing' a chimney to have been on fire on October 14th.

Then on Wednesday, October 18th 1916, at the Divisional Petty Sessions special constable H. I. Middleton gave evidence regarding an incident on the night of October 1st. He had been in charge of the patrols of special constables in the town, and during an air raid alert at about 10.30 p.m. special constable J. Short, in the company of another member, reported a light shining across the North bridges from the back window of a house in Mill Street. The matter was investigated, and in court the person responsible was fined 10s, with 2s 6d expenses for each of the special constables. After six years as chief of the county police for the Divisional Petty Sessions of Newport Pagnell, Stony Stratford, Fenny Stratford, and Winslow, on Monday, November 6th 1916 Superintendent James Pearce severed his connection with the district, on being transferred to the Slough division. His replacement would be Inspector Dibbin, who had been promoted to Superintendent. Since the outbreak of the war Superintendent Pearce had been instrumental in raising and training several companies of special constables, and he was accordingly paid glowing tributes at the Newport Pagnell Petty Sessions on Wednesday, November 1st 1916. Then on the eve of his departure, at the police station on the evening of Saturday, November 4th he was presented by the special constables with two armchairs. Cyclists riding without lights were increasingly a problem for the special constables, such as for special constable W.C. Chapman who, when on duty at Cannon Corner, apprehended a student of Lathbury Park at 5.45 p.m. on October 31st 1916. As for special constable A. Lott, it was a stray dog running loose in Silver Street that he had to contend with on December 17th 1916. Due to sheep worrying in the district in consequence Herbert Hawkins, of 13, London Road, was summoned, but since he was engaged on munitions work at Bedford his father appeared in court, where he admitted that he had taken the dog for a run, but it had got loose. Inebriates were another menace, and at a special police court on Saturday, May 5th 1917, three men of no fixed abode, one describing himself as a pedlar, were charged with having been drunk the previous day. One had been found in the town by special constable W.C. Chapman, another was arrested for being drunk and disorderly by police constable Bonner, and at 11.30 p.m. special constable T. Sim had found the third, who said that he hadn't gone into lodgings because the £9 15s in his possession might be stolen. He was fined 10s and 2s 6d costs but despite his affluence he declined to pay, and opted instead for seven days in prison. However, under a new order the Bench was empowered to deduct a fine from any money found on a prisoner, and this they duly did.

Cannon Corner.

In the first week of 1921 work to improve safety at Cannon Corner was completed, with a new pavement finished and the roadway at this point built up with tarmac. When it became known that the London Joint City and Midland Bank Ltd. had purchased the premises (seen on the left hand side of the photo) where Mr. Sawbridge had carried on a large butchering business, Mr. J. Short J.P. visited London and met the bank directors. They intended to build a new bank on the site and pointing out the danger of the street corner he asked if they could set their premises back for an improvement to be made. They agreed and as a result the new bank was set back to give an extra three feet of road space from near the Plough in the High Street to Mr. Lawman's confectioner's shop in St. John Street

Another case brought by a special constable was heard at the Divisional Petty Sessions on Wednesday, September 5th 1917, when Marion Waterlow, of the Manor House, was summoned for having failed to screen the lights at her house. In court she said she came to live in the countryside because of the air raids, and for the offence a fine of 5s was imposed, plus 5s expenses for the special constable. Emphasising the importance of complying with the lighting restrictions, a letter from the Superintendent of Police was read at the monthly meeting of the U.D.C. on Tuesday evening, November 6th 1917, in which he complained that during a recent air raid alert it had taken, despite notice having been given at the Gas Works, half an hour before all the street lamps were extinguished. In fact it had been necessary to send a police constable to hurry the matter along, and but for the help of the special constables the task would have taken longer. Apart from air raids, there could also be apprehension regarding escaped prisoners of war, with such an occasion being one Friday in late December, when around dusk two Germans broke out of the Husborne Crawley Camp. The police and special constables were immediately called out, and at about 9.30 p.m. special constables E.F. Dant and A.G. Ellingham, who were on duty as a picket at Cannon Corner, Newport Pagnell, saw two 'strange looking men' turning the corner from Silver Street. Captain C. M. Wilford happened to be with the constables, and after their swift arrest the men were taken to the police station, where it was found that they were the two wanted men; Johann Pietzik, and Ernst Schneider. Then as a pleasing sequel, in January 1918 the Chief Constable of Bucks, Major Otway Mayne, wrote a letter of congratulation to special constable Captain C. M. Wilford and the Newport Pagnell Special Constabulary. As well as the reading of the King's Proclamation, portions of special forms of prayer and thanksgiving, which had been issued by the Archbishops of Canterbury and York, were used on Sunday, January 6th 1918, at the services at the parish church, where amongst those present at the Soldiers' Church Parade was a large muster of the special constables under special constable Captain C. Wilford, Lieutenants F. O.Butler and P. C. Gambell, and Superintendent Dibben. As for more mundane matters, at the Divisional Petty Sessions on Wednesday, March 20th 1918 a Royal Engineer pleaded guilty to having ridden a bicycle without lights in the town on February 27th. Special constable W.C. Chapman, who had brought the case, declined expenses, and a fine was the penalty imposed.

In fine sunny weather, on Market Hill the Red Cross Sale was held on Wednesday, April 24th 1918. The opening ceremony took place at 2 p.m., and as part of the guard of honour the Newport Pagnell Company of Special Constables was under the command of Lieutenant F. O.Butler and also Captain C. M. Wilford who, assisted by his wife, had organised the numerous side shows and competitions etc. Following the outbreak of the war, one of the first to join the special constables had been George Daniells, whose house in Caldecote Street had recently become one of the many in that part of town to be flooded by the recent deluge. Through this he caught a chill, and following the onset of other symptoms died at the age of 42 on Friday, May 3rd 1918. Like his father he had been a familiar figure at local auctions in his business as a furniture dealer, and his death bereaved a widow, four sons and a daughter. Being in the Army in France, sadly two of the sons could not be present at the funeral, which on the following Tuesday afternoon was attended by several members of the P.S.A. Brotherhood, since the deceased had been a member of the committee. The first part of the service was held at the Wesleyan Church, from where under Captain C. M. Wilford about 20 of the town's special constables headed the cortege to the cemetery. Having been found lying hopelessly drunk on the path near the Post Office, at about 10.15 p.m. on Sunday, May 4th 1918 a homeless man was conveyed to the police station by special constable T.H. Sim, who by the subsequent conviction received expenses of 2s 6d. Then in August he was no doubt amongst the special constables who, under Captain C. M. Wilford and Lieutenant F. O.Butler, attended the ceremony in the town to mark the fourth anniversary of the war. Yet little could they know that the war would soon be over, and to mark this occasion they attended a thanksgiving service at 11 a.m. on Sunday, November 17th 1918, at the parish church. Afterwards, having reformed on North Square with the Royal Engineers, the Volunteers, and the wounded soldiers from Tickford Abbey V.A.D. Hospital, they then marched in the procession headed by the town band to Market Hill, to be dismissed.

With the conflict finally at an end, by the invitation of a small committee, comprised of well known local gentlemen, the Newport Pagnell Special Constables enjoyed a first class supper at the Swan Hotel on Thursday evening, February 6th 1919. Being an appreciation of their work, this marked the winding up of the movement in the town, and the prime mover in organising the event had been Mr. William Coales, in association with Messrs. G. Tayler, F. W. Taylor, P. C. Gambell, and W. J. Hobbs. The excellent catering was undertaken by Miss Howard, the manageress of the Swan, and with 77 persons present apologies were received for the absence of Section Leader E. Glanley and special constable C. A.Branford. Mr. J. Short presided, and after the supper the toast of 'The King' was given from the chair. The chairman next submitted 'The Imperial Forces,' and apt replies were made by Captain T. Bawden, Lance Corporal E. Stapleton, Privates F. W. Roberts, A. J. Roberts, C. Bavington, and also C. Dickens, and all spoke of how their special constable training had proved of great value prior to joining the Army for active service. In reminiscence, the chairman said that when first established he had joined the force with much trepidation, and in fact had only muddled through by keeping his eye on the man next to him "and doing something like he did." He then recalled some of his experiences, and also the humorous incidents which had occurred whilst on duty. Captain C. M. Wilford then thanked the men for their loyal co-operation, and said that the demobilisation of the specials had been discussed with both the Lord Lieutenant and Colonel Finlay (the chairman of the Bucks Standing Joint Committee) at a meeting attended by himself and other captains of companies of special constables. A sub committee with Major Otway Mayne as chairman was the consequence, and the details would be forthcoming. However, one detail was certain, for as a memento of their service the special constables would be allowed to keep their equipment, although the warrant cards would have to be handed in. In recalling the progression of the contingent, he said that in January 1915 on the formation of an ambulance class 28 members had availed themselves of Dr. Bailey's instruction, whilst regarding enemy air raids special classes of observation had been held in June 1918, although only one 'point' was made, this being on August 6th at 12.15 a.m. 47 of the 73 men on the present strength had been sworn in during 1914, and of past members 27 had joined the Forces, three had resigned to become Volunteers, 13 had resigned for other reasons, and four had died.

By Mr. J. E. Whiting, during the evening appreciation was expressed for the early work of instruction performed by Superintendent Pearce. Similar thanks was afforded to the work of his successor Superintendent Dibben, who spoke of the value of the work of the special constables, and recalled how the trips at night to Woolstone, the patrols along the canal side, and the visits to the water tower at 5 a.m., had made them realise that the lot of a policeman was not a happy one. However, that night he could announce that this would be the last of their parades, and in the ordinary way none of them would be called upon for any further patrols. In fact, he said to applause, he would grant their release that night. Other members then gave addresses, and of the ensuing toasts Mr. F. W. Taylor proposed that to 'The Hostess,' speaking highly of Miss Howard's management of the hotel. Contributing a musical entertainment were 'The Merrymakers,' a pierrot troupe from Northampton, and making for an interesting memento of the evening the printed invitations, and the cards, contained a clever and suitably themed original sketch by Miss K. W. Coales of Market Harborough, niece of Mr. W. J. Coales. With the singing of the National Anthem the evening then closed at 11 p.m. Yet it would not be until Saturday evening, October 25th 1919, that the Newport Pagnell Company of Special Constables was officially disbanded, this being at an occasion at the Police Court where, expressing thanks for 'good and efficient public service,' printed certificates were presented. These had been signed by the Marquis of Lincolnshire (Lord Lieutenant of Bucks), Lieutenant Colonel A. Finlay (chairman of the Bucks Standing Joint Committee), and Major Otway Mayne (Chief Constable), and at the top of the address was the county crest worked in gold. Due to business or other reasons some of the 'Specials' were unable to be present, as also the Marquis, on whose behalf the certificates were presented by Mr. W. Carlile O.B.E., a deputy lieutenant of the county. Being supported by Superintendent E. Dibben, Captain C. M. Wilford, and Lieutenant F. O. Butler, he said that he was there to thank them on behalf of the Marquis, Major Otway Mayne and himself, and concluded by saying how indebted they were to Captain Wilford and Lieutenant Butler, who had done so much to bring the town's company to a state of perfection.

Also present was Superintendent Dibben, who said that he had been asked by the Chief Constable to state that a scheme was now in hand to continue the Special Constabulary, albeit under new control and as a new organisation. Regarding the conditions of service he could not give any details at present, but anyone who had served as a special was eligible to join, and those interested could give their names to Sergeant Roberts that night. There would be an annual premium for the services rendered, and all the members would be expected to attend a certain number of drills. With suitable thanks the specials were then presented with their certificates by Mr. Carlile, to whom appreciation for attending that evening was expressed by Captain Wilford. This was seconded by Lieutenant Butler, who said that at the outbreak of war they all felt they should do something. Since that first night when they 'formed fours' in the back yard at the police station they had tried to do their bit, and he thanked the men for the way in which they had supported the officers. This approval was echoed by Captain Wilford, who to applause thanked Superintendent Dibben for his harmonious style of management. In conclusion Mr. Carlile then said that the Bucks Standing Joint Committee had passed a resolution that all specials could keep their equipment as a memento of the war, although warrant cards had to be returned.

Memories of his time with the 'Specials' by Alfred Bullard

Several years after the war, Mr. Alfred Bullard spoke to an audience in the Town Hall, Newport Pagnell, of nearly 100 ex-servicemen about his wartime experience as a special constable. In a humorous speech, punctuated by much laughter, he said that despite a hard day's work some of them were called out on the Market Hill to go through military drill - "form 3's and 4's, present arms and do the double shuffle" - and then had to go and patrol the streets in the dark nights. In fact with no lights allowed they couldn't even have a cigarette, or if they did they had to hide it. One of his duties had been to go to the water tower to see that the Germans were not stopping the wind from working the wind motor. And then he had to go as far as the Workhouse, and see that there were no Germans demanding admittance.

But the worst job - he hated it - was to patrol the canal bank from the Black Horse to Woughton on the Green. They called upon him more than anyone else for that particular duty, and it was no use getting under a bridge when the wind was blowing, because he had to make a point and report. Sometimes it took him all his time to know which was the towing path and which was the canal, and if he had not been a teetotaller in those days he wouldn't be alive to tell the story. And the ladies helped them in those days, and if they had formed an army of Amazons, and made him captain, they would have had a fine troop in Newport Pagnell. The ladies had to work making shirts and knitting socks, digging up gardens and rooting up flower beds to plant cabbages, and in fact one lady even went in for chicken farming. She purchased a piece of land, erected chicken houses and then went to a poultry dealer and ordered 30 hens and 30 cockerels. However, the poultry dealer said two or three cockerels would be quite enough, to which she replied "You go on, this is my show; I don't believe in polygamy."

Some years after the war, in a speech at a British Legion dinner Alfred Bullard recalled how near North Bucks, and Wolverton in particular, had been to a serious raid by German Zeppelins. Plans had been made for an attack to destroy not only the great railway carriage works but also the viaduct bridge and the amazing story is told in his own words:

"While I and another special constable were patrolling the streets of Newport, between 2 and 3 o'clock in the morning, a sudden burst of light in the sky in the direction of London was so brilliant and at such an elevation, that one could easily have seen to pick up a pin from the roadway. We knew what it meant, because we had been listening to the distant droning of the engines of a Zeppelin, and I felt confident one had burst into flames up in the air.

The other special said, "Come on, let us go, it is only between Broughton and Woburn." He had not good eyesight. I said, "It is nearer St. Albans; let us go and report what we have seen at headquarters," which was the police station. 'Phone wires were set ringing and we soon learned that the Zep. had been brought down at Cuffley. ... We had not been troubled much by enemy aircraft round Newport, but it is evident from what I am about to relate, and make public for the first time, that the enemy did intend to pay a visit, but they were not taking any unnecessary risks in doing so.

I was in a gentleman's house not many miles from Wolverton discussing a matter of business with the owner. As I was preparing to leave the daughter of the house came running up to me and said, "Can you tell us, Mr. Bullard, if there are any anti-aircraft guns kept at Wolverton?" I replied I did not know, but, I said, "You need not be afraid, the enemy airships won't come to an isolated place like this." They said, "Oh, we are not afraid in the least but we do so want to know." I then thought they knew some young aircraft gunner. I said, "If you will tell me his name I will try and find out."

"We don't know anyone at all in it, but we promised to find out if there are any aircraft guns kept there." I said I had some friends in Wolverton, and I would enquire. Then, to my surprise, they said, "What we promised particularly to find out was, are there any soldiers guarding the bridge that crosses the river." I said, "Do you mean the viaducts?" "Yes," was the reply; "do find out and let us know how many in the day time and how many at night." I said, "Before I go to all that trouble you must tell me why you want this information." The reply was, "We promised not to tell any one." I said, "Then if you don't tell me I shall not make enquiries." "Well, if I tell you, you won't know who it is - a particular friend of ours up in London." I said, "Ask your father; he can find out." "Oh, we promised not to mention it to him."

I thought there was something very unusual and suspicious about these enquiries and I thought I would report it. Then I thought after all it is perhaps only a mare's nest. However, I saw the housekeeper, who did not know anything of our conversation, and asked her if she could tell me where the young ladies had been staying. She readily gave me the address. I then thought I would go up to London and see if I could find anything out, intending to go and ask the trades people and shopkeepers if they could give me any information about the people at that particular address. But when I got there it was a residential neighbourhood, with good, large expensive houses. For a minute I was nonplussed. Then suddenly I thought I could go to the rating office and ask the rateable value of this particular house. This I did. The official turned over the papers and said it was rated so much gross and so much nett. I thanked him and, in an off-hand way, said, "Can you tell me anything about the people living in it?" He replied, "I cannot, but perhaps the rate collector could give you some information." I said, "You can tell me if they have been there long?" "Oh, yes!" and turned back in the book; "They have been there four or five years, and by-the-by, they are Germans. Perhaps that is why they want to sell it."

I thanked him, knowing I had all the information I required. I went straight to headquarters and reported the incident as I am relating it now. The official thanked me, and took my name and address. I did not expect to hear anything more about it, but thought I had done my duty by reporting it. Two days after a special messenger came to Newport saying he was sent to thank me for the information and would I keep it secret; it had been of the greatest value. Within two hours of my report the house was entered; all in it were placed under temporary arrest while a search and investigation was being made. The searchers found positive evidence that the persons in the house were in communication with the enemy. Further, they discovered that a chain of espionage was at work, of which the authorities knew nothing. Within 24 hours all the aliens in the house were deported to Germany and other arrests were imminent. I was also informed that evidently the Germans were intent on sending aircraft to blow up Wolverton Works, where munitions of war were being made. And the bridge over the viaducts spanning the Ouse was one of the most vital points on the whole of the L.M.S. railway. If the bridge could have been blown up there was no possibility of a loop line or a detour being made, and it would probably have taken longer to repair or reinstate than any other section of the line."

Of the Zeppelin incident, special constables at Bletchley had also witnessed the spectacle, except for Joe Fennell and his fellow officer:

"One cold night when I was on duty with Tom Coffee of The Grange Lodge, a Zeppelin was brought down near Barnet. All the others saw it except we two and our Lieutenant, Mr. Hedley Clarke, said he could not understand why we had not seen it. He thought we must have been in the Park Hotel. We truthfully denied this for the truth was that when in Bletchley Road Mr. Edwards (butcher) came to his door and said, "You've got a cold job - would you like a drop of Scotch? Come in." Did we say no? Who would on a cold frosty night."

Of the espionage incident, Mr. Bullard would himself be arrested as a suspected spy. During the war he played a prominent role in the local P.S.A. Brotherhood's campaign to collect food and clothing for the poor people of Belgium and Holland and eventually sufficient was amassed to fill four railway trucks. The National Brotherhood also collected such huge quantities that a special train was chartered and Mr. Bullard was amongst those persons nominated to distribute the goods in the war zone. He had been too old to enlist in England but once across the Channel he offered his services as a sniper, holding several certificates for rifle shooting and being qualified to shoot at Bisley. However in no uncertain terms the senior local officer told him this would not be possible although permission was granted for the party to visit the deserted mining township of Vermells. Enemy shelling then prevented this and during his stay in the neighbourhood he slept in a miner's cottage, through a skylight in the roof of which he could witness the sights of war with the flash of the shell bursts and the continual Verey flares. Of the next events Mr. Bullard recalled:

"The morning we were due to leave that district we were all under arrest, suspected of being spies. Mounted soldiers surrounded the house we had met in, and we were all driven in a motor a long way to a guardhouse or prison in a village named Guinchy. While we were there a British Tommy was to be shot for desertion. He had deserted several times and was always found drunk in some estaminet with undesirables, who may have been seeking information. After being interviewed we were sent to St. Omar to be interviewed by General French, and were ordered to leave the country within a few hours."

THE TAYLORS

FREDERICK JAMES TAYLOR

Lovat Bank.

In 1825 William Taylor began in business next to the old Fire Station in the High Street, moving a few years later to premises across the road at 34, High Street. There he continued as a chemist, druggist and soda water manufacturer and in 1830 from a secret recipe developed the first ready prepared English mustard. This was made in a factory in Union Street and in 1863 he passed his business to his sons Thomas and Frederick James Taylor, trading as 'T. & F. J. Taylor.' From Matthew Featherstonehaugh, a woolstapler, in 1876 Frederick purchased workshops and premises in Silver Street and on the land in 1877 built Lovat Bank, with Edward Swinfen Harris as the architect. At his own expense he had the street widened to remove a dangerous corner and at the palatial house he would live with his mother, Catherine, and his three sisters Emma, Clara and Fanny. They were all chemists whilst as for Frederick he retired from active business 10 years later. Having a reputation as a marksman, taking part in several rifle shooting competitions on the Wimbledon ranges, in his younger days he had been a member of the 6th Bucks Volunteer Rifles but following the outbreak of the First World War due to illness he was unable to take an active role in the local war effort. Indeed, having been the honorary secretary for many years he was unable to attend a meeting of the Soldiers' and Sailors' Families Association at Gayhurst House on Tuesday, August 4th 1914. In fact due to his health he was unable to accept any appointment although the following day Mr. A. Lott, his head gardener at Lovat Bank, sent a grand display of cut blooms to the Newport Pagnell Flower Show. Then as a former chairman of the Board of Managers on Tuesday afternoon, December 22nd 1914, he sent the pupils of the Newport Pagnell Council Schools boxes of oranges, which were distributed to the children before they left for the Christmas holidays. Unfortunately Mr. Taylor was also unable to be present when for the forty eighth time the members of the Newport Pagnell Church Institute were entertained on New Year's Eve to a supper. This was given at Lovat Bank where on February 25th 1915, his sister, Emma, died aged 76. Greatly involved in church work for 50 years she had been involved with the Sunday Schools and at the funeral the mourners included Miss Fanny Taylor, sister, Mr. F. W. Taylor, nephew and the household staff - Mrs. Fuller, Miss Kate Welch, Miss Alice Brown, Miss Elizabeth White, as well as Mr. A. Lott, the head gardener, Mr. D. Reynolds, coachman and the gardeners, Cecil Hedge and Fred Bristowe. Again through illness on Tuesday, March 23rd 1915, Mr. Taylor was absent at the annual meeting of the shareholders of the Newport Pagnell Gas and Coke Co. Ltd. This took place at the registered office in Union Street where for his services as Managing Director during the past year a vote of thanks was proposed. On the afternoon of Thursday, July 29th 1915, thanks were also expressed for the monetary prizes which he had given in connection with the annual swimming tests for the Council Boys' School. These were held at the Bathing Place and Mr. Taylor had never been happier than when rowing his boat down the Lovat to watch the competitions. Annually he also gave money prizes to those boys of the elementary schools who accomplished distances in swimming. In other benefactions he gave the prizes for the table decoration and the wild flower collection by the members' children at the fifth annual flower show of the Unionist Working Men's Club. This was held on Saturday, September 4th 1915, whilst in November 1915 the competition for his championship silver cup, open to members of the Newport Pagnell Bowling Club, was won by Mr. G. Chasty. In 1915 as usual when the Council Schools broke up for the Christmas holidays each child received his gift of an orange. However, the New Year didn't begin too well for Cecil Webster, clerk at Messrs. T. and F. J. Taylor's mineral water works, for on Wednesday afternoon, January 5th 1916, when getting onto a lorry he fell onto some mineral water cases. Having fractured his leg he was taken to Northampton Hospital where he was detained. Throughout the year Mr. Taylor maintained his benevolence by giving the usual monetary prizes for the annual schoolboy swimming tests. As customary on Thursday afternoon, August 3rd 1916, these were held at the Bathing Place and although confined by serious illness to his home he also sent his customary Christmas gift of oranges to the pupils of the Council Schools. Then for a large agricultural and general auction jumble sale, held in the town during March, he sent a cheque for £100. However his serious illness sadly culminated in his death towards the end of the month aged 83 and on the afternoon of Monday, March 26th 1917, the coffin, covered with flowers, was borne from Lovat Bank on the hand hearse to the parish church. During the service all business in the town was suspended and blinds at the windows drawn and with the full choir in attendance Mr. C. K. Garratt presided at the organ. The body was laid to rest in the family vault in Newport Pagnell Cemetery with amongst the mourners his nephew, Mr. F. W. Taylor, the household staff of Lovat Bank (the Misses Kate Welsh, Amos, Peto and Cobb,) the outdoor servants (Messrs. A.H. Lott, D. Reynolds, Fred Bristowe and Fred Humphreys) and from the Council Schools the headmaster, Mr. O. H. Bull, Messrs. Herbert I. Middleton and Tracey Higgins, assistant masters, plus 32 pupils of the boys' department, each of whom as they filed past placed bunches of snowdrops on the coffin. Also present was Miss K. James, headmistress of the Girls' School, and representatives of the School Managers. For 45 years Mr. Taylor had been an honoured member of the SS Peter and Paul Lodge of Freemasons and as their mark of respect members placed sprigs of acacia on the coffin. In full uniform also paying their respects were the members of the Town Fire Brigade who were accompanied by two retired members.

For a long while Mr. Taylor had been the chief officer of the Fire Brigade, from which he retired in 1891, and it was largely due to his efforts that a magnificent steamer and the most modern fire-fighting appliances had been acquired. In fact the new engine was christened 'Lovat' in the grounds of Lovat Bank. Also at the funeral were many people from the business community and during the evening the full muffled peal rung on the church bells was a well deserved tribute, for he had financed many improvements and renovations. Indeed in 1895 it had been on his initiative that a house in the High Street was pulled down to give a better view of the church and when the chimes were installed to commemorate the Queen's Jubilee he presented a new clock bell. He also subscribed £1,000 towards enlarging the organ and providing a gas engine and additionally gave generously to the new vestry fund. Elsewhere he was the biggest subscriber to the cost of building and equipping St. Luke's Mission Church. At the monthly meeting of the U.D.C. on Tuesday evening, April 3rd 1917, a vote of sympathy was passed to the Misses Taylor, of Lovat Bank, on the death of their brother who it was revealed in June 1917 had left estate of £63,826, bequeathing £500

'Lovat,' now to be seen at Milton Keynes Museum.

for the upkeep of the parish church organ and £150 to the Newport Pagnell Feoffees. Postponed from August Bank Holiday, due to the Bathing Place being in flood, a grand water carnival organised by the Newport Pagnell Hospital Week Committee took place on Thursday afternoon, August 23rd 1917, and continuing the benevolence of their late brother the Misses Taylor gave money prizes for the swimming tests. Then also in the aftermath of his death at the meeting of the Newport Pagnell, Wolverton and District Model Building Society, held at The Poplars on Wednesday evening, December 19th 1917, Mr. F. O.Butler was appointed in his place as arbitrator. On the domestic scene, at Lovat Bank in February 1918 Miss Taylor had the need for a good plain cook. The need then arose again in June, with applicants to be 'not under 30,' and the two sisters, Clara and Fanny, would continue to live at Lovat Bank until their deaths in 1928. The next occupant would be their nephew, Francis William Taylor, until his death, followed shortly by that of his wife, in 1953. Then in 1969 the U.D.C. moved to the premises which in

1974 on being passed to Milton Keynes Borough Council was subsequently let as offices.

Francis William Taylor

In business as a chemist in the town, and resident at The Limes, on the evening of Wednesday, August 26th 1914, Mr. Francis William Taylor was amongst those supporting a proposal to restart the Rifle Club and reopen the range. This was discussed at an adjourned meeting at the Town Hall and his sons were also becoming involved in the war effort with Frederick Thomas Taylor, who as a chemist was in business with his father, volunteering the next month for the Public Schools and Universities Corps. Another son was serving with the Inns of Court Officers' Training Corps and in December 1914 it was announced that Frederick had been gazetted second lieutenant in the 21st Manchester Regiment. As for his father he joined both the Special Constables and the Newport Pagnell Company of the County Volunteer Defence Corps. In his business life in February 1915 he had the need for a well educated youth as an apprentice at his pharmacy whilst in July 1915 his chief assistant and dispenser, his brother Francis Taylor, who was a fully qualified chemist, joined the R.A.M.C. as a private, to be stationed at Aldershot. Having been a member of the tribunal under the Derby Scheme, at a special meeting of the Newport Pagnell U.D.C. on Tuesday evening, February 8th 1916, Mr. Francis William Taylor was appointed with the other members to the tribunal to consider local appeal tribunals under the Compulsory Military Service Act. His wife was also involved in civic life and as honorary secretary was amongst those present at a large meeting of the Newport Pagnell Deanery Mothers' Union, held at the Electric Theatre on Thursday afternoon July 13th 1916. Tragically the month also brought sadness when her third son, Francis Maurice Taylor, of the Royal Fusiliers, was killed in action aged 19. This was whilst carrying a wounded soldier to safety in the face of withering machine gun fire and also during

Urban District Council of Newport Pagnell.

MILITARY SERVICE ACT, 1916.

Unattested Men.

The LOCAL TRIBUNAL for the above District hereby GIVE NOTICE:—

THAT ALL MEN who have NOT ATTESTED and desire exemption MUST, whether they are starred or not, make application to the Local Tribunal under the above Act.

Forms can be obtained from the undersigned, and must be returned, properly filled in, on or before WEDNESDAY, 1st MARCH, 1916.

E. P. WARD,
Clerk to the Tribunal.

Council Offices,
60, High-street, Newport Pagnell.

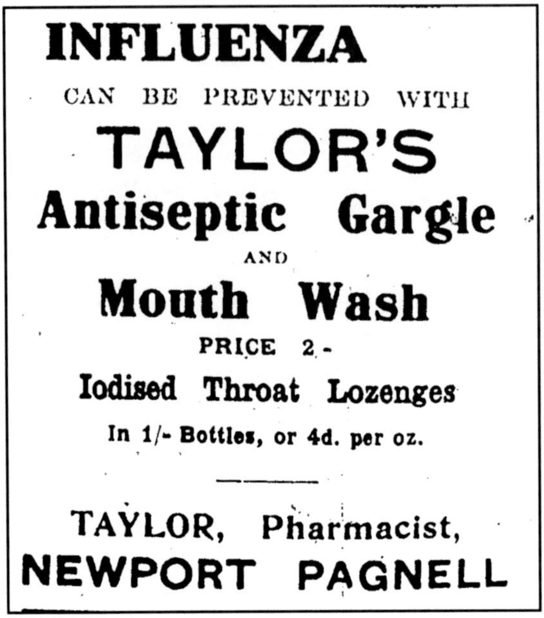
INFLUENZA
CAN BE PREVENTED WITH
TAYLOR'S
Antiseptic Gargle
AND
Mouth Wash
PRICE 2/-
Iodised Throat Lozenges
In 1/- Bottles, or 4d. per oz.
TAYLOR, Pharmacist,
NEWPORT PAGNELL

Bucks Standard, February 17th, 1923

the month Frederick, the eldest son, was wounded in action by a shell burst. After recovering he would be sent in November 1916 to Salonica, where he was given his company. Then in June 1917 news arrived that as a captain in the 13th Manchesters he had been awarded the M.C. During heavy fighting in Salonica on April 24th, when British troops stormed and captured Bulgar trenches, this was for having lead his men with great dash, with his coolness and courage under fire being highly praised by the Divisional Commander. In fact a height captured by his company would be named Taylor's Hill. In Newport Pagnell, on the evening of Thursday, February 21st 1918, the assistant at Mr. F. W. Taylor's pharmacy, Mr. J.J. Marshall, on stepping from the entrance hall at the Union Club to the side passage fell over a bicycle which was being taken down the passage. Assistance was quickly rendered and he was taken to his lodgings nearby. He was later attended by Dr. H. Wickham and Dr. Digby White and on Saturday was removed to Northampton Hospital for an operation on his fractured knee cap. At the final committee meeting regarding the town's Aeroplane Week, on Tuesday evening, July 23rd 1918, the vicar reported that the use of a room at 36, High Street, had been promised by Mr. F. W. Taylor who, to mark the winding up of the Special Constable movement in the town, was one of a small committee of well known local gentlemen that organised a first class supper at the Swan Hotel on Thursday evening, February 6th 1919. Then at a church parade to the memory of the fallen from the county amongst those present on Market Hill on Sunday, April 4th 1919, was his recently returned son Captain Frederick Taylor, M.C., who now returned to the family business. In 1919 he married Florence Whiting, the daughter of Mr. and Mrs. Harry Whiting who farmed at Willen, and in 1920 was elected to the Urban Council, being the chairman from 1926 to 1929. In 1928 on December 31st his partnership with his father 'carrying on business as Pharmacists and Mineral Water manufacturers at Newport Pagnell' was then dissolved by mutual consent and he took over the running of the family business. In 1955 the business became two limited companies with himself at the head - T. & F. J. Taylor (Newport Pagnell) Ltd. and F.T. Taylor (Pharmacy) Ltd. Newport Pagnell. He died the following year in a London clinic aged 67 leaving two sons and also a daughter, whose father in law was Dr. Julian Huxley.

Bucks Standard, May 7th, 1932

TROOPS IN THE TOWN

(BEDS. YEOMANRY, HIGHLANDERS, ROYAL ENGINEERS)

Beds. Yeomanry

For the drilling of men in the new Army, early in the second week of April 1915 came rumours of military negotiations to acquire a local field. Having inspected a field which seemed suitable the authorities then sought assurance that prominent residents in the town would welcome the arrival of the military and in consequence stabling was guaranteed for the fifty horses which were to arrive with the squadron of one hundred and fifty Yeomanry. However on the Thursday night notification was received that for unknown reasons the negotiations had fallen through. However, in September 1915 a squadron of Beds. Yeomanry were billeted in the town and it was thought they would probably remain for quite awhile. Therefore since the town had been previously approached about the long term accommodation of troops Mr. O. H. Bull, as chairman, called an urgent meeting of the U.D.C. on Saturday evening, September 18th 1915. This was to decide if the War Office should be petitioned to consider the town as a suitable billeting and training centre for soldiers and the members present were Messrs. O. H. Bull, F. Littleboy (vice chairman), W.R. Chantler, G. Tayler, W. J. Coales, J. Short, F. J. Sharp, J. Parrott, C. Holland with Mr. E.P. Ward, clerk, and Mr. A. J. Roberts, deputy clerk. As the chief recruiting officer for the town also in attendance was Superintendent J. Pearce, who told the chairman that if the Council made an application they might be able to get a large company of Artillery billeted in Newport Pagnell and he thought the authorities would seriously consider an approach if it came from the Council. Newport Pagnell already accommodated a few of the Bucks Yeomanry and the townspeople would welcome a much larger body of troops. In fact at the request of the chairman the previous day Mr. Walter Carlile, of Gayhurst House, had called on Superintendent Pearce about the possibility of billeting some Artillery in the town and it was thought that billets could be provided at Olney and Stantonbury and the neighbouring villages if there was insufficient room in the town where St. Paul's School (Silver Street) and St. Peter's School (Priory Street) could accommodate large numbers of troops. The elementary schools would not be used but the Town Hall was a possibility and if they could secure 'Olympia,' the large three storey building of Salmons, then the problems would be overcome. In fact a farmer had offered to stable 100 horses and billet 200 men in his barns and in reply to Mr. Holland,

Superintendent Pearce said that he had been making enquiries in the town as to the accommodation for ordinary billeting. This entailed finding out the potential of spare accommodation in every house in the town but his returns were not yet complete. Speaking of the recent levels in the well, and saying their first duty was to the ratepayers and townspeople, Mr. W.R. Chantler raised a concern about the water supply for 1,500 men and 100 horses but Mr. Tayler said the horses would not be watered from the public supply. As for the chairman, he reminded the Council that when the Army manoeuvres were carried out in the district the town water had been laid on to Bury Field. Mr. Short said that some 300 men were now away from the town fighting and Superintendent Pearce gave a reminder that it was not necessary for all the troops to be billeted in the town. However continuing concerns about the water supply, and the reaction of the townspeople if there were problems, were voiced by Mr. Littleboy but Mr. J. Short said the tradesmen had had a roughish time and the Council should help in any way. Mr. Tayler then asked how long the Beds Yeomanry would be in the town to which Superintendent Pearce replied for the duration of the war, as a depot supplying drafts to the fighting regiments. After some discussion Mr. J. Short then moved: "That this Council, on behalf of the town, would welcome additional soldiers when the Army authorities are prepared to send them." Mr. Tayler duly seconded but Mr. Chantler took exception to the wording, contending that the town would not accept an indefinite number of soldiers and suggesting that the troops should not be sent until the end of October, as the water supply was not adequate. However, Mr. Short said he thought the water supply would not fail and remodelled the resolution: "That this Council will welcome a further number of soldiers in the town, such number not to exceed the billeting accommodation available." Mr. Chantler then said it was not a question of accommodation, to which Mr. Short said, "You say it is." In clarification Mr. Chantler replied, "I say it is a question of water and not of accommodation" after which, with the aid of Mr. Tayler, the motion was amended by Mr. Short, "That this Council do (sic) welcome on behalf of the town a further number of soldiers as far as billeting accommodation will allow." This was adopted and thanks were expressed to Superintendent Pearce for his attendance. For the entertainment of the Beds. Yeomanry now training in the town, organised by the Newport Pagnell P.S.A. Brotherhood the first of a series of smoking concerts took place at the Town Hall on the evening of Friday, October 1st 1915. The P.S.A. committee presented the troops with cigarettes and supported by Second Lieutenants Woodhams, Dalmage and Haddock the chair was occupied by Lieutenant Halliday. With the piano accompaniments by Miss Amy Harris, Mr. Pat Levin and Mr. C. K. Garratt those performing the songs and musical sketches included Mr.

Pat Levin, Mr. O. Critchard, Trooper Pollock, Trooper Mann and also Mr. C. K. Garratt who rendered a comic song, 'The Bedford Boys.' Then at the Unionist Club, on Thursday evening, October 7th 1915, their first smoking concert of the season proved a great success. Mr. G. Tayler, J.P., occupied the chair, supported on the platform by local gentlemen and officers of the Beds. Yeomanry, and the entertainment included piano solos by Mr. C. K. Garratt and songs by amongst others Fred Walker, of Aspley Guise, Mr. O. Critchard, the Reverend Father Walker, Trooper Pollock, Mr. C.R. Line and Trooper Mann. Then at the same venue on the eve of their departure from the town the members of 'A' Squadron Beds Yeomanry held an enjoyable and hastily raised concert on Monday, October 25th 1915. Trooper Tom Pollock sang several Scotch songs in his inimitable style and other members of the regiment also contributed to the programme. On Tuesday the Yeomanry then marched out from the town for a destination 'somewhere in England,' having during their short stay become very popular.

In September 1913, Army manoeuvres were carried out in the local district, the schedule of which is described in this contemporary notice.

The object of this Guide is to give in brief compass intending and useful information about the Annual Army Manoeuvres, which, during this month of September, will bring into Northamptonshire, Buckinghamshire, and adjacent country armies of British troops, with a total strength of about 50,000. History records no such great massing of troops in this part of the country.

It should be understood that the operations this year are different from anything that has before been attempted. Instead of the usual manoeuvres, with two opposing forces of approximately equal strength, each with equal liberty of action, the Army Manoeuvres this year will take the form of an Exercise in which a Brown Force of Four Divisions and a Cavalry Division, all under the command of Field Marshal Sir John French will operate against a White Force, the main part of which will be in skeleton. That Exercise, which will take place on the five days beginning on Monday. September 22, and ending on the following Friday morning, will be preceded by the Divisional Trainings and Inter-Divisional Manoeuvres at camps, of which the most important in this district is at Wolverton. Other camps hereabouts are at Daventry, Spratton Bridge, and Boughton Park, Kettering.

For the closing week's Exercise the King and Queen come from Balmoral to Althorp, where they will be the guests of Earl Spencer. K.G., Lord Lieutenant of Northamptonshire.

Field Marshal Sir John French, third from the left, is seen standing outside the Swan Hotel, Newport Pagnell. Photo courtesy of Ken & Joyce Graham

Troops are seen marching along the High Street, Newport Pagnell, in September 1913. Sent on September 26th 1913, the wording on the postcard reads;

'Dear Reg, Another P. C. as promised. Hope you will like it. This was taken the other day of the soldiers passing through the High Street. Love and kisses M.' Photo courtesy of Ken & Joyce Graham

The Highlanders

In training at Bedford, and being this week engaged in field manoeuvres in the villages around the town, on the night of Thursday, November 19th 1914, a company of about 150 non commissioned officers and men of the Gordon Highlanders (Territorials) were billeted in Newport Pagnell Town Hall, with the officers accommodated in the houses of private gentlemen in the town. Then regarding further accommodation the School Correspondent reported that with two of the N.C.O.s the headmaster had visited him, to say that billets might again be needed in the town for a number of soldiers on the evening of Thursday 26th. For this it was possible that the schools might be needed but in the event the accommodation was not required. However, should there be a further need the Correspondent was given authority to place the premises at the disposal of the military. In such occurrences the following day the children would be given a holiday to allow for cleaning the premises, which was no doubt the case when from Bedford a Battalion of the Argyll and Sutherland Highlanders (Territorials) visited the town on Thursday, December 3rd 1914, being also billeted for the night in the Mission Hall and the Town Hall. Then having been on daytime reconnoitring work in the district, on the night of February 26th 1915, a party of 35 Gordon Highlanders, also from Bedford, were billeted in the town. On Monday, April 15th 1918, having seen active service since the beginning of the war, and been wounded twice, at the parish church Lieutenant Hilary A. Agnew of the Highland Light Infantry, the only son of the late Mr. and Mrs. H. Agnew, of 'Rocquaine', Newport Pagnell, married Miss Wilfred Emily (Freda) Coales. She was the younger daughter of Mr. and Mrs. W. J. Coales of 'The Lodge' and assisted by the Reverend Gunnery the ceremony was performed by the Reverend Bale. He was the cousin of the bride who was given away by her father with her brother, Lieutenant J.L. Coales, of the Munster Fusiliers, acting as best man. However the ceremony was of a quiet nature, as the groom had unexpectedly received orders to return to the Front on Wednesday. Joining the Stanmore Military Hospital since March 1915 the bride had been a V.A.D. Nurse and for two years and three months had been nursing at No. 2 Red Cross Hospital at Rouen and the Duchess of Westminster's Hospital at Le Touquet. Thus it was appropriate at the end of the marriage ceremony that from Tickford Abbey V.A.D. Hospital the Commandant, Miss McFerran, the Quartermaster, Miss Wood and the nursing staff lined up at the north door of the church to form a Guard of Honour.

Royal Engineers on parade - February 1916 Photo courtesy of Ken & Joyce Graham

This postcard was sent from Newport Pagnell in May 1914. Few could realise that in the coming months this would be a familar venue for those engaged in a far more desperate struggle for liberty. (The postcard was sent by 'Daddy' to his son Noel, at Bartholomews Close, Nelson Street, Norwich, Norfolk, and reads; "In case mother would like my address it is 31, Curry St., Hertford."   Photo courtesy of Ken & Joyce Graham

During September 1914 Walter Wright, the eldest son of Eli Wright, of 28, Tickford Street, joined the East Lancashire Royal Engineers for service in Egypt. Then in late December 1914 a married man of the town, Mr. F. Iliffe, a saddler and harness maker, volunteered for the Colours but was rejected on medical grounds. He then tried again and passed, and would subsequently serve with the Royal Engineers at Shorncliffe. Engaged in a staff ride through North Bucks, in the last week of March 1915 a section of troops, undergoing training in the districts of Wing and Leighton Buzzard, were billeted in the town on the night of Wednesday, March 24th. Comprising about 240 officers and men the ride was composed of units from various regiments, and upon their arrival in the early afternoon they had soon became a source of fascination for the many people who gathered in the High Street, to witness the issue of their billeting instructions. The 'ride' was then continued on Thursday morning, when the men marched on to Northampton. Well known in Newport Pagnell, in 1915 Sapper Leonard Knight, of the 12th Company Royal Engineers, was severely wounded near Armentiers on March 11th, when hit in the shoulder by three machine gun rounds. He was returned to England for hospital treatment at Southsea, but on contracting a fever was then sent to a hospital on the Isle of Wight. As he always did when on leave, he would then spend a week - subsequently extended to a fortnight - with his sister, Mrs. Wallace Dale, of Church Street, but afterwards when ordered to Chatham he contracted pneumonia, and died there in hospital on Wednesday, June 16th. The youngest son of a boot maker of the town, the late James Knight, and his wife, of 27, Bedford Street, he had enlisted in the army six years ago, and was stationed mostly in Ireland. However, shortly after the outbreak of hostilities in August he was sent to the Front, and subsequently took part in much action. Afforded full military honours, his funeral was held at Newport Pagnell. Before the war, for some eight years he had been employed at Salmons, as also had been W. Daniells, who was now a sapper in the Royal Engineers.

The son of Edward Daniells, of Greenfield Road, he had volunteered early for service, and mention of his sporting renown is made in the chapter on Salmons. Many having seen active service, by December 1915 about 620 members of the Royal Engineers (Signal Section) were billeted in the town, and, with the Town Hall as their depot, daily parades took place on the Market Square. For instructional purposes the Congregational Church Sunday Schools had been placed at the military's disposal, with the Baptist Schools in use as a reading room, and it was expected that the troops would remain in the town for some months. In fact for instructional purposes they would be joined one Friday in late December 1915 by a party of soldiers who had served under General Botha in German South West Africa. On the evening of Friday, December 17th the Royal Engineers in the town, assisted by members of the Tyringham Hospital staff, gave a concert at the Workmen's Social Club, and as a further integration into the social scene on the evenings of Monday and Tuesday, December 20th and 21st they played a billiards match with the Unionist Club, whose team proved victorious by 85 points. Visiting various parts of the town, on Thursday evening, December 23rd 1915 a party of Royal Engineers and members of the Congregational Church Choir sang carols to raise money for the Red Cross. This they repeated on Sunday evening, and by their efforts raised the sum of £4 7s. On Tuesday evening, December 28th 1915, at the Masonic Centre there was a happy gathering of the locally stationed Royal Engineers. This was for the formal opening of the building as a recreation, games and refreshment centre for the military, and, with the large hall having been comfortably furnished, and with newspapers and literature placed on the tables, suitable facilities would be afforded for the men to write letters. The Reverend F. Gunnery presided, and, with Mr. C. K. Garratt at the piano, in a long programme of vocal and instrumental entertainments the excellent violin solos of Sapper Steele were greatly appreciated, which was hardly surprising since he had performed in the Carl Rosa Opera Company. After travelling from Wolverton, Miss Elsie Cooke and Miss Wilkes rendered songs, and in other contributions Mr. A. Bullard and Mr. O. Critchard were in fine voice, loud applause greeted the humorous songs by the popular local comedian Mr. Ernest Platt, and similarly applauded was a recitation by Miss Wilford.

During the interval the vicar, explaining that the rooms had been opened by a small committee representative of the town, welcomed the soldiers to the room, and in response on behalf of the detachment Captain Bradley expressed his thanks to the vicar and the people involved, saying in conclusion; "I call upon you men to show your appreciation in a real good cheer - a cheer like that you will give when you man all the offices in Berlin." To this the soldiers immediately gave three rousing cheers, which were then repeated when the vicar announced that the library and billiards table of the Church Institute, situated below, would be open to the men. A feature of the institute was to be a temperance refreshment stall, and this was to be under the charge of Mrs. Gunnery, Mrs. Mitchison, Miss French, Miss A. Coales, the Misses Allfrey, Miss Bull and Miss Wilford. Arranged by Mr. C. K. Garratt and others, at the Unionist Club on the following evening a smoking concert was held which, by permission of Lieutenant Colonel Lister, the Royal Engineers billeted in the town could attend. Sapper Steele again exercised his talents on the violin, and Sapper Horwill, Sapper Macdonald, and the Reverend Father Walker, from Wolverton, were all heard in good voice to the accompaniment of Mr. Garratt, who additionally contributed musical sketches. At the Girls' School, on New Year's Eve 1915 the Co-operative Society held a whist drive and dance, arranged by the general committee in conjunction with the Women's Guild and the Educational Committee of the local Co-operative Society. The proceeds were to augment the fund for sending parcels to some 150 Society members and their sons who were serving in the war, and many of the 700 or so Royal Engineers billeted in the town were present, plus a few soldiers from South Africa who, having been on active service, were now attached to the local contingent. A refreshment stall was managed by members of the Women's Guild, and with the Newport Pagnell Excelsior Silver Band having provided music for dancing, at midnight the party linked hands and sang 'Auld Lang Syne,' with the South Africans giving the war whoop of the veldt. In early 1916, Lieutenant H. Hooper, Division Officer of the Royal Engineers at Bedford, stated in a letter to the Council that on May 29th 1915 he had met the Surveyor, regarding a building that could be adapted for use as a bathroom for the troops quartered at Newport Pagnell.

This was subsequent to the Surveyor having found a shed with a concrete floor at the Council Depot which, measuring 24 feet by 13 feet, could be easily adapted by placing a temporary front between the eaves level and the ground, inserting two doors and some windows, creating a four inch half pipe channel leading to the gulley, which was adjoining, and extending the water supply to feed a couple of portable boilers for heating water for bathing purposes. The provision of a couple of gas lights would also be an advantage, as also a ventilator in the roof, and in his letter Lieutenant Hooper said "I should be glad to hear from you if you would allow us the use of the building. The cost of the adaptation and any re-instatement to the condition in what it was before would be borne by the military authorities. I need scarcely impress upon you the importance of the troops now quartered at Newport Pagnell having facilities for warm water bathing. The baths, of course, would be under the proper control of the officer in charge..." However, having met Lieutenant Hooper the Surveyor said that that if the suggestion was approved the Council would need to erect another shed for carts etc., and he therefore suggested that they select another spot in the March of Intellect yard, to which they would have access from the lane. To this Lieutenant Hooper agreed, being of the opinion that it would be just as well for the military to erect the proposed new bath house, as to put the Council to the expense.

On one side of the inn sign was a crude painting of a drawing room with a large piano at which was seated a chimney sweep with his rods and brushes laying on the floor beside him. He was playing the piano and singing his teeth as white as the piano keys. On the other side of the sign

Upper photograph: An early photo of the March of Intellect Photo courtesy of Don Hurst.

The lower photograph shows the premises today in Silver Street. It was converted into two private houses in 1985.

was painted a lot of brickwork a dark arched mass in the centre from which was emerging a man seated in a horse and trap and another vehicle ready to enter. The arched tunnel supposedly represented the tunnel under the Thames.He would therefore have a sketch prepared of the type of building required and invite four tenders. Also regarding facilities for the Royal Engineers, on December 29th 1915 the Surveyor had met several officers of the Royal Engineers at the public convenience at the Town Hall, and there it was suggested that more complete lavatory arrangements would be necessary to meet the requirement of the troops. It was considered that four w.c.s with pans and flushing arrangements could be erected in front of the urinal, although the Surveyor thought they might project too much. Since that meeting the military had interviewed the secretary to the Town Hall Company, and, having secured permission to erect the convenience on their property, the offer was made that if the Council erected the place, then the military would find the whole of the fittings. Should the soldiers leave the town then the facility would be left for the benefit of the townspeople. As for the bath house, in a Council debate some members thought that a building at the rear of the Council Offices, with an entrance from Union Street, would be suitable, but the Surveyor, Mr. Bransford, said Lieutenant Hooper required a place 20 feet square. The water would be heated in two 30 gallon boilers, but he understood that the military would not make a grant towards permanent baths, nor hand over the baths, boilers etc., when they were no longer needed. Each holding about seven gallons, they required wash baths, not body baths, and when the chairman asked if, considering the size, the place at the rear of the Council Offices could be fitted up as baths, Mr. Bransford thought that the military would readily agree. However, the building was presently let to Mr. Fleet, although since he might forego his tenancy, and put his carts in the March of Intellect yard, Mr. Bull, Mr. Littleboy, Mr. Chantler and Mr. Holland were appointed as a committee, empowered to act, to approach him, and to also confer with the military authorities regarding the provision of the baths.

As for the erection of the W.C.s near the Town Hall the Council unanimously agreed, and - being directed to prepare plans and specifications - the Surveyor was instructed to invite tenders as soon as possible. The national day of prayer and intercession was observed at the Congregational Church on the first Sunday of the New Year, with many of the Royal Engineers present at the morning service. Also during the month Mrs. Thomas, the organist at the Congregational Church, organised a concert at the Newport Pagnell Soldiers' Institute, where the packed audience of Royal Engineers encored many of the items, including a piano duet by Mrs. Thomas and Miss Lily Kempster. Other items were contributed by Miss Ellingham,

Sapper Hawitt, Mrs. Smith, Mr. C. Burgess, Master Harry Ward, Sapper Swaine, Mrs. Warren, Sapper Lucas, and Miss Wilford, and on Wednesday, January 19th 1916 at the same venue another concert was held, to a large attendance of Royal Engineers. Mr. C. K. Garratt presided at the piano, .and with his wife singing 'Take a pair of sparkling eyes' the performances by the other artistes were also greatly enjoyed. Then on Tuesday evening, January 25th at the Unionist Club a smoking concert took place, to which the Royal Engineers had been given permission to attend by Lieutenant Colonel Lister. Rendered by the Woburn Concert Party this featured an excellent selection of songs, recitations, duets, banjo solos etc., with the arrangements having been made by the Club Entertainment Committee. Mr. C. K. Garratt was the accompanist, as he would also be at a first class sacred concert which, in conjunction with the entertainment committee of the Soldiers' Institute, he arranged for the evening of Sunday, January 23rd 1916 at the Electric Theatre. Here before a packed audience Miss Wailey, a soprano from Crewe, who was very popular in the district, sang several numbers, the Reverend Father Walker performed songs in his powerful bass voice, Miss Mabel Wilford gave recitations, and Mr. O. Critchard performed tenor solos. The event raised £5 10s 6d for the upkeep of the Soldiers' Institute, and at the same venue another enjoyable evening was then spent on Monday, January 31st, when a concert arranged by Sapper J. Hewitt took place. Sapper Arlett presided, and the entire programme consisted of items by the Royal Engineers, who, as stewards, were present in the afternoon the next day at two grand concerts at the Electric Theatre, held under the auspices of the Newport Pagnell War Charities Committees in aid of the Serbian Relief Fund. By now the bathing shed for the military had been erected, and was ready for use at the Council's depot in Silver Street. Thus at the meeting of the U.D.C. on Tuesday evening, February 1st a report from the Army Baths and Latrines Committee was read, in which the thanks of Division Officer Hooper was expressed both for the construction, and for the Council's approval regarding the arrangements made with the Surveyor to provide latrines at the Town Hall. He estimated the cost of appliances at £6, and suggested that the work should be carried out by the Council, who would be repaid the £6 and be in control of 'the hire and use of the latrines.' However, the Surveyor estimated a cost of £36 12s for constructing suitable latrines, and the Clerk had duly communicated with the Division Officer with a view to the military authorities paying a larger contribution. In reply, by a letter dated January 13th Division Officer Hooper stated that all that was necessary for the troops was a light structure of timber and corrugated sheets, with a concrete floor and drain, and of his estimated cost of £16, £6 would be repaid by the War Office in the form of rental, the revenue being brought into the town by the 500 or so troops being sufficient for that contribution. In fact the Surveyor had submitted plans and specifications for the construction of four permanent latrines, but after fully considering the question the Committee resolved that he be instructed to prepare plans and specifications for two permanent and two temporary latrines, and that the tenders be submitted to Messrs. Littleboy and Chantler.

Subsequently tenders were duly received from Wilford Bros., £31 13s, W. Read and Co., £29 15s, and T. and C. Shelton, £28 13s, and that of the latter was accepted. On Sunday evening February 6th 1916 a good number of Royal Engineers attended a sacred concert at the Soldiers' Recreation Room, where Sapper Oxburg sang 'Lorraine,' Miss Eva Garratt sang songs to include 'Bid me discourse,' and, with Mr. C. K. Garratt at the piano, other items were contributed by Mr. A. Bullard, Mr. C. Line, Mr. O. Crithcard, Miss Wilford and Miss Allfrey. Then on Monday evening, February 14th 1916, given by the Royal Engineers and friends another concert took place at which, in opening the event, Corporal James, occupying the chair, thanked the kindness of the local people for providing such a comfortable room for recreation and reading for the 'boys,' as also those who provided refreshments night after night, and those responsible for the upkeep of the hall. For the occasion Sapper R. Lucas had arranged an interesting programme, and of the artistes the fine singing of Miss Olive Ellingham and Mr. Oliver Critchard resulted in encores. Amongst other items Sapper L. Brown contributed 'The Kaiser - I want to meet him,' whilst Corporal Ellingham delighted the audience with his violin solos. A copper collection amongst the soldiers towards defraying the expense of gas, cleaning, etc. raised £1 1s 9d. In other entertainments, on Thursday, February 17th 1916 a pleasant musical programme was held at the Wesleyan Schoolroom. Sapper G. Rowland occupied the chair, and the performances included a piano solo by Mrs. Shedd, songs, to include 'Till the boys come home,' by Miss Eva Garratt, and recitations by Lance Corporal Thompson. Other artistes were Sapper O'Shaughnessy, Miss Middleton, Miss Wagstaff, Sapper Greaves, and Sapper Bates, and during the interval a collection was taken to purchase new hymn books, since soldiers were now attending the church. Elsewhere, on the same evening at the Unionist Club the return billiards match took place between Mr. A. Orton's team (Stony Stratford) and Mr. T. Sim's team (Newport Pagnell). The home team comprised military and civilian players, and by permission of Lieutenant Colonel Lister an extension of time was granted to enable the soldiers to see the match, which the home team won by 254 points. For the benefit of the Royal Engineers, on the following Sunday a fine programme of sacred music was performed at the Soldiers Recreation Room (Masonic Hall), with the voluntary artistes being mainly from Wolverton. This had been organised by Mr. C. K. Garratt, and due to two of the performers being indisposed his wife, as a soprano, and Mr. O. Critchard, tenor, stood in, being thanked, as were all the performers, by Lance Corporal Atkins before the close. Arranged by the Royal Engineers, on Monday evening, February 21st 1916 a smoking concert took place in the Masonic Hall, and, on his taking the chair at 7.30 p.m., the announcement by Lieutenant K. Armytage of an extension until 11 p.m., granted by Lieutenant Colonel Lister, met with hearty cheers. The lengthy and varied programme commenced with the song 'Three for Jack' by Sapper Pear, and during the event Miss Kathleen Powell sang numbers in a pleasing soprano voice, Miss M. Wilford was well received for her recitation, Miss Grace Middleton sang as a contralto, and Miss Wagstaff excelled in a violin solo.

For the upkeep of the Institute a collection was taken during the interval, and amongst other performances much laughter and applause was caused by a musical sketch performed by Mr. C. K. Garratt, and despite having a cold the popular Sapper Reg Lucas, a baritone, sang commendably. In fact also commendable would be his performance later in the war, when for bravery during the Messines offensive he would be awarded the Military Medal in September 1917. Again at the Institute, a smoking concert was held on Monday evening, February 28th, with the attendance being such that many had to stand, with some even turned away. An excellent programme had been arranged by Sappers Lucas and MacManus, and in the chair Sergeant Roberts was supported on the platform by Sergeant Legge and Sapper MacManus. Played on the piano by Mr. C. K. Garratt the programme began with Grieg's 'Wedding Day,' and apart from the local artistes, amongst whom were Miss K. Powell, Miss G. Middleton and Mr. C. Line, contributions were also given by several sappers of the Royal Engineers, including a violin solo by Corporal Wilkinson, from Canada. Having been made temporary members, for additional recreation the Royal Engineers could now attend the Unionist Club, several of the members of which who had joined the Forces had been killed. However, the Institute remained the main venue for concerts, such as that arranged by Mr. C. K. Garratt for the Royal Engineers on Thursday evening, March 9th 1916. So many attended, including the soldiers' wives, that many had to be turned away, and supported by Captain Stevens, Captain Needham, Lieutenant Yates (Bletchley), and Lieutenants Haines and Ashby (Newport Pagnell), Lieutenant Colonel Lister took the chair, having motored over from Bletchley. For the event Mr. Garratt had not only enlisted the voluntary help of the Woburn Concert Society and two or three of the Royal Engineers, but also the help of Miss Christine Larkin (Mrs. A. T. O'Rourke) of Wolverton, who, being a soprano formerly of Queen's Hall, London, and principal provincial concerts, began with 'The merry month of May.' Responding to an encore she then gave 'The Kerry dance,' and on needing to leave early was thanked by Lieutenant Colonel Lister for having attended from Wolverton. Cheered and encored for each of his numbers, also of professional status was Lieutenant Yates, for prior to his appointment to a commission he had been a well known London professional vocalist, who had appeared with considerable success in grand opera. For their contribution the Woburn Concert party included humorous numbers, songs, and banjo solos by Bob Lansom, whilst as for Miss Wilford she recited 'Mr. Winkle on skates.' Amongst other items Sapper Jezzard, of Bletchley, sang the humorous song 'The ideal home,' and throughout the concert Mr. Garratt played the piano accompaniments. £2 was raised by a collection at the interval, and with the Reverend Gunnery being present in the second half at the close he thanked the officers and Lieutenant Colonel Lister, who in return thanked the residents for their kindness to his men, and for establishing the recreation room. He also thanked the artistes, and the event was brought to a close by the singing of the National Anthem. Given at the Institute, with Lance Corporal Dodderidge in the chair on Sunday evening, March 5th 1916 a fairly large number of Royal Engineers listened to a sacred concert, at which songs were sung by some of the soldiers, Miss West, and Miss Wilford. Mr. C. K. Garratt, who had arranged the event, played the accompaniments.

By four goals to one, on Saturday, March 4th 1916 the Royal Engineers beat a team from the town at football on Bury Field, and on the ground a collection was taken for the Town Band. They now played the Royal Engineers to and from church on Sunday mornings, but it was the Royal Engineers who made the musical arrangements for a concert held in the Institute on Monday evening, March 13th 1916. With the latter being loudly applauded for his songs, a surprise visit by Captain Stevens and Lieutenant Yates added to the importance of the occasion, and amongst the Royal Engineers Sappers Harding and Hunter contributed two piano duets to the programme, which was presided over by Sapper Hawitt. A collection to help defray the expenses realised 19s 0½d, and a penny stamp! The concert hall was packed for a whist drive held at the Unionist Club on Friday, March 10th. With many sappers present there were 100 players and by the grant of an extension of time by Lieutenant Colonel Lister the event finished at about 10.30 p.m. Arranged by Mr. C. K. Garratt, who with Miss Amy Harris provided the accompaniments, on Sunday evening, March 19th 1916 a sacred concert for the Royal Engineers took place at the Institute, with Lance Corporal Stevens occupying the chair. The various items included those by Mrs. Broadhurst, of Liverpool, Miss K. Fleet, Miss M. Wilford, Dudley Gardner, Oliver Critchard, and Sappers Prescott and Sharp, 'who possessed a very fine tenor voice.' Sapper Lucas also contributed, and in aid of funds for the Royal Engineers' Club he arranged the smoking concert on the evening of March 16th, held at the Unionist Club. The room was crowded, and with Lieutenant Colonel Lister in the chair, supported by other officers and Major W. Dodds, the officer commanding the Newport Pagnell depot, amongst the audience were many Royal Engineers from Fenny Stratford. Much laughter was caused by the anecdotes of Frank Hudson, whose living marionettes were later greatly appreciated, and the programme included the fine singing of Lieutenant Yates. The solo singing of Sapper Baird, also Mr. A. Bullard, was appreciated on Sunday evening, March 19th, when members of the P.S.A. Brotherhood visited the Workhouse for a service for the inmates, with the accompaniments played by Miss Amy Harris. At the Institute, on Monday evening, March 27th 1916 a smoking concert was held for the entertainment of the Royal Engineers. Supported by other officers, and also the vicar, Major W. Dodds occupied the chair and for the occasion the organiser, Mr. C. K. Garratt, who played the accompaniments throughout the event, had secured the services of Mrs. T. Gale of Bletchley, soprano, the Reverend Father Walker, bass, and, also from Wolverton, Mr. W. Liddle, solo clarinet. However he and Harry Ridge, a humorist, had to leave early to catch the 9 p.m. train. Other performers were Miss Mabel Wilford, elocutionist, Mr. Cole, humorist, Sapper Lucas, baritone, Sapper Sharp, tenor, and Sapper L. Bishop, as well as two members of the Royal Engineers who, preferring to be styled as 'The Brothers Mac,' told hilarious jokes and performed an amusing sketch.

With friends, the Royal Engineers also performed at a concert at the Workhouse on Friday evening, March 31st. Lieutenant Moreton, baritone, occupied the chair, and the artistes included Miss G. Middleton, contralto, Miss K. Powell, soprano, Mr. A. Bullard, bass, and Sappers Sharp, tenor, Lucas, baritone, and Hanlan, bass. Sapper Jackson performed a musical sketch, and instrumental numbers were given by the trio of Mr. and Mrs. W. Charlton and Sapper Manson. There was a happy gathering of over 200 children at the Workmen's Club on Saturday afternoon, April 1st. These were the children of the members, and the occasion was the annual tea and entertainment provided by the club management. Under the supervision of Mrs. A. Andrew, stewardess, tea was served in the concert hall, and afterwards the Magpie Concert Party provided a varied entertainment. Then in the evening, arranged by Mr. C. K. Garratt a concert was held in the hall to a large attendance of the members and their wives. Assistance was given by the Royal Engineers, and although a special feature was to have been the appearance of the popular artistes Sam Tilley and Gertie Lee, due to traffic dislocation, caused earlier in the week by a blizzard, they were unable to

be present. Instead, with Mr. Garratt playing the piano accompaniments, and also giving a musical sketch, voluntary assistance was given by Mr. O. Critchard, Cecil R. Line and a young man calling himself 'De Civa,' who aptly performed conjuring feats. Whilst taking a walk around the allotments, Sapper James Gordon came to the assistance of 73 year old Thomas Sharman on Tuesday afternoon April 4th when, whilst digging on his son in law's plot in Fox Gate Piece, he collapsed. However, despite every effort nothing could be done to revive him. During his working life Thomas had been an agricultural labourer, and having previously resided at Willington, near Bedford, about two weeks ago after the recent death of his wife he had come to live with his daughter, Mrs. Whitlock, at 2, Greenfield Road.

In appreciation for all the entertainments that had been staged for them, at the Electric Theatre on Wednesday evening, April 5th 1916 the Royal Engineers gave a special concert for Mr. Garratt. Assisted by Sappers Jaggard, Jackson, and Sharp, this had been most ably arranged by Sapper R. Lucas, and amongst those occupying the reserved seats was Lieutenant Colonel Lister. The fine singing of Sappers Sharp, Lucas, and Vezey, was greatly appreciated, and, apart from employing his talent as an accomplished pianist, Sapper Jackson convulsed the audience with his story of a village concert. Miss Mabel Wilford, elocutionist, also performed, as well as Miss Beatrice Walley, a soprano from Crewe, who sang beautifully, and Mr. G. Webb, who gave piccolo solos. The humorous side was provided by Frank Hudson, of London, who firstly appeared as a ventriloquist and later told the story of Old Mother Hubbard. This was in the form of a parson's sermon, and as a finale he introduced his clever display of living marionettes. As the piano accompanist, Mr. Garratt had opened the programme with the National Anthem, and during the interval Lieutenant Colonel Lister, on behalf of the Royal Engineers, presented him with a silver salver and a cheque. To this Mr. Garratt suitably responded, and after expenses it was found that the concert had made about £22. On the following evening, arranged by the Royal Engineers a musical programme was given in the Wesleyan Schoolroom, with the artistes being Miss Punter, of Bradwell, soprano, Miss Grace Middleton, who recited a poem of her own composition entitled 'To His Mother,' Mr. O. Critchard, Mr. C.R. Line, Sapper Greaves, Sapper Baird, Mr. H. Green, solo cornet, and Miss Amy Harris, who presided at the piano. After playing for the Royal Engineers' Church Parade, on Sunday morning, April 9th 1916 the Excelsior Silver Band, under Mr. A. Green, gave a sacred concert in front of the Royal Engineers' headquarters at the Town Hall. Then on Thursday evening, April 13th, a concert was held at the Institute arranged by ladies from Emberton and district. They were assisted by Oliver Critchard, Harry Colson, and Sapper Vezey, and with Captain Stevens, from

The Magpie Concert Party, from Wolverton.

During the war the performers gave many concerts to boost local morale. On the evening of Saturday, November 22nd 1919, they gave a masquerade ball at Newport Pagnell in the suitably decorated Town Hall where, secured by the manager, Mr. F. Bavey, this flashlight photo was taken. Many of the 130 persons present were in fancy dress and, with Mr. H. Nicholson's string band providing an up-to-date and popular programme of music, 'there was a general atmosphere of real enjoyment throughout the evening.' As members of the party Mr. W. Holloway and Mr. H. Coward acted as M.C.s and during the last set of Lancers a quantity of coloured paper ribbons were thrown amongst the dancers, who quickly became entangled in the web. Refreshments were served by Mrs. Bavey and also Mr. and Mrs. Temple, whose assistance as well as that of Mr. Kingham was greatly appreciated. By popular request another ball was arranged for Monday, December 29th.

Fenny Stratford, presiding, Miss W. Cotton and Mr. C. K. Garratt opened the concert with a piano duet. Of the other performers Captain Brett, from Fenny Stratford, contributed 'I want to meet the Kaiser,' a well received humorous item, and also contributing to the entertainment was a party brought by Mrs. Savory, of the Manor House, Emberton. This consisted of the Misses Savory, Mrs. Young, of Clifton Reynes, and also Miss Bertha Richens, who received encores for each of the four times that she sang. Sapper Vezey performed three songs. Mrs. Young played two violin solos, the piano accompaniments were the province of Miss Savory and Mr. C. K.

Garratt, and at the refreshment stall the Misses Allfrey and Mrs. Mitchison were amongst the ladies in attendance. The following evening a concert arranged by Pioneers Prager and Wright, of the Royal Engineers, was held at the Workmen's Social Club where, with Lieutenant Colonel Lister having granted an extension of time, the items included piano solos, comic songs, a cornet solo, and a sentimental song by Miss Cole. Also performed was an amusing sketch entitled 'Army Headquarters,' in which with the scene being ten miles behind the firing line the characters were General Sir Drury Lane (Pioneer Prager,) Colonel Cheesewinks (Sapper Hanley,) Private Sausage (Pioneer Wright,) and Sergeant Crumpet (Mr. C. Cole.)

Arranged by Mr. C. K. Garratt, the next concert in the town took place at the Institute on Tuesday evening, April 25th. Lieutenant Colonel J.F. Lister presided, and amongst those present were Lady Farrar, Miss Helen Farrar, Mrs. Mitchison, the Misses Allfrey, Miss Dorothy Wickham, Miss Monica Gunnery, the Reverend F. Gunnery, and officers of the Royal Engineers. Lady Farrar apologised for the absence through indisposition of her daughters Muriel, soprano, and Gwendoline, cellist, but had brought Miss Hilda Mynard, a soprano, from Emberton, as an addition to the programme. Mr. O. Critchard and members of the Royal Engineers sang well received songs, Miss Wilford gave two recitations, and Captain Brett's humorous items caused such amusement that they were encored. Also causing much amusement was his humorous duet with Lieutenant Yates, whose fine baritone voice had been heard to great advantage with his songs, which included A Perfect Day, being deservedly encored. Mr. C. K. Garratt presided at the piano, and the singing of the National Anthem brought the evening to a close. Again arranged by Mr. C. K. Garratt, under the auspices of the Newport Pagnell Girls' Club a concert was given at St. Paul's School on Wednesday evening, April 26th. The programme featured Sappers Sharp, Lucas and Jackson in songs and humorous stories, and other contributions were given by Miss Allfrey and Miss Elsie West. Under the supervision of Mrs. Mitchison members of the Girls' Club gave pleasing drills, and a musical sketch entitled 'Our bazaar,' whilst as for Mr. Garratt he performed the piano accompaniments and played the music for the subsequent dance. Arranged by Pioneer Prager, a well attended concert was given at the Workmen's Social Club on Friday evening, May 5th. Mr. J. Roberts presided over a varied and interesting programme which, with Mr. A. Levin playing the accompaniments, and contributing two piano solos, featured songs by Sappers Hanlon and Kirby, Mr. C. Cole and Miss Cole. Pioneer Prager gave a very amusing recitation, the 'Brothers Mac' were loudly encored for a duet, and were inimitable in a new song and dance entitled '1915,' and a member of the Town Band gave a musical selection. Mr. C. K. Garratt played the accompaniments at a concert he had arranged for the Royal Engineers on Monday evening, May 8th. This was held in the Institute, and in the chair Lieutenant Murray, from Fenny Stratford, was supported by Lady Farrar, the Misses Helen, Muriel, Gwendolyn and Marjorie Farrar, Miss Berry, Captain de Mowbray, Captain Stevens, Lieutenant Yates, Lieutenant Phillips and others. Including many of the wives and friends of the Royal Engineers the room was crowded, and, having a fortnight ago been prevented from performing through indisposition, the Misses Muriel and Gwendolyn Farrar gave contributions. Performed in a mezzo soprano voice, the songs by Muriel were loudly re-demanded, and also encored were the cello solos by Gwendolyn. As for their duet, double encores were demanded. For each of her songs Mrs. Percy Lovett, of Bletchley, was also encored, as were the songs by Lieutenant Yates, Mrs. Yates, and no doubt Miss G. Middleton, and towards the close the chairman proposed a vote of thanks to Lady Farrar, her daughters, and to all the performers. This was carried with loud acclamation, and in response her Ladyship briefly replied. Mr. Garratt then proposed a similar compliment to the chairman, and the event concluded with the singing of the National Anthem.

On Friday morning May 12th, due to having lost his directions in low cloud the pilot of an army biplane landed his machine in Bury Field, damaging one of the wheels. During the afternoon hundreds of people from the town and neighbourhood came to look at the machine, and a number of the local Royal Engineers were deployed to mount guard, to keep those who became too inquisitive at a safe distance. Later in the afternoon mechanics arrived to repair the damage, and afterwards the pilot took off to resume his journey. At the parish church, after evensong on Sunday, May 21st a musical programme was given by Mr. C. K. Garratt, who opened with the C minor overture by Hollins. Then without organ accompaniment the choir sang Tennyson's 'Crossing the Bar,' and Lieutenant Yates of the Royal Engineers performed two sacred solos. Watched by large crowds of people who had assembled in the field, after some months of being billeted in the town the Signal Section of the Royal Engineers took up quarters under canvas on Bury Field on Thursday evening, May 25th. The location - to be fenced off, to prevent damage by cattle - was at the far end of the 'broad acred playing field,' where on a level expanse of ground rows of bell tents had been erected. Running in a parallel line with the hedge was the wet canteen and the cookhouse with its field ovens, boilers, etc., whilst the dry canteen and stores were situated so as to command ready access, with three large marquees being near at hand for use as dining tents. The men would be 'told off' into messes, and having taken their seats would have their meals served to them by camp orderlies. As for the officers they had their own

Bury Field was the site of a sad fatality on the evening of Wednesday, August 25th 1915, when an infant was kicked by a horse. As on several occasions the children of Mrs. John Clare, the wife of an antique dealer of the High Street, had been taken to the field by Dora Percival, a 14 year old domestic, with those in her charge being four brothers and sisters. One of these was Herbert who, not yet two and a half years of age, was in his pushchair. While the other children went off to play, on arriving at the field an older sister of the boy, Phyllis, sat down on the grass to do some knitting with Dora. For a while one of the children, Ella, sat with them but a little later Dora saw her waving her hat at two loose horses, making a horse gallop in front of her. When the child ignored her calls Dora left her knitting to run and fetch her back but whilst her attention was diverted Herbert climbed out of his push chair and began to follow. On looking round Dora then saw him lying on the grass and was told by the older brother, Clifford, that he had been kicked by 'a big horse,' which was standing a little distance away. Swiftly picking up the infant, Dora on seeing Mrs. May Glidewell nearby asked if she would take him to the doctor, as she might get there quicker, and in compliance the boy was immediately taken to Dr. C. Bailey. However the infant died at his premises soon after, the cause being from internal injuries due to a blow to the stomach. The following morning the District Coroner, Mr. E.T. Worley, held an inquest at the police station where Police Sergeant Roberts acted as Coroner's Officer with the foreman of the jury being Alfred Simpson.

During the First World War, Bury Field was the site for a summer camp of the Royal Engineers and during the Second World War was requisitioned by the War Agricultural Committee for food cultivation. However somewhat belatedly, since they had previously been given every opportunity to purchase the field, the townspeople began to take a critical interest and protested about bushes being pulled up at the far end of the field (since a great deal of fuel was used by the machinery) and the temporary buildings erected to store the equipment. An assurance was sought that these would be removed after the emergency.

mess, as also the sergeants. Men of the detachment carried out the general cooking for the camp, and with Messrs. Morris and Co., of Ampthill, being the contractors for the wet canteen, Messrs. Fortnum and Mason, of Piccadilly, had charge of the dry canteen. Flour for the camp was supplied by the Army Service Corps, and for baking bread the contract had been awarded to Mr. J. Roston, baker and confectioner of St. John Street. As for the supply of eggs and milk, the contract from Mr. J. E. Whiting, of Willen, had been accepted. The officer in charge of the section was Captain G.B. de Mowbray, of the King's Royal Rifle Corps, and his officers were Second Lieutenants Haynes, Brown, and Goldsmith. The 'staff' comprised Q.M.S. W. Gallagher, Company Sergeant Majors H.F. and T. Smith, Company Q.M.S. C.W. Smith, Sergeants Menzies, Walker, Flannigan, Simpson, and Campbell, and although the camp initially accommodated 380 of all ranks, it was anticipated that this would probably be increased to 500. In the strict routine of the camp reveille was at 5.30 a.m., first parade at 6 a.m., breakfast at 7 a.m. (Sundays 7.30 a.m.), and second parade at 8 a.m. The men would then attend their instruction, and after dinner, taken at 1 p.m., parade again for school at 2 p.m. Tea was at 5 p.m., retreat at 7 p.m., first post 9.30 p.m., last post 10 p.m., and lights out at 10.15 p.m., with the section trumpeter sounding all the calls. Guards would patrol the camp at night, whilst during the day the regimental police would be on duty.

Soon the soldiers became quite reconciled to life under canvas, and on the evening of Sunday, May 28th enjoyed, as did hundreds of people from the town and locality, a sacred concert played in the vicinity of the camp by the Excelsior Silver Band, which had played the soldiers to church that morning. The camp was supplied with the town water, but although the lavatory arrangements complied with the town's bye-laws there was increasing difficulty in getting the privy soil removed since, with 80 buckets a day to be emptied, due to the scarcity of labour local farmers would not undertake the work. In fact the matter would be discussed at the meeting of the U.D.C. on Tuesday evening, June 6th, for in a letter from the Bedford depot of the Royal Engineers the council's assistance had been requested. However, the Surveyor said that arrangements had been made with Mr. J. Holes to do the work, and although the military authorities at Bedford had been notified of this, via the Clerk, no reply had as yet been received. With so many Royal Engineers now in the town romances with local girls were bound to blossom, and by special licence on Tuesday, June 6th the wedding took place of Miss Olive Ellingham, the eldest daughter of Mr. and Mrs. Ellingham, of Park Avenue, Newport Pagnell (late of Woburn Sands) and Sapper Frederick Westlake, the fifth son of Mrs. and the late Mr. W. Westlake of Plymouth, Devon. However, the ceremony was of a quiet nature due to the bridegroom being called away for military service abroad. On Thursday evening, June 15th 1916 about 45 of those Royal Engineers who worshipped at the Nonconformist churches were entertained by the Newport Pagnell Free Church Council. As the venue Mrs. W. Bull had granted the use of the garden at Ouse Bank, and there after a splendid tea, provided by the lady members, games and amusements took place. Regarding his workman who removed the night soil from the Bury Field camp, on Thursday evening, June 22nd 1916 a farming and carting contractor applied for military exemption at the Newport Pagnell Urban Tribunal, saying that not only did the man perform this role, be he also looked after the stock and gave general assistance. After considering the details the members then postponed the case for a month, so that enquiries concerning the scavenging contract could be made. Elsewhere, on the same evening teams of Royal Engineers from the Newport Pagnell and Fenny Stratford Signal Depots opposed each other in a rifle shooting match. This took place on the town's miniature range, and the home team won by 120 points. During the day Captain G. de Mowbray had met the Clerk of the Council, Mr. E. Ward, asking if the town's water supply would be sufficient if another 1,000 men were encamped in the town. The Clerk had told him to put the enquiry in writing, and so on the following day the letter was considered at a special meeting of the U.D.C. where the Surveyor, Mr. C. Branford, said that the proposed site of the camp was near Midsummer Holme in Bury Field. Taking in the cricket pitch it would be near the Mill Street entrance to the field, and, confirming that the men would be accommodated in huts, he said that the soldiers would be Territorials belonging to a pontoon section, and would have a number of horses.

With the question of sewerage arrangements next being raised, it was pointed out that being near Mill Street there would be no difficulty in connecting up to the main sewer. As for the question of water, the Surveyor thought that sufficient could be obtained by using the Council's equipment to extract quantities from the river. Continuing, he said that the Royal Engineers now camped in Bury Field used 1,000 gallons of water a week, whilst regarding sewage disposal Dr. Digby White, the Medical Officer of Health, said another 3,000 gallons a day would be entailed. However, he was of the opinion that this could be dealt with by connecting to the main sewer, although he urged the Council to insist on a water closet system, as the only way to deal with the sewage. Having pondered all the considerations, in conclusion the Council agreed that, despite the addition of some of the soldiers' wives and children, the facilities of the town would be able to cope. Between the showers, the sports at the annual fete for Northampton Hospital took place on Saturday, June 24th, and, with the prizes having been provided by tradesmen in the town, included was a tug of war between two Royal Engineer teams - England and Ireland - and a town team. Ireland won against England, but in the final the town defeated Ireland. Held at the Council Offices, at the meeting of the Tribunal on Wednesday evening, June 28th a baker's assistant was applied for by his employer, who had been awarded the contract to supply bread to the Royal Engineers camp at Bury Field. However, the military representative, Donald Fraser, said he thought that a woman could be taught the business if a month's exemption was allowed, but to this the employer replied that it was impossible to put a woman in a man's place. They were working 18 hours a day, and besides his regular customers he had to supply the camp with from 180 to 200 loaves a day. Three months exemption was allowed. On the town's miniature range, teams of Royal Engineers from the Newport Pagnell and Fenny Stratford Signal Depots opposed each other in a rifle shooting match on Thursday evening, June 22nd. The home team won by 120 points, and they also gained a victory over a team from the civilians in the town on Wednesday evening, June 28th, with the civilians scoring 1,338 and the Royal Engineers 1,558. Another shooting match then took place on the range of the Rifle Club on Thursday evening, July 6th. This was between the officers of the Royal Engineers (Signal Section) stationed in the town and a town team, which included Superintendent Pearce, Mr. H. Middleton, Mr. J. Butler, Mr. F. Wilford and Mr. G. Tayler. Due to heavy rain and bad light it only proved possible to fire at 500 yards, and so the match was continued in improved weather on Thursday evening, July 20th, with the soldiers winning by 66.

Despite having caused disruption to the shooting match, the recent bad weather had also compounded the state of the ground at the entrance near to the Royal Engineers camp at Bury Field, and this was a condition that in early July 1916 the Surveyor was instructed to remedy. Yet there was more bad weather to come, and indeed it proved unfavourable for the annual garden party of the Congregational Church which, organised for the benefit of the London Missionary Society, was held in the grounds of The Lodge on Thursday, July 13th. Nevertheless, a fruit and flower stall was set up under the charge of Mrs. A. J. Roberts, assisted by other ladies, and Mrs. Lee and others had charge of the tea and refreshment tent. Bowls, croquet, golf and other sports were all enjoyed, as also the pretty flower garden, and in the evening under Miss James the girls of the Council School performed costume dances. In other events Miss Eva Garratt organised a baby show, and an egg and spoon race took place. Sappers Frost and Hall were amongst those who performed in a concert, and also involving the Royal Engineers was a tug of war, which resulted in their defeat by the A.S.C. However in a second tug of war the soldiers, after a struggle, beat a team of civilians, and received a plate of strawberries as their reward. Superintendent Pearce was the coach for the soldiers, whilst Admiral's Mate Gregory, of H.M.S. John Moore, acted for the civilian team. One of the largest patriotic meetings since the beginning of the war took place on Market Hill, on Friday, August 4th, with some 2,000 people attending. This was to affirm their determination to crush Germany, and all classes of society were present. Many soldiers were in attendance and their inspiring presence in the town was especially mentioned in the address by Mr. O. H. Bull, who presided. The following afternoon a cricket match was played on Bury Field between the Newport Pagnell Town Club and the Royal Engineers from the Fenny Stratford Depot. Then near the Bury Field camp on the following evening the Excelsior Silver Band, conducted by Mr. A. Green, gave an open air concert to a large attendance. In August 1916, at a special police court the wife of a lance corporal of the Royal Engineers, encamped at the town, was charged with having falsely represented that she had 11s credit in the Post Office Savings Bank, and the story is told in the chapter 'Crimes and Punishment.' For the entertainment of the Royal Engineers, the first concert of the season, prepared and accompanied throughout by Mr. C. K. Garratt, took place at the Institute on Tuesday evening, September 26th. Accompanied by his wife, Major Hamilton Barrie presided, and with Lieutenant Haines and several officers also present the attractive programme comprised, having come over especially from Wolverton, Mrs. E. Oliver, who performed operatic and revue songs, Miss D. Eady, a soprano, and Miss Dorothy Coker, who performed solo dances. Miss Mabel Wilford gave two recitations, Mr. Oliver Critchard, tenor, contributed songs, and as a baritone Sapper J. O'Connor was loudly encored for each of his songs, especially the Toreador's song from Carmen. Sapper Trevitt's contribution was humorous sketches at the piano, and at the close Mr. Garratt proposed a vote of thanks to the Major, with the evening then concluding with the singing of the National Anthem.

On the morning of Saturday, September 23rd 1916 it was made known that at the end of the camping season the Royal Engineers Signal Section would move to another centre for training. This caused some consternation in the town, for in terms of trading and behaviour their presence had been greatly appreciated. So much so that in consequence on Wednesday, September 27th the U.D.C. was petitioned by 42 influential tradesmen to persuade the military to reverse their decision. Thus with Mr. O. Bull as chairman a special Council meeting was held the same evening, with Superintendent Pearce, the chief billeting officer for the town, amongst those present. Having read the petition, the chairman said that not only had he secured an interview as to the requirements of the military authorities, but he had also approached Mr. Walter Carlile about using his influence, and in fact General Boyes and a staff officer had met Mr. Carlile and himself that afternoon. As a remedy to overcome the difficulty of messing accommodation Salmons had offered the use of a portion of their large motor garage, where, as long as room could be found for the firm's cars elsewhere, the soldiers could be fed in two relays. Both the Mission Hall and the Town Hall would continue in use as schools for the Royal Engineers, whilst as for the accommodation of the 800 to 1,000 men, which had been the figure given to Superintendent Pearce, if they could not all be billeted in the occupied houses then the remainder could sleep in the empty houses, as also the large buildings that were available. The military would find beds for the empty rooms, and in view of this at the U.D.C. meeting the following resolution was proposed and seconded; 'Provided Mr. Pearce can find the accommodation required by the military this Council would be very pleased to retain the soldiers in Newport Pagnell, and congratulate officers and men on their excellent behaviour during the time they have been in the town.' Under orders from Superintendent Pearce the town was subsequently canvassed by special constables, and at the conclusion it was pleasingly found that the number of billets available, including arrangements to occupy certain empty houses, exceeded all expectations. The figures were then placed with the military, who had also been supplied with the dimensions of those buildings that were available either as billets or schools, and in early October 1916 arrangements were made whereby the Royal Engineers Signal Section would remain in the town for the winter months. For the instructional requirements the vicar and the churchwardens had offered the military the use of the church schools in Silver Street, Priory Street, and River Side, and the committees of the Unionist and Working Men's Clubs had also offered to place their large concert halls at their disposal. Despite being billeted out the men would all take their meals together, since Salmons, as per their recent offer, had donated the major portion of their building known locally as Olympia which, measuring 110 feet by 50 feet, would be the mess room where from 800 to 900 men would be able to take their meals at one sitting. On the evening of Wednesday, October 4th a company of Royal Engineers appeared as pierrots behind the footlights at the Electric Theatre, and with the assistance of talented local lady vocalists gave to a packed audience a concert for the benefit of regimental charities. The troupe performed under the name of 'The Quaints,' and the items covered all tastes. Mr. C. K. Garratt, Company Sergeant Major F. Smith (the honorary treasurer), Corporal Permain, and Sapper J. O'Connor had made the arrangements, and Corporal W. Peet and Sapper W. Elms were the joint honorary secretaries.

The occasion was given under the patronage of Lieutenant Colonel J.F.

Lister, and with many of the Royal Engineers present the programme sellers were the Misses Austin, W. Cotton, I. Powell, N. Fleet, West, and Ellingham. In typical pierrot dress the troupe consisted of Miss Marjorie Choules, L.R.A.M., violin, Miss Kathleen Fleet, soprano, Miss Grace Middleton, contralto, Corporal J. Cahill and Lance Corporal R. Hector, tenors, Sapper T. Steven, baritone, Sapper J. O'Connor, bass, Sapper W. Elmes, humorist, and Sapper A. Hyde, pianist, and with the programme having been opened with the chorus 'Cheereo,' Miss Kathleen Fleet was heard to excellent advantage in the Japanese song 'Butterfly Land.' In other numbers she sang 'If you were the only girl' as a duet with Sapper R. Hector, who with Miss Grace Middleton sang 'They wouldn't believe me.' Being deservedly encored, in her first visit to the town Miss Choules played brilliantly and indeed all the performances were much appreciated. The concert ended with the Good Night chorus by the whole troupe, who on Thursday evening then visited the Workhouse and repeated the programme. The Institute was crowded on Wednesday evening, October 11th 1916 for an excellent concert arranged for the Royal Engineers by Mr. C. K. Garratt. Lieutenant Dean was in the chair, accompanied by Mrs. Dean, and having kindly motored over from Tyringham, Miss Wood was encored for each of her songs, her rendering of Tosti's 'Good-bye' being particularly fine. Many performances were given by the Royal Engineers, Miss Mabel Wilford gave a charming recitation, and Miss Winnie Cotton played a piano duet with Mr. Garratt, by whom with Sapper Amos the accompaniments were furnished. After playing the Royal Engineers to church, the Excelsior Silver Band, under Mr. A. Green, gave a first class concert near the Town Hall on Sunday morning, October 15th. Then on October 18th a concert for the Royal Engineers was given in the Electric Theatre, with most of the items performed by the soldiers assisted by three Newport Pagnell ladies; Miss Dorothy Pettit and Miss Kathleen Fleet, sopranos, and Miss Grace Middleton, contralto. Major J. Hamilton Barrie presided, and amongst those present were Mrs. Barrie, Lieutenant Haines, and officers of the Newport Pagnell Royal Engineers Signal Depot. The arrangements had been made by Corporal Peet and Corporal Permain, and a number of the N.C.O.s acted as stewards. As for the piano accompaniments, these were shared between Corporal Banks and Sappers Huggins and Trevitt. The event had been eagerly anticipated, as also was Saturday, October 21st 1916 when the soldiers moved into their billets in the town, having been encamped on Bury Field for several months. In fact the reason they were staying in the town, and not being transferred to Leighton Buzzard, was due to the finding of 400 extra billets by the special constables acting under the orders of Superintendent Pearce, to whom glowing tributes were paid at the Newport Pagnell Petty Sessions on Wednesday, November 1st.

Soldiers can be seen in this photo of the High Street. In fact perhaps the sender of the card was a soldier for, saying, 'I am T. Mills 81820 same address,' he writes to his wife, Gert, at 52, Trinity Road, Halstead Essex, 'Just a card to let you know what Newport Pagnell is like: not a bad little place.'

Thus there were many Royal Engineers present at two concerts which were given at a sale of work on Saturday afternoon, November 4th. Held in the Council Schools these were for the funds of the village churches associated with the Congregational Church, and in the afternoon and evening the central hall of the girls' school was busy with stalls of useful and fancy articles, of which many had been made by the church ladies. Under the direction of Miss Amy Harris and Miss Eva Garratt a party of children gave entertainments, and the event raised £132. At the Electric Theatre, another concert was held on Sunday evening, November 12th 1916, this being for the Christmas Presents Fund. Among the artistes were Sapper V. Earl, tenor, Pioneer W. Huggins, baritone, and Sapper C. Watson, bass, and the role of stewards was taken by Corporal Peet and other members of the Royal Engineers. With the refreshments supplied by Messrs. C. Lawman and Son, at the Unionist Club the N.C.O.s of the Royal Engineers arranged a whist drive and dance on Thursday evening, November 23rd 1916. Twenty games were played, and Major Hamilton Barrie presented the prizes. A short programme of dances then followed, with Sapper Huggins at the piano, and the master of ceremonies was Corporal Peet, who was mainly responsible for a concert organised by the Royal Engineers in the town on Monday evening, December 4th 1916. This took place in the Electric Theatre, and for the event he had secured the services of Madame Humphrey Lees, a soprano vocalist. With this being her first visit to North Bucks her songs stirred the patriotism of the audience and merited much applause, as also did those of Miss Bertha Richens. Possessing a fine bass voice, the Reverend Father Walker also contributed to the programme, whilst of the Royal Engineers Sapper Aspinwall was greatly appreciated as a humorist, as also, paying a return visit, Frank Hudson with his living marionettes. Mr. C. K. Garratt accompanied throughout on the piano, and at the close Madame Humphrey Lees sang a new version of the National Anthem, which called for God's blessing on the boys at the Front. The event concluded with the artistes being personally thanked by Major Hamilton Barrie, by whom plants had been lent for the decoration of the stage. The event raised £5 for the Royal Engineers Prisoners of War Fund and the Royal Engineers Comforts Fund (Chatham.) However, out of his comfort zone had been Sapper Alfred Vines, for explaining why he had been cycling without a properly screened front glass of an acetylene lamp he said "I am not accustomed to the lighting orders, they are so different everywhere." Nevertheless he was fined 5s. As for Sapper Thomas Orchard, who was fined 10s for riding a bicycle without a red rear light, his explanation was that when he went to fetch his bicycle from the Neptune Inn yard he found that the lamp had gone. Another Sapper in contravention of the cycling laws was James Morrison, who was summoned for riding a bicycle on the footpath at Newport Pagnell on December 10th. His excuse was that the road was bad, but when the police constable contradicted this he said "Well, I did it for devilment." Saying that he came from the camp at Biggleswade, he had second thoughts when asked to produce his pass, and admitted that he was billeted in Newport Pagnell. A fine of 10s was imposed.

Sapper G. Bennett, also of the Royal Engineers Signal Depot in the town, was another to face a summons, for not having properly obscured the acetylene lamp on his bicycle on December 13th. He pleaded not guilty, and said that his eyesight was bad through having been severely injured in action. He thought that the lamp was the responsibility of the person from whom he had hired the cycle, but a fine of 2s 6d was imposed. Major Hamilton Barrie being in the chair, a smoking concert was held in the Unionist Club on the evening of Monday, December 18th. This had been organised by Sergeant Flannagan and other N.C.O.s of the Royal Engineers Signal Depot, several members of which gave assistance to the Congregational Church Choir when, at different parts of the town, they sang carols on the evenings of Friday 22nd and Saturday 23rd. This was under the leadership of Mrs. Thomas, the church organist, and their efforts raised £4 10s 6d for the Red Cross Society. In the town and local villages, also singing carols was a party organised by Mr. C. K. Garratt, the members of which - to include Mrs. C. K. Garratt, Mrs. V. Earl, the Misses Allfrey, Miss K. Fleet, Messrs. Oliver

Critchard and H. Colson, and Sappers Earl, Huggins, and Steer, Cecil Line and Lance Corporal Jerry O'Connor - gave up much of their Christmas holiday to provide financial help for St. Dunstan's Home. The annual Christmas treat to the infants attending the parish church Sunday School took place on Wednesday, December 27th 1916, but due to St. Paul's School being occupied by the military it was held in the Council Schools. Miss F. Taylor, superintendent, and her teaching staff made the day a pleasure and each child received a present from the Christmas tree, and also an orange and a mince pie. An invitation whist drive and dance took place at the Unionist Club on Tuesday, January 2nd 1917, held by the warrant officers and N.C.O.s of the Royal Engineers. Sergeant Flannagan, Sergeant Burrows, Sergeant Jayne, Corporal O' Donohoe and Corporal Permain had been responsible for the arrangements, and with other officers present Major Hamilton Barrie presided. For the whist drive, for which valuable prizes were offered, Sergeant Jayne was the master of ceremonies, whilst for the dances, which were preceded by songs from the soldiers, Sergeant Burrows performed the duty.

Then on the following evening the Unionist Club hosted another event, when the wives and children of the Royal Engineers spent a happy time in the concert hall, which had been transformed into a miniature fairy palace. This had been the idea of Sapper Williamson, and from a magic cave Father Christmas (an appropriately dressed Corporal Aspinwall) brought forth with his magic wand gifts to include dolls that closed their eyes (and had names such as Philip and Archibald) which the children stepped forward to receive. Delighting the children with his antics, Lance Corporal O'Connor appeared as Joey the Clown, and subsequently a large Christmas tree, given by Major Hamilton Barrie for the special benefit of the soldiers' children, was lit up, and from which Major Barrie, assisted by Mrs. Digby White, Sergeant Peet and other members of the Royal Engineers, distributed a variety of gifts until each child had an armful of presents. Major Barrie then called for cheers for Father Christmas, and with these having been enthusiastically given the children on leaving for home each received an orange. The following evening the officers of the Court 'Unity' Ancient Order of Foresters held their annual supper at the Workmen's Social Club. A splendid repast was served by Mr. and Mrs. A. Andrews, the steward and stewardess of the club, and as secretary of the Court Mr. J. Short was chairman. After the toasts the Royal Engineers joined the gathering, and Sapper Rogers opened the evening by singing 'The Trumpeter' and 'Glorious Devon.' Sapper Williamson, a gold medallist for elocution, told amusing stories, and a toast was proposed to Mr. J. Roberts, the treasurer, and to Mr. Short. In fact having served on public bodies in the town for many years, Mr. Short had now been nominated to represent the town on Buckinghamshire County Council, and in his reply he said that he had been the secretary for some 12 years, and that with there now being 820 voluntary contributors those members in the Forces, some 200, were having their subs paid by a 3d levy per quarter on the members at home. Songs and piano selections then took place, and the evening concluded at about 11 p.m. with the singing of Auld Lang Syne and the National Anthem. During the month it was announced that temporary Lieutenant Herbert Coales, Royal Engineers, the grandson of the late Francis Coales and Mrs. Coales, of Beechwood, Newport Pagnell, had been awarded the Military Cross, whilst of those seeking exemption from military service, at the Newport Pagnell Urban Area Tribunal, held on Wednesday evening, January 17th 1917, the U.D.C. asked for further exemption for their water works engineer and fitter. He was aged 38 and married, and the Surveyor said that if he went the town would go short of water. Since the man was practically under military service, through supplying the Royal Engineers' depot with water, six months was granted.

After a few hours illness, Sapper T. Keen, of the Royal Engineers Signal Depot, Newport Pagnell, died on Thursday morning, January 25th. Single, his home was at Weybridge, and in civilian life he had been a post office employee. It had been on December 29th 1916 that he first came to Newport Pagnell, and being present at the whole of the parades on Wednesday, January 25th he seemed t to be in good health. In fact that evening he went to the Unionist Club, but shortly after returning to his billet he was taken ill. Subsequently his condition became of such concern that an attendance had to be made by Dr. Digby White, by whose advice the man was taken by motor ambulance to the Military Hospital at the Council Schools, Aylesbury. However, his condition became critical and he later died. On a central site in the High Street a Y.M.C.A. hut, of modest lines and an external plainness of structure, had now been erected. For those who were billeted in the town this was for the recreation of the soldiers, and at the opening ceremony on the night of Saturday, January 20th 1917 their commanding officer, Major Hamilton Barrie, who was present with his wife, said in his address that he had personally seen the good work that the Y.M.C.A. was doing in France. A concert then followed, with the fine programme having been provided by Captain Williamson, R.A.M.C., Mrs. Lecky, and Mr. Hedges. The premises, where the men could play games, read, and write letters, was under the charge of Mr. C.O. Robson who, having been sent by the Y.M.C.A., had the assistance of a Boy Scout from St. Leonards. As for those giving voluntary assistance at the canteen, which would be run on temperance principles, they included the Misses Allfrey, Miss Bailey, Mrs. W.R. Chantler, Miss A. M.Coales, Miss Farrar, Miss Carr, Mrs. Littleboy, Miss Odell, Miss Trevor,

Mrs. C. Wilford, Miss Williams and Miss Wickham. Thus at this additional centre for entertainment on the evening of Saturday, January 27th 1917 many of the Royal Engineers were present for a concert arranged by Mr. C. K. Garratt. Among the performers were Sapper Jordan, Lance Corporal Aspinwall, Sapper Cahill, Sapper Victor Earl and also Sapper J. Kellet, who performed the following evening at a concert held at the Electric Theatre which, with men of the Royal Engineers acting as stewards, was for the benefit of the National Egg Collection. Of the acts Lance Corporal Jerry O'Connor was indisposed, but despite having met with an accident earlier that day Sapper Victor Earl still performed, albeit with two stitches above his right eye. The annual meeting of the Unionist Working Men's Club was held on Friday evening, March 2nd 1917, with Mr. W. Carlile presiding. Including 2,500 temporary members of the Royal Engineers the membership was now 3,167, and, with £100 having been spent on the building and fittings, the concert hall was under the direct control of the military authorities. As for the Workmen's Social Club, of which some 200 members were now in the Forces, there was a large gathering on the evening of Saturday, March 17th, when, including Corporal G. Keay, talented members of the Royal Engineers gave a concert. In fact this proved a favourable opportunity to recognise the services rendered by the secretary, and one of the founders of the club, John Roberts, who was presented with a cheque by Mr. J. Harris, the chairman. In his reply Mr. Roberts said that the club had been started in 1895 in the premises now occupied as an N.C.O. mess, and that later they had secured larger premises. The concert was greatly enjoyed, and for the welcome and hospitality afforded to the soldiers the club was thanked by Corporal A. Harris, on behalf of the Royal Engineers.

Having given up the use of their largest building, as a mess room for the Royal Engineers, Salmons were now storing the motor chassis as they arrived from the works in the principal malting of the Newport Pagnell Brewery Company. This was situated in the High Street, and for the purpose the premises had been suitably adapted. Held in the town on Wednesday, March 21st 1917, a large agricultural and general auction jumble sale took place. The role of sale porters was performed by members of the Royal Engineers, two members of which would be the soloists the following afternoon at a special open meeting of the Newport Pagnell P.S.A. Brotherhood. They were Sapper Steer and Sapper Norman Raff, of the Australian contingent. Sixteen members of the Royal Engineers formed a guard of honour at the parish church when, on Tuesday afternoon, March 27th 1917, Miss Dorothea Elaine Wickham, the only child of Dr. H. Wickham and Mrs. Wickham. of The Close, married Lieutenant Temple George Hillyard, the only son of the Reverend A. Hillyard and Mrs. Hillyard of The Parsonage, Upton

Royal Engineers on parade outside the premises of the Newport Pagnell Brewery.

The scene today.

Pyne, Exeter. As the bridal party left the church the guard, on the orders of Corporal Keay, formed up in two lines under the direction of Lieutenants Roberts and Robey, and being equipped with the long poles used in carrying telephone wires brought these smartly to the slope. By now quite a few of the Royal Engineers in the town were from overseas, and a dance had been recently held in the Council Schools under the auspices of the Overseas Committee. Then on the evening of Monday, April 2nd 1917 a function was held at the Plough, when a company of 40 Royal Engineers and their guests sat down to a dinner. After the toast to the King the chairman, Sapper Sydney

Mason, from Wairoa, New Zealand, gave a few well chosen remarks, and the toast of 'The Overseas Troops' was proposed by Quartermaster Sergeant Gait, who said that having been associated with overseas men, in Egypt and elsewhere, he found them to be "most excellent fellows and thorough good sports." Sapper Raff, from Australia, responded, and the 'Army and Navy' was proposed by Sapper Gregory from the Transvaal, who 'eulogised' their performance. The response was given by Sergeant Flannagan, after which Corporal O'Donoghue proposed 'Success to the British armies all the world over.' The chairman then made the response in 'Bonza' fashion, and a musical evening followed in a both humorous and sentimental style. Indeed, the rousing war cry of the South Africans was rendered with full gusto, with Sapper Siebert (South Africa) taking the part of chief 'Induna' The singing of the National Anthem and Auld Lang Syne finally brought the evening to a close. Sensational charges regarding the alleged theft of Army food were partly heard at the Newport Pagnell Police Court on the afternoon of Friday, March 30th. In fact the premises had the appearance 'of a small provision merchant's shop,' since before the magistrates was displayed a huge quantity of foodstuffs, alleged to have been surreptitiously removed from the Royal Engineers messing quarters at Newport Pagnell. The full story is told in the chapter 'Crimes and Punishment.'

With the need for local billets the landlord of the lodging house in the town had now taken in soldiers, which was no doubt quite lucrative. However, the matter of accommodating tramps who had been the usual occupants was becoming a consequent concern, especially since private houses would not take them, and so a committee would be formed regarding the problem. On Tuesday evening, May 1st, at the monthly meeting of the U.D.C. there was concern at the amount of water being wasted in the town. It was therefore resolved that a thorough investigation should be made by the Surveyor, with meters to be installed at the two clubs and at the military camps. Also of concern were the rumours now circulating in the town about alleged waste at the military cookhouse, and in response a swift denial was made by Major Hamilton Barrie who, inviting an inspection of the kitchens and of the dinners served to the men, said "I might add that not only is there no waste but that the amount of dripping recovered per 1000 rations is very much higher than the average in the whole of the Eastern Command. ... Even from the water in which the dishes are washed is collected all the fat, and this is rendered down into dripping for munitions." Also during May, Edgar Moore, of the Royal Engineers, pleaded guilty following a summons for riding a bicycle without a light in the town on April 24th, and for showing no rear light. Police constable Nicholls said that the accused had ridden away when called upon to stop, but had fallen off in Caldecote

Street. When spoken to he then said "I expect it will only be a five bob touch. Never mind, I'm a policeman here as well as you are." Stating that he had been to the Front twice, been wounded once, and suffered from malaria, the defendant said that on the night in question he thought he was going to have a recurrence of the fever. Therefore he had a couple of drops of rum, and not having heard the policeman calling him to stop he turned into Caldecote Street. However, in trying to avoid two women he collided with the pavement and fell off. In view of his 14 years of good conduct in the Army the Bench imposed a lenient fine of 2s, with the chairman saying that they didn't like dealing harshly with a wounded soldier. Also during the month, at a special police court on Saturday, May 19th a 48 year old married woman of The Butts, Coventry, was charged with having stolen on August 7th 1916 two blankets, two sheets, one mackintosh and £10 in money, this being from her husband of Union Street. The case involved a Royal Engineer who had been billeted for a time with her, and the story is told in the chapter 'Crimes and Punishment.' Also on the wrong side of the law was Garvin Fernio, a South African soldier attached to the Royal Engineers Signal Section at the town, who was summoned for having ridden a bicycle without lights on the Wolverton Road at 10.40 p.m. on June 19th 1917. When stopped he said he had a puncture on the return journey, otherwise he would have been back before lighting up time. A fine of 11s was imposed.

With their relatives and friends, officers, N.C.O.s and men of the Royal Engineers crowded the Electric Theatre on the evening of Friday, June 22nd for a visit by the Francis L. Isaacs Camp Concert Company. This comprised a number of first class London artistes, and practically every item was encored, and on more than one occasion twice or three times recalled. The artistes included Miss Dora Labbette, a soprano of Queen's Hall and principal London concerts, Miss Dorrie Courtney, an accomplished banjoist, Miss Evelyn Cooke, violin solos, Mademoiselle Aimee Floretta, a dancer, Miss Annie Trilnick, elocutionist, Miss Lilian Hoare, Percy Khan, a brilliant pianist in rag time numbers, and Harry Russon, a comedian. At the conclusion, on the initiative of Major Hamilton Barrie a hearty vote of thanks was accorded to Mr. Isaacs and his talented friends, and the theatre rang with the cheers of a delighted audience. Raising £21, and given by permission of Mrs. W. Rogers Bull, under the auspices of the Congregational Church a garden fete and sale of work, enhanced by fine summer weather, took place in the grounds of Ouse Bank on Thursday, July 12th. The proceeds were for the London Missionary Society, with the secretarial duties being undertaken by Miss Gertie Cowley, assisted by Miss A. M.Coales and others. Of the many stalls arranged about the lawn that selling flowers was under the charge of Miss Bertha Garratt and Miss Eva Garratt, amongst others, whilst Miss M.

Ellingham presided at houp la. Teas and refreshments were available, and amongst the evening attractions was, directed by Miss Amy Harris and Miss Eva Garratt, a missionary dialogue by the Sunday School children, dressed in native costume. Trained by Miss James, the headmistress of the Council Schools, and her assistants, a party of school children gave Old English and character songs, dances and a tableau, whilst arranged by Mrs. Thomas, the organist of the church, an open air concert took place assisted by members of the Royal Engineers. As a championship holder, and being in civilian life a gymnastic instructor at the General Post Office, London, Corporal Keay gave a sword swinging display, and in a water tournament soldiers and civilians took part, with the event causing much amusement. As for a tug of war across the river, this resulted in a dunking for the Royal Engineers, their team having been captained by Corporal Keay, and that of the civilians by Mr. W. Cowley, who impersonated a policeman. In beautiful summer weather, the annual fete to raise funds for Northampton Hospital took place in Bury Field on Saturday, July 21st. Of those participating, in a tug of war the Royal Engineers were hopelessly outclassed by a team lead by Tom Bavington, who had been a successful coach in past years, although they redeemed themselves by giving three concerts, under the direction of Lieutenant A. Speight. At the July meeting of the U.D.C., held on the evening of Tuesday the 17th, a letter from the Reverend Gunnery regarding St. Paul's School was read, in which he said that he had immediately protested to the military authorities on becoming aware that the closets were being used by the soldiers.

Having been acknowledged by both Major Barrie and Lieutenant Haines the school had been taken on the clear understanding that there was no lavatory accommodation, and that the closets should not be used. Further he stated that the attitude of the Surveyor had been unsatisfactory, but an enclosure from Lieutenant Haines reported that the latrines had now been cleared out and fastened securely. There was a crowded attendance at the Y.M.C.A. Hut on Wednesday evening, August 8th when, with the management having allowed the Royal Engineers to bring their wives and lady friends, the 'Doh-Nuts' Concert Party gave a performance. They had travelled especially from Bedford, and were afforded a hearty vote of thanks by Major Hamilton Barrie. Postponed from August Bank Holiday, due to the Bathing Place being in flood, a grand water carnival, organised by the Newport Pagnell Hospital Week Committee, took place on Thursday afternoon, August 23rd. Assistance was given by members of the Royal Engineers, who on Tuesday evening, September 11th gave a charity concert at the Electric Theatre. This was under the patronage of Major Hamilton Barrie, and the programme opened with 'Danse des Bouffons,' a piano duet played by Lance Corporal G. Uttridge and Mr. C. K. Garratt, the latter of whom shared the duty of accompanist with Pioneer H. Williams. Being heartily welcomed, Miss Bertha Richens sang firstly the war ballad 'A carol of bells,'which was encored, whilst at the conclusion of her song 'The garden of your heart' the applause was deafening, and much cheering followed as Major Barrie stepped forward to hand her a bouquet of roses. She then returned to sing 'The Stars,' and of the other performers delightful renditions were made by Mrs. Oliver's Concert Party from Wolverton. Superb in song and dance, the participants were all children, who later concluded their performances with 'Toy Town,' in which they had the assistance of Mrs. Oliver. Each of the 'little ladies' was then presented with a box of chocolates. In other items the Reverend Father Walker sang in fine voice, and Corporal G. Uttridge employed his talents as an accomplished elocutionist, having formerly held a leading position in the famous Oscar Asche Company. Corporal G. Keay received an ovation for his demonstration of Indian club and swords swinging and the humorous part of the programme was well sustained by Lance Corporal R. Aspinwall, who also gave humorous duets with Lance Corporal Uttridge. Members of the Royal Engineers also contributed to a concert held at the Electric Theatre on Sunday, September 30th 1917, organised by Mr. C. K. Garratt. Raising about £11 this was in aid of the Good Samaritan Society, with the chief attraction being a visit by Miss Doris Carter, the Australian soprano. She received quite an ovation in the second part with three encores, and as popular as ever were Miss Bertha Richens and Oliver Critchard.

Early October saw the conclusion of a series of billiard matches played between the Royal Engineers and the Unionist Club. The soldiers won two of the trio of games, but on aggregate the Unionist Club won by 16 points. It was now announced that after a stay of two years in the town the Signal Section of the Royal Engineers was to leave for new quarters at Bedford, and, as a mark of the town's appreciation for their past presence, Mr. C. K. Garratt organised a farewell concert at the Electric Theatre. With Mr. J. Short, chairman of the U.D.C., presiding, this took place on the evening of Monday, October 15th 1917 and present were members and officials of the Council, leading residents and business people, the nurses and patients from Tickford V.A.D. Hospital, and the soldiers home on leave. Supporting Councillor Short were Major and Mrs. Hamilton Barrie, officers of the Detachment, the Reverend F. Gunnery and his wife, and the Reverend R. S. and Mrs. Mitchison, and of the performances particularly enjoyed were the brilliant violin solos by Miss Sybil Keymer, who had just returned from a world tour. With Miss Bertha Richens as popular as ever, other contributions were made by some of the residents and also the Royal Engineers, in praise of whom Mr. Short made a speech during a break. Light refreshments for the artistes had been arranged by Miss James, and at the end Miss Phyllis Simpson presented Mrs. Barrie with a beautiful bouquet. As for Major Hamilton Barrie, saying that he came to the town two years ago he expressed his appreciation of the townspeople, the clubrooms in the Masonic Hall, in which their chaplain, the Reverend Gunnery and his wife had taken a deep interest, the club for the soldiers' wives, in which Mrs. Gunnery and Mrs. Mitchison had taken a great interest, the Y.M.C.A. Hut, which had been due to the enterprise of the residents, the local clubs, which had admitted them, and Dr. Digby White and certain ladies, for the unofficial hospital all through last winter. Also to the proprietors of the Electric Theatre, to Mr. Garratt, and to Salmons for providing the messing accommodation. On the proposition of the chairman a vote of thanks was then passed to Mr. Garratt and to Mr. Short, for being in the chair, and the evening closed with the singing of the National Anthem and Auld Lang Syne. Subsequently many residents of the town turned out early on Sunday morning, October 21st 1917 to witness the departure of the soldiers. The men, some 340 in number, paraded on their camping ground in Tickford Abbey at about 9 a.m., and half an hour later in fine weather marched out under the command of Major J. Hamilton Barrie for their new quarters at Bedford, with the Excelsior Silver Band playing them down to the Sherington crossroads.

Details of the Wireless Section, Royal Engineers, had arrived in the town the previous week, and, as with an additional 500 men who arrived on Thursday, October 25th and Friday, October 26th, were being billeted in private houses. At the Y.M.C.A. Hut on Saturday, November 3rd, at a concert arranged by Mr. C. K. Garratt many Royal Engineers were in attendance, and some contributed songs to the performance. Company Sergeant Major Harrod occupied the chair, and in response to a vote of thanks from Mr. Garratt he expressed appreciation for the persons who had provided the entertainment, and for the hearty welcome that had been given to the Wireless Section by the residents. The presence of the soldiers may have been heartily welcomed, but on Wednesday, November 21st there was hardly a hearty welcome for one of those who had been formerly encamped with the Signal Section at the town, when he appeared at a special police court charged with stealing a gent's bicycle and bell. Valued at £3 10s this was the property of Fred Chapman, a boot maker, of 28, Caldecote Street, and the story is told in the chapter 'Crimes and Punishment.' At the Y.M.C.A. Hut another concert was held on Wednesday evening, November 21st 1917, with Lieutenant Sturgess in the chair. Performed to a packed attendance the programme included the song 'Shipmates o' mine' by Sapper Dadwell, a humorous song, encored, by Sapper Adams, and the song 'So you want to be a soldier, little man,' by Sapper Inglis. The following evening there was also a large attendance at the Unionist Club for a billiards match between a team of Royal Engineers and the Club, which won by 169 points. For the fund to send Christmas gifts to those men from the town in the Forces, the last of a series of three whist drives and dances took place in the Council Schools on Friday evening, November 30th. This had been organised by Miss James, and during the event a clever acrobatic display was given by Sapper Collett, and in a flag competition Sapper Adams was the winner. There was a packed attendance at the Electric Theatre on the evening of Sunday, November 25th for a sacred concert. This had been arranged by Mr. A. Bullard and the P.S.A. Committee, and as chairman in his address Captain J.B. Mowatt, the commanding officer of the Wireless Section of the Royal Engineers, said that he had spent two Christmases at the Front, where the Christmas puddings sometimes didn't arrive until April, and when they did they were often smashed up, with the sweets stuck together in a gluey mess. Assisted by local musicians, during the concert the orchestra of the Royal Engineers Wireless Section played three selections, Sapper Fuller performed brilliant violin solos, and by a silver collection at the door £9 was raised, to be added to the some £180 of the Christmas presents fund.

On the Autos Ground, on Saturday, December 8th Newport Pagnell Rovers played the Royal Engineers, whose team had now changed due to men having to leave the town. Both teams were unbeaten and would remain so, for with the local team winning the toss the result was a draw. For augmenting the funds of St. Dunstan's Hostel, a carol concert was held at the Electric Theatre on Monday evening, December 17th, raising about £15. With Mr. C. K. Garratt as musical director and accompanist, the performance was given by the Newport Pagnell Parish Church Girls' Club, and they were superintended by Mrs. Mitchison assisted by Miss Bale, Miss M. Coales, Miss P. Taylor and Miss E. West. A chorus of 70 girls sang the carols, being assisted in the tenor and bass parts by members of the Royal Engineers, and in both parts of the concert the beautiful singing of Miss Bertha Richens was deservedly encored, as was that of Miss Mabel Wilford, who stepped in for Lance Corporal Utt Ridge, since he was now in Bedford on military duties. Also encored were the violin solos of Sapper Fuller, and other contributions were made by Mr. C. Line and also Oliver Critchard, for one of whose songs the music had been specially composed at short notice by Mr. Garratt. For the chorus Mr. W,J. Cole, builder and contractor, had gratuitously erected the tiered platform on the stage, with the materials having been kindly loaned by Mr. F. W. Taylor. On Christmas Day, after dinner the festivities at the Y.M.C.A. Hut took the form of competitions, with 'Impromptu Speech' being won by Pioneer Beecroft, 'Hat Trimming Competition' by Pioneer Hedderley, 'Blindfold Sketch on Blackboard' by

Pioneer Timmings, 'Best Representation of a Lady' by Pioneer Grey, and 'Paper Hats' by Pioneer Jones. Then after the competitions came a lengthy programme of songs etc., provided, with Lieutenant Marris in the chair, by the Royal Engineers and local artistes. Organised by Captain Mowatt, and on behalf of the local Royal Engineers Benevolent Fund, on the afternoon and evening of Wednesday, January 2nd 1918 Captain R.E. Priestly, Adjutant of the Royal Engineers at Bletchley, gave a lecture at the Electric Theatre entitled 'Antarctic Adventure.' In fact this was the title of his book recounting his experience as a member of the Shackleton Expedition of 1907 to 1909, and the Scott Expedition of 1910 to 1913, and with Mr. Walter Carlile presiding at the afternoon lecture, Captain Mowatt attended in the evening.

For illustrations on both occasions Mechanist Sergeant Major Price projected photos onto the screen, and including Lance Corporal Semple six patients from the Tickford V.A.D. Hospital acted as stewards for the afternoon lecture. As for that in the evening members of the Royal Engineers officiated. The first general meeting of the members of the newly formed Town Institute was held on Thursday evening, January 24th, and it was agreed that the Royal Engineers stationed in the town, and any visiting soldiers, should have the free use of the rooms when open. Also, agreed, unanimously, was an application made on behalf of the Royal Engineers Drill Instructors. This was for the use of the gym for one hour for three nights each week, and under their direction in other sporting arrangements boxing entertainments and exhibitions were now to be given twice a week in the Y.M.C.A. Hut. Presided over by Mr. Walter Carlile, the annual meeting of the Working Men's Club was held on Wednesday evening, February 27th 1918, and in a lengthy report the secretary, Mr. T.H. Sim, said that 200 members were now in the Forces, with a large number of Royal Engineers on the books as temporary members. In fact the military authorities had taken over the concert hall at 10s a week, whilst amongst the soldiers a rifle club had been formed, whose members would use the Club's range and pay 5s a week for the same. Perhaps they also needed practice in other forms of shooting, for at a billiards match at the Unionist Club, held on Thursday evening, March 14th 1918 they lost to the resident team by 197 points. At the Divisional Petty Sessions on Wednesday, March 20th 1918, George Hampson, of the Royal Engineers in the town, pleaded guilty to riding a bicycle without lights at Newport Pagnell on February 27th. Special constable W.C. Chapman, by whom he had been appended, didn't wish to claim expenses but a fine was imposed. It was therefore ironic that Harold Moore's Cantata 'The Darkest Hour' was sung that evening by the choir at the parish church. They were augmented by several ladies from the town and a number of the billeted Royal Engineers, but it was a Royal Engineer who had been formerly billeted in the town who made a welcome local reappearance on Friday evening, March 22nd, at an entertainment organised by the Congregational Church Girls' Club, under the superintendence of Miss A. M.Coales. In aid of the starving children of Palestine this was held at the Council Schools, and Corporal Utt Ridge was afforded a hearty welcome. Indeed all his elocutionary items were encored at this re-acquaintance with a Newport Pagnell audience, but unfortunately they could not be acquainted with the orchestra of the Royal Engineers, which did not appear due to several of the members being on leave.

On Good Friday, at 10 a.m. a special service was held at the parish church for the Royal Engineers stationed in the town. Then at 7 p.m. the congregation assembled for the singing of Stainer's 'Crucifixion' by the choir, who had the assistance of a number of ladies and several Royal Engineers. The solos were taken by Messrs. O. Critchard and C.R. Line, with the minor passages being sung by Mechanist Sergeant Major Price and Corporal Verity. For Easter an attractive programme of entertainments was arranged by Leader D. Ashton Davies at the Y.M.C.A. Hut, and on the afternoon of Easter Monday a cross country race of seven miles was held in which 20 Royal Engineers competed. All completed the course, with first place going to Sapper Mitchell, second place to Sapper Thwaites, and third place to Sapper Clare. In the evening a concert was given, and during an interval Captain Mowatt presented the prizes. In fine sunny weather, the Red Cross Sale took place on Wednesday, April 24th 1918 on Market Hill, and forming three sides of a square the Royal Engineers ensured a safe distance was kept between the dignitaries on the temporary platform and the large crowd hearing their address. At the Petty Sessions on May 1st a woman of Priory Street was brought up in custody, charged with an offence regarding a member of the Forces who was suffering from venereal disease. The offence was stated to have occurred between April 2nd and 30th, and in court Superintendent Dibben said the warrant had been issued that morning on information supplied by Captain Mowatt. With the soldier now in hospital Superintendent Dibben produced a medical certificate from Dr. White, the Medical Officer, and police sergeant Roberts gave evidence of having arrested the prisoner at 11.15 that morning. Acceding to Superintendent Dibben's request the Bench remanded the prisoner to Northampton gaol until the following Wednesday. On Monday and Tuesday evenings, May 6th and 7th, The Giggles, a concert party of Royal Engineers from the Staple Hall depot, Fenny Stratford, performed at the Electric Theatre. On Monday there was a fairly good attendance, but on Tuesday, when it was given free to the soldiers for their benefit, the attendance left something to be desired. However, the Royal Engineers Orchestra added to the pleasure of the evening.

In glorious summer weather the Red Cross Gala day and Gymkhana, held on Whit Monday, was a great success. The Royal Engineers performed a gymnastic display, and not only gave assistance in erecting and preparing the sports ring, but on the following day also assisted Messrs. Lawman and Son to take down and pack the tents. On the evenings of Thursday, May 23rd and Friday, May 24th 1918 Mr. J.W. Moodie, late of the Seaforth Highlanders, paid a visit to the Y.M.C.A. Hut. On Thursday he related his experiences while serving with Lord Roberts at the Relief of Kandahar, with Lord Wolseley at the Battle of Tel-el-Kebir, and with Sir Redvers Buller at the Relief of Ladysmith. Then on Friday evening he spoke of 'How I became a soldier,' describing his experiences with the B.E.F. in the early part of the war. On both evenings the Hut was crowded, and the audience of Royal Engineers listened with rapt attention. On Saturday, June 29th 1918 the Royal Engineers played St. Andrew's Hospital, Northampton, at cricket. The match took place at Northampton, and in an easy win Corporal Dennis took seven wickets for 34 runs. In aid of Northampton Hospital, the annual fete was held on Bury Field on Saturday, July 20th. Including a tug of war between three teams of Royal Engineers, and a three legged race for men in the Forces, a sports programme had been arranged, whilst at the concerts in the evening Sapper Morgan gave a piano solo and an encored recitation. On the fourth anniversary of the war, of the special services held at the parish church that conducted at 11 a.m. was attended by members and officers of the Wireless Depot of the Royal Engineers under Captain Mowatt. Also that month, one Wednesday a 21 year old married woman, from Moulsoe, pleaded not guilty to a charge brought under D.O.R.A. Regulation 40D. This concerned a member of the Forces who was suffering from venereal disease and Dr. Digby White, the Medical Officer of the Royal Engineers stationed in the town, said that the sapper had reported sick on July 25th. Subsequently, on August 6th Captain Mowatt gave instructions for the warrant to be issued, and in consequence police sergeant Honour arrested the defendant at 9.30 a.m. the next day. However, when he examined the woman at her home Dr. H.T. Wickham found absolutely no sign of the alleged complaint, and in consequence she was remanded by the Bench for another seven days, to allow time for a report from the Medical Research Association to be obtained. There was also trouble for a member of the Royal Engineers in September, when at the Petty Sessions he was charged with having stolen Treasury Notes. These were the property of a fellow soldier, and the story is told in the chapter 'Crimes and Punishment.' For the fund to send Christmas presents to those men from the town in the Forces, an entertainment was held at the Electric Theatre on Wednesday evening, September 25th, at which members of the Royal Engineers acted as stewards. As for those who had served in previous wars, Sergeant Major John William Fowler, late of the Royal Fusiliers, died on Sunday, September 22nd aged 88. He was born in the town in 1830, and having on November 4th 1846 enlisted in the Army at Weedon, during his career he would serve in the Mediterranean, at Corfu and Cephalonia, where his regiment lost a number of men from cholera. When the Crimea War broke out he landed with his regiment at Varna, marching through Bulgaria to the scene of operations, and after this campaign he proceeded to India where, having fought all through the mutiny, he remained for 11 years. Then in 1868 he was discharged through ill health, retaining the Crimean Medal with clasps for Sebastopol, Inkermann, and Alma, the Turkish Crimean Medal, the Indian Mutiny Medal with clasp for Umbeyla and the medal for long service and good conduct. His home had been in Union Street, and at his funeral on Friday afternoon, September 27th full military honours were accorded with, under Quartermaster Sergeant Cousins, the Royal Engineers stationed in the town forming a firing party, with their bugler sounding the Last Post. Major William Trevor, of Lathbury, was amongst the mourners, and the floral tributes included one from Colonel Good, of Broughton, and one worded 'In proud memory of Colour-Sergeant J. Fowler, from the Officers, Warrant Officers, Non commissioned Officers and men of the Royal Fusiliers (City of London Regiment.')

In aid of the Town Christmas Presents Fund, for those men from the town in the Forces an autumn fair and 'razzle dazzle' took place on Saturday, October 12th. The location was the Council School playgrounds, and during the afternoon the winners of a men's tug of war were a team from the Royal Engineers, the commanding officer of which lent a shop in St. John Street for the 'Our Day' effort in the town on Wednesday, October 16th. This was in aid of the Red Cross Prisoners of War Fund, and with all kinds of produce for sale among the helpers were Mrs. Gunnery, Mrs. Glanley, Mrs. G. Tayler, Misses K. James, and A. M.Coales, Mr. A. Goodman, Mr. T. Shelton, Mr. J. Short, and some of the school girls. Trolleys laden with vegetables etc. were paraded in the streets, and by operating a piano organ the Misses I. and K. Powell, amongst others, raised £5 0s 6d, with the takings for the day amounting to £31 17s 7d. Organised by Leader T.W. Allen the following day in aid of the Town Christmas Presents Fund a concert was held at the Y.M.C.A. Hut, to a crowded attendance of Royal Engineers and friends. Yet there was a different type of entertainment at the Y.M.C.A. Hut on October 25th, when around 9.30 p.m. a disturbance was caused by a 19 year old private in the Labour Corps, Royal Engineers, stationed at Newport Pagnell. Police sergeant Roberts told him to return to the Camp, but instead he went with another soldier round the back of the Town Hall and, taking off his coat, shouted "I want to fight the Germans." Police sergeant Roberts then took him into custody, and in court Superintendent Dibben said that when brought to the police station the man was hopelessly drunk on rum, whiskey and ale. Captain Mittell, the officer commanding, said the man had a clean sheet in the Army and a good name, and although he was formerly in a low category he had since been passed A1, and had got very excited about being found fit for active service. The Bench let him off with a caution, but he would be disappointed in his ambition to fight the Germans, for news of the Armistice was only a couple of weeks away. In fact in Newport Pagnell the news arrived some time before noon on Monday, November 11th and as they marched to their mess room for dinner the Royal Engineers made the streets ring with their hurrahs, and lusty cheers. Then having been given a half day holiday they paraded the town with flags, and spent the time shouting and cheering. Later, some of the more enthusiastic members lit a bonfire on Market Hill, and on being joined by the local females danced around the fire and enthusiastically made merry. In the evening a public meeting convened by Mr. J. Short was held in the Electric Theatre, where those on the platform included Captain Mittell, who was now the Commanding Officer of the Newport Pagnell Wireless Depot. Addressing the audience, after regretting the absence of the troops from that meeting, on account of influenza restrictions, he gave a brief resume of the work of the Wireless Section at the Front, showing how the men trained at Newport Pagnell had gone over the parapet with the infantry, since the wireless was the only means of conveying messages back to headquarters when the German barrage came down. Following cheers he then concluded by urging the audience to lift up their hearts with joy, now that the end for which so many of his pals had fought and died had been consummated.

Special services of thanksgiving for the cessation of hostilities, and the coming peace, were held at the parish church on Sunday, November 17th, with the service at 11 a.m. attended by the Royal Engineers under Captain Mittell and the other officers. Then in the continuing celebrations a concert was given at the Y.M.C.A. Hut on Wednesday evening, November 20th to a crowded audience of Royal Engineers and friends. The chair was occupied by Lieutenant Bell, and with Captain Eastman as one of the accompanists the artistes included Sapper Barrett, piano selections and 'Yeomen of England,' Sapper Dadswell, humorous recitations, which were encored, and Lieutenant Jacobs, who sang 'Love's own kiss.' Rather too exuberant in the Armistice Day celebrations had been Lieutenant Patrick McInerney, of the Royal Engineers, Fenny Stratford, for at a Petty Sessions on Wednesday, November 27th he was summoned for his escapades on a motor cycle, one charge being for riding without lights. Superintendent Dibben explained that the proceedings were being taken under instructions from the 'Competent Military Authority,' but the case was dismissed, with the chairman, Mr. W. Carlile, saying that many people broke the Lighting Regulations on Armistice Night. However, there was a further charge of driving a motor cycle at a dangerous speed at the same time and place, and giving evidence Superintendent Dibben said that between 9.30 p.m. and 10 p.m. whilst on duty near the Town Hall he saw a motor cycle being driven down the street with no lights. The rider was dressed in white night attire, as was his pillion passenger, and with the speed being about 40 m.p.h. there was a large crowd about. The rider had sped towards Wolverton and then a few minutes later returned at the same speed, causing the crowd to scatter to make room. Superintendent Dibben said it was the most dangerous driving he had ever seen, and on the 18th at Fenny Stratford the man admitted that he was the driver. In court he apologised, and said that because it had been the night of the Armistice he was exhilarated. He was let off with a caution. At Christmas 1918 a tea was provided for the Royal Engineers at the Y.M.C.A. Hut, and with Lieutenant Bell in the chair in the evening entertainments Sergeant Ellingham, of the Royal Engineers, gave a violin solo, and by impromptu speeches the soldiers kept the audience in a merry mood, with their impersonations of women being very good! Preparations were now being made for the military to leave the town, and in view of this imminent departure in January 1919 householders in the town were advised to take heed of a notice issued by the Army Authorities, in which it was stated that any property of any kind left behind in billets, or received from soldiers, was to be handed in at the Mission Hall. The entrance was behind the Y.M.C.A. Hut, and the hours of opening would be daily until 7 p.m. Then in further measures, with the pans taken out and the drains disconnected during April 1919 removal was made of the temporary structure outside the Town Hall, which had been erected for the convenience of the military.

Nevertheless, certain legacies still remained in the town, for at the Petty Sessions on Wednesday, May 18th 1919 a pioneer, late of the Royal Engineers at Bedford, was summoned by a single woman of 36, Mill Street to answer why he should not contribute to the support of her illegitimate male child, of which he was the alleged father. At first he denied being the parent, until two of his letters were read out, in one of which, written from Hitchin, he told her that he had been doing orderly corporal's duty, and she should not be surprised if he came home a field marshal. Having been billeted for a while in Newport Pagnell, he had 'walked out' with the woman for five months, despite being married with two children. Now, recently demobilised, he was out of work, and with the Bench making an order for 5s a week, until the child was 14, he was directed to pay the costs of £4

17s 6d. There was a large attendance at the Electric Theatre on Wednesday evening, November 19th 1919, when a dramatic recital was given by Mr. Utt Ridge, who for awhile had been stationed in the town during the war as a corporal in the Royal Engineers Signals. His finest performance was the Orations scene from Julius Caesar, by Shakespeare, whilst his touching rendition of the story by Robert Blatchford of 'The men of Whitby' was told with pathos and pride, and 'which stirred the audience to great enthusiasm.' 'In his verses with music he was equally successful, as also his child studies.' Serving for awhile with the Middlesex Hussars, another soldier who had been stationed for a while with the Royal Engineers in the town was Horace Badham, the only son of Mr. and Mrs. F. Badham, of Forest Gate, London. He had made the acquaintance of Miss Joan A. Ellingham, a young lady well known in local musical circles, and at the parish church they were married on Thursday, October 21st 1920. Joan was the youngest daughter of Mr. A.G. Ellingham, who ran a high class hairdressing and tobacconist business in the town, and since he was also the proprietor of the Swan Hotel it was there that the reception, for some 60 guests, was held. Then in the evening he and his wife entertained a company of about 50, with the newly weds leaving for London the following morning. Another wartime romance between a local girl and a Royal Engineer stationed in the town culminated on Tuesday, September 13th 1921, when at the parish church Miss Lilian Wright and Herbert Holmes were married. The groom, who had served throughout the war, seeing much service in East Africa, was the only son of the late Mr. William Holmes and Mrs. Holmes, of Tottenham, and had been stationed in Newport Pagnell for awhile with the Royal Engineers Wireless Section. As for the bride, she was the youngest daughter of Mr. and Mrs. Isaac Wright of the High Street, and having been employed at Newport Pagnell for seven of her 11 years service, as a wedding present she received a silver cake basket from the postal staff of the town. Having possibly been spruced up for the occasion by Mrs. Wright, who carried on the business of a painter and decorator in the town, the bride's home was the venue for the reception, and in the afternoon the couple journeyed to Bletchley station to board a train for a honeymoon in Freshwater, Isle of Wight.

During the war a number of South Africans had been stationed with the Royal Engineers at Newport Pagnell, as also at Fenny Stratford, and it seems they were so well treated by the locals that they were reluctant to be sent to the Continent. In fact when there it was their desire to get back as soon as possible and physical complaints were not infrequently feigned to achieve this objective. Indeed so infamous did this become that it gave rise to a saying in common usage at the Defence Headquarters at Roberts Heights, Pretoria. This was the training camp for non combatants and during drill instruction for any misdemeanours the instructor would issue the reprimand, "Ons speel geen Newport Pagnell veneeuky hier!" which translates from the Africaans as "No Newport Pagnell tricks here!"

Y.M.C.A. HUT

William Earl, a carpenter living in Church Passage, suffered an accident on Friday, December 22nd 1916, whilst engaged with other workmen in erecting the Y.M.C.A.'s soldiers' hut near the Town Hall. He had been on the roof preparing to lay the felt covering when the ladder slipped and he fell 18 feet onto the road. Promptly taken home, there he underwent a medical examination and although no bones were broken some evidence of internal injuries meant that he was confined to bed. Of modest lines, with an external plainness of structure, the building, in front of the entrance to the Mission Hall, was located on a central site in the High Street and, being for the recreation of the troops billeted in the town, facilities were provided for the soldiers to play games, write letters, read the papers and other literature. Also incorporated was a canteen run on temperance principles, where the voluntary helpers would include the Misses Allfrey, Miss Bailey, Mrs. W.R. Chantler, Miss A. M.Coales, Miss Farrar, Miss Carr, Mrs. Littleboy, Miss Odell, Miss Trevor, Mrs. C. Wilford, Miss Williams and Miss Wickham. Having the assistance of a Boy Scout from St. Leonards, Mr. C.O. Robson had been sent by the Y.M.C.A. to take charge of the premises which on Sunday, January 20th 1917, opened with a concert, of which the fine programme had been provided by Captain Williamson, R.A.M.C., Mrs. Lecky and Mr. Hedges.

As the officer commanding the Royal Engineers Signal Depot at Newport Pagnell, Major Hamilton Barrie was present with his wife and in his address he remarked upon the good work that he had seen the Y.M.C.A .doing in France. A week later another evening concert then took place, arranged by Mr. C. K. Garratt. For the performance he had secured the services of friends from Wolverton but their visit was only short, as the last train now left Newport Pagnell at 8 p.m. With a short break for refreshments the two and a half hour entertainment began at 7 p.m. and with Mr. Garratt at the piano songs were given by Mr. O. Critchard, Miss Elsie Cook, of Wolverton, Miss Jessie Dixon, also of Wolverton, Mr. C.R. Line, Sapper Jordan, Lance Corporal Aspinwall, Sapper Cahill, Sapper J. Kellet, Miss Grace Middleton, and Sapper Victor Earl, Harry Ridge, of Wolverton who contributed a humorous song. Also enjoyed was a cornet solo by Mr. J.W. Webster, of Wolverton. Then on Wednesday evening, August 8th 1917, there was again a large attendance when the 'Doh-Nuts' Concert Party travelled from Bedford. For this occasion the management had allowed the Royal Engineers to bring their wives and lady friends and at the conclusion Major Hamilton Barrie proposed a hearty vote of thanks to all the performers. After a stay of two years in the town the Signal Section of the Royal Engineers would leave for new quarters at Bedford on Sunday morning, October 28th 1917, and as an appreciation of their well behaved presence Mr. C. K. Garratt organised a farewell concert at the Electric Theatre on Monday evening, November 15th.

During a break Mr. Short made a speech in praise of the Royal Engineers' stay and during the proceedings Miss Phyllis Simpson presented Mrs. Barrie with a beautiful bouquet after which, saying he first came to the town over a year ago, Major Hamilton Barrie expressed appreciation for the welcome afforded to the troops by the townspeople, through whose enterprise the Y.M.C.A. Hut had been provided. Following the departure of the Signal Section, at the end of October 1917 hundreds of soldiers of the Royal Engineers Wireless Section arrived in the town. They were billeted in local houses and for their recreation an appeal was made for books and magazines at the Y.M.C.A. Hut where on Saturday evening, November 3rd 1917, a concert for their entertainment was arranged by Mr. C. K. Garratt. Before a crowded attendance he opened the performance by playing Grieg's 'Wedding Day' on the piano and subsequently accompanied all the songs including those by Miss Bertha Richens, Mr. O. Critchard, Mr. C. Line and members of the Royal Engineers. Occupying the chair, in his response Company Sergeant Major Harrod proposed a vote of thanks to Mr. Garratt and the performers and for the hearty welcome given to the Wireless Section by the residents. However that evening there was a more muted welcome for a man dressed in the uniform of an English sailor, for as he was leaving the Y.M.C.A. Hut he was approached by Police Sergeant Roberts who asked him what he was doing. The man said he had signed an agreement with the Admiralty 'to go with trawlers' and duly produced a seaman's discharge book which he asked the officer to inspect. As it was dark Police Sergeant Roberts said they should do this at the police station and he then noticed apparent irregularities with the uniform. In consequence the man appeared at a Special Petty Sessions on Saturday, November 3rd 1917, charged with wearing Naval uniform contrary to the Defence of the Realm Act. In evidence Police Sergeant Roberts said at 7 p.m. he saw the man leaving the Y.M.C.A. Hut and during his questioning noticed his uniform and hat, which bore the words 'H.M.S. Pekin.' He then asked the man to explain and was informed, "They issue them out to us on our discharge. I am making my way to Baker Street for my pension." As for the hat, his reply, which raised laughter in court, was "Well, I am entitled to wear it, and yet I am not." "That ain't a ship at all; that is the cookhouse where they send you all when you join up."

Explaining his situation the man said he was a Grimsby fisherman and belonged to a trawler, but he could leave on giving 24 hours'notice and join another boat. As for the uniform, he thought he was entitled to wear this since the clothes were issued to him to mark a distinction between a fisherman and 'the Admiralty's naval men.' However, he admitted he was an absentee from the trawlers and had been absent for about two weeks. In court Superintendent Dibben said the man had been in Northampton police station on Thursday night but, again causing laughter in the court, they turned him out as a conundrum. The defendant was then remanded for enquiries to be made and at the adjourned hearing on Wednesday it was said that a message had been received from Grimsby police. This stated that having signed on as a fisherman under Admiralty agreement the man was entitled to wear the Naval uniform with the distinctive badge. As to him being a possible absentee no information had been received regarding Naval discipline, and in consequence he was discharged. With Lieutenant Sturgess in the chair there was a packed audience at the Y.M.C.A. Hut on Wednesday evening, November 21st 1917, with the attendance not disappointed by the concert which included a duet by Mrs. Westlake and Miss Ellingham, a song 'Shipmates o' mine' by Sapper Dadwell, a humorous song, encored, by Sapper Adams, a song 'So you want to be a soldier, little man,' by Sapper Inglis, 'There's a land,' encored and 'An old fashioned town' given, by Mr. Davies, 'The Blue Grenadier,' by Corporal Doyle, 'My Ships,' by Miss Ellingham, 'When you come home,' by Mrs. Westlake, and 'Blue Eyes,' by Miss Webster.

Apart from the concerts musical entertainment at the Y.M.C.A. Hut could be provided by a gramophone and consequently in late November gifts were sought of gramophone records. Yet the most appreciated entertainments were the live performances and not least that on Thursday evening, December 6th 1917, when with Mr. Davies in the chair songs were given by Miss Grace Middleton, Mr. Davies, Corporal Doyle, Sapper Dadwell, Sapper Thompson, and Sapper Adams. Sapper Fuller contributed violin solos and Miss Wilford recitations. The premises had been packed and there was also a crowded attendance on Wednesday evening, December 12th 1917, when Miss Armstrong and three talented artistes from London gave a concert. Every item was encored and there was another much appreciated event on the following Wednesday with a programme provided by Mr. J. Goddard, of Leicester, and from Northampton Madame Sturges, who, with Mrs. Westlake presiding at the piano, contributed several songs. Other items included ventriloquist sketches and singing and dancing marionettes. It was now decided that on Christmas Day 1917, the military authorities would provide tea for the 'boys' at the Y.M.C.A. Hut, the interior of which was subsequently decorated with holly and evergreens, whilst the incandescent lights were covered by coloured shades. Leader D.A. Davies and his assistants had made the special arrangements and after grace, said by the Vicar, over 400 sat down to a tea. This was served in two sittings, with the ladies presiding being Mrs. Clutton, Mrs. P. C. Gambell, Mrs. Westlake, Miss S. Sams, Miss A. M.Coales, Miss M. Coales, Miss M.A. Coales, Miss Weeks, Miss Mason, Miss Bailey, Miss V. Cameron and Miss Ellingham. After the tables had been cleared various competitions were enjoyed with much laughter and the winners of the first prizes were Pioneer Beecroft, for 'Impromptu Speech,' Pioneer Hedderley, 'Hat Trimming Competition,' Pioneer Timmings, 'Blindfold Sketch on Blackboard,' Pioneer Grey, 'Best Representation of a Lady,' and Pioneer Jones, 'Paper Hats.'

The prizes had been provided by the ladies and after the competitions came a lengthy programme of songs etc. performed by local artistes and the Royal Engineers, of which Lieutenant Marris was in the chair. Then on Boxing night a first-class entertainment was provided by a London concert party from the Three Arts Club, whilst on Friday, January 4th 1918, Enoch Bacon, an entertainer provided by the Y.M.C.A., gave a first-class programme. The following day a cross-country run organised by Leader D.A. Davies took place over about six miles. Completing the course in about 45 minutes Sapper Thwaite proved the winner with Pioneer Grey second and Pioneer Walsall third. As for any outsiders who wished to join the harriers' club, Mr. Davies would be pleased to welcome them. At an entertainment at the Y.M.C.A. Hut on Wednesday evening, January 9th 1918, amongst those contributing songs were Mr. A. Bullard, Pioneer Adams and Leader Harris. Pioneer Matthews gave recitations, Miss Ellingham presided at the piano and there were various competitions to include 'Eating the Apple,' 'Impromptu Speech,' and 'Blackboard Sketch.' The prizes had been given by the lady workers at the Y.M.C.A. Hut and there was also a competition for the Boy Scouts. On the evening of Saturday, January 19th 1918, Mr. Reynolds of Northampton, the Y.M.C.A. Divisional Secretary, occupied the chair when Miss Armstrong's concert party from London performed a concert at the Y.M.C.A. Hut. Every item was loudly applauded and Leader D. Ashton Davies contributed songs as he would also do at the Electric Theatre on Thursday afternoon, January 24th 1918, when members of the Newport Pagnell Habitation of the Primrose League assembled for their annual entertainment. On Tuesday, January 22nd 1918, Bob Barry and Miss Sheilah McCarthy paid a welcome return visit to the Y.M.C.A. Hut, where on Friday evening, January 25th 1918, an evening entertainment was given by the Merry Makers' pierrot troupe from Northampton. In fact this was the largest audience ever seen at the Y.M.C.A .Hut. Then on the Sunday evening a sacred concert took place organised by Mr. C. K. Garratt.

The programme consisted of Miss Bailey, Miss E. Garratt, Major Smith, Sapper Fuller, violin, and Leader D. Ashton Davies, and afterwards an address was given by Mr. Reynolds. Fred Hall and a party from Bedford received an encore for practically every one of their items at a concert on January 31st 1918, whilst on Thursday, February 7th an illustrated lecture on Palestine was given by Major Clutton of Sherington Manor, who had recently been invalided home from the front due to illness. Beginning with the operations around Gaza and followed by the various actions up to the capture of Jerusalem, he gave a graphic account of the campaign and as Assistant Provost Marshal it was he who had the honour of receiving the keys of Jerusalem, being responsible for making the arrangements for the official entry into the city by the Commander-in-Chief, as well as for preserving law and order. Captain Mowatt, C.O. of the Royal Engineers Wireless Depot, presided. At the Divisional Petty Sessions on Wednesday, February 20th 1918, a motor driver of Northampton was summoned for having unscreened front lights on his car on Sunday, February 3rd 1918. Also for having no side lights and for not producing his driver's licence. Having been at the Front for four months he had been discharged due to a gunshot wound in the knee, and on the night in question had been engaged to drive a preacher to the Y.M.C.A. Hut. However, in his haste he forgot that his licence was in his work clothes. In court Mr. Reynolds, the Divisional Secretary of the Y.M.C.A., spoke in his favour and in consequence the Bench decided not to record a conviction although the defendant would have to pay the costs.

As for another motoring case, Alfred Dean, a motor driver of Bedford, was summoned for using petrol, or petrol substitute, for unauthorised purposes at Newport Pagnell on January 31st 1918. Police Sergeant Roberts said on Thursday, January 31st at 10.45 p.m. he saw the man in the High Street driving a motor car with a hackney carriage plate. When stopped outside the Dolphin public house the man said he was driving Fred Hall and a party from Bedford to the Y.M.C.A. Hut, where they were to voluntarily entertain the troops, and explaining the situation he said that whilst plying for hire at Bedford he had been asked by Mr. Hall to take the party to Newport Pagnell. However, the car he was driving broke down and he had to use another. Questioned in court Mr. Hall said he brought two ladies and three men over to the town, with the Y.M.C.A. paying for the hire of the vehicle. He had been rejected for military service but being due to go up for reclassification was presently employed on munitions and in his spare time arranged concerts for the troops, sometimes voluntarily and sometimes for payment. In fact he considered it an essential public duty to encourage and entertain the fighting men. His wife was a semi professional singer and he had acted as a concert agent for some ten years. As for the offence, he was unaware that he could have obtained a permit for special purposes by applying to the proper authorities. Taking a lenient view, since he was driving a concert party for the Y.M.C.A., the Bench fined the driver 10s, or imprisonment for seven days, whilst as for the Y.M.C.A. they were advised to apply to the Board of Trade for a petrol permit for such concert parties. In conclusion Superintendent Dibben said he had been in communication with the Y.M.C.A. and had given them the necessary instructions.

A sacred concert was held at the Y.M.C.A. Hut on Sunday, February 10th 1918. Miss Bertha Richens sang beautifully and Leader Davies' baritone voice was heard to distinct advantage. Mr. C. K. Garratt presided at the piano. Then on Friday, February 15th Miss Sheilah McCarthy and Bob Barry paid another visit. Their performance was thoroughly enjoyed and in other activities boxing entertainments and exhibitions were now to be given twice a week under the direction of the Royal Engineers' gymnastic instructors. One Sunday in late February 1918 the Congregational Church Choir gave a sacred concert at the Y.M.C.A. Hut. The solos were sung by Mrs. Smith and Miss Platt, Mrs. Thomas presided at the piano, Mr. W. Cowley occupied the chair and an address was given by Mr. F. Maslin. There was a large attendance at the Y.M.C.A. Hut on Friday evening, March 22nd 1918, for a lecture by the Reverend Russell Parker of Birmingham entitled 'The Philosophy of Nothing.' Then for the Easter entertainments Leader D. Ashton Davies arranged an attractive programme including on Saturday evening, March 31st 1918, songs performed by himself and Miss Webster, with musical selections by the Excelsior Silver Band. On the Sunday evening a sacred concert was given by 'Northampton friends,' with Mr. H.G. Reynolds, Divisional Secretary, in the chair and on the afternoon of Easter Monday a cross-country race of seven miles took place, in which all the 20 Royal Engineers who competed finished the course. Sapper Mitchell was the winner with Sapper Thwaites in second place and Sapper Clare third. Afterwards tea for the competitors was provided in the Y.M.C.A. Hut by Mrs. Gambell, Mrs. Snell, Miss Coales, Miss Bailey and Miss Vi Cameron. During the evening four members of the Three Arts Club, London, performed a concert and during an interval Captain Mowatt, Officer Commanding the Newport Pagnell Company of the Royal Engineers (Wireless), presented the prizes for the cross-country race.

Continuing the Easter events, on the Tuesday evening an entertainment was provided by Madame May Sturgess and Walter Langford, of Northampton. On Wednesday, April 10th 1918, a large number of Royal Engineers attended an address by the Reverend Rutherford Lane, of London. This was at the Y.M.C.A. Hut where on the Friday evening a concert was given by Miss Lena Ashwell's Concert Party from London. Then on Thursday and Friday 23rd and 24th May 1918, Mr. J.W. Moodie, late of the Seaforth Highlanders, paid a visit to the Y.M.C.A. Hut, where on

Thursday he related his experiences while serving with Lord Roberts at the Relief of Kandahar, with Lord Wolseley at the Battle of Tel-el-Kebir, and with Sir Redvers Buller at the Relief of Ladysmith. The following evening he lectured on 'How I became a soldier' and described his experiences with the B.E.F. during the early part of the war. On both evenings the venue was crowded with Royal Engineers and afterwards 120 Y.M.C.A. War Roll cards were signed. The annual fete in aid of Northampton Hospital took place on Bury Field on Saturday, July 20th 1918, and in the newly introduced singing contest for school children Mr. D. Ashton Davies was one of the judges, with the Y.M.C.A. having lent some of the chairs for the festivities. As an endeavour on behalf of the Y.M.C.A. Huts Fund, two tennis tournaments initiated by the Newport Pagnell War Charities Committee, and organised by Mr. F. O.Butler, were held on the courts of the Bury Lawn Tennis Club on Thursday and Saturday, August 22nd and 24th 1918. Divided into three sections, on Thursday a ladies' doubles tournament was held, for which 18 couples had entered. In Section 1 the winners were Mrs. Carr and Miss W. Butler, in Section 2 Miss Adams and Miss Dover and in Section 3 Mrs. Norris and Miss K. Fleet, and Miss Duckett and Miss Weston (equal). The winners of the final were Mrs. Carr and Miss W. Butler. On Saturday 16 couples entered for the gents' doubles. This was to be played in two sections but owing to failing light the final couldn't be undertaken. However, Messrs. S. Roddis and P. McInerney withdrew and so Messrs. A. Carr and E. McDermott were declared the winners. On both days the Newport Pagnell Golf Club lent the Club House free of charge and Miss W. Butler and Mr. Carr handed back their prizes for the fund.

As a special effort these 'Hut Weeks' were being held all over the country, the purpose being to obtain funds to replace the many Y.M.C.A. Huts lost during the last German offensive on the Western Front, and as the honorary treasurer for the Newport Pagnell and District Hut Week, Colonel Good, of Broughton Manor, would forward the sum of £20 8s 1d to Mr. H. Winter, the organising secretary of the Hut Weeks Fund. Under the direction of Leader T.W. Allen a musical service was held at the Y.M.C.A. Hut on Sunday evening, September 29th 1918, when a special choir, conducted by Mr. Allen, performed four anthems. Mrs. Thomas was at the piano, Miss Platt, soprano, sang a solo and Mr. C.R. Line performed a bass solo and two songs. Mr. C. K. Garratt played the piano accompaniments and Mr. Allen gave a short address entitled 'A Ministry of Song.' Organised by Leader T.W. Allen, a concert in aid of the Town Christmas Presents Fund for Soldiers and Sailors took place on Thursday evening, October 17th 1918, and before a crowded attendance of Royal Engineers and friends several glees were sung by a chorus of 20 voices. These were conducted by Leader Allen to whom during an interval a vote of thanks was proposed by Mr. O. H. Bull, as well as to the contributors who included Miss Wilford, Miss Platt, Miss G. Middleton, who as an encore performed 'Write to me dear' and Mr. C.R. Line. Mrs. Thomas and Miss Minnie Knott A.L.C.M. acted as accompanists, with the collection for the Fund making just over £3. In a case brought by Police Sergeant Roberts, a 19 year old private in the Labour Corps, Royal Engineers, at Newport Pagnell, pleaded not guilty to having been drunk and disorderly in the town on October 25th 1918. Giving evidence Police Sergeant Roberts said he had seen the defendant causing a disturbance outside the Y.M.C.A. Hut at 9.30 p.m. He told him to go to the Camp but instead with another soldier the man went round by the back of the Town Hall, took off his coat and shouted "I want to fight the Germans." Thereupon Police Sergeant Roberts took him into custody. In his evidence Superintendent Dibben said that when brought to the police station the man was hopelessly drunk on rum, whiskey and ale, whilst in his evidence Captain Mittell, the officer commanding, said the man had a clean sheet in the Army and a good name. Formerly he had been in a low category but having now been passed A1 he had got very excited about being classed as fit for active service. He was let off with a caution.

Before a crowded audience of Royal Engineers and friends, on Wednesday evening, November 20th 1918, a concert was given at the Y.M.C.A. Hut with Lieutenant Bell in the chair. The artistes included Sapper Barrett, piano selections, Sapper Dadswell, 'Yeomen of England,' Miss Marjorie Line, classical dance, encored and part repeated, Miss Cameron, 'Slave Song,' encored, Lieutenant Jacobs, humorous recitations, encored, and Miss Webster, 'Love's Own Kiss,' encored with 'Roses of Picardy.' The accompanists were Mrs. Gambell, Miss Knott and Captain Eastman. On Tuesday, November 26th 1918, the Doh-Nuts Concert Party from Bedford performed at the Y.M.C.A. Hut, which on the following evening was filled to capacity for a performance by the Three Arts Club, of London. The artistes included Miss Christine Kay, soprano, Miss A. Leon, cello, Miss Gladys Voile, comedienne, Selwyn Driver, 'the celebrated entertainer,' and Miss MacKenzie and Miss Brown, accompanists. Roars of laughter were caused by the amusing duets of Miss Voile and Mr. Driver, as by the humorous songs and stories of the latter, and encores were vociferously demanded. At the Public Library, Northampton, on Friday, November 30th 1918, as workers in the Newport Pagnell Y.M.C.A. movement service badges were presented by the Hon. Mrs. Stuart Wortley to Mr. F. Stayte, Leader, Mrs. Bucknall, Mrs. Geo. Tayler, Mrs. F. Littleboy, Mrs. W.R. Bull, Mrs. J.W. Clutton, Mrs. P. C. Gambell, Mrs. Symons, Mrs. F. Gunnery, Mrs. Huddart, Mrs. T. Robinson, and the Misses Allfrey, Bailey, Williams, A. M.Coales,

Weeks, Payne, Jessie Taylor and V. Cameron. There was a crowded audience at the Y.M.C.A. Hut on the evening of Wednesday, December 4th 1918 for a concert by artistes from the Three Arts Club, London. As a gifted soprano Miss Rogulski performed five songs, each of which was encored, Miss Florence Arnott was equally appreciated and the songs, stories and sketches by Mr. Thornley Dodge were cleverly done. The zither banjo solos by Mr. A.P. Nickolds proved popular as well as his piano playing and that of Miss Ivy Stephenson.

On the evening of Sunday, December 1st 1918 the Excelsior Silver Band performed a varied programme. During the event the Reverend Gunnery gave a short talk, whilst on the evening of Friday, December 13th 1918, Madame Strathearn, soprano, entertained a large company of soldiers at the Y.M.C.A. Hut, not least with her rapturously applauded imitations of a cornet and trombone. In a short address Mr. Reynolds, the Y.M.C.A. Divisional Secretary, thanked her for her performance and referred to the work of the Y.M.C.A. regarding the soldiers at home and on the battlefield. Christmas 1918 saw the interior of the Y.M.C.A. Hut decorated with bunting and evergreens. This was a credit to Mr. Stayte, the Leader of the Movement locally and the lady volunteers. In the afternoon a tea was provided for the Royal Engineers and between 6 p.m. and 7 p.m. the Excelsior Silver Band played musical selections. With Lieutenant Bell in the chair the evening also featured competitions of a novel and amusing nature and an entertainment in which songs were contributed by Miss Eva Garratt, Miss Webster and Mr. Cecil R. Line. A piano solo was performed by Miss Minnie Knott and also by Miss V. Cameron, Miss Marjorie Line gave two dances, Sergeant Ellingham of the Royal Engineers played a violin solo and Harry Ward gave bone (sic) solos. As with their impersonations of women, in 'Impromptu Speeches' the soldiers kept the audience in a merry mood and other competitions, for which the Y.M.C.A. Hut management had provided monetary prizes, included blindfold sketching, hat trimming and, with hands tied, eating apples suspended on a piece of string. In February 1919 since the troops had now left the town the U.D.C. ordered that the Y.M.C.A. Hut should be removed. However, to maintain a Y.M.C.A. presence Mr. A. Bullard suggested a Y.M.C.A. Institution as a permanent memorial for the fallen from the town, this being one of the schemes proposed at a preliminary meeting convened by the U.D.C. on Friday evening, February 21st 1919. Miss A. M.Coales supported the idea but it was the proposal for a Cottage Hospital that was carried. In April 1919 the Y.M.C.A. authorities confirmed their intention to have the Y.M.C.A. Hut removed but by May this had still not been done and they stated that if it was not removed by the end of the month they would have it dismantled and charge the expense to the owners.

More books by John A. Taylor

about the First World War

Stony Stratford during the First World War

A full account of life in the town of Stony Stratford during the war years, drawn from newspapers, letters, and other contemporary sources.

ISBN 978-1-909054-12-7

Home Fires:

Life in the North Bucks Towns and Villages during the First World War

The small towns and villages of North Bucks (now largely covered by present-day Milton keynes) contributed hugely to the war effort. John Taylor describes from newspapers, letters, and other contemporary sources.

ISBN 978-1-909054-20-2

Wolverton during the First World War

Wolverton was the largest town in the northern half of Buckinghamshire and with its railway works was at the forefront of the government's commitment to the war effort. This volume is in preparation and will be published August 4th 2014.

ISBN 978-1-909054-23-3

More books about North Bucks

from Magic Flute Publications

The Lost Streets of Wolverton

Bryan Dunleavy

The book describes the first settlement of the railway town in its first decade and reconstructs the "lost streets" from contemporary sources.

ISBN 978-1-909054-00-4

Manno's Manor

Bryan Dunleavy

Wolverton is a very old settlement and after 1066 was the centre of a large barony. The book decsribes archaeological discoveries of early settlements, medieval Wolverton and the development of Stony Stratford up to the day the railway arrived and changed everything.
ISBN 978-1-909054-05-9

I Grew Up in Wolverton

Ruth edwards

Memories and opinions are exchanged in this lively book recalling life in Wolverton before Milton Keynes. The reported conversations here took place online with 250 particpants from all over the world.

ISBN 978-1-909054-03-5

Lightning Source UK Ltd.
Milton Keynes UK
UKOW03f1330220414

230372UK00001B/2/P

9 781909 054134